Theodore Dreiser

A Picture and a Criticism of Life

NEW LETTERS, VOLUME I

THE DREISER EDITION

Sponsored at

the University of Connecticut

by

the Department of English,

the Thomas J. Dodd Research Center,

the College of Liberal Arts and Sciences, and

the University Research Foundations

and by

the University of Pennsylvania Library

Thomas P. Riggio

General Editor

Theodore Dreiser

A Picture and a Criticism of Life

NEW LETTERS

VOLUME I

Edited by

DONALD PIZER

University of Illinois Press
Urbana and Chicago

Photos on pages vii, 4, 12, 32, 59, 105, 128, 162, 208, 240, and 243 from the
Theodore Dreiser Papers, Annenberg Rare Book and Manuscript Library, University of Pennsylvania. Reprinted by permission of the Dreiser Trust. Photos
on pages 51 and 189 from the W. A. Swanberg Papers, Annenberg Rare Book
and Manuscript Library, University of Pennsylvania. Reprinted by permission
of the University of Pennsylvania. Photo on page 41 from *London Magazine*,
n.s. 3 (April/May 1991): 37. Photo on page 122 from D. Felicitas Corrigan,
Helen Waddell: A Biography (Victor Gollancz/Orion Publishing Group, 1986);
all attempts to trace the copyright holder proved unsuccessful.

Research for this publication was supported by a grant from the National
Endowment for the Humanities. This organization is not responsible for
the views expressed in the book.

∞ This book is printed on acid-free paper.

Library of Congress Cataloging-in-Publication Data
Dreiser, Theodore, 1871–1945.
A picture and a criticism of life : new letters /
Theodore Dreiser ; edited by Donald Pizer.
p. cm. — (The Dreiser edition)
Includes bibliographical references and index.
ISBN-13 978-0-252-03106-9 (cloth : alk. paper)
ISBN-10 0-252-03106-7 (cloth : alk. paper)
1. Dreiser, Theodore, 1871–1945—Correspondence
2. Authors, American—20th century—Correspondence.
I. Pizer, Donald. II. Title.
PS3507.R55Z48   2008
813'.52—dc22 [B]   2007046951

Dreiser in the 1920s.

The whole test of a book—to me—is—is it true, revealing, at once a picture and a criticism of life. If it measure up in these respects we can dismiss sympathy, decency, even the utmost shame and pain of it all.

—Dreiser to William C. Lengel,
14 April 1913

CONTENTS

ILLUSTRATIONS

PREFACE

Theodore Dreiser was an inveterate correspondent, writing an estimated 20,000 letters over the span of a half-century. Of this large body of correspondence, only some 1,300 have been previously published, mainly in Robert H. Elias, *Letters of Theodore Dreiser* (1959); Louise Campbell, *Letters to Louise* (1960); and Thomas P. Riggio, *Dreiser-Mencken Letters* (1986). With the exception of a handful of letters that have appeared in journals and books about Dreiser, the present collection gathers previously unpublished letters in this first edition of general correspondence to appear in forty-eight years. The editor has selected letters that shed new light on the novelist's well-known literary and social concerns, as well as letters that explore subjects not fully represented in earlier editions.

Dreiser's letters provide one of the fullest and most immediate records of his ideas, beliefs, and activities. As in the case of his diaries, they present a picture of the writer that complements the self-portraits he created in memoirs such as *Dawn* and *Newspaper Days*, together with other autobiographical works such as *An Amateur Laborer*, *A Traveler at Forty*, and *A Hoosier Holiday*. In addition, the importance of the correspondence derives from Dreiser's exchanges with many literary, social, and political figures who played key roles in the intellectual life of the twentieth century.

The provenance of the letters has been noted at the head of each selection. The Dreiser Papers at the University of Pennsylvania's Annenberg Rare Book and Manuscript Library include many copies of his letters to others, as well as scores of letters written to him. In his landmark edition of Dreiser's letters, Robert H. Elias depended heavily on carbons found in the Dreiser Collection. At the present time, however, Dreiser's correspondence is housed in archives throughout the United States, which contain thousands of letters that have been discovered in the last four decades. Consequently, the editor has been able to select letters from originals in some thirty-five libraries, in addition to those existing in private collections. Understandably, Elias's selection of letters in 1959 was also determined by consideration for persons alive at the time. Today, more than sixty years after Dreiser's death, this consideration no longer obtains, and in this edition, as well as in a forthcoming companion volume of Dreiser's correspondence with women, the editors have been able to draw upon a wider range of letters than was hitherto possible.

Because Dreiser seldom wrote letters for publication, this compilation has been prepared in conformity with widely accepted principles governing the editing of private documents. As has been true of other private papers published in the Dreiser Edition, Dreiser's handwritten letters are edited diplomatically, with an eye toward preserving the preliminary, personal nature of the original texts, to the extent this is possible in a typeset medium. Accordingly, his original misspellings, grammatical mistakes, slips of the pen, and other idiosyncrasies are almost all retained and presented in a clear text. In the case of typed letters (all done by secretaries), typographical errors have been silently corrected. These editorial practices are more fully discussed in the book's "Editorial Note." In addition, the editor's introduction offers a general account of Dreiser's career in relation to his correspondence. The headnotes provide the historical, personal, and thematic context of the letters at specific moments in Dreiser's life, and the historical annotations identify significant figures and references in the correspondence.

One characteristic of this edition deserves notice. Because of a forthcoming companion volume of letters in the Dreiser Edition, which is devoted exclusively to Dreiser's correspondence with women, the present edition contains only seventeen such letters. The one element that distinguishes them from those in the volume to follow is Dreiser's lack of personal relationship to the women. The later companion edition will contain more confidential correspondence, ranging from his courtship letters to his first wife to letters to former teachers, siblings, and lovers, as well as to writers, artists, and political activists with whom he often maintained both personal and professional relationships. The decision to devote the present volume to Dreiser's general correspondence and another to his more private exchanges with women derives in large part from the sheer number, variety, and richness of both types of letters.

* * *

This edition of Dreiser's correspondence is part of an ongoing series in the Dreiser Edition. Each book is a product of cooperative efforts. The general editor appoints an editor for each project and establishes the project within the framework of current editorial theory. At each stage of preparation, the editor and general editor proofread the text and authenticate its contents. This volume continues the Dreiser Edition's tradition of publishing texts that are not easily accessible, even to the specialist. Such an undertaking would be unimaginable without the sponsorship of two institutions: the University of Connecticut and the Library of the University of Pennsylvania. Several individuals at the University of Connecticut deserve special mention for their initiatives and continuing generous support of this project:

Robert Tilton, head of the English Department; Ross D. MacKinnon, dean of the College of Liberal Arts and Sciences; Thomas P. Wilsted, director of the Thomas J. Dodd Research Center; and Janet Greger, vice provost and dean of the Graduate School. The goodwill and special training of the staff at the University of Pennsylvania's Annenberg Rare Book and Manuscript Library have been essential to the progress of the Dreiser Edition. Director Michael T. Ryan has generously devoted his own time and the resources of his staff to facilitating the work of the Dreiser Edition. Nancy M. Shawcross, curator of manuscripts, continues to contribute her expertise and special service to the project. John Pollack has consistently and untiringly assisted Dreiser Edition editors in their work. Finally, Dr. Willis Regier, the director of the University of Illinois Press, continues against high odds to provide imaginative guidance and commitment to the project.

Thomas P. Riggio
General Editor
The Dreiser Edition

ACKNOWLEDGMENTS

I have benefited greatly in my research from the expertise and generosity of Michael T. Ryan, Nancy Shawcross, and John Pollack of the Annenberg Rare Book and Manuscript Library of the University of Pennsylvania Library. Thomas P. Riggio has guided this project from its onset and I owe much to his knowledge and skill. At an early stage of this project I benefited from a grant-in-aid from the American Philosophical Society. Lyn Hunter has been an ideal research assistant. I also wish to thank Richard W. Dowell, Jerome Loving, Richard Lehan, Maximillian E. Novak, Carol Pizer, and Frederic E. Rusch for various kinds of aid. My work on this project has been greatly facilitated by the goodwill and cooperation of the recent chairs of the Tulane University English Department, Michael Kuczynski and Molly Travis.

I wish to thank the trustees of the University of Pennsylvania for permission to publish previously unpublished letters by Theodore Dreiser and to reproduce illustrations in the Dreiser and Swanberg Papers of the University of Pennsylvania Library. I also wish to thank the following individuals and libraries for making available to me letters by Dreiser in their possession: American Jewish Archives, Cincinnati; Archives of American Art, Smithsonian Institute, Washington; Jonathan Auerbach; Bancroft Library, University of California Library, Berkeley; Bienecke Library, Yale University; Brown University Library; Columbia University Library; Cornell University Library; Dartmouth College Library; DePauw University Library; Emory University Library; Haverford College Library; William J. Heim; Houghton Library, Harvard University; Historical Society of Pennsylvania, Philadelphia; Huntington Library, San Marino; Indiana State University Library, Terre Haute; Kent State University Library; Library of Congress; Lilly Library, Indiana University; Newberry Library, Chicago; New York Public Library; Princeton University Library; Harry Ransom Humanities Research Center, University of Texas, Austin; Southern Illinois University Library; Temple University Library; University of California, Los Angeles, Library; University of Connecticut Library; University of Georgia Library; University of Illinois Library; University of Kentucky Library; University of Pennsylvania Library; University of South Carolina Library; University of Southern California Library; University of Virginia Library.

INTRODUCTION

Although Dreiser's letters tell many stories in the sense of the multifarious professional and personal aspects of his life that they touch upon, they also contain a single broad plot with several significant themes. The plot is that of a young man initially absorbed in his career as a writer who then gradually translates the specific difficult circumstances of his own professional life into efforts on behalf of all artists in America and who finally directs much of his energy toward improving conditions of life in the nation as a whole. The themes contained within this plot, however, often refer less to a narrative of change or development than to a portrait of a figure whose permanent underlying beliefs, values, and emotions can be described as sufficiently complex to border on the indefinable. Dreiser easily can be, and often has been, pigeonholed as a man and a thinker. To H. L. Mencken he was both a great novelist and an ignorant bumpkin, to Stuart P. Sherman a barbarian, and to W. A. Swanberg a lecher.[1] He may indeed have been all of these to some degree, but his letters reveal that he was far more and that any reduction of his mind and character to single dimensions does not do justice to the fullness and variability of his experience and nature. For example, a typical day's correspondence for Dreiser during the 1930s might have included warm letters to lovers and old friends; often demanding or recriminatory business communications with publishers, adaptors, and translators; letters reflecting his participation in current social issues and movements; and responses to queries about his philosophical and literary beliefs. This single day's correspondence might well have contained many unharmonious notes—anger and love, small-mindedness and generosity of spirit, a capacity for wonder and a closed mind, a love of life and dismay at its futility, and so on. Each of these reflects a facet of Dreiser, including the qualities that led Mencken, Sherman, and Swanberg to their estimates of his character and mind, but none constitutes the complete man.

Robert H. Elias's and Thomas P. Riggio's valuable collections of Dreiser's letters have already contributed greatly to the understanding of Dreiser's life and career, but they have done so in necessarily specific areas.[2] Elias, as is suggested by the title of his earlier biography—*Theodore Dreiser: Apostle of Nature*[3]—was especially interested in Dreiser's ideas, and his selection of letters thus tends to offer more of Dreiser's thought than of the practical and everyday in an author's life—for Dreiser, his work as an editor, for example, or his quarrels with publishers or his constant efforts to make authorship pay. There is much on these aspects of Dreiser's career in Riggio's edition of the Dreiser-Mencken correspondence, but the collection of course focuses more exclusively on the periods of the two authors' friendship and on matters of their mutual concern.

This new edition of Dreiser's letters aids in the understanding of Dreiser by filling in the "plot" and "themes" of his career in several significant ways. Moments such as his early hardships after the "suppression" of *Sister Carrie*, his staunch work on behalf of the *American Spectator*, his many dealings with Hollywood over the filming of his novels, and his time-consuming and fruitless efforts to protect his copyrights abroad are represented much more fully than earlier. In addition, our awareness of Dreiser's character, in all its conflicting aspects, is enhanced here. For a man reputed to have never maintained a friendship, there is the counter evidence of his close and lengthy relationships with Richard Duffy, William C. Lengel, and John Cowper Powys. There is also, in Dreiser's detailed advice during the period he worked as an editor regarding the contents and form of a successful article, an increased understanding of the basis of his rapid advance in the magazine field. Also made clearer is Dreiser's extraordinary career as an organizer. For almost thirty years, from the early 1910s to the late 1930s, he was engaged in seemingly countless attempts to establish literary groups dedicated to freedom of expression, to found magazines and movie companies with the same goal, and to support the formation of organizations seeking to guarantee basic constitutional rights for all Americans. Many of these efforts failed to get off the ground or failed in their goals even when founded. But as the most nationally recognized and the most fully socially engaged American writer during this period, Dreiser served as a willing leader in attempts to improve conditions by organized effort. And, finally, the more problematical side of Dreiser's character is also further clarified, principally his anti-Semitism, anti-Catholicism, and Anglophobia as well as some instances of sharp financial dealings.

* * *

The earliest stage of Dreiser's career reflected in his correspondence begins in 1898 with his full participation in the hectic life of a turn-of-the-century freelance journalist, soliciting editors for commissions, traveling around the country on assignments, and interviewing celebrities. Since it was uncommon at that time for a writer not fully established to have an agent, all these activities were undertaken without assistance. Dreiser's frequent associate in much of this frenetic activity and composition—he published more than 130 articles between 1897 and 1902—was his close friend of this period, the journalist and aspiring novelist Arthur Henry. With their quarrel in 1901, however, Richard Duffy, an editor at *Ainslee's* magazine whom Dreiser had met in early 1898, assumed this role. During the several years of Dreiser's collapse from nervous exhaustion after *Sister Carrie*'s appearance in 1900, it was the urbane and sympathetic Duffy who offered Dreiser the work, understanding, and cash which helped pull him through the crisis.

Dreiser's letters in the years between 1898 and 1903 often reveal the conventional ploys of a young writer on the make. He solicits the aid of Edmund Clarence Stedman, the major reputation-maker of young American poets during this period, and he writes with extraordinary obsequiousness to William Dean Howells in praise of Howells's work. He is also engaged in the creation of a public literary persona, as his long autobiographical letter to Duffy on 18 November 1901 suggests.* The life he sketches to Duffy is of a figure largely self-formed and self-educated who has struggled, first for survival and then for success, throughout his life and, he implies, will have to continue doing so in the future.

The years after the publication of *Sister Carrie* and before Dreiser began work for Street & Smith in the fall of 1904 were indeed years of struggle, as his letters to Duffy during this period reveal. Unable to work steadily on *Jennie Gerhardt*, Dreiser in mid-1901 began a life of aimless wandering. He soon had to borrow money to survive and began to slip into a Hurstwood-like decline toward oblivion. But he recovered, worked his way up the New York magazine-editing ladder, and by 1907 was the highly paid editor of Butterick's *Delineator*, a women's magazine with a circulation of more than a million.

Dreiser correspondence during this initial phase of his career reflects his ready adoption of the mix of positive public attitudes and less estimable private practices that make up success in the popular literature market-place. His February 1900 letter to Robert Underwood Johnson, editor of the prestigious and high-minded *Century* magazine, in which he proposes an article on advances in teacher training, is pervaded with contemporary Progressive assumptions on the role of government in achieving reform. In a like manner, as editor of the *Delineator*, he wishes the magazine "to be useful in an educational and instructive way" (Dreiser to Lester Frank Ward, 3 December 1908). This high-mindedness, however, functions side by side with his recognition that a successful magazine article or story is above all one which either appeals to or does not offend accepted taste and values.

---

* All letters by Dreiser cited in the text and notes of this introduction are present in the volume itself.

So, for example, in his August 1910 letter to Pitts Duffield, H. G. Wells's American agent, Dreiser asks Wells to tone down, in a novel offered to the *Delineator* for serialization, his critical depiction of the role of religion in marriages—this from a editor whose own unfinished *Jennie Gerhardt* depicts the pernicious effect of devout religiosity on family life! The *Delineator's* Child Rescue Campaign, undertaken during Dreiser's period as editor, is also a blatant appeal to popular sentiment.

Dreiser's editorial practice from 1905 to 1910, when he edited *Smith's*, the *Broadway*, and the *Delineator* magazines, often reveals other instances of his ability to work within the prevailing system. For example, in a letter to Richard Oulahan on 11 July 1907, he offers an associate of President Theodore Roosevelt a large commission, almost a bribe, if he will persuade Roosevelt to undertake an article for the *Delineator*. Dreiser's early letters, however, also suggest the qualities of mind and spirit that, in a confirmation of the self-portrait he offered Duffy, fueled his rise from a poverty-stricken Indiana boyhood to eventual literary fame and fortune. Like an Alger hero, he not only possesses boundless energy and ambition and an ability to take pains, but also a capacity, in the face of all opposition, to get the job done as he wishes it done. He desires that *Sister Carrie*, despite its sabotage by Doubleday, Page, have an "an honest hearing" (Dreiser to George P. Brett, 26 September 1901), and he eventually gets that hearing; he wishes, despite his nervous breakdown, to complete *Jennie Gerhardt*, and he eventually does so. Unlike an Alger hero, however, he has been aided in the achievement of these goals less by the intervention of good fortune than by his willingness not only to write about the "game [of life] as it is played"[4] but to himself participate with little hesitation in its various shadings.

The fifteen years between Dreiser's departure from the *Delineator* in October 1910 and the publication of *An American Tragedy* in late 1925 are characterized by his immense productivity in almost all literary forms and his equally prodigious efforts on behalf of free artistic expression in America. The two are related in that Dreiser had made the "suppression" of *Sister Carrie* inseparable from both his self-image as an artist whose destiny, he came to believe, was to have his work suppressed and his public image as a great writer whose freedom to express the truth had been, and was continuing to be, denied.

The initial reopening of the wound caused by Doubleday's refusal to have anything to do with *Carrie* except to print it was Harper's refusal, in early 1914, to issue *The Titan* despite having already prepared it for publication. ("Sister Carrie all over again," Dreiser wrote to Albert Mordell on 6 March 1914.) Since Dreiser soon found another publisher, this matter passed quickly. In July 1916, however, John Lane Co., which had published Dreiser's autobiographical novel The "Genius" in 1915, withdrew it from distribution after John S. Sumner of the New York Society for the Suppression of Vice threatened to bring suit against Lane on the grounds of obscenity. For seven years, until Boni and Liveright finally republished The "Genius" in 1923, Dreiser invested a great deal of energy in seeking to have the book reissued. He filed lawsuits, sought to interest other publishers in the novel, spoke and wrote constantly about its suppression, and participated in organizing protest groups against the actions of Sumner and the New York Society.

Even before the Titan affair, Dreiser had supported various attempts to provide more opportunities for "advanced" expression. In a letter to Floyd Dell on 23 March 1913, for example, he solicited Dell's aid in establishing a new publishing firm that would be a "thoroughly liberal, progressive house." The fiascos over The Titan and The "Genius" intensified and broadened these endeavors. He played an active, and frequently decisive, role during the late 1910s and early 1920s in efforts to establish new journals, publishing firms, and movie companies that would be receptive to literary expression not welcome in established outlets. He also sought to aid in the creation of literary societies that would aid writers outside the mainstream, either by defending their right of expression or by providing them with the financial means to do so. Literary historians have often attributed Dreiser's reputation as a champion of free expression in the early twentieth century largely to the mythic use made of the Sister Carrie incident by the generation of writers who followed him. In doing so, however, they have neglected the direct impact on this generation of his many efforts on behalf of artistic freedom. Of course, most of these attempts came to little in the sense of concrete accomplishments. But Dreiser persevered nevertheless. As he wrote on 18 August 1919 to Mitchell Dawson, who was trying to start a new, progressive magazine, "That this, or the efforts of others in a similar vein, have thus far borne much fruit I cannot say; apparently not. Yet that a better day may be near at hand I am still ready to believe." And of course eventually the efforts of Dreiser and other fighters such as H. L. Mencken did help to change the climate of opinion and hasten the formation of the actual magazines, publishing firms, and author societies Dreiser had failed to establish.

The continuing presence of the Sister Carrie incident in Dreiser's state of mind bore additional fruit during this period in his tumultuous relationships with his publishers. From Grant Richards to Harper's, John Lane, and Boni and Liveright, Dreiser distrusted his publishers' motives in almost all his dealings with them, yet he required their aid and understanding if he was to write the kind of fiction he wished to. "It isn't easy to do what I am trying to do," he wrote Willard Huntington Wright on 2 December 1912, by which he meant to write honestly and fully about life as he per-

ceived it and to make a living doing so. But it might also be said that it is
not easy to find publishers who gratefully and gracefully pay advances on
huge, ungainly works of fiction desperately in need of editing which will
sell only moderately at best, publishers who are then also berated by their
author for their insensitivity to his efforts, for their inadequate advertising,
and for their financial trickery and dishonesty. Each of Dreiser's publishing
relationships has the shape of a failed marriage. He is wooed by promises
of advances and publicity campaigns; his books, however, arrive late (and
in the instance of *The Bulwark* not at all) and then sell poorly; Dreiser is
angry and the publisher aggrieved; and the two part with recriminations and
lawsuits. "Someday I hope to find a publisher who will see me as a unity,"
Dreiser wrote Alfred Knopf on 21 March 1914, "not as a spring list, piece
meal, proposition." He was still seeking such a publisher at his death more
than thirty years later.

The semblance of a middle-class existence which Dreiser had created for
himself during the years following his collapse—a secure marriage, a well-
paying editorial position, and an attractive Upper West Side apartment—
gave way almost immediately after he left the *Delineator* for the kind of life
then often characterized as Bohemian. He traveled frequently, including a
lengthy European journey, lived in areas frequented by artists and writers,
acquired many new friends, and vigorously undertook what he called a "va-
rietistic" love life—that is, he moved openly and freely within a number of
concurrent sexual relationships. Some of Dreiser's most permanent personal
relationships were formed during the early years of this period. Visiting Chicago during the winter of 1912–13 (and again in early 1914) for research
on the Cowperwood Trilogy, he met Edgar Lee Masters, Floyd Dell, Carl
Sandburg, and Ben Hecht—several of the principal figures in what later came
to be known as the Chicago Renaissance. He also re-encountered William
C. Lengel, his former secretary at the *Delineator,* and met the young actress
Kirah Markham, who was to be his mistress for several years. Dreiser's primary
residence during the late 1910s, however, was New York, and more specifically Greenwich Village, where he settled in mid-1914 for a stay of more
than five years. The Village of these years, as Dreiser was later to recall it in
A Gallery of Women, was a hotbed of political and social radicalism as well
as a whirlpool of swiftly changing sexual partnerships. Dreiser established
friendships during his Village years with, among many others, the journalist
Edward H. Smith, the artist Franklin Booth, the Welsh novelist John Cowper
Powys, and the writer Hutchins Hapgood. And it was at his Village apartment in September 1919 that Dreiser met Helen Richardson, the woman
with whom he lived sporadically for the remainder of his life and who finally
became his second wife twenty-five tempestuous years later.

Helen had aspirations to a film career, and in October 1919 she and Dreiser moved together to Los Angeles, where they were to live for three years. Although Dreiser was enthusiastic about the southern California climate, he felt intellectually and socially isolated in Los Angeles and was most content when visiting the lively San Francisco Bohemian scene, where he established warm relationships with the poet George Sterling and the journalist George Douglas. In October 1922 he and Helen returned to New York and took an apartment in the Village. Soon after arriving he wrote to W. W. Lange on 22 October 1922 that "New York after California is like rapids after comparatively still & clean waters." But it is clear that Dreiser was very much at home in rapids; it was in New York over the next two years that he wrote *An American Tragedy*.

During this period Dreiser's literary credo maintained its essential character. "The whole test of a book—to me—," he wrote William C. Lengel on 14 April 1913, "is—is it true, revealing, at once a picture and a criticism of life. If it measure up in these respects we can dismiss sympathy, decency, even the utmost shame and pain of it all." To Dreiser, of course, the achievement of a true picture had always included an attempt to interpret life in its larger dimensions—to infuse his portrait with a philosophical reading of its meaning. From the earliest phases of his career, this effort had been shaped largely by his youthful encounter with the works of Herbert Spencer, Ernst Haeckel, and other late nineteenth-century figures who had sought to understand all existence in evolutionary terms. Dreiser's correspondence, however, between his return to fiction in late 1910 and the publication of *An American Tragedy*, reveals his unwillingness to rest easy in this belief. He responded eagerly to new ideas which might cast light on basic human conditions, warmly welcoming Freud's insights into the human psyche (Freud, he wrote A. A. Brill on 20 January 1919, is "like a master with a key who unlocks subterranean cells and leads forth the hoary victims of injustice") and Jacques Loeb's experiments in mechanistic behaviorism. (*Hey Rub-a-Dub-Dub*, Dreiser's 1920 collection of philosophical essays, is a potpourri of his old and newer ideas.) By late 1924, as his 14 September 1924 letter to Chauncey M. Depew suggests, Dreiser had reached a crucial point in his intellectual development. Using "the mystery of love" as a fulcrum, he posed to Depew a philosophical problem the resolution of which was to occupy him for the remainder of his life.

> Do you consider [the mystery of love], as did the late Jacques Loeb, and so many of the behaviorists of this day, the result of a blind and accidental physical and chemical formulae which had no beginning in any conscious mind anywhere, and that will pass as clouds pass, because of accidental

chemical and physical changes in the universe over which nothing has any control. Or do you suspect or perhaps just hope, since to some it is beautiful, that it was preconceived by a higher intelligence and by that same preordained. In other words do you believe in a higher and governing intelligence that consciously intends human happiness or not.

Despite some misgivings at the outset, Dreiser had been able to support himself by his writing during the fifteen years from his departure from the *Delineator* to the publication of *An American Tragedy*, and he had also established himself as a major American writer. The great critical and popular success of *An American Tragedy*, however, lifted his earning power and reputation into heights that had a significant impact on his career. In addition to royalties from the novel itself, Dreiser received large payments from its successful dramatic adaptation and from the sale of its film rights to Famous Players–Lasky. The novel's almost universal critical acclaim also raised him into the ranks of a world-class author. Very quickly he had become rich and internationally famous. He was touted as the next (and first) American Nobel Prize winner in literature, and he and Helen rented an expensive duplex apartment on Fifty-seventh Street, entertained frequently, and undertook a lengthy European tour.

Dreiser's new status soon affected his career in ways that are clearly manifest in his correspondence over the remainder of his life. A great deal of his time and energy over the next twenty years was expended in the business of authorship. His works were now in great demand for adaptation into plays and films and for translation into other languages. Eager to capitalize on this interest, Dreiser entered a period in which he engaged continually in the negotiations, disputes, and lawsuits often attendant on complex business transactions. Several aides and secretaries now helped him with his affairs, numerous agents sought his attention, and several law firms attended to his contracts and disagreements. In addition, as a major American literary figure, Dreiser was increasingly called upon, as the buoyant 1920s give way to the Depression and the rise of fascism, to participate in social and political movements and campaigns. His attraction to activists of all stripes, especially to those on the left, was matched by his own deepening engagement in issues of social justice. By the early 1930s, Dreiser was chair of an important organization seeking to preserve the civil rights of leftists (the National Committee for the Defense of Political Prisoners), had played major roles in the campaigns to achieve justice for Tom Mooney and the Scottsboro Boys, and had led a committee of writers into the chaos of the Kentucky coal fields to investigate the oppression of miners by both mine owners and civil authorities. Dreiser's social engagement also became increasingly international in character. He made a much-heralded trip to the Soviet Union during the winter of 1927–28, joined a number of organizations committed to fighting the spread of fascism, and visited Spain on behalf of the Loyalist cause during the closing phase of its civil war.

A welcome return to a more familiar literary territory appeared to offer itself in mid-1932 when Ernest Boyd and George Jean Nathan, two experienced editors, planned "a literary newspaper," the *American Spectator,* and asked Dreiser to become a member of an editorial board which would also include Eugene O'Neill and James Branch Cabell. The goals of the journal, to publish first-rate material by major writers without editorial restrictions, had been championed by Dreiser for more than twenty years, and he threw himself wholeheartedly into the project. From the beginning, however, he quarreled with Boyd and Nathan over their reluctance to publish socially pertinent material, and he resigned after a year and half of continuing controversy.

By the early 1930s Dreiser often complained to friends that his travels and social activism left him tired and ill and provided little time for his own writing. His unsuccessful attempt in 1932 to complete *The Stoic* and his huge efforts on behalf of the *American Spectator* from mid-1932 to early 1934 no doubt contributed to his belief that he was overextended and that it was time to concentrate his energies on the literary and philosophical projects which most engaged him. Dreiser's Los Angeles stay during the summer and fall of 1935 played a key role in this transition. He was refreshed by the Southern California climate, found stimulating intellectual companions in George Douglas and several Cal Tech scientists, and worked intensively on his book of philosophy, *The Formula Called Man.*[5] In a sense, Dreiser had discovered a cure for his physical and mental fatigue in the combined effect of the consolations of philosophy and his self-exile from the hectic New York political and literary scene.

Of course, it was not until 1938 that Dreiser and Helen were able to move permanently to Los Angeles, and he in fact did continue to participate selectively in political and social affairs until his death. Perhaps the most striking instance of this engagement occurred during 1940 and early 1941 in connection with the consequences of the Soviet-Nazi Pact of 1939. The Soviet Union argued that the pact was necessary to protect itself against possible aggression by European capitalist nations. The American left accepted this argument and translated it into a strident belief that America should not support Britain in its attempt to survive, and Dreiser himself endorsed these interpretations in what is no doubt his worst book, *America Is Worth Saving* (1941).

But for the most part, aside from his continuing difficulties with his publishers (now Simon & Schuster, with whom he had signed a long-term contract in 1934) and his fuller involvement, once he settled in Los Angeles, in efforts to sell his work to the movies, the final decade of Dreiser's career was characterized by attempts to put his literary affairs in order and to complete work that had long lay dormant. He arranged for his literary estate to go to the University of Pennsylvania, and he aided his biographer, Robert H. Elias, in his research. He labored on giving final expression to the philosophical ideas that had so long engaged him. And out of various trunks came the many fragments of *The Bulwark* and *The Stoic*, novels which had been promised again and again to publisher after publisher, to be at last completed—*The Stoic* just a few weeks before his death.[6]

* * *

It is difficult to broadly characterize Dreiser's friendships throughout his life except to note that his letters reveal more extended and intense relationships than his volatile temperament might suggest was possible. Sometimes, of course, as in the case of H. L. Mencken and Otto Kyllmann, his British publisher, the relationship was broken off for an extended period (almost ten years in Mencken's case) for personal or political reasons. And of course even the most permanent of his friendships waxed and waned over the decades, as in the case of Edgar Lee Masters. But though Dreiser was often socially awkward, he had the capacity to attract and maintain friendships with men who remained remarkably loyal to him and toward whom he was both appreciative and caring. Richard Duffy, his turn-of-the-century companion in New York journalism, was one, William C. Lengel, who served as his literary agent and advisor for more than thirty years, was another, and the poet and fellow iconoclast Masters was a third. Dreiser's letters to these figures are often personal correspondence at its best in that they range freely and expressively over the full extent of his temperament and interests and thereby render the man in all his richness.

Dreiser had many other friends, some of whom, like Burton Rascoe, Claude Bowers, and George Douglas, shared with him some particular enthusiasm or state of mind at a particular phase of his career; or, like Ernest Boyd and George Jean Nathan, were involved with him for a time in a common enterprise; or, like Edward H. Smith, John Cowper Powys, and Donald McCord, derived their association with him from contact within a specific setting. Dreiser also received a great volume of mail from strangers who were moved to write because of their admiration for his novels, and occasionally a correspondent of this kind, such as the ex-convict Joseph Fischler, became a friend. Dreiser's personal relationships sometimes made him vulnerable. His support of the crackpot theories of Charles Fort and John M. Maxwell no doubt stemmed in part from a loyalty to their ideas derived from his friendships with them.

Since it is common to share one's ideas with friends and, in Dreiser's case, on occasion even with total strangers who had written inquiring about some aspect of his belief, his letters provide an excellent insight into the full range of his thought. Indeed, as far as his philosophical ideas are concerned, his letters express his beliefs far more pithily, and thereby often more usefully, than the frequently muddy exposition of his essays. His early stress on life as a struggle is well-caught in letters to Willard Dillman on 7 February 1916 (the "keynote" of his philosophy, he explains, is that "life is a welter") and to Donald P. McCord in June 1920 ("Life is a grinding mess. . . . The individual amounts to nothing"). Almost two decades later, his shift to a more positive mechanism is succinctly summarized in his comments to Paul E. Lacosky on 24 June 1937 that "Philosophically a mechanist, I grant to the great process or machine whatever values it appears to establish in me or others" and to William C. Lengel on 5 July 1941 that "man, as well as the material universe of which he is a part, are both organisms or mechanisms put together by an immaterial and creative power which works through matter and energy as man works in and through clay or wood and stone."

Dreiser's use of scientific ideas in both his fiction and philosophy has aroused skepticism in that he frequently appears to apply scientific findings uncritically to enforce previously held conceptions. His correspondence, however, reveals both his willingness to examine material evidence objectively and his occasional prescience in difficult scientific areas. His 25 February 1931 letter to Mrs. Clinton P. Farrell, for example, chronicles his initial favorable response to her request that he support an anti-vivisection bill and his reversal of this position once he had discovered that vivisection has contributed to important medical advances. In regard to his insights, in an age when few intellectuals questioned the benefits of psychoanalysis in the treatment of mental disease, Dreiser expressed doubts about its efficacy and a belief that severe emotional disturbance often had both a chemical origin and a possible chemical cure (Dreiser to Paul E. Lacosky, 24 June 1937, and Mrs. Jerome S. Blum, 22 October 1936).

Dreiser took little interest in political affairs during his early career, but by the time he began to contribute to the socialist journal the *New York Call* in 1913, several of his long-standing social concerns—especially for the condition of the urban poor—had driven him, as was true of many writers of that period, toward the political left. He admired the socialist leader Eugene Debs and, as he noted in a 17 October 1922 letter to Debs, had voted for him for president on several occasions. By the late 1920s, however, stimulated both by the apparent success of the communist experiment in the Soviet Union and by the highly visible engagement of American communists in contemporary social issues, Dreiser began to participate actively in communist-led groups and movements. However, although Dreiser often identified himself in interviews during the 1930s as a communist and also often expressed economic and political views similar to those of the party, he was drawn into communist-led campaigns during this period primarily by the party's activism on behalf of civil and judicial rights. Present as a common thread in his participation in the Tom Mooney and Scottsboro Boys cases and the Harlan investigation was his belief that Americans of a specific class or race or political conviction were being denied their constitutional rights to freedom of speech and to justice.

As his correspondence reveals, however, Dreiser for most of his career was temperamentally incapable of resting easily within any organized political faith. He wrote his *Call* editor David Karsner on 9 August 1922 that though "the socialization of many things is important . . . even there best results are certain to flow from the presence of the individual and his ambitions." And he could not help teasing the committed socialist Upton Sinclair, in a letter of 18 December 1924, that "the brotherhood of man—(this entirely apart from some of the co-operative phases of socialism) is mere moonshine to me." His quarrel with communism for much of the 1930s was both with its absolutist ideology and with the frequent unscrupulousness and even dishonesty of its adherents. He complained to Lina Goldschmidt on 23 August 1930, for example, that the stage version of *An American Tragedy* which she and Erwin Piscator (both staunch German communists) had prepared was too doctrinaire:

> I am by no means as final in my conclusions in regard to the ills of society and the government or the way out as the text of this dramatization would indicate. For instance, by no means do I believe that the rich man is a scoundrel or the poor man an angel. Nor do I believe that the rich capitalist is always conscious of the injustices of a system of which he is an heir any more than I believe that the poor man is always conscious of the fact that society has benefited in the past, certainly by at least some of the methods of capitalism.[7]

In addition, he was irritated that his name was used by communist organizations without his approval, that he was constantly hounded for contributions to left-wing journals, and—most painful of all—that the state-owned and -operated Russian publishing houses appeared to be cheating him on his royalties. His sense of being used by the far left at home and abroad reached a climax in July 1938 when he accepted, after much urging, membership in a delegation of American writers to a communist-organized Paris peace conference. In a 16 July 1938 letter to Edgar Lee Masters, Dreiser adopted the comic device of pretending that he had been kidnapped and "when I get over in France they're goin to take me somewhere and stand me up and when they say '*say Peace*' I gotta say it. Now Doc, you know ordinarily I'm for peace—plenty of it—but this here way of makin me say it don't seem quite natural."

Whatever his inclination to think and act "natural," Dreiser fell into line on that occasion and, indeed, for the remainder of his life. Unlike many American writers and intellectuals on the left, he was not appalled by the 1939 Soviet-Nazi pact and in fact based his 1941 diatribe *America Is Worth Saving* on the strict party-line position of that period that the greater threat to peace was not Nazi Germany but European capitalist democracies. Dreiser had attempted to formally join the Communist Party in 1932 but had been turned down by its then chairman, Earl Browder, because he was considered ideologically unreliable. There was no question about this issue when he again sought membership in the spring of 1945. In an act symbolic of the character of this last phase of Dreiser's political belief and activities, his widely noted 20 July 1945 letter requesting membership was largely written by party hacks.

Dreiser's religious and ethnic prejudices constitute a significant though painful aspect of his social beliefs. His lifelong, often virulent anti-Catholicism stemmed from a youthful resentment against his father's efforts to impose absolutist religious beliefs and practices on the Dreiser family, a resentment that was later reinforced by his frequent encounters with Catholic censorship. He commented to Arnold Gingrich, in a letter of 31 October 1935, that behind the attempt by Chicago's mayor to censor *Tobacco Road* "is the Catholic Church, which, endangered by any show of real intelligence anywhere, is determined to fight all mental progress here and throughout the world"—a remark typical of the tone and substance of his belief in this area.

Dreiser's anti-Semitism is a more complex area. He himself, as in a 25 May 1938 letter to A. Heller, often denied that he was anti-Semitic, offering as evidence the many Jews with whom he was friends and the sympathetic portrait he had drawn of East Side Jewish life in his play *The Hand of the Potter*. Both of these appear to be valid arguments, since Dreiser did know and admire such Jews as Abraham Cahan, Jerome Blum, Horace Kallen, A. A. Brill, David Karsner, and Albert Mordell, and *The Hand of the Potter* was much praised by Cahan,[8] himself a novelist of Jewish life. The weaknesses in this argument, however, are that all the Jewish figures usually cited as friends by Dreiser were writers, artists, or intellectuals and that *The Hand of the Potter* was written in 1916. During the late 1920s and early 1930s Dreiser had a series of adverse business relationships with Jewish publishers and movie studio owners, producers, and directors which permanently affected his attitude toward the Jews.

Dreiser's suspicion of Jewish business practices initially focused on Horace Liveright, his publisher during the 1920s, who he believed was guilty both of falsely reporting royalties and of stinting on promised promotion. These suspicions came to a head in early 1926 in a notorious incident regarding the movie rights to *An American Tragedy*, an incident which also involved Jesse Lasky, head of Famous Players–Lasky film company. (Dreiser believed that Liveright and Lasky had conspired to lower the price of the rights in exchange for a higher agent's fee for Liveright.[9]) When *An American Tragedy* was at last filmed in early 1931, Dreiser may have seen his unsuccessful attempt to maintain control over the artistic integrity of the production as a struggle against a Jewish conspiracy to pervert the work and tailor it to popular expectations, since the movie's producer, writer, and director were Jewish.[10] In any case, in 1933 Dreiser advised Sherwood Anderson, in a letter of 12 May, to avoid employing a Jewish lawyer in any dealings with Hollywood, and in an *American Spectator* "Editorial Conference" on the Jew in America (published in September) Dreiser complained of the excessive shrewdness of Jews in their business dealings. The adverse reaction to the conference as well as to the publication in 1935 of his correspondence with Hutchins Hapgood on his possible anti-Semitism hardened Dreiser's attitudes.[11] Although he continued to deny publicly that he held anti-Semitic views, in letters of 1939 he asked Dayton Stoddart to provide him with a list of non-Jewish publishers, complained to William C. Lengel that his Jewish publishers Simon & Schuster were retaliating against him for his alleged anti-Semitism, and summarized to Stoddart his belief that Jews in Hollywood were "arrogant, insolent, and contemptuous."[12]

Dreiser's beliefs about the Jews, though not that uncommon during the 1920s and early 1930s among both the general public and many writers, received, and continue to receive, a great deal of attention for several reasons. One is that in this area, as in a number of others, Dreiser tended to translate personal pique into a general proposition. Jews in the movie industry, he appears to have believed, were untrustworthy because they were Jews. A different perspective is provided by Ernest Boyd in his response to Dreiser's letter of apology on 1 May 1931 after Dreiser had spoken negatively about Jews in the film business at a dinner party where one of the guests was, unknown to Dreiser, a Jew. Boyd noted in his letter of 4 May that his own point of view was that "Gentiles, trying to run the same racket today, have to and do adopt the same methods. If Hollywood, for example, were controlled by Gentiles but aimed at the same audience and profits, it would be just the same as we see it. Mass production and excess profiteering produce the same results in Jew and Gentile."

Another reason for the great attention paid to Dreiser's alleged anti-

Semitism was the historical moment in which it became a matter of conten-
tion. Throughout the middle and late 1930s, Dreiser's views about the Jews
were under especially close scrutiny because of the impact on the public
consciousness of the Nazi oppression of German Jews. This attention irritated
Dreiser, but it was perhaps an inevitable consequence of the seeming disparity
between his beliefs in this area and his reputation as a figure who had great
sympathy for the underdog in both his writing and political activities.

A great many of Dreiser's letters, in addition to their frequent expression
of his philosophical, political, and social beliefs, also reflect his profession
as an author and thereby provide a record of his work from *Sister Carrie* to
The Stoic. He writes of his plans for a book, his progress on it, his expectations about publication, his disappointment at its reception and sale,
and—in several notable instances involving *Sister Carrie* and *An American
Tragedy*[13]—recapitulates his intent in the work. His literary allegiances and
beliefs appear not only in comments about his own writing but also in correspondence dealing with the work of others. He is generous in promoting
the reputation of neglected realists of his own generation and, during the
1910s, the writing of the new poets and novelists, such as Carl Sandburg,
Edgar Lee Masters, and Sherwood Anderson, who were emerging, as he had,
out of the Midwest and out of Chicago in particular. In the last decades
of his life he writes revealing critiques of novels sent him for evaluation,
and, as he becomes an object of study in the history of late nineteenth- and
early twentieth-century American literature, he responds to questions from
students and scholars.

Much of Dreiser's professional correspondence also bears on his career-
long difficulties with his publishers. Scarred by his relationship with Doubleday, Page and Company in 1900 over the publication of *Sister Carrie*, Dreiser
tended to view all publishers, with one or two exceptions, as misguided and
excessively self-interested at best and as scoundrels and thieves at worst. The
long and tortuous history of his affairs with various firms—from Doubleday,
Page through Harper's, John Lane, Boni and Liveright, Simon & Schuster,
Putnam's, and (once again) Doubleday—is largely that of dashed initial
hopes followed by acrimony, lawsuits, and the search for a new company.
His list of complaints—many of them justified—included a firm's failure to
deliver on promised advertising, its overly swift withdrawal of books from
print, its untrustworthy royalty reports, and its excessive interest in the
publication of his novels at the cost of his work in other genres. Of course,
publishers had their own crosses to bear with Dreiser, most notably his failure
to deliver contracted novels which had been subsidized by large advances
and his insistence that they publish clearly unprofitable ventures such as
his philosophical essays and poetry.

One of Dreiser's major preoccupations during the last thirty years of his career was to gather all his works under one imprint and have them republished in a uniform edition (see, for example, his 9 April 1921 letter to Edward H. Smith). Indeed, in one of his last letters, to William C. Lengel on 17 November 1945, he returned yet again to this theme. There is some irony, therefore, in the fact that his one success both in this effort and in his establishment of a longtime cordial relationship with a publisher occurred with Constable and Company, his British publisher from 1926 to his death. He struck up a close friendship with Otto Kyllmann, his Constable editor, and during the late 1920s and early 1930s Constable issued a "New Uniform Edition" of Dreiser's novels and also republished much of his earlier work other than fiction.

Constable, however, was the one bright spot in Dreiser's otherwise disastrous relationships with European publishers. A good deal of Dreiser's correspondence from the late 1920s onward, after *An American Tragedy* had made him world famous, was devoted to issues stemming from the translation and publication of his work abroad. Many of these difficulties arose from the failure of the United States to ratify the 1886 Berne Convention establishing an international copyright, a lapse which permitted either the open pirating of Dreiser's novels by foreign firms or their cavalier attitude toward the payment of royalties even when a contract was in place. A notable but characteristic instance of the latter involved his German-language publisher, Paul Zsolnay of Vienna. Dissatisfied with what he considered Zsolnay's sporadic and insufficient reporting of royalties, Dreiser hired an American firm, the International Literary Bureau, to oversee the collection of his German-language and other European royalties. The European employees of the bureau, however, proved to be equally untrustworthy, and a highly irritated Dreiser had to ask M. Lincoln Schuster, of his American publisher Simon & Schuster (in a letter of 7 August 1935), to put his firm's accountant to work to sort out the mess. Even more disturbing to Dreiser was the failure of the Soviet Union to fulfill the terms of various publication contracts. Dreiser's highly visible move to the left during the late 1920s, his positive account of the Soviet Union in his *Dreiser Looks at Russia* (1928), and his fictional method of social realism had resulted in frequent Russian translations of his works during the 1930s. His 27 February 1934 letter to William C. Bullitt reveals, however, that even though the Soviet Union had found him doctrinally acceptable, this had not led to the satisfactory fulfillment of his contracts by Soviet publishers.

Like many early twentieth-century American writers, Dreiser often sought to tap into the rich vein offered by the adaptation of his fiction into films. His early desire, as is suggested by his 28 November 1915 letter to Ben

Hecht, was to use this new popular form not only as an income enhancer but to "give a new artistic twist" to his work. For much of his career, as his correspondence reveals, he found this attempt to combine profitability with artistic intent frustrating and time-consuming, and by the late 1930s he appears to have accepted the reality that the Hollywood film was primarily an industrial product.

Several incidents during the 1920s and 1930s dramatize the basis of Dreiser's frequently expressed suspicion of the business ethics and artistic integrity of those controlling film production. In 1923, Vitagraph produced the movie *On the Banks of the Wabash,* the title of which derived from the famous song by Dreiser's brother Paul Dresser, without any acknowledgment or payment to the Dreiser family. In 1931, in a highly publicized controversy, Paramount produced a version of *An American Tragedy* which Dreiser (and most other viewers) held to be a false representation of the themes of the novel. In 1935, Dreiser accused Universal of plagiarizing his *Jennie Gerhardt* in its film adaptation of Fannie Hurst's novel *Back Street.* Throughout the 1930s, Dreiser believed that the Hays Office, Hollywood's official censor, was responsible for his inability to find a studio willing to film *Sister Carrie.* It is no wonder that Dreiser's correspondence with movie executives stimulated extreme examples of his ability to deliver the epistolary insult. The Vitagraph company heads are charged with a "porch climbers capitalization of my brother's property" (Dreiser to W. Wallace Ham, 26 September 1923) and Robert Cochrane, a vice president of Universal, is told that "possibly you will apologize but I doubt it. What is needed is an apology from life itself for the existence of your type" (Dreiser to Cochrane, 1 October 1935).

Nevertheless, after Dreiser and Helen moved to Los Angeles in December 1938, his proximity to the Hollywood film marketplace and his desire to solidify his financial situation encouraged full-scale attempts to interest studios and individual actors both in adaptations of his own work and in totally new scenarios produced with a mass audience in mind. In these efforts he achieved two notable successes. In 1940 *Sister Carrie* was at last sold to a movie studio (it was not actually filmed until 1952) and in 1941 *My Gal Sal,* a musical comedy based on Paul's life, was sold to Twentieth Century–Fox and produced in 1942.

Like many writers, Dreiser attempted throughout his life to define himself in relation to his early experience. The richness of his Indiana boyhood, with its mix of ill-matched parents, children eager for life, and continuous poverty and movement; his work as a reporter in free-wheeling American cities of the 1890s such as Chicago, St. Louis, and Pittsburgh; and his struggle upward in New York as a freelance magazine writer and editor—all were available as sources for the representation of where he had come from and who he was. His autobiographies dealing with his early life and career—*Dawn* (1931), *A Hoosier Holiday* (1916), and *Newspaper Days* (1922)—are among his best works. But Dreiser also often dealt with these phases of his life in his correspondence, indeed increasingly so as his career advanced. This constant recapitulation of his life began as early as 1901, when in a remarkable autobiographical letter to his friend Richard Duffy on 18 November, he strikes many of the notes he would continually replay. His extensive correspondence during the 1920s concerning efforts to establish a Paul Dresser memorial in Terre Haute is more than peripherally related to his own autobiographical impulse. In honoring Paul he would honor as well the energy and talent which had propelled both of them from an obscure Indiana background into artistic fame. From the late 1920s until his death Dreiser was frequently, as his letters reveal, asked about specific moments of his career and often responded in detail. He recalls his Warsaw, Indiana, childhood,[14] including the importance of his teacher Mildred Fielding.[15] He tells of his years as a magazine journalist[16] and of his early literary enthusiasms.[17] He retells the story of the writing of *Sister Carrie*[18] and corrects Grant Richards's account of their relationship.[19] And finally, during his last years, he aids his biographer Robert H. Elias in shedding light on the more obscure recesses of his life and career.[20]

Notes

1. See H. L. Mencken's "Theodore Dreiser," in *A Book of Prefaces* (New York: Knopf, 1917), 67–148; Stuart P. Sherman, "The Naturalism of Mr. Dreiser," *Nation* 101 (2 December 1915): 648–50; and W. A. Swanberg, *Dreiser* (New York: Scribners, 1965).

2. Robert H. Elias, ed., *Letters of Theodore Dreiser*, 3 vols. (Philadelphia: University of Pennsylvania Press, 1959); Thomas P. Riggio, ed., *Dreiser-Mencken Letters: The Correspondence of Theodore Dreiser and H. L. Mencken, 1907–1945*, 2 vols. (Philadelphia: University of Pennsylvania Press, 1986).

3. Robert H. Elias, *Theodore Dreiser: Apostle of Nature* (New York: Knopf, 1949).

4. Otis Notman, "Talks with Four Novelists: Mr. Dreiser," *New York Times Saturday Review of Books*, 15 June 1907, 393; reprinted in *Theodore Dreiser: A Selection of Uncollected Prose*, ed. Donald Pizer (Detroit, Mich.: Wayne State University Press, 1977), 164.

5. Dreiser used a number of varying titles for this work during its long genesis. I have adopted one of these titles for all references to it within my own comments. When the work was posthumously published in 1974, its editors entitled it *Notes on Life*.

6. *The Stoic* was complete in the sense that Dreiser had finished a full draft of it. At the suggestion of James T. Farrell, however, he had begun a revision of its conclusion but had not completed this revision at his death.

7. For this letter, see Volume II, Dreiser to Lina Goldschmidt, 23 August 1930.

8. See Dreiser to Cahan, 23 December 1921, in which Dreiser notes Cahan's praise of the play.

9. See Swanberg, *Dreiser*, 306.

10. See Donald Pizer, "Dreiser and the Jews," *Dreiser Studies* 35 (Summer 2004): 3–23.

11. Hutchins Hapgood, "Is Dreiser Anti-Semitic?" *Nation* 140 (17 April 1935): 436–38. Portions of the corerspondence are also in Elias, *Letters*, II, 648–53; 657–64.

12. Dreiser to Stoddart, 10 May 1939; to Lengel, 6 May 1939; and to Stoddart, 22 June 1939.

13. For *Sister Carrie*, see Dreiser to Mr. Kohl, 8 February 1927, and to John Howard Lawson, 10 August and 10 October 1928; for *An American Tragedy*, see Dreiser to Elmer Davis, 15 January 1926.

14. Dreiser to Heath Bowman, 19 November 1940.

15. Dreiser to George T. Bye, 29 October 1939.

16. Dreiser to George A. Van Nosdall, 31 May 1921; to Edward McDonald, 25 November 1927; and to Francis H. Bangs, 9 January 1933.

17. Dreiser to Gabriel Lapique, 13 April 1939.

18. Dreiser to Sergei Dinamov, 14 March 1927, and to Burton Rascoe, 13 April 1931.

19. Dreiser to Albert H. Gross, 26 June 1934.

20. Dreiser to Elias, 28 January and 15 February 1945.

EDITORIAL NOTE

The letters included in *Theodore Dreiser: New Letters* are "new" in the sense that they were not published in the two major collections of Dreiser's correspondence, *Letters of Theodore Dreiser: A Selection*, ed. Robert H. Elias, 3 vols. (Philadelphia: University of Pennsylvania Press, 1959) and *Dreiser-Mencken Letters: The Correspondence of Theodore Dreiser and H. L. Mencken*, ed. Thomas P. Riggio, 2 vols. (Philadelphia: University of Pennsylvania Press, 1986). A small number, however, have appeared in various journals and books; they are included in these volumes to make available in convenient form Dreiser's significant correspondence not in the two earlier collections.

The textual principles underlying the representation of the texts of Dreiser's letters in this new collection derive both from general conventions regarding the transcription of authorial production not originally intended for publication and the specific nature of Dreiser's practice as a correspondent. Dreiser's handwritten letters, since they constitute a unique and authorially sanctioned expression of his intent, are reproduced as written without the editorial intervention of brackets or a "*sic*" to indicate errors of spelling or punctuation. (Dreiser, in fact, as a trained newspaperman, wrote with relatively few such errors except for lifelong difficulties with the "ei" and "ie" spelling distinction and in the use of the comma, apostrophe, dash, and parentheses.) The one major exception to this rule stems from his frequent careless failure to close a sentence with a period. Since little would be gained by reproducing this error, periods have been silently supplied to sentences of this kind. In addition, crossed-out words are not reproduced or noted unless there is some special significance to Dreiser's emendations. When a word cannot be deciphered, whether in a holograph or typescript letter, its site in the text is noted with an *illegible* between brackets. When a word necessary for the understanding of a sentence has been carelessly omitted, a *word omitted* within brackets has been placed at the site of the omission. Place names and word usages that were spelled differently in Dreiser's day (such as "Pittsburg" and "developes") are silently retained as they appear in the letters.

Dreiser's typewritten letters seldom have the textual authority of his holograph correspondence. Dreiser typed infrequently and with difficulty, and, except for a few letters to close women friends, did not type his own letters. Beginning in the years between 1905 and 1910, however, when he was a magazine editor, and quite frequently from 1919 to his death, when he privately employed a long series of secretary/typists, many of his letters are typewritten. Dreiser's typewritten letters are in two forms: original ribbon copies, signed by him, which are usually in collections other than the Dreiser Papers, and unsigned carbons in the Dreiser Papers. (The Dreiser Collection at the Annenberg Rare Book and Manuscript Library of the University of Pennsylvania contains the Dreiser Papers, including extensive files of correspondence to him and copies of letters by him.) There are also a few signed carbons in the Dreiser Papers, which are so noted. The carbons contain almost no correction of typist's errors, and very few of the signed ribbon copies contain such corrections, though a good many contain Dreiser's handwritten postscripts or marginal additions. To reproduce Dreiser's typewritten letters in the form in which they exist would be to preserve, especially when carbons are used, innumerable typographical errors. To correct such errors and to indicate each correction with a note would be to thicken the text and notes with a great deal of unproductive clutter. It has been thought best, therefore, to silently correct all typographical errors in typescript letters. In addition, the recipient's address has been omitted from all letters; the printed letterhead of some of Dreiser's typewritten letters—that of hotels, magazines, and organizations—has been silently shortened; and Dreiser's own return address, when it is that of an office, is omitted after its initial appearance. However, the often inconsistent and idiosyncratic punctuation of Dreiser's typists has been left unchanged unless it obscures meaning, in which case it also has been silently corrected.

The letters have been annotated in the following manner:

The nature and location of the document used to edit each letter are noted in the right-hand corner immediately following the name of the recipient, using the abbreviations in the list at the end of the Editorial Note.

A headnote provides relevant information about the recipient and the biographical or historical context of the letter. All letters to Dreiser cited or quoted in the headnotes and notes are in the Dreiser Papers.

The notes seek to identify specific people, events, works, allusions, and quotes. When possible, birth and death dates of individuals named in the letter are provided. When information about an individual or event is present in the annotation of an earlier letter, this information is not repeated but rather a cross-reference to that letter is provided. The cross-references in each volume of this edition of Dreiser's letters, however, refer only to material in that volume. The index at the close of each volume is limited to material in that volume.

ABBREVIATIONS

Description of Letters:

H—Holograph
HP—Photostat of holograph
Tel—Telegram
TC—Typewritten unsigned carbon
TCopy—Typewritten unsigned copy (not a carbon)
TCS—Typewritten signed carbon
TS—Typewritten signed ribbon copy

Location of Letters:

AAA—Archives of American Art, Smithsonian Institute, Washington
AJA—American Jewish Archives, Cincinnati
Auerbach—Personal possession of Jonathan Auerbach
BLUC—Bancroft Library, University of California, Berkeley
BLYU—Bienecke Library, Yale University
Br—Brown University Library
BRUP—Burton Rascoe Papers, University of Pennsylvania Library
Cor—Cornell University Library
CU—Columbia University Library
Dart—Dartmouth College Library
DeP—DePauw University Library
DPUP—Dreiser Papers, Dreiser Collection, Annenberg Rare Book and Manuscript Library, University of Pennsylvania
EU—Emory University Library
Hav—Haverford College Library
Heim—Personal possession of William J. Heim
HLHU—Houghton Library, Harvard University
HRHUT—Harry Ransom Humanities Research Center, University of Texas, Austin
HSP—Historical Society of Pennsylvania, Philadelphia
Hun—Huntington Library, San Marino, Calif.

ISU—Indiana State University Library, Terre Haute
JTFUP—James T. Farrell Papers, University of Pennsylvania Library
KSU—Kent State University Library
LC—Library of Congress
LLIU—Lilly Library, Indiana University
NL—Newberry Library, Chicago
NYP—New York Public Library
PU—Princeton University Library
SIU—Southern Illinois University Library
SLRC—Schlesinger Library, Radcliffe College
TU—Temple University Library
UCLA—University of California, Los Angeles, Library
UConn—University of Connecticut Library
UG—University of Georgia Library
UI—University of Illinois Library
UK—University of Kentucky Library
USC—University of Southern California Library
USoCar—University of South Carolina Library
UV—University of Virginia Library
WCLUP—William C. Lengel Papers, University of Pennsylvania
    Library

Other Abbreviations:

Elias, *Letters: Letters of Theodore Dreiser: A Selection*, ed. Robert H.
    Elias, 3 vols. (Philadelphia: University of Pennsylvania Press,
    1959).
Lingeman, *Dreiser, I:* Richard Lingeman, *Theodore Dreiser: At the
    Gates of the City, 1871–1907* (New York: Putnam's, 1986).
Lingeman, *Dreiser, II:* Richard Lingeman, *Theodore Dreiser: An
    American Journey, 1908–1945* (New York: Putnam's, 1990).
Riggio, *Dreiser-Mencken Letters: The Correspondence of Theodore
    Dreiser and H. L. Mencken*, ed. Thomas P. Riggio, 2 vols.
    (Philadelphia: University of Pennsylvania Press, 1986).
Swanberg, *Dreiser:* W. A. Swanberg, *Dreiser* (New York: Charles
    Scribner's Sons, 1965).

Theodore Dreiser

A Picture and a Criticism of Life

NEW LETTERS, VOLUME I

1888

To Judson Morris [H-Heim][1]

Two days short of seventeen, Dreiser writes Morris, the son of a Warsaw bookstore owner and a friend from Warsaw High School, about life in the great city. Dreiser's comment that "the country is far nicer" may derive in part from his series of miserable jobs since arriving in Chicago the summer before.

Chicago, Ill. Aug. 25, 1888

My Dear Judson,

I could not long remain away from Warsaw without writing back to you. I might as well apologize for this paper now. You will notice the extreme width between lines. Well it is "Home Rule" paper.[2] Chicago is quite lively now and there is plenty to see. I see a good part of it. You can sit at a window and amuse yourself for hours by just watching the people.[3] Sunday mornings one can lay in bed and hear the boys yell off the morning papers. They have elegant parks here and the Board of Trade[4] takes the bun. But after all the country is far nicer. When I think of how we went fishing at night and what fun we had in school it makes me long for the country again. I read Oliver Twist and Dr. Jekyll and Mr. Hyde this week and I read "Mr. Potter of Texas,"[5] the week before. All three of them are great. I will now mention a few jokes perpatrated by myself after which I will seal this missive.

I bought a spool of thread the other day. The man says "will you have Kerrs." I says "I don't Kerr if I do.[6]

I feel Joliet over that.

Well that will do for one time. I will try to do better in my next. Answer soon on about 10 sheets of paper.

I remain with best wishes to yourself and cousin.

as ever

Theodore Dreiser

(over)[7]

1. Published in William J. Heim, "Letters from Young Dreiser," *American Literary Realism* 8 (Spring 1975): 158–64.

2. Dreiser composed his letter to Morris on small sheets of blank paper on which he ruled lines. After "'Home Rule' paper" he placed an asterisk and, following a similar asterisk at the foot of the page wrote, "One on me." The joke lies in the allusion to the almost constant late nineteenth-century political controversy over Home Rule for Ireland.

3. Sister Carrie, it will be recalled, is fond of sitting by her window to view the street life below; see the opening to Chapter IV and the closing lines of the novel.

4. The imposing Chicago Board of Trade Building, at La Salle and Jackson (completed 1885), was then one of the city's landmarks.

5. Mr. *Potter of Texas* (1888) by the popular novelist Archibald Calvering Gunter (1847–1907), whose Mr. *Barnes of New York* (1887) sold over a million copies and was still widely read during the 1890s.

6. Kerr & Co. was a major thread manufacturer.

7. On the reverse side of this page Dreiser has added:

Address
T. H. Dreiser
489, Ogden Avenue.
Chicago, Ill.

1898

To Richard Duffy [H-HRHUT]

*Dreiser's turn to freelance journalism in late 1897 roughly coincided with the found-
ing of* Ainslee's Magazine *in February 1898, with Richard Duffy (1873–1949)
as editor. Over the next three years, Dreiser contributed almost thirty pieces to the
magazine and also established a warm and lifelong relationship with the congenial,
lively, and supportive Duffy. Duffy continued working in magazine journalism for
many years; he also wrote two novels and a play and translated a number of books
from French. During the late 1890s, Dreiser was a member of the Salmagundi
Club, which had many artists and illustrators among its members. He often used
its stationery for correspondence.*

Salmagundi Club,
14 West 12th St.

N.Y. May 25, 98

My Dear Duffy:—

Perhaps you have seen by now the nature of the poem in Colliers Weekly,
and if so you know where the suggestion came from. It was your remark
"Why dont you write something about him" that caused me to think of
sending some tribute to Colliers.[1] So you see how deeds come to be done.

I enclose two poems here for which I desire your consideration the one
"Night Song" I want published *quite much,*—so much so that if you are
willing to bring it out sometime during the summer you are welcome to it,
and it will do me a turn. If you think it advisable, I would like to have the
fourth verse excoriated, making the poem four verses long. Use your best
judgment however.[2]

The other poem "Broadway" is one that is submitted as all poems are. I
do not think any more of it than of the "Night Song", but it is to my interest to have the latter brought out soon. Hence the elimination of cost. You
will do me a favor by passing judgment, and a greater one by using the first,
as suggested.[3]

Is there any western subject you can think of? I am off for Chicago shortly,
sure![4]

Yours,
Dreiser

Dreiser with Richard Duffy and Friends.

1. The poem was "Of One Who Dreamed: W. Louis Sonntag, Jr., Obiit, May 11, 1898," *Collier's Magazine* 21 (28 May 1898): 2. (Sonntag had died of malaria in Cuba, where he had been working as an illustrator during the Spanish-American War.) Dreiser had come to know Sonntag (1870–1898), a young artist specializing in New York street scenes, in late 1895. He also wrote an essay on Sonntag's work, "The Color of Today," *Harper's Weekly* 45 (14 December 1901): 1272–73, which was collected as "W. L. S." in *Twelve Men* (1919).

2. "Night-Song," *Ainslee's* 2 (August 1898): 73. Dreiser appears to be using "excoriated" in the unusual sense of "stripped away." The poem as published in *Ainslee's* has four stanzas.

3. "Broadway" did not appear in *Ainslee's* or, apparently, in any other magazine.

4. Dreiser left for Chicago on 14 June to collect material for a series of articles, returning on 1 July.

To Richard Duffy [H-UV]

Salmagundi Club,
14 West 12th St.
Aug 24—98

My Dear Duffy:—

Enclosed find the poem, which I hope you will like.[1] I think it could be illustrated and I had a mind once to ask my friend Kelly[2] to make me sketch to accompany it, but have not done so yet. There is a poem of mine in the Sept. Success which I wish you would take a look at.[3]

The book you loaned me is fine.[4] Your photo wants your signature on it, and I will bring it down for that purpose shortly. Will you drop me a line stating when Zangwill is to arrive and what boat.[5] I've forgotten the exact day.

Sincerely,
Dreiser.

N.B. If you use the poem let me see a proof, will you.

1. Dreiser enclosed the twenty-four-line poem "Art Thou a Mourner"; it did not appear in *Ainslee's* or elsewhere.
2. Perhaps the New York sculptor and illustrator James E. Kelly (1855–1933), with whom Dreiser was friendly.
3. "Thou Giant," *Success* 1 (September 1898): 16.
4. Unidentified.
5. Dreiser was planning to interview the English writer Israel Zangwill (1864–1926), whose *Children of the Ghetto* (1892) and other novels of London's East End had received much attention. The article appeared as "The Real Zangwill," *Ainslee's* 2 (November 1898): 351–57.

1899

To Laura Stedman   [H-CU]

Edmund Clarence Stedman (1833–1908), a banker and poet, was a notable arbiter of public literary taste for much of his later career through his anthologies of American poetry. Dreiser wrote much poetry during the late 1890s and it was no doubt in response to Stedman's role as a supporter of American poets that Dreiser had sent him a book-length collection of his poetry in April. Not hearing from Stedman, who was ill, he directed this inquiry to Stedman's daughter, who often served as her father's aide during this period.

Salmagundi Club,
14 West 12th St.[1]
May 31—99

Miss Laura Stedman,
Dear Madam:—

   I do not wish to trouble Mr. Stedman concerning the verses which I sent him and yet I should be pleased to know if he will find time to look them over before the latter part of June. I leave for the West at that time for the summer.[2] Without disturbing him with any direct query perhaps you could inform me. I shall thank you very sincerely for your kindness.

Very Respectfully
Theodore Dreiser

   1. Although Dreiser and Sara White (often called by her nickname Jug) were married in December 1898 and moved into a New York apartment on 6 West 102nd St., Dreiser here continues to use his Salmagundi Club address.
   2. Dreiser and his wife left for Maumee, Ohio, in early July to spend several months with Arthur Henry and his wife at their house on the Maumee River.

To Ellen M. Boult   [H-CU]

Miss Boult, Stedman's secretary, wrote Dreiser on 9 June that Stedman had been ill but had nevertheless read the poems. Stedman, she reported, noted that Dreiser's "characteristic and best mood" was the contemplative, but that poems "lacking in dramatic or lyric quality" failed to appeal to the present generation. For that reason, "he does not venture to advise" Dreiser about publication.

[After 9 June 1899]
6W 102
Ainslee's Magazine
Street & Smith
Publishers
2–8 Duane Street, New York City

Miss Ellen M. Boult,
Lawrence Park.[1]
Dear Madam:—

I had only learned of Mr. Stedmans serious illness, through Mr. Torrence,[2] when I received your kind letter. I am sorry now to have troubled him so much, and intended, after hearing Mr. Torrence's report to write and ask that the matter of criticism be dropped. Still I am grateful for the opinion and believe it to be correct. Concerning the matter of popularity, poetry so far as I can learn has never been popular. A critically admired volume stands more as an exponent of a mans mental caliber than as a source of revenue or general fame. Possibly Mr. Stedman will be interested in knowing that these will be published in the fall.[3]

If you will express to him my sincere gratitude you will confer a favor upon me.

Very Respectfully
Theodore Dreiser

1. Stedman lived in a handsome large house in Lawrence Park, an artist's and writer's colony in the Bronxville section of northern New York City. The colony was the subject of one of Dreiser's earliest freelance articles, "New York's Art Colony. The Literary and Art Retreat at Bronxville," *Metropolitan* 6 (November 1897): 321–26, and he later devoted a full article to Stedman's house, "Edmund Clarence Stedman at Home," *Munsey's* 20 (March 1899): 931–38. Neither of these articles provides any evidence that he ever met Stedman.
2. Ridgeley Torrence (1875–1950), a New York journalist and poet whose work Stedman had sponsored; in late 1898 Stedman had sought, through Dreiser, to get Torrence a position at *Ainslee's*.
3. On 15 May 1898 Dreiser wrote Sara White (LLIU) that his book of poems would be published that fall, a claim he repeated in a McClure Syndicate interview in late July. The 1899/1900 *Who's Who in America* listing for Dreiser also noted a book of "Poems." However, the volume never appeared.

To Richard Watson Gilder   [H-NYP]

Richard Watson Gilder (1844–1909) was the editor of the Century, *one of the most prestigious magazines of its period, from 1881 to his death. Gilder wrote at the top of this letter, "Roosevelt could handle such a topic but I wouldn't commit myself to either of them before seeing." (Theodore Roosevelt was at this time governor of New York; Gilder is referring to Roosevelt's career earlier in the 1890s, when he did a considerable amount of freelance writing on popular topics.) Since an article of the kind Dreiser suggests was not published in the Century or elsewhere and is also not among Dreiser's surviving manuscripts at DPUP or UV, it is probable that it was not written.*

6W. 102nd St.

Dec. 12th 99

My Dear Mr. Gilder:—

Enclosed is the synopsis of the Country Legislature article which you wished me to send. I hope you gain from reading it that I have the Arkansas Legislature in mind and that my study of it will be sympathetic and impartial.

Along with this I enclose the synopsis of an idea of Mr. Arthur Henry's which he would be pleased to have you consider.[1] There is nothing local in his suggestion and I believe he would write something which would have broad intellectual significance, as well as much human interest.

Kindly let me know what you think of it and oblige

Very Sincerely

Theodore Dreiser

1. Dreiser had met Arthur Henry (1867–1934) in Toledo in 1894 while working briefly on the *Toledo Blade*, which Henry edited; they maintained their friendship between 1895 and 1897, when Dreiser was editing *Ev'ry Month* in New York and before Henry himself came east. With Henry's aid and encouragement, Dreiser was hard at work during the winter of 1899–1900 attempting to complete *Sister Carrie*, while Henry was working on his novel, *A Princess of Arcady*. However, it was also necessary for both of them to keep the pot boiling, as this letter suggests.

1900

To Robert Underwood Johnson [H-NYP]

A further attempt by Dreiser to sell an article idea to the Century. *Robert Underwood Johnson (1853–1937), a poet as well as an editor, was associate editor of the magazine from 1873 until he succeeded R. W. Gilder in 1909. Dreiser visited Washington for about a week in early February gathering material for various articles; Swanberg suggests (Dreiser, 84) that his proposal in this letter derived principally from material in government reports rather than, as Dreiser implies, from personal investigation. An article of this kind was not published and was probably not written.*

919 I Street
Washington
D.C.
Feb 8th 1900

My Dear Mr. Johnson:—

I say the policy or system of selecting and training teachers at Providence is *new* because I have investigated the nearest approaches to this ideal in New Jersey and Massachusetts.[1] Prof. Bumpus,[2] connected with the Massachusetts school system, is probably the most advanced educational worker in this country,—broad, scientific, human—and he told me that Fred Gowing,[3] of Providence has unquestionably approached nearer a true, working ideal in the matter of teacher selection and training then any other man in the country.

Furthermore, I have spread the knowledge of this Providence School among educators in high places and never has my description of the ideals and methods there in force failed to elicit expressions of astonishment and delight. Prof. Soldan, the head of the schools of St. Louis is a personal friend of mine, and upon my visit to St. Louis last November he reassured me that in all his search for some ideal normal system he had never heard of anything to equal this.[4]

Supt. Powell, here in Washington is one of the formost educators in the United States.[5] His local school system is today the subject of investigation by educators the country over, who come here to study the ideal in practice. Mr. Powell assures me that Gowing's system of selecting and training teachers is the best he has heard of yet—the one way by which the perfect teacher is to be obtained.

In the last place, if you please, I consider myself capable of judging in this matter. I have investigated the school systems,—grade and normal—of St. Louis, Kansas City, Chicago, Buffalo, Philadelphia, Boston, Washington, Providence, and New York and I know whereof I speak. For several years the improvement of the American school system has been the one thing that has aroused and retained my enthusiasm. I firmly believe that the welfare of man in the Western hemi-sphere depends solely upon the *genius*, the humanity, the Christ-like simplicity of the educators of our country—Powell, Bumpus, Gowing, Andrews, Soldan, Harper.[6]

Lastly, the school at Providence was not investigated with any idea of making a contribution to a magazine. What I have written is the result of an enthusiasm aroused by the sight of so perfect an ideal. I wrote it because I felt that the world should know and appreciate the perfect way. If what I have written does not convey the feeling that this is the best—if it does not show a high elation for the ideal then I have failed. To the best of my knowledge and belief the system at Providence marks the farthest line of advance in the matter of the right education of the people.

Very Truly
Theodore Dreiser

1. In response to Dreiser's earlier letter, in which he submitted a synopsis of his proposed article on recent educational advances, Johnson had written him on 5 February 1900 that he wished to know "what is the basis for your statement that the R. I. State Normal School policy is 'new.'"

2. Hermon C. Bumpus (1862–1943), a professor of comparative anatomy at Brown University, was to have a distinguished career as a biologist and educator, including the presidency of Tufts College from 1914 to 1919. During the 1890s he took a leading role in advocating reforms in laboratory science teaching.

3. Fred Gowing (1860–?), principal of the Rhode Island Normal School, 1898–1901; located in Providence, the school was devoted to the training of teachers.

4. Frank L. Soldan (1842–1908), superintendent of St. Louis schools (1895–1908).

5. William B. Powell (1836–1904), superintendent of Washington, D.C., schools (1885–1900).

6. Probably Elisha B. Andrews (1844–1917), superintendent of the Chicago schools (1898–1900), and William Rainey Harper (1856–1906), president of the University of Chicago and a member of the Chicago School Board (1898–1900).

1901

To Richard Duffy [H-DPUP]

With Sister Carrie *producing almost no income, Dreiser and his wife moved in early 1901 to a cheaper apartment at East End Avenue and Eighty-second St., where he began work on his second novel,* Jennie Gerhardt. *At this point, the novel was proceeding swiftly; hence Dreiser's certainty that he could complete it within a brief period.*

> 1599 East End Ave.
> N.Y.C.
> March, 19—1901

My Dear Duffy:—

I wonder if you could induce Messrs Street and Smith[1] to loan me a hundred dollars for a few weeks—long enough to allow me to finish my new novel. I am at that place where dropping it temporarily will be more than a distess to me, when a few weeks more will see it finished to my satisfaction and bring me what money I desire. I have not stopped to earn any money this winter—not an article since last October and my expenses have been rather heavy. I do not need any more than that however as I have an understanding with my next publisher which will see me through.[2] There [word missing] no one else I would care to go to but yourself for the simple reason that I would prefer to have the matter undiscussed and you understand. If you can accomodate me I will return the money in cash.

> Since Yours
> Dreiser

1. Street & Smith was the publisher of *Ainslee's*, the magazine Duffy edited and in which Dreiser had published many articles and poems.
2. Although Dreiser was seeking a publisher at this time, he had no formal agreement with one. That was not to come until 23 September 1901, when he signed a contract with J. F. Taylor and Co.

To George P. Brett [H-NYP]

The English-born Brett (1859–1936), president of the American branch of Macmillan & Co., *had shown some interest in* Sister Carrie *during Dreiser's controversy with Doubleday, Page & Co. over the novel's publication. Brett, in a letter of 19 April 1901, turned down the arrangement Dreiser proposes on the grounds that it was not Macmillan's policy to offer advances on incomplete manuscripts.*

> 1599 East End Ave.
> N.Y.C.
>
> March. 19 - 1901
>
> My Dear Duffy:-
>
> I wonder if you could induce Messrs Street and Smith to loan me a hundred dollars for a few weeks - long enough to allow me to finish my new novel. I am at that place where dropping it temporarily will be more than a detriment to me, when a few weeks more will see it finished to my satisfaction and bring me what money I receive - I have not shaped to

> earn any money this winter - not an article since last October and my expenses have been rather heavy I do not need any more than that however as I have an understanding with my next publisher which will see me through. There no one else I would care to go to but yourself for the simple reason that I would prefer to have the matter understood and you understand. If you can accommodate me I will return the money in cash.
>
> Since Yours
> Dreiser

Dreiser to
Richard Duffy,
19 March 1901.

1599 East End Ave.
N.Y.
April 16—1901

My Dear Mr. Brett:—

I desire to know if you would consider a portion of my new novel—the first fourteen chapters—with a view to advancing me $400.00, so that I might go forward with the work and complete it by midsummer. I have already written more than forty chapters, but an error in character analysis makes me wish to throw aside everything from my fifteenth chapter on and rewrite it with a view to making it more truthful and appealing.[1] I shall save considerable of that which is already done, but the new parts will necessitate three and perhaps four months additional labor—an amount of time I shall not be able to give without raising 400.00 either through some such method as this or by means of special writing for the magazines—the latter requiring the abandonment of my work on the novel for the next two months and possibly more. I do not know whether you will consider this a foolish intrusion or not but I cannot resist the temptation to help myself this way, rather then abandon my story. I would supplement the chapters in question with a synopsis of the remainder of the story and in case of its eventual rejection, when completed, would be glad to make any arrangement which would look to the speedy return of your investment.

I do not know how these matters are arranged but will thank you for an opinion, favorable or otherwise.

Very Truly Yours
Theodore Dreiser

1. Dreiser may be referring to his overreliance in his first draft on a depiction of Jennie as a beleaguered child of nature.

To George P. Brett [H-NYP]

1599 East End Ave
N.Y.C.
Sept 26th 1901

Dear Mr. Brett:—

Your kindness in speaking for Sister Carrie on the other side is very thoroughly appreciated by me[1] and I hope than I may some day be able to do something which will show my appreciation. I had hoped that in some way other I might make a valued connection with MacMillan but that seems to have been impossible. I have at last contracted with J. F. Taylor and Company who are to buy the plates, advertise the book very largely and aid me liberally in the completion of my next novel—which on the fulfillment of these terms is to go to them—a contract which I consider very generous indeed.[2] I have learned since that both Messr. Harper and Bros and D. Appleton and Co would have been glad to make me terms which would unquestionably have been advantageous but I seem to have been rather slow in finding it out. Mr. Heinemann informs me personally that he will "make a great fuss over the book" in England[3] and I hope that the wrong done the book here will now be undone. At any rate the struggle I have made to secure for the book an honest hearing is at last to bear fruit and I rest rather assured that no other publisher will attempt suppression in my case again.

I owe you a debt of gratitude for your kind words and good wishes in the past and I trust that this friendship on your part though not sealed by a financial contract may be enduring.

Very Truly Yours
Theodore Dreiser

1. Brett had noted in a letter to Dreiser of 21 September 1901 that he had spoken highly about *Sister Carrie* to a member of the William Heinemann firm during a visit to England. It was Heinemann which then published the English edition of *Sister Carrie* in August 1901.

2. For Dreiser's contract with Taylor and Co., see Dreiser to Richard Duffy, 19 March 1901, n. 2. Taylor and Co. supported Dreiser for eight months while he worked on *Jennie Gerhardt* but did not republish *Sister Carrie* when he failed to complete *Jennie*.

3. On 10 September 1901, Heinemann wrote Frank N. Doubleday, who of course had played the major role in the "suppression" of *Sister Carrie* by its American publisher, Doubleday, Page & Co., that the novel had achieved great critical success in England and congratulating Doubleday on having discovered Dreiser. He included in his letter a letter dated the same day, to be passed on to Dreiser, in which he also congratulated Dreiser. The phrase "a great fuss," however, occurs not in Heinemann's letter to Dreiser but in that to Doubleday in which he advises Doubleday to "make a great fuss" over Dreiser.

To Richard Duffy [H-DPUP]

Dreiser strikes a common note of this period in his claim that he will soon complete Jennie Gerhardt *but requires financial aid to do so.*

1599 East End Ave,
N.Y.C.
Oct. 4—1901

My Dear Duffy:—

If you conveniently can will you be good enough to befriend indigent genius to the extent of an extra hundred, and oblige etc. I have perfected all arrangements with Taylor & Co and will be able to draw upon them for a period of ten months or more, beginning November one, but meanwhile I am in need of about the sum mentioned and would consider it a great favor if you would let me have it.[1]

I could go to Marden[2] and get it or to Taylor and Company but I am rather averse to doing that as it puts the information where I would rather it would not be. With you it is different, as you see.

You have been so long my secret keeper in these matters that I feel that I can safely come to you and be served if you have it. Another month and I shall be out of deep water, never to get back in it I hope. Interest in my work has returned and I labor toward a very excellent conclusion.

As for the money again you can consider this letter as my note for $160.00 if you wish, due any time within six months, although I am sure you feel as I do that nothing of the sort is necessary between us. I will return it at my earliest convenience and shall always hold myself in readiness to do you a like service—should you ever require it.

Yours Sincerely
Dreiser

1. On 6 November 1901, Dreiser signed an agreement with J. F. Taylor Co. in which the firm was to pay Dreiser $100 a month for a year as an advance on *Jennie Gerhardt*.

2. Orison Swett Marden (1850–1924), the publisher of *Success* magazine, a publication which Dreiser had contributed to frequently since early 1898.

To Richard Duffy

[H—LLIU]

Troubled by financial worries and his inability to work on Jennie Gerhardt, *Dreiser, accompanied by his wife, had left New York for the South in early November 1901. They were to remain in Bedford City, a small town east of Roanoke, Virginia, until mid-December. In response to Duffy's request on 15 November 1901 for biographical information to be used in a sketch of Dreiser he was preparing for publication in* Ainslee's, *Dreiser offers this compressed account of his early life. The account is accurate in its broad outline, though it should be noted that, among other errors, Dreiser attended Indiana University one year rather than "several" and was supported at the university not by an "advance" from a "friend" but through the generosity of his former Warsaw, Indiana, high school teacher, Mildred Fielding.*

Bedford City
Va.
Nov. 18—1901

My Dear Duffy:

Thanks for the poem.[1] Had been intending to look it up long before I left New York but never got round to it. I was born Aug 27th 1871 at Terre Haute, Indiana. My father was a manufacturer of woolens and an expert buyer of such products. I was raised at Warsaw, Indiana, but it would be more truthful if my early life were ascribed to not so much to one place as to the whole state. All my life I have been a traveler. I spent my early years—up to 20—in such places at Terre Haute, Vincennes, Evansville, Sullivan, Switz City, Bloomington, Silver Lake, Indianapolis, with Warsaw as a centre. You can understand how this was. Our family had relatives and friends in these places and I knocked about a great deal. Bloomington was the site of the State University which I attended for several years acquiring absolutely nothing save a disrespect for cut and dried methods of imparting information. This is not wholly true however, for the beauty—natural and architectural—which invested the scene carried me to mental heights not previously attained.

The attempt to hire out as a farm hand was really my first effort to earn my own living. I was fifteen years old, in my second year in the local high school, and dreaming of earning something during the three months vacation which began in June. The result I have told you.

Two years later I ventured alone to Chicago, secured a position at three a week in a hardware store as a helper and was shortly discharged. Next I secured a position as clerk in a real estate office where I earned four, but never got it. The man finally paid my due bills for me which was almost as good. Then he failed.

I next secured a place with Hibbard, Spencer, Bartlett and Co—wholesale hardware as clerk and earned five a week. While working here a year I discovered I could go to College for a year, for $200 and made an arrangement with a friend of mine to advance me half of this. The rest I earned and in 1889 adjourned to Bloomington and nugaure[2] state again. What I acquired there, I have just told you.

Once out of college I went back to Chicago and secured several places—one in a real estate office, another in a laundry, a third in an easy payment house as collector and fourth in a better grade house of the same kind. Through these I toiled heaven only knows with what misgivings and gloom over my future. The last three positions mentioned were taken largely because of my lungs. Eight, nine, ten and twelve dollars—thus my salary arose.

All of this time—about two years—I was fearfully dissatisfied. Reading was my great resource—anything, everything. Eugene Field was then on the Chicago News—my friend Gunsaulus pastor of Plymouth Church. I knew neither of them then, but Fields delicate and humorous presentation of the delights of literature in the Daily News and Gunsaulus's sermons delivered Sunday evenings at Central Music Hall fired me immensely.[3] When the convention which nominated Cleveland in 1892 assembled in Chicago, I threw up my twelve a week job, sought the office of the Chicago Globe and hung around there in such a desolate and yearning frame of mind that I think the city editor hired me out of sympathy.

From there on I cannot tell the thousand and one influences, men, women, newspapers, cities, which affected and colored me. I was hired by telegraph by Joseph B. McCullagh, editor of the St. Louis Globe-Democrat,[4] was made traveling correspondent for the St. Louis Republic. Went to Toledo and met Henry,[5] for whose paper the Blade I did some work. Went to Pittsburgh and worked for the Dispatch its leading paper—where I was a free lance and not very hard pressed with work. From there I left to try my luck in New York. Was hired on sight by Brisbane of the New York World.[6] Stayed there about four months when I persuaded Howley Haviland & Co to found Every-Month. You ought to know the rest.

Plays, poems, operas, articles—Lord my trunk is full of them. I shall have a bon fire one of these days in honor of my escape from their influence.

It is very pleasing here as I have said to you. We are not in the mountains but at the very edge. I have been on one walking tour and made 25 1/2 miles in one day, to say nothing of climbing 6000 feet to the top of High Peak. We are thinking of going farther inland into the heart of the mountains. It will be colder but somewhat more picturesque.

Thanks again for the magazine. I hope my article on weeds is not out of date by now.[7] Regards to Mrs Duffy and the others. Mrs. Dreiser includes hers.

Yours

Dreiser

1. In his letter to Dreiser on 15 November 1901, Duffy noted that a copy of the poem "War" by Arthur J. A. Stringer, which had appeared in *Ainslee's* in 1900, was being sent to Dreiser.

2. Dreiser is here apparently attempting to use the Latin word for a "trifle," *nugae* (from the verb *nugari*).

3. Eugene Field (1850–95) wrote the very popular "Sharps and Flats" column for the Chicago *Daily News*; Dreiser had interviewed Dr. Frank Gunsaulus (1856–1921) for *Success* magazine in Chicago during the summer of 1898 and later shared a train journey with him.

4. McCullagh (1842–1896) was a major figure in late nineteenth-century journalism; Dreiser provides a vivid portrait of him in *A Book About Myself* (1922).

5. Arthur Henry, who was then an editor of the *Toledo Blade*; for Henry, see Dreiser to Richard Watson Gilder, 12 December 1899, n. 1.

6. Arthur Brisbane (1864–1936) was editor of Joseph Pulitzer's *New York World*; he later became nationally known as a writer for various Hearst publications.

7. Duffy had earlier accepted Dreiser's article "The New Knowledge of Weeds"; it appeared in the January 1902 issue of *Ainslee's*.

To Richard Duffy [H-DPUP]

Dreiser and Sara had left Virginia in mid-December to spend Christmas with her parents in Missouri.

Montgomery City
Mo.
Dec. 23rd 1901

My Dear Duffy:—

"Beauchamps Career" reached me at Bedford[1] and I was sincerely grateful but being in the throes of packing up I postponed an answer until I should reach here. Arrived safely and had two days with friends in St. Louis which took away my ability for anything but sleep.

I have not been unmindful of your kindness and now that your present of Whitmans poems has come I am set to pondering upon the value of your friendship and its continued expression through these several years. How much I appreciate the substance of kindness between men I have long hoped to make clear but I seem to have a poor medium for my thoughts. It is the best of life—old wine of thought—the stuff of which all better things are made.

Your friendship is a hearty thing. I think I have told you more than once that I like your wholesome stride through life. It is not attenuated or egoistically refined and there is good cheer by your fire. I would rather have it than more of the soulless intellectual.

We are here and the Christmas Day bids fair to be a rout of many children—a Christmas that I like. Green holly, a goodly show of candles, toys, candy, presents galore these are the elements of a Christmas for me.

I wish I knew something that you liked—and yet I will not attempt a present this year. They are only signs to me of something better and that you already have my friendship and good will.

So Merry Christmas for me to Gerald, Fernand,[2] Mrs. Duffy and all the others. I wish them that—a long life and a merry one. As for you—lift up a good glass of wine for me Christmas eve and pledge me in it. I will give your good wishes for the year.

Always
Dreiser

Will write you later.

1. In a letter of 2 December 1901, Duffy noted that he had sent George Meredith's 1876 novel to Dreiser some time earlier and was now sending him a volume of Whitman's poems.
2. Duffy's children.

1902

To Richard Duffy
[H-DPUP][1]

Dreiser and his wife had just arrived in Red Sulphur Springs, West Virginia, a small resort town and spa in the southern portion of the state close to the Virginia line. They were to stay in this area, principally at Hinton, West Virginia, until late March while Dreiser attempted to work on Jennie Gerhardt.

Red Sulpher Springs
West Va.
Feb. 2nd, 1902

My Dear Duffy:—

Ground hogs day is upon us—lowering clouds with now and then a flare of sunshine that he may see his shadow and the wind blowing 50 miles an hour. Red Sulpher is deep in the mountains and a little colder because of that, then would otherwise be the case. Red Sulpher Water is supposed to be good for insomnia. Hence my presence.

Received two letters from you last night—one addressed to Montgomery, Mo.[2] also two magazines and 8 poems, for all of which thanks. Hardys poems are rousingly beautiful to me. I do think that man is the greatest figure in all English literature. I know of no one to place beside him. The poem by Henley is good also. I have a little book of his now—"London Voluntaries and others" some of which are very fine indeed.[3] If you come across any others send them on.

I was interested to see Henry's Island Cabin story and have been wondering whether McClures ever accepted it.[4] Do you know? Hen has rather gone out of my life recently and so a bit of news now and then would be welcome.

You see you are my only New York connection now. I write to my publishers but on business merely.

The novel is proceeding slowly but proceeding. I suppose I will get it done on time. Have meant to tell you what a joy Whitmans poems are to me. Time will put him above all other American poets up to now. He is better than oriental in his pantheism—universal I should say. Thank you again so much for that, for the novels, poems, letters and good will. I appreciate them all.

Yours
Dreiser

1. Published in William White, "Dreiser on Hardy, Henley, and Whitman," *English Language Notes* 8 (December 1968): 122–24.

2. Dreiser and Jug had spent Christmas with her parents in Montgomery City, near St. Louis.

3. On 30 January 1902, Duffy sent Dreiser the poem "Epilogue" by W. E. Henley (1849–1903), which had appeared in Henley's *Hawthorn and Lavender* (1899). Henley's *London Voluntaries and Other Poems* was published in 1893.

4. Dreiser and his wife and Henry and Anna Mallon, whom Henry was soon to marry, had spent part of the summer of 1901 on a small island off Noank, Connecticut, sharing a cabin. Dreiser's and Henry's friendship began to unravel during their stay on the island, and Dreiser was no doubt apprehensive over his possible portrayal in Henry's fictional recreation of the experience. *An Island Cabin* was serialized in the *New York Post* starting in January 1902 and was published by McClure, Phillips, & Co. in March 1902. It contains an unflattering depiction of Dreiser.

To William Dean Howells [H-HLHU][1]

Dreiser had moved from Hinton to Lynchburg, Virginia, and then, after a stay of a few days, to Charlottesville, where he was to remain until early June. At the turn of the century, William Dean Howells (1837–1920) was perhaps the dominant figure on the American literary scene. Although Dreiser had written two complimentary articles on Howells (see note 3 below), they had met, if at all, only in passing. There is no evidence that Howells responded to this letter.

Charlottesville,
Va.
May 14th 1902

My Dear Mr. Howells:—

In looking over the Harpers for April the other night I came across this statement of yours.

"The beauty of such art (Longfellow's sonnets) and the truth of it in these later poems, are traits which become more apparent to the reader's later years, when impartial chance decimates the rank in which he stands, and

leaves him safe only till the next round at best. They who fall become the
close friends to those who remain untouched, and as everything is dearer
since it dies, all memories of such as have lived and labored within touch of
us take the tinge of a personal grief, and we know too late how much they
were to us who can be nothing more."[2]

This is very touching. There is something so mellow, kindly, and withal
so lovely about it that I venture to offer, if I may, a word of fellow feeling and
appreciation ere the "next round" take you and it be too late. It has been
my good fortune to say elsewhere and in another way what I think of you,[3]
but here and now I would like to put down a few thoughts the purpose of
which is to convey my spiritual affection for you—to offer my little tribute
and acknowledge the benefit I have recieved from your work. In a little
scrap-book I have been keeping for the past five years I have pasted a small
collection of poems—Studies in Monotone I think they were called—which
I cut from Harper's Magazine and which I treasure as highly as any verse
I have ever encountered. "The Bewildered Guest," is one, "Company" is
another, "Friends and Foes," a third, "Respite" a fourth "Hope," "Question,"
"Living" etc. still others,[4] all of which to me breathe the quintessence of
tender, soulful doubt, and "show the wisdom of the man humbled to the
universal conditions." These poems, if you would be pleased to know, have
been a source of never-failing delight to me and I have often turned to
them, the very uncertainty of hope in them seeming to answer some need
of fellowship when I can no longer feign to believe that life has either a
purpose or a plan.

Thomas Hardy has provided some of this spiritual fellowship for me.
Count Tolstoy yet some more.[5] Of you three however I should not be able
to choose, the spirit in each seeming to be the same, and the large, tender
kindliness of each covering all of the ills of life and voicing the wonder and
yearning of this fitful dream, in what, to me, seems a perfect way. I may be
wrong in my estimate of life, but the mental attitude of you three seems
best—the richest, most appealing flowering-out of sympathy, tenderness,
uncertainty, that I have as yet encountered.

I have sometimes wondered that your expressed estimate of Hardy is what
it is—he who reaches out to you, as you do to him—the same sympathetic
solicitude for life, sorrow for suffering—care for the least and the greatest
even to the fall of a sparrow, which is so marked a feature of both of your
natures. I had rather hoped to find an acknowledgment of the soul of the
Englishman, equal to that of the Russian—a chain of spiritual sympathy
binding you together.[6]

However I am not writing to criticize. The beauty of your mental attitude is enough for me. If the common ground is to be credited with the

flowering out of such minds as yours I shall not be disturbed to return to the dust. There is enough in the thought to explain the wonder of the night, the sparkle of the waters—the thrill of tender feeling that runs abroad in the odours and murmers and sighs. Buried Howells and Hardys and Tolstoys shall explain it for me. I shall rejoice to believe that it is they who laugh in the waters—that it is because of such that the hills clap their hands.

Sincerely Yours

Theodore Dreiser

"Would that my songs might be
What roses wake by day and night—
Distillments of my clod of misery
Into delight."
Sidney Lanier[7]

1. Published (with a number of inaccuracies) in Ellen Moers, *Two Dreisers* (New York: Viking, 1969), 175–76.

2. Quoted, with some minor inaccuracies, from Howells's "Editor's Easy Chair," *Harper's Monthly* 104 (April 1902): 836.

3. Dreiser had published two laudatory articles on Howells, "How He Climbed Fame's Ladder," *Success* 1 (April 1898): 5–6; and "The Real Howells," *Ainslee's* 5 (March 1900): 137–42.

4. The poems named by Dreiser are in Howells's "Monochromes," a collection of nine poems which appeared initially in *Harper's Monthly* 86 (March 1893): 547–50.

5. Dreiser's portraits of Sister Carrie and Jennie Gerhardt have frequently been linked to that of Hardy's Tess. There is an echo of Tolstoy's aesthetic ideas in Ames's advice to Carrie at the close of *Sister Carrie*.

6. It is difficult to determine what "expressed estimate" Dreiser is referring to, since Howells deeply admired Hardy's fiction and strongly defended *Tess of the D'Urbervilles* and *Jude the Obscure* when they were attacked during the mid-1890s. See, for example, his review of *Jude* in *Harper's Weekly* 39 (7 December 1895): 1156.

7. The first stanza of "Rose-Morals" (1876) by Sidney Lanier (1842–81).

To Richard Duffy [H-UV]

Increasingly ill with a form of nervous exhaustion, Dreiser had moved to Philadelphia—where he sought treatment—in mid-July 1902. Although he expresses the expectation that he will soon complete Jennie Gerhardt, *he gave up the effort in December.*

210 Sumac St.
Phila. Pa.
Oct 20—1902

My Dear Duffy:—

Yours with enclosures safely to hand and mental gratitude registered. I have often thought of you between whiles but in these urgent times of literary composition it has passed my ability to correspond with even the merchantmen let alone my friends. Life has taken on a very strenuous phase and I have had to work hard to accomplish what I have.

I see you have changed the magazine radically and I trust for the better. Hall told me that the purely literary was to be your watchword and that the special was ruled out.[1] You can hardly have erred in this, unless it would have been in your power to obtain the most original and exclusive features of the world such as the Ellen Stone story etc. in the future.[2] I hoped you make a success of it.

My last sketch in your magazine seems to have struck a peculiarly resonant note in so far as personal feeling is concerned.[3] I have heard from over a dozen strangers who have addressed me through "Whos Who" (I judge so from the old address)[4] and a number of my acquaintances. Some of them seem to consider that I must possess some of the qualities of Mr. Potter,[5] which of course is humorous. Altogether I have been rather entertained by it.

I do not know that I can give you any interesting information about myself except that I am still working on my story and hope to finish it in time for the spring trade. Errors and insomnia have cost me a good deal of time. However I still retain the faith of my publishers and my own unwavering confidence in myself which is something.

Wish you could run over to Philly some Saturday afternoon and spend the evening Sunday with me. I should like very much to see you again. Old friends are best.

Yours Ever
Dreiser

1. Up to the issue of October 1902, *Ainslee's* published a mixed selection of fiction, poetry, and articles. With that issue, however, the journal was subtitled "A Magazine of Clever Fiction" and was devoted almost entirely to novelettes and short stories. Gilman Hall (1866–?) was associate editor of *Ainslee's*.

2. Ellen M. Stone (1846–1927), an American missionary, had been kidnapped and held for ransom in Turkish-held Macedonia in September 1901. The story was headline news until her release in February 1902.

3. "A Doer of the Word," *Ainslee's* 9 (June 1902): 453–59; collected by Dreiser in *Twelve Men* (1919). The sketch deals with a Connecticut fisherman, Charlie Potter, who attempts to live his life by Christian principles.

4. The 1901/1902 edition of *Who's Who in America* lists Dreiser's address as 1599 East End Ave, New York City.

5. See note 3 above.

To Richard Duffy [H-DPUP]

Dreiser was now near the end of his financial resources. He had placed very few articles in recent months, and since he was also unable to work on Jennie Gerhardt, *he determined to stop the monthly stipend which he had been receiving from Taylor and Co. The specific "financial squall" he refers to may be his need to raise money to send Jug to live with her parents in Missouri.*

210 Sumac St.,
Philadelphia
Pa.
Dec 5th 1902

My Dear Duffy:—

Since writing you the other day I have been struck with one of those little financial squalls which makes it imperative for me to raise a moderate source of money in several directions. Although indebted to you allready in the sum of eighty or thereabouts I still turn to you because of all men I know that you have the most long suffering confidence in me. I would like you to loan me fifty dollars, either in the form of anticipating a contribution one of these days or in some other manner which your fertile imagination may suggest. You have the book of poems of mine—perhaps you could find a few things in it which would cover the amount in a temporary way.[1] They might do to raise a check upon and leave me time to return it to you in another form. Your own good judgment must decide this as the possibility of such a thing may have utterly passed with the new arrangement.[2]

I do not wish you to feel that I am in any way counting upon the success of this or that I will be in the least disappointed if you cannot aid me. I know only too well that you would if you could. I have several avenues out of my predicament but none so available and so free from entangling complications as your good friendship has always proved. Do not hesitate to say no, if no it must be, and believe me always the same,

Dreiser.

My best regards to Mrs Duffy. I would add Mrs. D's but I have not included her in my confidence in this. She would send a good word if she knew.

D.

1. No doubt Dreiser's unpublished manuscript, *Poems,* which he announced for publication as early as 1898 (see Dreiser to Ellen M. Boult, after 9 June 1899, n.

3) but which never appeared. Duffy replied in a letter also dated 5 December 1902 that *Ainslee's* accepted three poems from Dreiser's manuscript and was sending him a check for $50.

2. For the "new arrangement" at *Ainslee's,* see Dreiser to Richard Duffy, 20 October 1902, n. 1.

1903

To Richard Duffy [H-UV]

210 Sumac Street
Phila. Pa.
Jan. 6th 1903

My Dear Duffy:—

For some days past I have been intending to drop you a line "just to let you know" etc but have been rather busy doing nothing. Nervous Prostration (which I have shortened to N.P. for family use) still holds a restraining finger on me and I cannot do as much in a day as I used to. I am "getting along though" as the expression saith and am slowly coming into my own. Some day I will turn up in New York with a completed novel in my grip and some ideas that will "shake the universe" as my fighting German friend would say.[1] Meanwhile I am doing my best to hold my own,—my patience, faith, etc.

We had a very merry Christmas over here. Mr. Gray, a lawyer friend of mine,[2] came over from New York and spent the day with us and we had a cheerful time entertaining him. Later we went to a foolish extravaganza which passed away the evening. The visits of friends from New York and elsewhere are the only that make Phila endurable.

What is Norman Duncan doing? I heard he was professor of something in a Pennsylvania college but am not sure. He is very kind to enthuse over Carrie. I have done as much over "The Soul of the Street." If you see or write to him give him my best regards.[3]

Enclosed is a letter to Mr. Preston[4] which I wish you would forward. He was cheerful with New York anticipations when I saw him last. I hope he succeeds.

Give my regards to Hall[5] and say what you wish for us to Mrs. Duffy. She is our French model. Thanks for the clippings.

Always
Dreiser

1. Unidentified.

2. Probably Charles Norman Gray, a New York acquaintance of this period.

3. Canadian-born, Duncan (1871–1916) had worked for the *New York Evening Post* during the late 1890s; his short story collection *The Soul of the Street* (1900) deals with New York Syrian life. In 1903, he was teaching at Washington and Jefferson College in Washington, Pennsylvania.

4. Unidentified.

5. Gilman Hall, an editor at *Ainslee's*; see Dreiser to Richard Duffy, 20 October 1902, n. 1.

To Ripley Hitchcock [H-CU]

A prominent figure in the New York literary and art scene for three decades, Hitchcock (1857–1918) was in early 1901 an editor at D. Appleton & Co. when Dreiser offered Jennie Gerhardt, in the form of its early chapters, to that firm. Although unwilling to subsidize Dreiser at that time, Hitchcock continued to inquire about his progress on the novel, as he did in a letter of 24 February 1903. When Dreiser finally completed Jennie in late 1910, it was Hitchcock who accepted it for Harper's, where he had become an editor.

113 Ross Street
Brooklyn
N.Y.
March 2nd 1903.

My Dear Mr. Hitchcock:—

I will pleased to show you the fragment of the story which is at present typewritten, although that is not so very much more than you saw once before.[1] I have been making some radical changes which make it impossible to offer more. There are certain things relating to this story which make it impossible for me to offer any hope that we can come to any arrangement concerning it, but I am still taking advantage of your kind interest to speak to you. I will come Friday night; not to stay all night however, and will talk to you then.[2] I trust you will base no conclusions on anything I have written as I have not really given you any clear conception of this situation. Accept my sincere thanks for your invitation and good will and believe me

Very Sincerely Yours
Theodore Dreiser

1. Presumably the fourteen typescript chapters Dreiser had salvaged from his early draft of the novel and which he had offered to a number of publishers in early 1901 (see Dreiser to George P. Brett, 16 April 1901).
2. Hitchcock was living in Nutley, New Jersey, just north of Newark.

To Joseph H. Coates [H-DPUP]

Following a down-and-out period in Brooklyn and an initial period of recuperation in Muldoon's sanatorium (see Dreiser's autobiographical An Amateur Laborer *[1983]), Dreiser continued his recovery by securing a job as a manual laborer and clerk for the New York Central Railroad. He was assigned to its Spuyten Duyvil shop on the Hudson just north of Manhattan and took a room in nearby Kings-bridge. Joseph Coates (?–1930) was a Philadelphia writer, editor, and business-man whom Dreiser had come to know and admire during his recent Philadelphia stay. Coates was later to supply Dreiser with a newspaper file dealing with the Philadelphia career of Charles T. Yerkes, the prototype of Dreiser's Frank A. Cowperwood.*

Nathalie Ave.
Kingsbridge, N. Y.
c/o Schill
Sept. 19th 1903

My Dear Coates:

Where, by the Beard of the Prophet, is the opening chapter of the once promised novel?[1] I don't understand or approve of your shirking. Last April I heard from you and since then never a word. How is this?

About a week or ten days ago I received the proofs of an article of mine which you are about to publish, I suppose.[2] I also received a letter saying that you were sending me proofs of some pictures for which you had no explanations or captions. I corrected the proof at once and returned it but the pictures never came.

As you can see we[3] are living in Kingsbridge at present. I am working on the New York Central as a masons helper for my health. It is out of door work and very interesting. I went completely to pieces with neuresthania after I left Philadelphia.

If ever you come over to New York let me know. Mrs. Dreiser often speaks of you and you know what pleasant feelings I have [word omitted] you. Run over, and anyhow if you don't do that send on the opening chapters. Would like to know how you do.

Yours Sincerely
Theodore Dreiser

1. Coates had written to Dreiser on 9 March 1903 that he was beginning a Civil War novel entitled *The Conflict* and would soon send him its opening chapter.

2. "The Problem of the Soil," *Era* 12 (September 1903): 239–49. The *Era*, a Philadelphia-based journal, was edited by Coates.

3. Jug had recently rejoined Dreiser.

1904

To Hamlin Garland   [H-USC]

Fully recovered from his nervous collapse, Dreiser at the time of this letter to Garland had just begun working for the New York Daily News *as a feature writer and part-time editor while living with his wife in the Bronx. Garland (1860–1940), who had achieved recognition during the early 1890s as a realistic portrayer of Midwest farm life, had written Dreiser on 3 January 1904 praising* Sister Carrie.

399 East 144th
The Clara
Friday, Jan 8th 1903[1]

Dear Mr. Garland:—

Such cordial goodwill as you express is never late and always welcome. Years ago (1894) when I was a newspaper writer in Pittsburgh I made the acquaintance of "Main Traveled Roads" in the lovely Carnegie Library of Allegheny while lounging away the long afternoons of my "city hall" assignment.[2] I have never forgotten it. Like the other beautiful things of life those fresh flowered stories of yours became identified with my dearest remembrances and I have always followed your work with interest. Only a year ago I read "Rose of Dutchers Coolly."[3]

I am not of Chicago in the way you seem to think[4] though I did live and work there for a time. Indiana is my home and New York City my present abode. In between there come many places, but who has not wandered.

Your kind wish to know more of me is reciprocated, though in a public way I seem to know much of you already, and I sincerely hope that we may meet and soon.[5] If you have the wish and the time I am sure it will not be long before we do.

Sincerely Yours
Theodore Dreiser

1. Although Dreiser dated his letter 1903, the fact that he is replying to Garland's letter of 3 January 1904 indicates that he intended 1904.

2. *Main-Traveled Roads* was published in 1891; Dreiser is referring to his job as a reporter for the *Pittsburg Dispatch* from April to November 1894. In *A Book About Myself* he recalls his fruitful period of self-education in the Allegheny Carnegie library, across the river from Pittsburgh.

3. *Rose* (1895), the last of Garland's midwestern realistic novels, resembles *Sister Carrie* in that it depicts the experiences of a Wisconsin farm girl in Chicago.

4. Garland, in his letter of 3 January 1904, had remarked, "I take it that you are from the West and specifically of Chicago."

5. The two met in Chicago in late 1912, but soon became estranged because of Garland's increasingly conservative views on the depiction of sexuality in literature.

1905

To Phoebe A. Hearst   [TS-BLUC]

Dreiser began working in Street & Smith's pulp-fiction "factory" in August 1904 and then, in early 1905, became the editor of Smith's, the firm's new popular audience magazine. Mrs. Hearst (1842–1919) was the wife of the mining millionaire George Hearst and the mother of William Randolph Hearst. During the late 1890s the Hearsts built a palatial Spanish-style home at Pleasanton, thirty miles east of San Francisco. The letter contains a note in an unknown hand: "Mrs. H. has gone to Europe. Regret cannot be granted. Send a nice note."

SMITH'S MAGAZINE
79–89 Seventh Ave
New York
Editorial
November 3rd, 1905.

Dear Madam:

We have in preparation for publication in *Smith's*, an article on "The Best of American Houses," and as your home seems to be one of those representative of the improvement in architecture in America, we would very much like to use it in the illustrating of the article.

Would you be kind enough to lend us one or several views, either or both exterior and interior,—those which you consider give the most comprehensive idea of the building or landscape architecture or the interior furnishings.

We assure you that the favor will be greatly appreciated both by us and our readers and that the pictures will be taken care of and carefully returned.

Thanking you in advance for an early response, we are,

Very truly yours,
Theodore Dreiser
Editor.

1907

To Richard V. Oulahan [TS-UK]

From Smith's, Dreiser's upward spiraling career as an editor of popular magazines took him to the Broadway Magazine *and then, in the summer of 1907, to the pinnacle of Butterick's* Delineator, *which he continued to edit until late 1910. Dreiser had just become editor of the* Delineator *when he sought to enlist Oulahan in interesting President Theodore Roosevelt in writing for the magazine. Oulahan (1867–1931), a prominent newspaperman and diplomat based in Washington, was at this time chief European correspondent for the* New York Sun. *No such article outlined by Dreiser appeared in the* Delineator.

THE DELINEATOR
New York
[11 July 1907]

Dear Mr. Oulahan:

At the suggestion of Mr. Samuel G. Blythe[1] I am writing you to see if you can carry out a scheme which interests me very much.

Recently in the daily papers there appeared a supposed interview with Admiral Sakamoto, of the Japanese Navy,[2] in which he was made to say:

The Editor of the
Delineator, 1907.

"Should hostilities break out between Japan and America, the result would be indecisive, owing to a want of proper bases of operation. Even if the Washington Government should decide on war, it is doubtful whether the Americans serving in the Navy are sufficiently patriotic to fight. American Navy officers are brilliant figures at balls and social gatherings, but they are very deficient in professional training and practice. It is too much to expect burning patriotism from the American naval service in case of war with Japan. It is likely that most of the crews would desert and leave the ships".

This statement suggested to me that an article on PATRIOTISM, particularly from the women's point of view, the American wives and daughters of the Civil War, the Spanish American War and other significant stages of American history, would be most important, if it were done with considerable feeling and enthusiasm by some person whose name stood for sentiment and patriotism in this country. But the thing which I want you to do is to put this proposition up to President Roosevelt, with a view to having him do it.

I may as well speak frankly. I understand from Mr. Blythe that to a certain extent, you have a claim on the President's friendship which ought to lead to the construction of an article of this kind. If you can use your friendship with Mr. Roosevelt to get him to write me an article of say 2,000 words on this subject, something that will be a ringing call to the patriotic spirit of this country, I would be willing to pay you $500 for your services and your expenses from Washington to Oyster Bay and return.[3] I should want you to take action at once, and let me know what the result is, so that if possible, the article could be got in our October number, which we are working on now. If it cannot be had for that number, of course I would be willing to use it in the November number, but would much prefer for the other. The all-essential thing is immediate action.

Mr. Blythe is writing you in reference to the matter. If you can put this matter through for me, I shall not only consider it well worth the money, but will see if some other material cannot be thrown your way.

Very sincerely yours,
Theodore Dreiser
EDITOR.
July 11, 1907.

1. Blythe (1868–1947) was a New York journalist who at one time had edited *Cosmopolitan* magazine.

2. Admiral Gombel Yamamoto (not Sakamoto), a former minister of naval affairs in the Japanese government, had just arrived in New York; the source of the quote attributed to him which follows has not been identified.

3. Roosevelt's summer residence was at Oyster Bay, Long Island.

To Dear Sir [TS-Cor]

The November 1907 issue of the Delineator *announced the magazine's Child Rescue Campaign, an effort to create a national organization devoted to the placing of orphans in foster homes. The campaign continued through Dreiser's editorship and brought widespread attention to the magazine.*

Editorial Rooms
Butterick Building, New York

THE DELINEATOR
London: Paris: New York
November 15th, 1907.

Dear Sir:—

We beg to call to your notice "The DELINEATOR Child-Rescue Campaign." Our Magazine is bending every effort to bring the child without a home and the home without a child together. You yourself know the need of such a work done in a national way.

We are giving to this task the earnest endeavor of our whole editorial staff, with the belief that ultimately our reward will come in the sum of increased happiness in many lives. We are in a position to do great good. We want to do it. The November and December numbers of THE DELINEATOR give you the details of our progress up to date.

We now have a common note with you; we have set out with the honest determination to effect a permanent betterment among those of God's creatures whom humanity has seemingly forgotten. Whatever encouragement you might be moved to give us would, indeed, find great appreciation.

Earnestly yours,
Theodore Dreiser
EDITOR

P.S. We are sending you a sample copy of the December issue of THE DELINEATOR. Will you kindly read the pages devoted to our "Child-Rescue Campaign."

1908

To Lester Frank Ward [TS-Br]

One of the founders of American sociology, Ward (1841–1913) had worked as a government geologist until 1906, when he became a professor of sociology at Brown University. His many works of the 1880s and onward laid down the principle of the important role of sociological research in aiding social progress. Although Dreiser's invitation is couched in language which should have appealed to Ward, Ward did not contribute to the Delineator *and there is no evidence that he replied to this letter.*

Editorial Rooms
Butterick Building New York

THE DELINEATOR
London: Paris: New York
Theodore Dreiser, Editor
Dec. 3, 1908.

My dear Sir:—

Your name has been suggested to me as that of some one who is interested in the sociological progress of America, and particularly in matters which concern the development and well-being of the on-coming generation of Americans. I am the editor-in-chief of the three publications, The Delineator, The Designer and The New Idea which have a combined circulation of 1,800,000. It is the object of these magazines to be useful in an educational and instructive way—presenting to the average person those subjects which will demonstrate the practical workings of life. We endeavor to teach at every turn new ways, new theories in all that relates to the well-being of the individual and the family. Naturally it is necessary to be aware of the advisable things to discuss at any time, and I write to ask if you will not make some suggestions for subjects which could be discussed either by you or by some one who may dwell in your mind as the ideal person to present a certain phase of life in a helpful way. I should very much appreciate it if you would give this proposition your serious consideration, and if there is any subject you have in mind which you could present personally let me know.

Very truly yours,
Theodore Dreiser
Editor.

1909

To Mrs. M. Landon Reed [TC-LLIU]

Mrs. Reed was a freelance journalist who published several articles in the Delin-
eator during Dreiser's editorship but has otherwise not been identified. Dreiser's
letter reveals the pains he was willing to take to spell out to contributors the
characteristics of a successful popular article.

New York, April 19, 1909

My dear Mrs. Reed:

Doing something significant always follows the long and rather per-
sistent course of taking thought. I found your little articles on what you
consider your specialty only fairly good. Somehow you didn't crowd into
them all the information which it seemed necessary should be there, and
you didn't sweep around the circle of your proposition in what I must call
a full breathing way. On the other hand, taking so general a topic as "The
Hard Work of a Foreign Tour" you made an exceedingly good thing of
that.[1] It was humorous, full of keen observation and illuminating. From
that I should say that you would be the person to write many an interesting general article. It all depends on your experience and your powers of
concentrating your mind on some single proposition. Most good articles
flow from a full heart or a full intellect—whatever you choose to call it. If
a man writes on Banking entertainingly it is usually because he knows all
about Banking and can tell you, not only the practical phases of it, but the
human interest that goes with it. If it is Farming an author is interested
in he can usually write well on that. I remember as a special writer I was
particularly interested in educational projects of all kinds and loved to find
out some phase of development in some state or other which showed a
number of human beings bestirring themselves to accomplish a great good
or a forward step, and could always write an interesting article about a thing
of that kind.[2] I have always liked articles on an outing experience of any
kind, whether it was a lone trip up a river, or through some unexplored val-
ley on horseback or on foot in Germany or Ireland. Anything of that kind.
I like to read articles on the Home Life of the New Northwest, or making
a homestead in any country where a person has to fight a battle for success
and then succeeds. I am interested in pictures of social life, whether they
be in Washington or in Paris, so long as they are really intimate pictures
of interesting people. There is something for me always in any new movement which affects the family or develops the people in any way, but the

person who attempts to write anything of this kind must be familiar with what they are writing about.

Now you ask whether you can be of service to me. I can only answer that in one way it depends on yourself. If you have something within the range of your experience which you know all about, which makes for the betterment or entertainment of humanity, or our American people, which is as much of humanity as we can deal with at present, you probably have an article which your can write entertainingly about and which I can buy. Your article on "The Hard Work of a Foreign Tour" pleased me and if I had some subject which I thought you could do (basing my judgment of what you can do on this particular article) I would let you try it. If anything occurs to me I will be glad to let you know. Meanwhile you must look through your experiences or your personal knowledge of any one worth while subject and let me know what you have to offer.

Very sincerely yours,
Editor.

1. Published in the *Delineator* 73 (June 1909).
2. See Dreiser's 8 February 1900 letter to Robert Underwood Johnson, of the *Century* magazine, in which he proposes an article on the training of public school teachers. In fact, however, this article appears not to have been written, and there is no evidence of other articles on education by Dreiser.

1910

To Clarence S. Howell [TC-LLIU]

Howell was an army officer and engineer. Dreiser's full expression to Howell of his beliefs of this period is an early manifestation of a characteristic Dreiserian mix: contempt for human greed and ignorance, demand for greater efforts in achieving social progress, and stress on the inevitable workings of natural law.

New York, May 17, 1910

My dear Mr. Howell:

I have your very interesting letter of May 10th with its statement of the present economic and sociologic troubles of our day. You propound an exceedingly subtle problem which involves the life and growth of a nation. I would not be much of an editor if I did not have opinions and convictions in this matter. How sound they are is another matter. I believe actually that the law of supply and demand has something to do with the increased cost of living. I think the easy manner in which certain classes of Americans have made money has led those classes to make an extra display of their wealth and so corrupt the economic judgment of the people and fill them with delusions in regard to the importance of making a show and spending money.[1] I believe that this nation, being a young nation, has the weakness of youth, that actually, man for man, woman for woman it is prone to show a lack of thought for the future, which only real distress can remedy. I actually believe that the farmers of the country are not possessed of the essential knowledge of their work and are not making the best use of their land, and I still further believe that the tendency of a large percentage of our people is to crowd the cities, there to waste their sustenance in riotous living which is making for stress and difficulty in the financial condition of the majority. But having said these things I believe also that there is a conspiracy among the strong and subtle to get control of and manipulate for their own purposes the necessities of life. I believe that the tariff is juggled to suit the various needs of the various interests in various sections. I believe that transportation and methods of distribution are centralized and made a source of profit for the few as against the general advantages of the many. I believe that there is generally a low political, religious and moral level of thought, which permits, not only these men of wealth and power, but their tools to execute the various laws and judgments, which permit and bring about these conditions. But at the same time I would be, in my own judgment, foolish if I felt that this conditions was due entirely to any group of individuals. I believe that in fact the American attitude, man for man, and woman for woman is coarse, greedy, calculating and insincere. The intention of every individual is to get as much as he can as quickly as he can, with as little work as he can, and his desire when he gets it is to make as great a show as possible in order to belittle and make insignificant the lives and aspirations of those whom he finds about him. No, this is not a class condition. It is the American temperament, and we will have to outgrow it eventually through slowly reaching maturity or by lessons of poverty and tragedy. If the moral judgment of the nation were higher, the moral and physical condition of the people would be sound. You and I know that the moral judgment of this nation is not high. We rise to great heights in time of stress. We have fought for ideals; for the freedom of man; the freedom of the slaves; the freedom of the seas; the cause of the oppressed beyond our limits as in the case of the Cubans. Having done this we seem to sink back, the majority of us in a state of comfortable acquiescence in the theory that life is to be lived for the joy it can produce and for the amount of superiority it can give the individual over the many.

I would be a wise man, indeed, if I could offer a remedy. I actually think that things will be worse before they are better. I think the rich will be richer, the poor poorer, and the ignorant more ignorant, until that saving spirit which abides in men and makes for right and justice will rise in disgust and lay about itself with a view to cleansing or destroying the things which are holding it back. When this comes you will see another great enthusiastic struggle for an ideal in this land and we will move up one peg. I believe that the next time the nation will take a long step toward the better organization of its facilities, its means of transportation and its means of distribution, that it will insist upon a higher standard of justice and fair play as regards the commercial relationship of men. I think you will find after this next fight, whether it be mental or physical, that the whole nation, man for man, will have a higher sense of justice and duty in the conduct of public affairs, and they will not be so eager and greedy to show off, each for himself, at the expense of all. I actually believe that in the course of time that society will eliminate from its various constituencies the type of individual who wishes to rule and show at the expense of all others and without regard for any one. How soon this is coming I do not know. There is a strong drift toward it at present. We, all of us, feel the unrest and dissatisfaction in the air. Those who are in power are not working fast enough to remedy the evils that are creating the unrest. I do not say that these evils will not be remedied. I do say this, that there is not much evidence at present that they will be remedied in time. We who feel that justice is not being done have but one thing to do and that is—fight, by argument, by example, by insistence on fair play where ever we have the power to compel such. The rest is in the hands of the Lord, or nature which swings like a pendulum from one extreme apparently to another. Depend on it, that from every condition of distress or evil there is a great reaction, and the greater the evil or distress, the greater the reaction. If we do not get a reaction quick, we will get it long when it does come.[2]

With best wishes, I am.
Very sincerely yours,
Editor

1. Dreiser's comments regarding the relationship between money and display echoes one of Thorstein Veblen's principal ideas in his *The Theory of the Leisure Class* (1899).
2. An early statement of Dreiser's belief in an "Equation Inevitable," one of his principal philosophical ideas as well as the title of an essay in *Hey Rub-a-Dub-Dub* (1920).

To Grant Richards [TS-BLYU]

Dreiser had been corresponding with the English publisher Grant Richards (1872–1948) for several years over various matters pertaining to the Delineator *as well as Richards's effort to secure the English rights for* Jennie Gerhardt.

Editorial Rooms
Butterick Building New York

THE DELINEATOR
London Paris New York
Theodore Dreiser, Editor
New York, May 27, 1910

My dear Richards:

Our health keeps the even tenor of its way, our prosperity some times appears to have a slightly faded complexion, but at other times appears to be very hale and rosy. I think it varies with the weather. Last Winter I told Mr. Gilbert Christie of Chatenay, S. Borough Rd—Surbiton, Eng. to look you up. He is a wholesale chemist by trade—or profession—(I don't know what you call it in London) but by mental qualifications he is a gentleman and a scholar. Actually, he is very fascinating—familiar with literature, art, science, a traveler and a cosmopolitan. In addition he has a charming wife. I wish you and Mrs. Richards would look them up. I believe you would like them very much.

The details of running the Delineator keep me pretty busy. I put in eight hours a day at the office and sometimes a little at night, and then I do not

Grant Richards.

think I do all that I might. We dream of coming to London, Mrs. Dreiser and I, and of seeing you and meeting some others who have said they would be pleased to see us. If I do not get over there pretty soon, however, I think I will make up my mind not to go at all, because I have become so fixed and settled in my ways that stirring around would be a hardship. That sounds pessimistic, doesn't it?

I was really greatly shocked personally when I read of King Edward's illness and death.[1] From various articles and scraps of personal information that have come my way I had come to think of him as a really remarkable person with a charming broad minded point of view and it seems a pity that he had to be removed. As a matter of fact English affairs are interesting and clearer and more intelligent to me than American problems although I am right here on the ground. I am, as you know, always strong for the British because of the profound admiration I have for their intellectual leadership.[2] If I had the means I would live in England, but not having them I will stay in New York and hope that Grant Richards, Gilbert Christie and W. J. Locke,[3] and a few others may occasionally come my way.

Please extend the joint good wishes of Mrs Dreiser and myself to your wife, but say that we have no use for her husband who is obviously a bad lot.

Yours as ever,
Theodore Dreiser

1. Edward VII, a flamboyant Prince of Wales for many years during the reign of Queen Victoria, was crowned in 1902 and died on 6 May 1910.

2. This admiration was to shift radically in later years as Dreiser came to view class oppression and imperialism as distinctive British evils.

3. Locke (1863–1930) was a prolific and popular English novelist whose *The Beloved Vagabond* (1906) had been a great success.

To Pitts Duffield [TCopy-UI]

Pitts Duffield (1869–1938), an American publisher (Duffield & Co.), published the American edition of several of Wells's novels and also acted as his American agent. Wells's novel, here named Marjorie's Expenditures, was not written until the summer of 1911; it appeared in 1912 under the title Marriage.

THE DELINEATOR
LONDON-PARIS-NEW YORK
New York, August 7, 1910

My dear Mr. Duffield:

I am returning for your possible use this outline of Mr. H. G. Wells' new novel, but the return of this does not mean that I am not considering the use of this novel serially. It is the best proposition that has been presented to me this Fall, and I am anxious, not only to see the first half of the Ms, but all of it as quickly as possible, but the first half by express, if possible.

In regard to the serial: The theme, with some modifications is all right for the Delineator, but Mr. Wells will handle it in such a manner, that while it might delight the highly intellectual woman, it would possibly offend the rank and file. It seems to me that Mr. Wells has grown to be, in his latest work, the most sophisticated of modern writers. His sophistry is stinging, especially when he writes of religion and society, and because of this I would like to express a few opinions for his guidance in regard to the 60,000 words he submits to me, because I would like to publish his stuff and because I admire him greatly.

(1) Specifically, Mr. Wells should restrain himself a little at the start. Some of the keen things he says about religion and society will hurt some people, yet they are trifles, easily left out.

(2) He should be careful to delineate Marjorie's character without dragging in her religious training, or permit us to edit it out.

(3) To make clear that Marjorie's mother is a liar, because her maternal love is stronger than her sense of morality.

(4) To modify or eliminate in the remainder of the book the keen thrusts at religion and society, or permit us to do so.

(5) To make the girl's spendthrift qualities obvious from her actions.

Another point that is desirable in a serial, and which is not quite possible here, but which you might assist a little in bringing about, is divisional climaxes. We can use about 7000 words to an installment, and of course, each installment ought to have some hold over power. That is, it ought to have a kind of climax which would inspire the reader to get the next number of the magazine. It sounds silly to say to Mr. Wells that divisional climaxes are desired. Still, there is a way of giving a sort of dramatic fillip to the end of each division, which would grasp and hold the reader. I say this, not so much in the spirit of making a condition, as in the hope that he can do a little something to assist this desired idea. These things done, it is probable I can use "Marjorie's Expenditures", and I would like to have it come to me, as I say, as expeditiously as possible, as time is a great factor.

Will you extend to Mr. Wells my personal compliments. I have read his stories from the time he wrote "The War of the Worlds" until recently I finished "Tono-Bungay", a cruel, brilliant, sophisticated and utterly forceful story.[1] He is one of England's greatest writers.

Very sincerely yours,
Theodore Dreiser,
Editor.

1. *The War of the Worlds* (1898); Dreiser was later to write a laudatory introduction to *Tono-Bungay* (1909) for the Sandgate Edition (1927) of Wells's works.

To Fremont Rider [HP-DPUP][1]

Rider (1885–1962), who had published three volumes of poetry by 1910, was one of Dreiser's editorial assistants at the Delineator *and also aided him in 1909 in the editing of the* Bohemian, *a small independent magazine. Dreiser had been forced out of the* Delineator *in early October because of the threatened scandal arising from his infatuation with Thelma Cudlipp, the young daughter of a Delineator colleague.*

439 W. 123rd St[2]
N.Y.C
Oct. 11th 1910

My Dear Rider:

I do not consider my resignation in the light of a loss. The big work was done there. We were in smooth waters. I had been fighting interference for sometime & finally stood the whole thing out. There are several things I can do at once, even to editing a newspaper, but I believe I will finish my book.[3] Mrs. Dreiser is getting on slowly but I don't believe shall be able to keep house this winter. She's not very strong.[4] Sorry about Mrs. Rider. Give her our regards.

Yours

Dreiser

1. The letter is extant in the DPUP in photostat form; its original has not been located.

2. The address of the Park Avenue Hotel, where Dreiser had taken a room on 3 October when he temporarily left Jug.

3. Writing rapidly, Dreiser did finish *Jennie Gerhardt* by the end of December 1910.

4. Jug was indeed ill, but Dreiser fails to mention, at her insistence, that they are not living together.

1912

To Grant Richards [H-Dart]

Dreiser had returned on 23 April from a five-month trip to England and the continent, a journey largely engineered by Richards (see Dreiser to Grant Richards, 27 May 1910), who had both brokered a publication contract with the Century Company to finance the trip and served as Dreiser's unofficial tour advisor. Still to be finalized between the two, however, were the English rights to Dreiser's future work, especially The Financier, *which Dreiser would soon complete.*

> Sixtieth Street & Columbus Avenue
> St. Paul Hotel
> New York
> May 4—1912

My Dear G.R.:

Kindly pardon delay. On investigation I find that Harpers have sold exactly 12,717 copies of Jennie Gerhardt to date and 1026 copies of the new edition of Sister Carrie. This makes, for Sister Carrie, from first to last a little over 19,000 copies in the United States. This can be verified from the books of Doubleday Page & Co. B. W. Dodge & Co., Grosset & Dunlap and Harper & Brothers.[1] I am glad I did not leave on the Titanic.[2] I am now soundly at work again & making some progress. Your Snugtex Fabric Belt is being searched for,[3] as you give no location for its purchase, & when found will be forwarded. I am profoundly glad that I am on my home ground and out of your clutches.[4] I will write you later when I have anything to say. Lunched with Doty yesterday.[5]

Th.D.

1. The four publishers of *Sister Carrie:* Doubleday, Page in 1900; Dodge and Grosset and Dunlap in 1907; and Harpers in 1912.

2. Dreiser's laconic reference to the fact that he had planned to leave Europe on the *Titanic* but had postponed his trip for a few days to take a cheaper ship. The *Titanic* sank on the night of 14–15 April 1912 on its maiden voyage.

3. Snugtex is a braided, non-elastic fabric used for belts, straps, and the like.

4. Dreiser had been displeased by the high cost of the continental touring arranged for him by Richards. The jocular tone of his reference to this issue soon gave way to more intense feelings (see Dreiser to Richards, 7 July 1912).

5. Douglas Z. Doty (1874–1935), an editor of the Century Publishing Company, which was to publish several of Dreiser's European travel articles in the *Century* magazine and then *A Traveler at Forty* (1913).

To Grant Richards

Richards had written on 11 June 1912 requesting that Dreiser confirm their agreement of 5 December 1911 that Richards was to be granted the English rights to The Financier. *However, if Dreiser decided to remain with Harper's as his American publisher, Richards would probably be closed out as the novel's English publisher, since Harper's had an active British branch and would, as Dreiser comments, wish to include the British rights in any contract.*

605 W. 111th St[1]

N.Y.C

July 7th 1912

My Dear Richards:

I have your very carefully constructed letter in regard to The Financier. Do you really think you ought to have it? Personally I get very dubious when I think that the one financial thing I really wanted you to do you did not do and rather wilfully & inconsiderately I think.[2] However this makes no difference in my personal feeling toward you. You might do worse & still have me like you. Harpers will pay me 20% & spend some money on advertising. You offer me no definite program. (I can see a wry face here.) However the book is not finished even at this late date & I am having considerable difficulty with it. I hope for the best. Parts II and III will carry separate titles as I see it now. I have no contract with Harper & Brothers concerning these and no understanding. I am doing my best to modify their feeling in regard to part one and the English rights. When I get proofs I shall have time enough to decide. I will then let you know. But meantime I think you might well meditate on your sins and how easy it is for the wicked to be punished at times.

Th.D.

I am glad the childrens opinion of me has improved under proper parental guidance as Lane[3] would say.

1. Possibly the address of Dreiser's sister Emma.

2. Dreiser refers to his earlier expressed desire to Richards that on making arrangements for Dreiser's European travel, Richards keep his expenditure under a specific amount. See also Dreiser to Richards, 4 May 1912, n. 4, and 24 July 1912.

3. Sir Hugh Lane (1875–1915), Irish-born art collector who joined Richards and Dreiser during a portion of Dreiser's European tour. He is portrayed as Sir Scorp in *A Traveler at Forty* (1913).

To Grant Richards [H-HRHUT]

Richards brought the issue of the rights to The Financier *to a head in a letter of 12 July 1912, when he noted that publication and advertising deadlines required him to know Dreiser's plans for the novel's English edition. Dreiser, in his reply, found a basis for his desire to stay with Harper's in his claim that he had been betrayed by Richards's handling of his expenditures during his European journey. Dreiser's letter and Richards's bitter 8 August response severely damaged the friendship between the two men.*

606 W. 111th St
N.Y.C
July 24—1912

My Dear G.R.

It is very plain that I shall have to talk out in school and I don't like it. What I am going to say has little to do with my personal liking for you which remains unchanged. I am decidedly impersonal in most of my affairs anyhow. The thing I wanted to do—which I indicated in New York before I started, which I spoke of in Paris before we started for the Riviera, which I indicated very plainly at Monte Carlo and which I was quite angry about in Rome when I saw that it was not going to materialize was that I wanted to return to America with $800 or $1,000 and that I was not going to be permitted to do so. I use the word permitted after due consideration. My money was in your hands—all but 60£s or thereabouts. You told me that you would "arrange it". Did you? We won't argue ten thousand points that can be made into a confusing dust. The main facts are as I say. It gave me pause. I am a fair observer—a reasonable psychologist and I follow closely sometimes where I am not wanted. This whole money matter discolored the trip for me greatly. You should have been wiser than to irritate me on a point that could have been so easily adjusted. An accounting and lessened expenditures would have been simple. But no—that was too much to ask. You carried your point in an easy, good natured tolerant way. I may have seemed easy I admit. I am in most things—willingly so. The point I have made however is important for me to consider in any commercial dealings. I did not care to sign the letter because I did not care to be rushed into any understanding I might regret.[1] I am glad I didn't. I am debating this matter of English publication. I will transfer if I wish. Sincerely, without ill feeling of any kind, with the greatest pleasure in many of your personal qualities I am not sure that I want to. I will let you know. Then you can do as you choose without hurting my feelings in the least.

Sincerely
Dreiser

My regards to Lane[2] if you see him.

1. In his letter of 11 June 1912, Richards noted that though he and Dreiser had agreed on 5 December 1911 that Richards would have the English rights to *The Financier*, Dreiser had not signed the agreement.

2. For Lane, see Dreiser to Grant Richards, 7 July 1912, n. 3.

To Willard Huntington Wright [H-BLYU]

Wright (1888–1939) was literary editor of the Los Angeles Times *at this time. A strong supporter of Dreiser's work, he later achieved recognition both as an art critic and, under the name of S. S. Van Dyne, as the writer of the Philo Vance crime novels.*

3609 Broadway

N.Y.C

Dec. 2nd 1912

Dear Mr. Wright:

Your letter of November 20th cheered me greatly.[1] It isn't easy to do what I am trying to do unless I shut my ears almost entirely to current American opinion. The tide, at times, seems almost all again me.[2] While I personally grieve over the obvious defects of The Financier—defects which more time and means would have permitted me to correct[3] I live in the hope that I shall earn enough at this work to go on for I always feel that if I can only keep at it sufficiently long I shall be able to do one or two things which will have the fused materiality and essential illumination which life requires to transfigure it into literature.

Theodore Dreiser

1. Among other words of encouragement, Wright had written, "Sooner or later America will wake up to the fact that she has a real novelist."

2. Since the reviews of both *Jennie Gerhardt* (1911) and *The Financier* (published in late October 1912) were mixed, Dreiser's characterization of the response to his work appears to be overstated.

3. Under pressure from Harper's to complete *The Financier*, Dreiser was unable to avail himself of friends and editors, as was his custom, in the editing of the novel. He was especially sensitive to the derisive comments by some reviewers about its length and in 1927 published a severely cut new version of the novel.

1913

To Major Frederick T. Leigh [HP-DPUP]

Leigh (1861–1914) was treasurer of Harper & Brothers and an officer in the New York State National Guard.

3609 Broadway N.Y.C
Feb. 24—1913

My Dear Major:

This is to acknowledge the new arrangement which we entered into the other day covering sufficient cash to finish The Titan. I figure I will require five or six months—possibly even seven—but say five or six—during which time you are to send me $200 on the first of each month.[1] To affect this & other advances already made you are permitted to charge these and other advances & payments previously made and not yet satisfied by me to my general royalty account which includes Sister Carrie, Jennie Gerhardt, The Financier & The Titan after you publish it. As I told you the Mss of *The Genius* is now in Chicago but will come back in a month. When it comes back I will turn it over to you. If my general indebtedness has not, say, by Sept or Oct 1914, been cleared up by royalties earned by these other books Harper & Brothers may publish the Genius and include the royalties on that in the general adjustment.[2] I reserve the right even under these conditions however to withdraw *The Genius* and substitute for it some completed work (novel) which I may then be anxious to see published first. If you will send me the letter concerning Jennie Gerhardt I will write Miss Holly.[3]

Theodore Dreiser

1. In fact, Dreiser did not complete *The Titan* until December 1913.
2. *The "Genius,"* which Dreiser was having read by several Chicago friends, had been completed in July 1911. Dreiser did indeed turn over the manuscript to Harper's; when he and Harper's parted ways in early 1914, with Dreiser owing the firm a large sum in advances, Harper's claimed its rights in the novel until the matter was settled.
3. Flora Mai Holly (1868–1960), Dreiser's agent.

To Floyd Dell [H-NL]

Dreiser became acquainted with Dell (1887–1967), a prominent figure in the "Chicago Renaissance" of this period, during the winter of 1912–1913, when he was in Chicago doing research for The Titan. *Dreiser also wrote H. L. Mencken, among others, about the scheme he outlines, one which never came to fruition. Throughout his career, and especially during this phase, Dreiser was attracted by plans for new publishing firms, magazines, and movie production companies which would be committed to the unrestricted expression of quality work.*

3609 Broadway, N.Y.C
Mch 23rd 1913

My Dear Dell:

B. W. Dodge, who used to be with me in B. W. Dodge & Co has gotten in with a fellow by the name of Hill who is primarily a banker, rich & has written one book, not absolutely vile.[1] Dodge, for Hill, controls a publishing company called the Morningside Press. It is not doing so very well as you might suspect. Dodge, for Hill, wants me to come in on a new company to be organized (no name chosen) as "consulting editor" with the privilege of naming an office manager and a reader. That & cash are fairly satisfactory. Question: do you think my name as consulting editor would be a bad thing for me to use in this way? There is need for a thoroughly liberal, progressive house. Under contract no book could be accepted or rejected without my consent. No work beyond advice & appointing people whose judgment I could trust would be demanded. The firm—some part of it—could be made an intellectual and artistic center. What do you think? Let me hear from you & oblige

Theodore Dreiser

My name would not appear in the firm title—only here & there in letters & possibly on stationary as "consulting editor." I should not allow the company work to interfere with my writing in any way.

1. Dreiser was largely responsible for setting up Benjamin W. Dodge (?–1916) as B. W. Dodge & Co. in 1907. (The firm published the second edition of *Sister Carrie* that year.) William S. Hill (1863–1940) was a banker and the vice president of a realty company. Hill's novel, *What a Man Wishes*, was published by the Morningside Press of New York in 1913.

To William C. Lengel [H-CU]

Dreiser had left a copy of the manuscript of The "Genius" *in Chicago, where it was read by several literary figures, including Lengel (1888–1965), who had been Dreiser's secretary when he edited the* Delineator *and who was now working in Chicago as editor of a building trades journal. The version of* The "Genius" *in question was that completed in July 1911; in 1914 Dreiser revised its conclusion extensively. For thirty-five years, from their meeting in 1910 to Dreiser's death, Lengel served him in various professional capacities while also remaining a loyal friend.*

William C. Lengel.

[After 31 March 1913][1]

My Dear Lengel:

This an interesting comment on The Genius.[2] I think in the main you are right. I don't know however in just how far you are influenced by your knowledge of some things relating to me & your fondness for me. I have to smile when I read of "the pain" it caused me. You don't know how practically I went about it or how cheerfully it was executed. That may be the cause of its weakness in spots. Three other people have read it but they do not agree with you. Miss Tobin of Harpers[3] is violently opposed to any idea of changing it. Let us see what Masters says.[4] Did you really get me a straight opinion from the Red Book man?[5]

Well it can't be published for two years anyhow & possibly three.[6] I had thought of changing it & may. If I do it over it would be altered so very much.[7] I wonder what particular elements or colors you think will or might be eliminated in 5 years. Does "getting the sympathy of a reader" make a great book? I'm not at all sure. Witness Vanity Fair.

However write me more. I'd like to hear your second thoughts. I read your little story & liked it.[8] It struck me as reasonably true. Why don't you sell through an agent—Miss Holly or Reynolds or Curtis Brown.[9] I like Reynolds best or Curtis Brown. Write me all the news. The Dodge-Hill matter still hangs fire.[10]

Th D.

1. The letter is undated but see note 2 below.
2. On 31 March 1913, Lengel had sent Dreiser a lengthy critique of *The "Genius."*
3. Unidentified.
4. Dreiser had met the poet and lawyer Edgar Lee Masters (1868–1950) in Chicago in late 1912. Masters would soon achieve fame with his *Spoon River Anthology* (1915). The two men struck up a lifelong friendship, one which was to become especially important to Dreiser late in his career.
5. Perhaps Ray Long (1878–1935), at that time editor of the *Red Book*, a Chicago-based magazine.
6. Dreiser's agreement with Harper's was that he would complete, and they would publish, the three volumes of the Cowperwood Trilogy before *The "Genius"* appeared. In April 1913, *The Financier* had been published, *The Titan* was still in progress, and *The Stoic* was unwritten.
7. See also Dreiser to William C. Lengel, 14 April 1913.
8. Lengel had written Dreiser on 7 March 1913 that he had finished writing a short story and was sending it to him.
9. Flora Mai Holly had aided Dreiser in the republication of *Sister Carrie* in 1907 and was often used by him an as agent for several years afterwards. Paul Revere Reynolds (1864–1944) established the first literary agency in America in 1893; Curtis Brown (1866–1945) founded a major British literary agency in 1899.
10. See Dreiser to Floyd Dell, 23 March 1913.

To William C. Lengel [H-CU]

On completing his reading of the manuscript of The "Genius," *Lengel had passed it on to two other Chicago literary figures, Floyd Dell and Lucian Cary, who then wrote Dreiser their own critiques. In response to their and Lengel's comments, Dreiser counters with his own battery of more positive readings.*

3609 Broadway
April 14—1913

My Dear Lengel:

Very shortly I think I will send you six or seven or eight reviews of The Genius by different people of ability from which you will see how easy it is for people to disagree utterly as to the merits of the same thing. Floyd Dell[1] dismisses the whole thing as a failure but saves himself by saying that he has not read it all—an easy out. Now I am not and never have been ready to admit that this book is not done exactly as it ought to be done. I am not sure for to say that I would really have to read it from end to end consecutively which I have not done in two years. Be that as it may. What I want to find out is whether Dell & Cary[2] are really influenced by current opinion—other reviewers and what they think men like Mencken and Edgett[3] will say. When you get these reviews drop round casually & get in touch with them. Let them read these & then see if you can see any uncertainty manifested—any change of front. You know I have never been sure of Dells inmost convictions about anything and I am not now. Men like Mencken, Edgett, T. P. O Conner in England and Hersey here in N. Y.[4] say what they mean—also Reedy, Jim Ford & others[5]—but not all reviewers really review truly. Its a curious point with me. As for your opinion I always take you to say what you feel. Don't ever disappoint me in that. I want to add one thought. It doesn't follow that a character in a novel need ever be admirable. The whole test of a book—to me—is—is it true, revealing, at once a picture and a criticism of life. If it measure up in these respects we can dismiss sympathy, decency, even the utmost shame and pain of it all. Do what I suggest will you.

Th D

Write an editorial on the American Building Laws—the pros and cons. Berlin is limited to a single height & width of street & it is beautiful. New York is not & and it is strangely splendid. Which is right.[6]

1. For Dell, see Dreiser to Floyd Dell, 23 March 1913.
2. Lucian Cary (1886–1971), literary editor of the *Chicago Evening Post* during this period.
3. Edwin F. Edgett (1867–1948) was a reviewer and literary editor of the *Boston Evening Transcript* from 1901 to 1938.
4. O'Connor (not O Conner) (1848–1929), an Irish-born journalist and politician; Harold Hersey (1893–1956), a young poet and editor, was in 1916 to play a major role in aiding Dreiser in fighting the charge of obscenity against *The "Genius."*
5. William Marion Reedy (1862–1920), a supporter of Dreiser's work and editor and publisher of the St. Louis–based *Reedy's Mirror* (1893–1920); James L. Ford (1854–1928), journalist, author, and editor.
6. Dreiser has written in the margin of the postscript: "Our building [illegible] reflects our national character. Reread Kiplings 'The American Spirit.'" No Kipling work with this title has been identified, but Dreiser may mean Kipling's *American Notes* (1899).

To Albert Mordell [H-UV]

A prolific Philadelphia-based literary journalist and critic, Mordell (1885–1965) had in 1912 published The Shifting of Literary Values, *a work that Dreiser refers to at the opening of his letter.*

New York, Sept. 25—1913[1]

Dear Mr. Mordell:

It is pleasing to recieve your very interesting letter. Several people during the past year have spoken to me of you but who they were I cannot recall now. Your book evidently made a deep impression on many. I surely welcome an additional able critical intellect and I will read your book with pleasure.[2]

Why cannot we have a talk some day? It would be pleasant to go over anything in the literary field which would interest either of us. I have but few literary prejudices I think, though not so many literary favorites. Concerning The Financier I should like to talk to you more fully than I could by letter perhaps. It is but volume *one* of a three volume essay to which I gave the general title "A Trilogy of Desire". Harpers would not put the statement on volume one but I shall force it on volume II the special title of which is "The Titan". The third volume is entitled "The Stoic" and will be done next year. Whether I am wasting my time remains to be seen. We have never yet seen a complete dramatic financial life. This ought to prove one. "The Financier" lacks in drama and condensation in spots but I expect to go over it and re-issue it much improved for the final set.[3] Whatever one may think of "The Financier" as a segment it may take on new lustre as the base-stone of a trilogy or complete life.

Be that as it may I am glad you like "Jennie". Most critics, including Harris and Bennett, prefer "Sister Carrie."[4] William Marion Reedy and Thomas B. Mosher—men whose judgments I set very high—prefer "The Financier" to either.[5] In the current Smart Set is my first play—a one act affair[6]—and in the Century (August, September and October) chapters of a forthcoming travel book—"A Traveler at Forty" which the Century Company will publish next month. I will send you a copy. In January next, Harpers will publish Volume II of the trilogy entitled "The Titan".[7]

I do not count myself a Neithchean.[8] I have merely (and always) felt that I must achieve and maintain a personal point of view—as free from bias and prejudice as a conditional interrelation with the mortal stream will permit. But who is without prejudice.

Theodore Dreiser
Address P. O. Box 39
Hamilton Grange Branch
New York City
Do you come to N.Y.—ever?

1. Dreiser placed in a box to the left of the opening date: "My house address is 3609 Broadway. Phone 1980 Audubon. If not there try 1946 Bryant c/o Hyman."
2. Mordell's long appreciative letter of 19 September 1913 included a flier for *The Shifting of Literary Values*.
3. A revised and much condensed version of *The Financier* appeared in 1927.
4. Frank Harris (1856–1931) and Arnold Bennett (1867–1931); see Harris's "American Novelists Today. Theodore Dreiser," *Academy* 85 (2 August 1913):

133–34, and Bennett's "The Future of the American Novel," *North American Review* 195 (January 1912): 76–83.

5. Reedy, "Reflections: Dreiser's Great Book," *St. Louis Mirror* 21 (2 January 1913): 2; the comment by Thomas Mosher, founder and editor of *The Bibelot*, has not been identified.

6. "The Girl in the Coffin," *Smart Set* 41 (October 1913): 127–40.

7. Harper's, however, cancelled publication of *The Titan* while it was in press (see Dreiser to Albert Mordell, 6 March 1914); it was published by John Lane in May 1914.

8. Dreiser, who habitually misspelled Friedrich Nietzsche (1844–1900), had been introduced to his ideas through Mencken's *The Philosophy of Friedrich Nietzsche* (1908), though it is not certain whether he read him firsthand. His characterization of Frank Cowperwood in *The Financier* and *The Titan* as a figure who believes himself superior to common morality has frequently been considered Nietzschean.

1914

To Alfred A. Knopf [H-HRHUT]

Knopf (1892–1965), who was later to become a major publisher, was at this time employed by Doubleday, Page and Co., Joseph Conrad's American publisher. Knopf had written Dreiser and many other prominent American authors seeking public support for Conrad's work.

3609 Broadway, N.Y.C
Jan 21—1914

My Dear Mr Knopf:

Since writing you I have read "The Heart of Darkness", "*Youth*" and "The End of the Tether".[1] Of the three "The Heart of Darkness" is easily first—a splendid tale done in a new way with the first attempt at painting the brooding metaphysics of life which is to me successful and richly agreeable. It suggests a great art & that the same man might do more wonderful things if he took great pains. I understand from some of his strong advocates that some of his things are not so good and it would be easy to know that they would not be. There are not many hearts of Africa or rich & new themes. Back of all is a sea of metaphysics however (I mean all life) and from it we have drawn as yet but a few tin cups full. Shall I say more—need I?

I never go to luncheon save under compulsion (business). It breaks into & spoils my working day. As a rule I eat nothing between breakfast & dinner. All my evenings are gone this week. If you care to suggest one the latter half of next week I shall be glad to meet it if I can. With best wishes

Theodore Dreiser

As to using my opinion I fancy you had best consult Mr. Doubleday. He may not care to quote so immoral a man—I suggest this seriously.[2]

---

1. All three works named by Dreiser appear in *Youth: A Narrative and Two Other Stories* (1902).

2. Dreiser is here recalling for Knopf's benefit the alleged "suppression" of *Sister Carrie* by Doubleday in 1900. Knopf recalled Dreiser's remark about Doubleday in his 1965 autobiography *Portrait of a Publisher*.

To Albert Mordell [H-UV]

*Dreiser was in Chicago to complete his research on Charles T. Yerkes for the
Cowperwood Trilogy. For Mordell, see Dreiser to Albert Mordell, 25 September
1913.*

Hotel Bradley
N.W. Corner Rush & East Grand Ave.[1]
Chicago, March 6 1914

Dear Mr. Mordell:

There may be some noticeable delay in connection with The Titan. After
printing a 1st edition of 10 000 Harpers have decided—(for reason of its
cold realism perhaps)[2]—not to publish. They feel that it will do their house
harm. There is no doubt of the books early issue by one of several firms but
I merely notify you in order that the fact may reach you first hand.

Sincerely
Theodore Dreiser

Sister Carrie all over again only my position happens to be by no means
so insecure.

1. Dreiser has written "For the present" above the Hotel Bradley letterhead address.
2. An unlikely reason given Harper's awareness of the work's emphasis on Cowperwood's sexual conquests before it was set up in print. More probably, Harper's
was responding to information from its London branch that *The Titan* would be
found libelous in England because of its portrayal of Emilie Grigsby, one of Yerkes'
mistresses, as Berenice Fleming, since Miss Grigsby was still prominent in British
society.

To Alfred A. Knopf [H-HRHUT]

*Knopf had become an editor for the publisher Mitchell Kennerley and was soliciting
The Titan for that firm. Lengel, now again in New York, was acting as Dreiser's
agent in placing the novel, sending proof copies to a number of publishers.*

Hotel Bradley
N.W. Corner Rush & East Grand Ave.
Chicago, March 13 1914

My Dear Mr. Knopf:

I have your letter[1] and am asking Mr. W. C. Lengel, Editor of the Real
Estate Magazine, 165 Broadway to see that you get a copy of The Titan.
Call him up. I think his phone number is Cortlandt 4790 but I'm not sure.
His room there is 1437. I have as you must know small faith in the prelimi-

nary or subsequent emotions of publishers. I really would not object to any publisher so long as he saw me as a commercial possibility. Mr. Kennerley doesn't interest me because he doesn't see me. If he has enthusiasms they are not in my direction I fear. His presumed feeling over the Mss I mentioned is purely a courtesy of trade. I know him well.

However. The Mss of The Titan contains the objection that it has been rejected by another house—that it is hard, cold, immoral. It would never occur to any American publisher to tie up with a man on the basis of his career. The book of the season is the thing and the opinion of small fry critics. My contempt for the situation is so great that I heartily desire to drop out at times. However read the book, if you wish. I stipulate but one thing—that you do me the service of rendering a frank honest opinion.

Sincerely,
Theodore Dreiser

And the reading must be speedy as well as the decision.

1. Knopf wrote Dreiser on 10 March 1914 requesting that Dreiser arrange for Knopf to receive an advance copy of *The Titan* from Harper's.

To Alfred A. Knopf [H-HRHUT]

Continuing his efforts to land The Titan *for Kennerley, Knopf wrote Dreiser on both 18 and 19 March that he was reading the novel and would seek to reach a decision about it as soon as possible.*

Hotel Bradley
N.W. Corner Rush & East Grand Ave.
Chicago, March 21 1914

My Dear Mr. Knopf:

You are almost too late. John Lane wires a proposal this A.M.[1] It is quite satisfactory, other things being equal though I have wired Lengel to talk to you over the phone & see what he thinks. I cannot authorize Major Leigh to speak for me.[2] Lengel should not have made that suggestion. Harpers are entitled to say anything they please this side of libel regardless of me. Someday I hope to find a publisher who will see me as a unity—not as a spring list, piece meal, proposition. *Supposing* I did fail in one book—what of it? It is safe to suggest now that I might sell in a set sometime isn't it? I hope so anyhow. A courageous publisher might gamble so anyhow. My pontifical curse on all commercialized best seller houses & pseudo patrons of the fine arts. I shall be in New York Monday P.M. late perhaps & will call you up Tuesday.

Theodore Dreiser

1. The English publisher John Lane had a New York branch. Dreiser accepted Lane's offer to publish *The Titan* shortly after his return to New York on 23 March 1914.

2. Major Frederick T. Leigh, the treasurer of Harper's (see Dreiser to Frederick T. Leigh, 24 February 1913). Knopf, in his letter of 18 March, reported that Leigh needed Dreiser's permission before he would discuss with Knopf Dreiser's current relationship with Harper's.

To Upton Sinclair [H-LLIU]

Almost from the onset of the World War in August 1914, the German forces were accused of destroying Belgian and later French art treasures. Sinclair (1878–1958), who had achieved fame with The Jungle *(1906), wrote Dreiser on 1 October 1914 seeking his participation in a protest of these actions by a committee of American authors. During the first two years of the war, both Dreiser and H. L. Mencken were strongly pro-German in their sympathies.*

Dreiser in His Tenth St. Greenwich Village Apartment, Late 1910s.

165 W. 10th St. N.Y.C[1]

Oct 8th 1914

Dear Mr. Sinclair:

I am not convinced that the Germans any more than any other nation—difficulties being equal—are destroying monuments and works of art. Until I am satisfied of that I am in no mood to protest.

Very Truly

Theodore Dreiser

1. In July 1914, Dreiser moved to this Greenwich Village address, where he was to remain for over five years.

1915

To Carl Sandburg [H-UI][1]

Sandburg (1878–1967) and Edgar Lee Masters (see Dreiser to William C. Lengel, after 31 March 1913, n. 4) had met in Chicago in the spring of 1914. When Masters visited Dreiser in New York during the summer of 1915, he brought along a collection of Sandburg's poems for Dreiser to read with the hope that Dreiser might interest a New York publisher in their publication.

165 WEST 10 STREET
NEW YORK CITY
Aug. 6th 1915

My Dear Mr. Sandburg:

Sometime ago I asked Mr. Masters to get you to gather your poems together and let me see them. Last Monday he came in, bringing them, and I have since had the pleasure of examining them. They are beautiful. There is a fine, hard, able paganism about them that delights me—and they are tender and wistful as only the lonely, wistful, dreaming pagan can be. Do I need to congratulate you? Let me envy you instead. I would I could do things as lovely.

Mr. Dell[2] was in here the other night as we were reading them and he said that once he had seen some earlier poems of yours, many of which were lovely and some of which should surely have been included in these. Will you be so kind as to let me see them. My idea is that if so many as a hundred and twenty-five or a hundred and fifty poems can be gotten together a publisher can be found for them. I sincerely hope so,—I mean now. A publisher will certainly be found for them eventually. If I had the others perhaps we could select a few more and complete the proposed material of the book.[3]

Incidentally Mr. Dell, hearing your poem on Billy Sunday read wanted me to let him submit it for consideration at the Masses. I loaned it to him, subject to further advice from you, of course.[4]

My sincerest compliments. When I next get to Chicago I will look you up.

Sincerely
Theodore Dreiser

1. Published in Robert Carringer and Scott Bennett, "Dreiser to Sandburg: Three Unpublished Letters," *Library Chronicle of the University of Pennsylvania Library* 40 (Winter 1975): 252–56.

2. Floyd Dell (see Dreiser to Floyd Dell, 23 March 1913) had moved to New York from Chicago and had become managing editor of the *Masses*.

3. In fact, Masters himself submitted the poems he had brought to New York to John Lane, Dreiser's current publisher, unbeknownst to Dreiser, who was in Indiana at the time. Lane turned them down, and they were published, in 1916, by Holt as Sandburg's first volume, *Chicago Poems*.

4. "To Billy Sunday" appeared in the September 1915 *Masses*; it was republished in *Chicago Poems* as "To a Contemporary Bunkshooter."

To Ben Hecht   [H-HRHUT]

William C. Lengel had approached Dreiser in the fall of 1915 on behalf W. J. Hoggson, a building contractor and also the publisher of Hoggson's Magazine, who wished to start a movie production company devoted to quality films. (The New York City area was at that time the center of the American film industry.) In addition to Hecht (1894–1964), a Chicago journalist and writer, Dreiser wrote similar letters to H. L. Mencken, Carl Sandburg, Arthur Davison Ficke, and several others.

165 WEST 10 STREET
NEW YORK CITY
Nov. 28—1915

My Dear Hecht:

It looks to me, at the present writing, as though I were about to take literary and art charge of an important American film corporation. In that capacity I will be open to suggestions as to books, plays, poems, legends, panoramas, pageants and the like—for purchase of course, and to original scenarios. I desire to give a new artistic twist to things that I do or have done and I do not expect to be bound by the straw and water standards now prevailing. If you have any thoughts at any time perhaps you will trouble to write me. I will see that things used or taken advantage of are paid for. Pass the word along, if you choose, to all the ambitious.

Theodore Dreiser

I liked your summary in the Little Review.[1]

1. Dreiser may be referring to "The Dionysian Dreiser," *Little Review* 2 (October 1915): 10–13, an article in praise of *The "Genius,"* which is signed "The Scavenger."

1916

To Willard Dillman [H-UV]

Dillman (1872–1949), the proprietor of a Minneapolis printing firm, was an admirer of Dreiser's work and the author of two books of poetry, Across the Wheat *(1898) and* Monoscripts *(1912).*

P.O. Box 282
Savannah, Ga.
Feb. 7th 1916

Dear Mr. Dillman:

Your graceful letter of the 28th follows me here.[1] I'm suffering from grippe and only last week had to get out of New York. The undertakers were doing an unpleasant large business. Many people are kind enough to write me—thanks be—but it is very rare that I get a letter as sincere, as frank and as entertainingly philosophic as this. People who think logically and incisively are rare. As I get along in years I marvel more and more at how cleverly the world is run—not by any inherent current wisdom, or much—but by tradition and people. Did you ever stop to think of that. We live largely by things we have been told—things written in books. If we want to know or act we first run to a book—or a neighbor—or a lawyer—or a doctor—millions of us. Who has knowledge—and what does it amount to.

You put your finger on the keynote of my philosophy when you suggested that perhaps I meant that life is a welter. It is—to me. I do not see that tragedy pacifies. I do not see that prosperity weakens or destroys anything. I do not see that the world is getting better—or worse. Mechanically it improves. Spiritually it is static. I do not see that love is necessarily rewarded, or is a solution—or that hate is punished. A balance is struck—roughly—very roughly—but it is a varying balance.[2] Pari passu, other things being equal.

However I didn't mean to philosophize. I merely meant to tell you something about myself. I am now 44 and really not illusioned or disillusioned. Life looks as pleasant and agreeable to me as it ever did. No more so. I don't often find people with whom I can be intellectually happy, but when I do I am very happy. Here and there in America I have struck a man—intellectually. Most often they are mere mechanical toys, lay figures—church goers, religionists, moralists, law worshippers. I cannot endure limited men—or women—pseudo intellectuals. I would rather deal and live with the ordinary blind day laborer who doesn't think at all—but acts, like a dog, from impulse.

Be that as it may. I like your letter and it pleases me of course that you like my books. I wish I might see something of you, at sometime or other. Possibly you come to N.Y. When the cold weather breaks—April I should say, or May, I'll be back there. My address there is 165 W. 10th Street—Phone 7755 Chelsea. Here it is as above. If you come east be good enough to look me up. In the meantime, luck.

This is a charming place—Southern, warm, and different. It is really beautifully laid out. Just now the peach trees are blooming—something that happens about May 1—in New York.

Theodore Dreiser

1. In his initial letter to Dreiser, on 28 January 1916, Dillman noted that he had recently completed and liked The *"Genius"* and also spoke highly of Dreiser's work in general.
2. A brief summary of Dreiser's idea of the "equation inevitable," a philosophical belief present in much of his fiction and essays of the period.

To Willard Dillman   [H-UV]

165 WEST 10 STREET
NEW YORK CITY
July 31—1916

Dear Mr. Dillman:

I fancy you think I'm a very poor correspondent and you are quite right—I am. I liked your letter about the plays,[1] not because I agreed with it exactly but because you were so forthright about the whole affair. I have always intended to do a few three or four act plays but have never arranged my themes just right. After your opinion of the seven one act ones I fancy you think I ought to stick to novels exclusively.

I have been working quite hard this summer but not all the time in New York. There are so many places just around here that I am in and out from week to week almost. Once or twice I have thought of Minneapolis, but it's a long way.

A friend of mine is planning an automobile trip from Denver west to the Coast and south to Los Angeles for next spring.[2] If it goes through I may stop off at your city enroute. I got to thinking last night that you might judge by my silence that I was offended—hence this note.

And just now comes the cheering intelligence that the Anti-Vice Society here (successor of Comstock) and the Anti-Vice Society of Cincinnati have joined hands to suppress The "Genius".[3] It's already done, save for the prosecution which will follow in case any more copies are sold. The John

Lane Co. proposes to fight but we may be beaten in our Puritan Courts. I suppose from now on all my new works will be [illegible] with care.

My compliments and I hope to hear from you at your convenience.

Theodore Dreiser

1. *Plays of the Natural and the Supernatural*, published in February 1916. Dillman expressed reservations about Dreiser's abilities as a playwright and suggested that he return to the novel form.

2. Perhaps Franklin Booth, with whom Dreiser had made an automobile trip to Indiana in August 1915.

3. Dreiser had just learned of the action of the New York Society for the Suppression of Vice, founded by Anthony Comstock (1844–1914) and led at this point by John S. Sumner (1876–1971). He was to be engaged in a struggle against the ban until the novel was republished by Boni and Liveright in 1923. See also Dreiser to Arthur Davison Ficke, 21 September 1916.

To Arthur Davison Ficke [H-BLYU]

The "Genius" *was published by John Lane in October 1915; in late July 1916 the New York Society for the Suppression of Vice threatened to bring charges against Lane for publishing an obscene and blasphemous work. Although Lane's American representative, J. Jefferson Jones, refused to contest the charge and instead withdrew the novel, Dreiser, with the advice and aid of H. L. Mencken, determined to fight Sumner both in the courts and the media. Ficke (1883–1945) was ideally positioned to help, since he was both a poet sympathetic to Dreiser's work and a practicing lawyer.*

165 WEST 10 STREET
NEW YORK CITY
Sept. 21—1916

My Dear Ficke:

I have been so busy taking care of the details of this fight for the John Lane Co. that I have not had time to answer your very helpful letter of Aug. 25. (Think of it! Nearly a month ago!) And still the thing isn't settled. The P.O. department at Washington has still to say whether it will or will not bar the book from the mails—a very important matter. That is why the creation of a favorable public sentiment is so important now—beforehand, as it were. At the same time the suit here is delayed purposely by the John Lane Co. in order to win over the Government beforehand. No books are being sold however and none distributed, so unless the suit is eventually won and the government refuses to act the censor has triumphed and one more book has gone under. It seems ridiculous and impossible but so it is.

I am still working to get enough help to beat these people and if we do it will be a real victory—one worth trying for. They (Vice Commission N.Y.) have already taken action against two other works—August Forels "The Sexual Question" (imagine!) and Louis Wilkinson's "The Buffoon."[1] It's a scream, really.

My regards and my thanks. For what you have done and what you may yet be moved to do still more thanks. Smite the vice-crusaders hip & thigh until they win sense enough to let literature & art alone.

You heard of Jerome Blums Japanese prints in Chicago, of course.[2]

Theodore Dreiser

1. Auguste Forel (1848–1931), *The Sexual Question: A Scientific, Psychological, Hygienic, and Sociological Study* (1908), and Louis Wilkinson (1881–1966), *The Buffoon* (1916), a novel.
2. Dreiser admired the artistry of Jerome S. Blum (1884–1956) and was also his friend. Chicago-born and educated, Blum made a trip to the Orient early in his career which deeply influenced his work.

To John Lane   [H-HRHUT]

Lane (1854–1925) was the founder and owner of the John Lane Company of London, which, under the imprint "The Bodley Head," published many of the notable new writers of the 1890s and later, including Oscar Wilde. His New York branch, which published Dreiser's The "Genius," *was founded in 1896. By December 1916, Dreiser and Mencken had enlisted a formidable group of American writers in opposition to the suppression of* The "Genius."

Dec 15—1916

Dear Mr. Lane:

For sometime I have been intending to write and thank you not only for your personal interest in the outcome of the effort to suppress The "Genius" here, but also for the cable from Messr's Locke, Walpole, Wells, Thurston and Bennett,[1] which whether through your good offices or no was cabled to your house here and to the Author's League.[2] If it was *not* a suggestion of yours I am sure you were personally pleased and wished it and will gratefully do me the favor of thanking these gentlemen individually for me. I would write each one—and hope to soon, but what between a play, a book, the lawyers and several critics who have organized an offensive and required my aid I have been worked twelve hours a day and still am. A large body of correspondence has had to go without comment of any kind.

It may and I think will interest you to know that one of the formost law firms in America—Messrs Stanchfield & Levy,[3] and Joseph S. Auerbach, the personal counsel of August Belmont[4] have interested themselves in the case to the extent of preparing actions to be tried before the U.S. Commissioner for this District (Federal Attorney) and the Appellate Division (State Court of Appeals) a branch of which is here. Five judges will pass on it in this latter instance and Mr. Stanchfield will argue the case in person. As you may see by the enclosed, the United States District Attorney for this district (N.Y.) has already ruled in the books favor.

The cablegram—(will you say as much to the gentlemen who signed it)—proved most helpful and just at the right time. A petition containing four hundred names of American authors and playwrights, attached to which is the cable in question is being filed with the respective courts and later will be largely circulated. Considerable headway has been made—so much so that the agent for the vice society[5] has already offered to drop the case providing in the actions which are so soon to come before the court he be not censured. I am sincerely obliged to you and to these several gentlemen . . . to whom please convey my sense of obligation.

Theodore Dreiser

1. Five of the most popular and, for Wells and Bennett, critically esteemed English novelists of the period: W. J. Locke (1863–1930), Hugh Walpole (1884–1941), H. G. Wells (1866–1946), Ernest T. Thurston (1879–1933), and Arnold Bennett (1867–1931). Their cable to the American branch of John Lane and the Authors League was sent on 13 September 1916; it is reprinted in Riggio, *Dreiser-Mencken Letters*, I, 262n1.

2. The Authors League of America was a loosely organized society of professional writers; Dreiser's strong advocate Harold Hersey (see Dreiser to William C. Lengel, 14 April 1913, n. 4) was employed by the league and played a major role in promoting its protest of the suppression.

3. John B. Stanchfield (1856–1921) prepared Dreiser's "friendly suit" against John Lane to force Lane to distribute the novel. The suit was dismissed in 1918 and *The "Genius"* was not available until 1923, when it was reprinted by Boni and Liveright.

4. Joseph S. Auerbach (1855–1944), a prominent New York attorney; August Belmont (1853–1924), a banker and financier.

5. Probably a reference to John S. Sumner, who in 1915 had succeeded Anthony Comstock as secretary (or head) of the New York Society for the Suppression of Vice.

1917

To Willard Dillman [H-UV]

Dillman had written on 28 December 1916 expressing his appreciation of A
Hoosier Holiday and inviting Dreiser to visit Minneapolis the coming summer.

165 WEST 10 STREET
NEW YORK CITY
Jan 11—1917

Dear Mr. Dillman:

I am so pleased that you like A Hoosier Holiday so much—it is important for a writers work to be liked by somebody, isn't it? What you say about returning to Catholicism amuses me. Could it possibly be prompted by the profitable idea so industriously furthered by the church that all renegade (?) Catholics do return. I admire the Catholics for spreading it—good business I would call it—but I don't believe it. They even claimed that Voltaire returned on his death bed. But place his works against his alleged return and weigh their relative import. My present faculties will need to change greatly if I do.

What you say of your home interests me. I cant say about next summer. But if I am out that way & you still want me I'll come. A boat and a machine—well. Write me at your convenience.

Yours
Theodore Dreiser

1918

To Edward H. Smith [H-DPUP]

A journalist on the New York Sunday World, Smith (1881–1927) was a good friend during Dreiser's Greenwich Village years and remained a supporter of his work for some time afterward. Dreiser portrays him as "Jethro" in his sketch "Olive Brand" in A Gallery of Women (1929). Dreiser's letter reveals the efforts that various New York writers were making on his behalf in response to the continuing suppression of The "Genius."

165 WEST 10 STREET
NEW YORK CITY
Feb. 26—1918

My Dear Smith:

In regard to the Society in question Hapgood yesterday made the same suggestion—to call a dozen or so people together and discuss this pro and con—organize if necessary.[1] If I did not seriously wish to avoid being the prime mover in the thing I would issue fifty invitations and ask the individuals to meet here. If it cannot be forwarded any other way & soon, I will so do, but I prefer the other way.

In regard to Arnold Daly, I wish I might meet him.[2] It would be interesting so to do whether he produces my play or not. By the way galley proofs are coming in and I will soon have rough printed copies to supply.[3]

In regard to the dinner that is a good idea—not bad at all.[4] You would have to include the attorneys in the case—John B. Stanchfield, Louis Levy, Joseph S. Auerbach[5] and again such relative figures as J. Jefferson Jones the manager of the American John Lane Co—Boni & Liveright and a list of others whom I would furnish—people whom to neglect would mean bad feeling toward me. For instance Franklin Booth, the artist, Randolph Bourne, Abraham Cahan, Robert H. Davis, Douglas Doty, Edgar Lee Masters, Lawrence Gilman of the North American and a number of others.[6] I tell you frankly however that if you go to The Authors League with this you will be frost bitten. They do not like me there—why—perhaps you can find out.[7]

Theodore Dreiser

Why not make tentative soundings here & there and see how the idea is recieved.

1. Smith, in a 24 February 1918 letter to Dreiser, noted that he had discussed plans for a new writers association (to supplant the established Authors League) with Hutchins Hapgood and John O'Hara Cosgrave. Hapgood (1869–1944) was a writer and Greenwich Village friend. He and Dreiser were later to quarrel over the issue of Dreiser's anti-Semitism (see Dreiser to Joseph Fischler, 30 May 1935, n. 2). Cosgrave (1864–1947) was a writer and editor. Although Dreiser continued to discuss the need for a progressive association of American authors, no such organization was formed during this period.

2. Daly (1875–1927) was a well-known actor who had made his reputation in plays by George Bernard Shaw and other "advanced" dramatists.

3. Although Dreiser's play *The Hand of the Potter* was printed by Boni and Liveright in early 1918, publication was delayed until September 1919 as Dreiser sought to arrange a stage production.

4. Smith had proposed that the upcoming court hearing on *The "Genius"* case be followed by a dinner honoring those involved in fighting the ban on the novel. The dinner did not occur.

5. Three lawyers who were aiding Dreiser in the *The "Genius"* case; see Dreiser to John Lane, 15 December 1916, n. 3–4.

6. Named besides Jones (see Dreiser to Arthur Davison Ficke, 21 September 1916), Cahan (see Dreiser to Abraham Cahan, 23 December 1921), and Masters (see Dreiser to William C. Lengel, 31 March 1913, n. 7), are Booth (1874–1948), an Indiana-born artist; Bourne (1886–1918), a radical essayist and Village resident; Davis (1869–1942), a journalist and dramatist; Douglas Doty (1874–1935), an editor of the Century Co.; and Gilman (1878–1939), a prominent music critic.

7. The Authors League (see also Dreiser to John Lane, 15 December 1916, n. 2), the only national organization of American writers at the time, had earlier, in 1916, supported Dreiser's struggle to lift the ban on *The "Genius."* It had then gradually withdrawn from the effort under pressure from its more conservative members.

To Churchill Williams [H-HSP]

Having revised his 1901 story "Butcher Rogaum's Door" for inclusion in his collection Free and Other Stories, *which was scheduled for summer 1918 publication by Boni and Liveright, Dreiser now also sought magazine publication of the revised version, prior to its book appearance, in the well-paying Saturday Evening Post. The Post declined the offer and the revision did not appear before its book publication.*

March 20—1918

Dear Mr. Williams:

I am offering the enclosed story—*Old Rogaum and His Theresa* subject to the following information. It was first attempted in 1900. The first short version, 3000 words in length, was sold to The Mirror of St. Louis (William Marion Reedy) at that time (1900) for $35.00 and was published by him at once.[1] As he now informs me the paper then had a circulation of about

8000. Recently I came accross the old tale and revised it, straightening out its psychology and adding to its narrative until it reached its present length—about 8000 words. Since it seemed more or less a new tale—the name also having been changed I wrote to Mr. Reedy and explained the matter. He has advised me to sell it. With this data I am offering it and will be glad to know if you can consider it.

Theodore Dreiser

1. "Butcher Rogaum's Door," *Reedy's Mirror* 11 (12 December 1901): 15–17. Reedy (1862–1920), owner and editor of *Reedy's Mirror*, was an early supporter of Dreiser's work.

1919

To Edward H. Smith [H-DPUP]

For Smith, see Dreiser to Edward H. Smith, 26 February 1918. On 8 January 1919, Dreiser held a meeting at his Village apartment, attended by about twenty artists, writers, and critics, to discuss a proposal for the establishment of a private foundation to aid struggling workers in the creative field. Harold Hersey (see Dreiser to William C. Lengel, 14 April 1913, n. 4), who was also aiding Dreiser in The "Genius" *case, acted as temporary secretary of the group. Few major donations were received and the plan soon collapsed.*

Jan 11—1919

My Dear Smith:

I am grateful for your letter though I don't believe I deserve all the nice things you say. I don't know quite what to think of the result—nor whether I was wise in proposing it. Mencken insists that it is cheap—even moralistic (!) propaganda for something that isn't needed—more jobs for poseurs.[1] Nathan as you saw was of the same mood. On the other hand I consider Lewisohn one of the sanest of brooders on life—and he is for it.[2] It looks now that whether I do anything more or no—and I desire to do nothing—something would come of it. In re all this Knopf[3] has remarked that I have a "persecution complex"! As a matter of fact—and as I told you—I merely moved because I have been urged by many to do so. I can live without any court of critical aid or approval.

Young Heresy whom you saw here has since recieved money from Pinchot, Dr. Grant[4] & one or two others—to enable him—(and it is there wish)—to continue to try to round up groups for discussion. Bellows, I believe is also behind him.[5] They want him as a kind of temporary Secretary or runner. If you want to help anybody—help him. I have given him your address.

Th D

1. See Mencken to Dreiser, 3 January 1919, in Riggio, *Dreiser-Mencken Letters*, II, 330.
2. Both George Jean Nathan (see Dreiser to George Jean Nathan, 27 April 1932) and Ludwig Lewisohn (see Dreiser to Ludwig Lewisohn, 5 July 1933) attended the meeting.
3. For Alfred A. Knopf, see Dreiser to Alfred A. Knopf, 21 January 1914.
4. Gifford Pinchot (1865–1946), a pioneer conservationist and later governor

of Pennsylvania; Dr. Percy Stickney Grant (1860–1927), an Episcopal priest and poet noted for his radical social and religious views.

5. George W. Bellows (1882–1925), a realist painter.

To A. A. Brill [H-DPUP]

Brill (1874–1948), an Austrian-born psychiatrist, was Sigmund Freud's principal American exponent and translator. Dreiser had met him in late 1918.

> Hotel Traymore
> Atlantic City, N.J.
> Jan 20—1919

Dear Dr. Brill:

Several days since I finished your book on Psychoanalysis[1] and have been awaiting a favorable moment ever since to write you concerning it. Its directness and daring have impressed me greatly. Somehow the facts here, and your interesting cases, have the appeal of great tragedy for me. I feel as though I were walking in great halls and witnessing tremendous scenes. Life as revealed thus is sad to me,—in view of all the obvious and yet unseen pitfalls through which we move. "The blind leading the blind." Again a book like this and the wisdom of Freud, is like a master with a key who unlocks subterranean cells and leads forth the hoary victims of injustice. It is a science that a man should love to practice. I can only congratulate you on the pleasure your work must give you.

> Theodore Dreiser

1. *Psychoanalysis: Its Theories and Practical Application* (1912).

To Eugene O'Neill [TS-BLYU]

Horace Liveright, Dreiser's publisher, had agreed to back a new magazine devoted to "distinguished" expression, with Merton Yewdale serving as managing editor and Dreiser supervising selection of material. In addition to O'Neill (1888–1953), who at this early stage of his career was closely allied with the Provincetown Players, Dreiser wrote similar letters to, among others, H. L. Mencken, Eugene Debs, Edgar Lee Masters, and Randolph Bourne. The project never proceeded beyond the planning stage.

165 WEST 10th STREET,
NEW YORK CITY,
May 7, 1919

Mr. Eugene O'Neill,

Dear Sir:—

With the assistance of some friends who are planning to relieve me of most of the mechanical burden, I am getting up a magazine to appear quarterly or semi-annually which will be somewhat broader in its scope than most of those now on the market. The contents will consist of short stories, essays, one-act plays, poems, critical studies, etchings and fine illustrations in halftone and line; each issue to be limited to ten miscellaneous contributions, and each contribution to be, in so far as possible, as distinguished in quality as the other.

The magazine will be brought out over the imprint of some first-class publisher; it will be published in book form and sold in the bookstores at a price that will enable the publisher to allow a royalty of twenty per cent on all copies sold.

Thus instead of paying each contributor a stated sum in advance for his contribution, as is customary with the regular magazines, we propose to apportion the royalty among the contributors on the basis of the relative merit of each contribution, this apportionment to be determined by myself.

The aim of the magazine is to present in the most artistic form, the best in American art and letters, but meritorious works of foreign contributors will receive consideration.

Now that you are familiar with the general plan of publication, perhaps you will be willing to submit something for our examination.

Yours sincerely,
Theodore Dreiser

To Jacques Loeb   [H-LC]

Loeb (1859–1924), the principal exponent of biological mechanism (or tropisms) as the key to all life, was a member of the Rockefeller Institute at this time. He and Dreiser did not meet until early 1923.

165 WEST 10 STREET
NEW YORK CITY
May 29—1919

Dear Mr. Loeb:

Several years ago I read your book on the Mechanistic Interpretation of Life.[1] I have been wondering if, since then, you have developed much additional data and if these are to be found in any published form. I will appreciate information.[2]

Theodore Dreiser

1. The correct title is *The Mechanistic Conception of Life* (1912).
2. In his 3 June 1919 response, Loeb noted that Dreiser might find of interest two of his recent books, *The Organism as a Whole, from a Physiochemical Viewpoint* (1916) and *Forced Movements, Tropisms, and Animal Conduct* (1916).

To Mitchell Dawson   [TS-NL]

Dawson (1890–1956), a prominent Chicago lawyer as well as an occasional contributor to magazines, had written Dreiser in early August 1919 outlining a plan for a magazine devoted to fresh and original expression to be called The New Moon. *He also requested that Dreiser write a letter endorsing the project that Dawson could use to enlist support for the venture. Dreiser's response resembles his comments on the state of American writing expressed in his "Life, Art and America," published initially in the* Seven Arts *in February 1917 and reprinted in* Hey Rub-a-Dub-Dub *(1920). The magazine never appeared.*

165 West Tenth Street, New York City
[August 18, 1919]

Dear Mr. Dawson:

I have your very urgent letter in regard to the New Moon. Naturally the idea appeals to me, for for some years I have attempted to interest the public in one magazine venture and another, as well as in books, and have contributed freely to efforts of this kind. Whether the time has come remains to be seen. Others working in allied fields have done as much. Whether their efforts are to remain entirely without fruit also remains to be seen. Certainly no vast success has crowned the efforts of any serious American artist or writer or magazine editor thus far. The laurels are all to those who work in a lighter vein or who come with a foreign reputation. Any European or Asiatic, in so far as the American mind is concerned, so far outstrips anything which any American could possibly achieve that any seriously inclined American is apt to feel at the outset the weight of an almost unendurable handicap. While a foreign name and reputation may easily lead the shy and morally secretive American to contemplate the spring of realism or fact, the American never. At every book counter, as well as at every library and magazine door, stands the religious and moral American, glasses on nose, thin lips firmly set, one hand raised, exclaiming "Thou shalt not," "Too strong," "Too coarse," "Too realistic," "Too true," "Too sad," "Too brutal," "Too vulgar," "Too unhappy", "Not uplifting enough," "No moral," "Fails to end happily." Such are the comments and the condemnations. And behind these again are the newspaper and magazine critics agreeing and crying the same thing and with one accord singing of the undefiled sweetness of life, the purity and hope that must forever and ever be inculcated, in order to preserve the young. And behind these again are ranged priests and preachers, moral prophylaxers, women and men, vice crusaders of every faith and phase, all bent upon one or two or three things: a salary, publicity, and the suppression or destruction of everything which fails to inculcate a moral or content the mass with their lot.

Now this were excellent if all agreed and if there were never, anywhere, a call for anything different. But is this true? Is it not right now the fashion of the day for literary censors to decry the decadence of English and the absence of American letters? Do they not bemoan the utter banality of "the best seller" and sometimes all but shed tears because no one is essaying real "literature"? All of which is quite touching. But let any American-born seriously address himself to letters for art's sake, and woe betide him. The slurs! The contempts! The brutal where not inane falsification! Moved by some inexplicable resentment against an American attempting—or, worst of all, achieving—a work of art, or at least a true picture of American life, they are out upon him for a scoundrel with cries of rage and even hate. The dog! The prostitution of the Temple and the Sacred Fire!

Now I for one have no very great complaint to make, for despite various mishaps I have done well enough. But it does seem to me nevertheless that intellectual America should seriously bestir itself and do something by way of encouragement to American letters and art. As I have elsewhere said, a fund might be raised, some magazines supported, some phases of serious effort encouraged.

For in America, as it seems to me, the artist and thinker in any field works under too many discouragements. His rewards are much much too small, little or nothing. He is too much chastened and repressed. A Carnegie lives and dies, devoting hundreds of millions to libraries and the support of college professors, and the result is what? The two groups combine to debar or contemn the serious worker and so prevent him from earning a living. Religious organizations are given almost wholly to the same labor. Vice societies the same. There are far, far too many art baiters. It is even becoming the fashion, a popular pastime, as it were.

The chief trouble with our people today is that they are too narrowly religious and too full of mistaken notions of what is intellectually and morally to their advantage. Ignorance and prudery are the millstones that grind thought to nothing in America. We are all too much shocked by many things publicly stated that we know privately to be true. Our money-makers and trust-builders conform to few of the things which the current American ethical and moral code demands. Yet few have the courage to arise and admit what they know to be true, especially where the latter runs counter to current notions or beliefs. And when some one occasionally insists upon our admitting publicly that which we privately know to be true or do, the average American arises and feigns an outraged sense of decency. Our public modesty or pretence is injured. What we really fear is that our private moods and desires may be scathingly revealed.

Well and good. I have no quarrel with that, only I still insist that somewhere in this great dreariness there should be an oasis. We cannot really be as perfect as we maintain that we are.

In most of the publishing houses, libraries and offices, and even newspapers, today there are too many men of straw, too many absolutely trivial time-servers without experience or breadth of vision or vitality, who are deciding upon the mental bait wherewith the public is to be tempted, and the public must—or at least should—always be tempted with some worth while bait. If a fact agrees with current religious or moral beliefs it is marvelous to the present-day editor or publisher or librarian or professor. If not it is a scandal, something to be hidden deep in the lowermost dungeons of secrecy. Similarly with any poem, play, story. We are becoming so amazingly self-protective that we fear to live—and, what is worse, fear to let others live. Personally what I most resent is the constant crowding in between myself or any other serious writer or artist of men of lesser understanding and less courage who insist that all must be made to conform to their pygmy theories and a pygmy understanding of life. The intellectuals are barred from reaching each other. Rabelais cannot come to you because some thin-souled puritan cannot endure him. Similarly with Boccaccio, Zola, France, Moore.[1] The reading of serious and vital things today is everywhere discouraged because the puling stomachs of a puling and absolutely negligible mass cannot stand them. And even the stage, hitherto more or less ignored, now appears to be as carefully studied for the possible intrusion of serious thought as any book. True, the undressed chorus and the bedroom farce still remain, because free of serious thought. But not so a really serious play.

Now if, in the face of this, any one is interested to venture a publishing scheme of any kind—magazine, book or other—I for one am ready to hail him and cry "luck". Personally I feel that I have done as much as any one via free contribution of material to aid such ventures. I have persistently attempted to ally those of an intellectual artistic turn in order that they may be rallied to the aid of superior things. That this, or the efforts of others in a similar vein, have thus far borne much fruit I cannot say; apparently not. Yet that a better day may be near at hand I am still ready to believe. It certainly should be possible to found one or two good magazines, and it is also entirely possible that the current magazines and newspapers, feeding our public as they do on mush and sweet milk, may at last surfeit them and so create a market for something different. Meantime the best I can say for your scheme for The New Moon is that it appeals to me. If you have a genuine sense of what is new and valuable in letters and can secure or create a temporary subsidy you will be doing the discriminating a favor by publishing it. There is—should be, even if there is not—a small and growing audience for something real and vital in America. In time it should be possible to marshal this to the support of a first-rate magazine. In the meantime—as the revered Wilson is so fond of saying—may I not hope that it will prove to be The New Moon.[2]

Very truly yours

Theodore Dreiser

Aug 18–1919

1. These were the authors conventionally attacked as salacious by Anthony Comstock, John S. Sumner, and other suppression of vice reformers who sought to protect American readers from unsuitable literary works. For Comstock and Sumner, see Dreiser to Willard Dillman, 31 July 1916, n. 3.

2. An ironic allusion to President Woodrow Wilson's predilection for the "may we not hope" construction.

1920

To Edward H. Smith   [H-DPUP]

For Smith, see Dreiser to Edward H. Smith, 26 February 1918. Dreiser had met Helen Richardson (1894–1955) in New York in September 1919, and in November he moved with her to Los Angeles, where they settled in the northeast suburb of Highland Park. Throughout most of their three-year stay in Los Angeles, Dreiser continued to use a post office box as his mailing address.

P.O. Box 181
Los Angeles
Calif
Jan 5—1920

Dear Smith:

You entirely wrong in thinking I might object to anything in the Kramer article.[1] It was excellent and I had been intending to write & tell you so. I'm only sorry you couldn't get him a 5th Ave. show. However Kennerley[2] is not so bad. He seems to have some standing. I'm very hard at work here trying to finish another novel for my friends the critics.[3] They toil & sweat over my productions. Sometimes I think it is the only real work they do. As for this supposed book of philosophy Liveright, Fleischman, Yewdale & some others seem to think that my forthcoming book of essays contains a new one.[4] To me it seems a very old one—a seeming rough balance or equation holding in all things—Newtons law of gravitation applied to thought & human action.[5]

I am told a rainy season soon follows here now. The holidays were hot & clear. I have a porch overlooking the mountains back of Pasadena although I am in Highland Park. Can't say whether I'll be back by May or not. May be not. If they keep shoving up my studio rent in N.Y. ($7 more beginning Jan!) I may seek to sublet ½ of your place—the top floor say. I promise to be a respectable tenant.

The woods here are full of authors, playwrights, scenario writers & what not. Movie stars bump into you at every corner. I keep very much to myself as I need to.

Greetings. Best wishes for your trip & this year. If you see anyone I know & respect give them my regards.

Dreiser

1. Edward Adam Kramer (1866–1941), a New York–based landscape painter. The article Dreiser refers to has not been identified.

2. The publisher Mitchell Kennerley (1878–1950); see also Dreiser to Alfred A. Knopf, 13 March 1914.
3. Dreiser was attempting to complete *The Bulwark*.
4. *Hey Rub-a-Dub-Dub*, published by Boni and Liveright in January 1920. Dreiser refers to Leon Fleischman, vice president of Boni and Liveright, and Merton Yewdale, an editor who had been at John Lane and was now at Harper's.
5. See Dreiser's "Equation Inevitable," an essay in *Hey Rub-a-Dub-Dub*.

To Dr. P. Charles Green [H-Auerbach][1]

Dr. Green, a Philadelphia physician, had written Dreiser for his opinion on the recently enacted Eighteenth Amendment.

P. O. Box 181
Los Angeles
Calif.
June 8—1920

Dear Doctor Green:

My feelings concerning Prohibition are various. I long for the days of the Bushmill High Ball and the Gin Rickey. Again I have always felt that certain aspects of the saloon as a dispensary were horrible. Too often it was coupled with cheap or crooked politics, graft & protected vice. Many people who dislike prohibition intensely despised the saloon & would rather suffer drink-less than let the saloon *as it was* come back. Again thousands—possibly hundreds of thousands of families—that suffered via a boy, a girl, a father or mother or some other relative becoming an addict & irresponsible turned their faces against the saloon & against liquor in general, not because they were moralists or religious but because they were hurt or tortured. My mother suffered agonies over one boy—one of my brothers—who literally drank himself to death & in so doing stole, got in jail etc.[2] A sister of mine has had 30 years of poverty & misery because hubby is a souse. Now in his old age when he cant get it he seems to be a fairly respectable person intellectually.[3] These cases—this type of case—started the moralists & the religionist & the vice crusader—all drawing salaries—on the war path. As you point out business at last saw that it could divert liquor money into shoe money, etc. and thats what turned the trick. Personally I long for the pleasant cafe & the gin rickey. Liquor never hurt me. I like it. It made a grand evening. And I don't believe human weakness or its craving for pleasure & surcease can be permanently restrained by law. But I may be wrong. Look at the *Bee* family. Behold the ant. Are there any drunkard *Bees*? Any souse ants? Maybe—maybe. But I haven't heard, as yet. Nevertheless I regret that humanity or to come closer—the American people are such poor truck that they cant drink & regulate drinking so that it wont be a disgrace. At the same time I thoroughly believe that moon-shine & all other drinks will soon be common in homes. Every liberty loving drunkard will have a small still still[4] of his own. Would that I had one myself.

Theodore Dreiser

now if you know where I stand its almost more than I do. I would like to see the individual strong enough to stop this side debauchery.

1. Previously published in Jonathan Auerbach, "Dreiser on Prohibition," *Dreiser Studies* 30 (Fall 1999): 35–38.
2. Dreiser's brother Rome (1860–1940), whom Dreiser at this time believed to be dead. See also Dreiser to Arthur Pell, 5 November 1926.
3. Dreiser's sister Mame (1861–1944) and her husband Austin Brennan.
4. The repetition is in the holograph text.

To Donald P. McCord   [H-DPUP]

McCord, a retired army doctor, was the brother of Peter McCord, Dreiser's great friend when both worked on the St. Louis Globe-Democrat *in the early 1890s. He and Dreiser met in 1906; they were to become good friends after both settled in Los Angeles in the late 1930s.*

P.O. Box 181
Los Angeles
Calif.
June 12—1920

Dear McCord:

Glad to hear from you again and more than sorry that your long army service has resulted so unsatisfactorily.[1] I remember the Christmas all right and I remember how much Peter thought of you—but I can't get back your first name. Please sign your next letter legibly & in full. As you see I am here in Los Angeles and I'd like to hear the story. If you go East[2] why not come up this way. If the tale has the color that I believe it is likely to have I might do something with it. Life is a grinding mess as you knew. The individual amounts to nothing. He knows he's a thin shadow & in danger of disappearing at any moment. I only wish all our lives could appear more substantial than they are. But I'll be glad to see you & I hope you'll come to see me here. Personally I've done very well—much better than I expected—but it has been largely luck at that.

Theodore Dreiser

1. McCord, in his letter to Dreiser of 1 June 1920, reported that he had been forced to retire from the army after being slandered by the wife of a superior officer.

2. Since McCord lived in San Diego, Dreiser appears to be assuming that he would travel east through Los Angeles.

To Benjamin W. Huebsch [H-DPUP]

Huebsch (1876–1964) was the founder in 1914 of B. W. Huebsch, a firm which published many prominent European and American writers, including James Joyce, D. H. Lawrence, and Sherwood Anderson. John Maxwell, an editor on the Chicago Globe *during the 1890s, had aided and instructed Dreiser in 1892 during his first job as a newspaper reporter. Dreiser had visited him in Indianapolis in June 1919, where Maxwell worked on the* Star, *and learned of his book on the authorship of Shakespeare's plays. (Maxwell held that the plays were written by the Earl of Salisbury.) Despite many efforts over the years, Dreiser was never able to interest a publisher in Maxwell's book.*

P.O. Box 181
Los Angeles,
Cal.
June 21—1920

Dear Huebsch:

There is a man—John Maxwell—address c/o Hotel Seminole—Indianapolis Ind—who has solved the question of who Shakespeare was. It is a large work—about two thick volumes when printed. I have read it and it is masterly. Do you know of a publisher who would be interested. It is a book that would be bought by professors—libraries, students of Shakespeare and the well to do lovers of letters generally. I think something ought to be done about it. The work needs a patron—(publisher-patron or otherwise). I see where Thomas Looney—of England has issued another work, making another guess[1]—but this man has the goods. Please advise me & him to the best of your ability. Would Francis Hackett read the Mss?[2]

Dreiser

1. J. Thomas Looney (1870–?), *"Shakespeare" Identified in Edward de Vere* (1920).
2. Hackett (1883–1962), a journalist and critic, was at this time literary editor of the *New Republic*.

To David Karsner [H-Cor]

Karsner (1889–1941), the editor of the New York Call, *a socialist newspaper to which Dreiser contributed frequently during the late 1910s and early 1920s, was the author of* Debs: His Authorized Life . . . *(1919). He had also in early 1918 provided Dreiser with some of the Jewish background for* The Hand of the Potter.

> P.O. Box 181
> Los Angeles
> Calif
> July 26—1920

Dear Karsner:

That is a fine resume of my spirit and import so far.[1] It is interesting to me to note that you are the very first to "bear down hard" on the philosophic import of the works in general and Hey, Rub—in particular. I read the first sane estimate of it clipped from the New York Tribune about a week ago.[2] Thanks.

I am in the best of health & spirits and enjoying an ideal summer climate—the most delightful I have ever known. This fall, if I vote, I vote for Debs.[3]

> Dreiser

Wired you about some copies. Hope I get them.

1. Karsner, "Theodore Dreiser: A Portrait," *New York Call Magazine*, 18 July 1920, 6–7.

2. An anonymous review of *Hey Rub-a-Dub-Dub*, *New York Tribune*, 4 July 1920, Magazine and Book Section, 11. Reprinted in Jack Salzman, ed., *Theodore Dreiser: The Critical Reception* (New York: David Lewis, 1972), 390–92.

3. Eugene Debs (1855–1926) was the Socialist candidate for president despite being in prison during this period for anti-war activities. He received almost a million votes.

To Jacques Loeb [H-LC]

For Dreiser and Loeb, see Dreiser to Jacques Loeb, 29 May 1919.

P.O. Box 181
Los Angeles
Calif.
Aug. 26—1920

Dear Mr. Loeb:

For sometime I have been intending to write and thank you for the pamphlets you so kindly sent me—those relating to some of your experiments. Quite recently I read The Science of Human Behavior—by Parmelee—a most involved and poorly presented version of *behavior*.[1] Isnt there some clear readable summary of the Science of Human Behavior—to date—which you can recommend? I am without scientific training and only a good writer can interpret science for the layman. I find no difficulty in reading & following you—but so often writers present their data so poorly that it is slavery to follow them. I will thank you.[2]

Theodore Dreiser

1. Maurice Parmelee (1882–1969), *The Science of Human Behavior* (1913).
2. Loeb replied on 11 September 1920 that "No exact work has been done on human behavior."

To Benjamin W. Huebsch [H-DPUP]

Huebsch (see Dreiser to Benjamin W. Huebsch, 21 June 1920), who had recently published Sherwood Anderson's novel Poor White, *had asked Dreiser to write in its support.*

P.O. Box 181
Los Angeles
Nov. 24—1920

Dear Heubsch:

I read *Poor White* the other day—or rather finished it—and while I am the man who induced J. Jefferson Jones to publish *Marching Men* and *Windy McPhersons Son*[1] I cannot say that I like this story. As a matter of fact while I think the theme excellent and the workmanship *in places only*—not bad—on the whole the thing is poorly executed—miserably so—so much so that I cannot write what you would like me to write. The color is muddy—the characterization uncertain. There is much of repetition & and what I consider weak deduction. But for heaven sake don't show Anderson this let-

ter—for after all he is a realist—and working in the right direction and I
don't want to discourage any realist anywhere or at any time.

I regret this all the more because just after *Poor White* I read a most
excellent realistic novel by Floyd Dell—(Moon Calf)[2] and have just written him an enthusiastic letter. I think it a fine piece of work—all that new
American realism should be and call it to your attention. You know, if
you know anything about me—that if could like Andersons new book I
would say all that I could everywhere. Let him do another—and give me
a chance at that. After reading the book I encountered Menckens review[3]
but cant see it all. I think, eventually Mencken will hurt himself if he fails
to discriminate more accurately.

How are you? I hope thriving. Have you ever been to L.A. If not take
my advice & come between April 1 and Nov 1—not earlier or later. Their
summer here is ideal. No rain, no flies or mosquitoes—cool nights always.

Theodore Dreiser

1. Anderson (1876–1941), who had met Dreiser in Chicago in 1912, sent him the
manuscript of his first novel, *Windy McPherson's Son*, in late 1915; Dreiser recommended it to Jones (1880–1941), head of the American branch of John Lane and
at that time Dreiser's publisher, who then published both it (in 1916) and *Marching
Men* (in 1917).

2. *Moon-Calf*, an autobiographically based novel, was published by Knopf in
1920.

3. Mencken's largely positive review of *Poor White* appeared in the *Smart Set*
(December 1920): 138–39 (though dated December, the issue appeared in late
November).

To Horace Liveright [TC-DPUP]

*Horace Liveright (1886–1933) became Dreiser's publisher—first under the Boni
and Liveright imprint and then that of Horace Liveright, Inc.—in 1917 after
Dreiser broke with John Lane over its failure to fight the suppression of* The
"Genius." *The association was Dreiser's longest with an American publisher and
also one of his most tempestuous. Dreiser's irritation in this letter no doubt stems
from his failure to complete* The Bulwark *after a year in Los Angeles despite
Liveright's anxious queries about the novel. In addition, he had recently put* The
Bulwark *aside for* An American Tragedy, *a work which, he realized, would
require a long gestation.*

P.O. Box 181
Los Angeles,
Calif.
Nov. 28, 1920.

Dear Liveright:

First, in regard to a novel.[1] I am fairly along in one which suits me so far but much more than that I do not care to say. Having made promises with every intention of keeping them and not having been able to fulfill them I now prefer to say nothing until I can lay a completed thing down. My indebtedness to you is certainly taking care of itself and the obligation to pay out a debt with a novel when the debt is taking care of itself automatically certainly ceases, doesn't it? I should say so.[2] I may want to turn this over to you and everything else which I do, only assuming that we can keep on reasonable terms, but I have had so many irritating rumors drift out here that I don't know what to think, or rather, at times, I certainly think I do know what to think. One and another person in touch with you during the past year have written me on one pretext and another and the burden of their song, once various silly little preliminaries were cleared away has been that it is so important for me to do another novel, that the public expects it of me, that my reputation as a writer somehow hangs not on anything I have done in the past but on what I may hope to do in the future, that I must achieve a *new* and smashing success in order to restore or at least retain my waning reputation.

Your own last letter is full of the same sweet song. Floyd Dell has written a novel which strips me of all my alleged laurels. Sherwood Anderson the same. Sinclair Lewis the same. Ben Hecht the same.[3] As a matter of fact long since there have been many others who have done the same. Willa Sibert Cather, H. B. Fuller, Owen Johnson, Joseph Hergesheimer, Will Payne, George Bronson Howard, Stephen French Whitman and a number of others.[4] In fact the competition has been so keen and I have so often been exposed in the public prints as reduced to ashes by some lusty young rival that I have long since despaired of success fully contending with so many upspringing brilliantly outfitted rivals and have contented myself with trailing along behind, a tenth rate competitor. I could not hope to knock out the [word missing] even supposing that I were so vain as to believe that I might or, failing that, were interested to try. Well you know how one feels when he sees the game going against him.

Seriously, I get just a little tired of all this silly palaver about the great American novel,[5] a sole and glistering luminary blazing unrivalled in the literary heavens, my own alleged claim to be the same, etc. As a matter of fact I have never laid claim to being this person or star and I do not so do now. If I have not already written the Great American novel than I never will, for I have already written as good a novel as I will ever write. I might hope and wish, as I sometimes have that I might write a dozen more as good, not in the hope of adding to or staying my waning reputation but in the hope that one of them might sell more furiously than any that I have ever written ever have. But since my energy is limited and my tastes vary slightly so that betimes I prefer to do a short story, at other times a play, at still other times an essay or a poem, why,—Sincerely, I wish I might write a novel so appealing to the public at large that it would earn me sufficient to retire once and for all or, at least, for a period of years but I am by no means satisfied that I have the Knack. If Harold Bell Wright or Jean Stratton Porter would only kindly open a school I would begin on a best seller course at once.[6]

Quite frankly I am not running a race with anyone. It is not a contest I have entered upon but the labor, such as it is, of expressing myself. For years I have seen the limelight occupied by many generally conceded to be much more efficient and appealing than myself. So be it. I am reasonably contented. But that is why, when, in these late days inspired letter writers descend on me with advice and appeals to look out for my enormous career I am but slightly moved. Put yourself in my place.

N. B. I have just read, by request, Sherwood Anderson's new novel. It is a failure, very poorly executed and not so very capably conceived. On the other hand Floyd Dell has really got down a brilliant piece of autobiography in novel form. It is beautiful and I have so written him. Since I am the man who induced Jones to publish Anderson's first two books you will credit me I think with being free of jealousy or envy in Andersons case.[7]

1. Liveright had written Dreiser on 8 November 1920, "How about the novel for the Spring list?" On 22 November, he wrote, "I have asked you any number of times whether you will have 'The Bulwark' ready for publication say in April."

2. Dreiser's reference is to his belief that the advances he had received for *The Bulwark* were being paid off by royalties on other books of his published by Liveright.

3. Liveright, in his letter of 22 November 1920, had remarked, "We simply must not let Sinclair Lewis, Floyd Dell, Sherwood Anderson, etc., do the writing of the 'great American Novel.'" Dell's *Moon-Calf* (1920), Anderson's *Winesburg, Ohio* (1919), and Lewis's *Main Street* (1920) had all received strongly positive reviews. Hecht's first novel, *Erik Dorn*, was not published until September 1921, but perhaps Dreiser had advance notice of its quality and appeal.

4. A very mixed group: Cather (1873–1947), Fuller (1857–1929), and Hergesheimer (1880–1954) were well-known novelists with considerable reputations; Owen Johnson (1878–1952) was a popular novelist best known for *Stover at Yale* (1911); Will Payne (1865–1954), the author of *The Story of Eva* (1901), and

Stephen French Whitman (1880–1948), author of *Predestined: A Novel of New York Life* (1910), were scarcely known figures; and Bronson Howard (1842–1908) was a dramatist who wrote no novels.

5. See note 3 above.

6. Wright (1872–1944) wrote popular romances; his *The Winning of Barbara Worth* (1911) sold more than a million copies; Gene (not Jean) Stratton-Porter (1863–1924), author of *A Girl of the Limberlost* (1911), wrote popular girls' stories.

7. For Dreiser and the publication of Anderson's early novels, see Dreiser to Benjamin W. Huebsch, 24 November 1920.

To David Karsner [TS-UV]

For Karsner, see Dreiser to David Karsner, 26 July 1920.

P.O. Box 181
Los Angeles,
Cal.
Dec. 12, 1920

Dear Karsner:

Hereafter you are David only, as per your wish. Thanks for the copies of The Call containing the P. D. article.[1] It is very good. And evidently the copies you so kindly mailed have reached their destination for I am in receipt of letters from Indiana indicating a surprise at the "nationwide"(!) interest. So much for a judicious and timely word. So, once more, thanks.

How are you? I hope all right. One of your letters some time ago seemed to me at least to indicate a low state of mind but since you live and work, and apparently the latter with interest, you will come out all right. Nothing like work as a cure for every ill. Believe me, I know whereof I speak.

Read your article, *If the Light Should Go Out* and agree with it entirely.[2] These sniffy intellectuals give me a pain. They spend their days in sniffing and die sniffing. They are pointless—mere gum on the axles. A man like Lenine or another like Trotzky are worth 8,000,000,000 Wells or Wallings.[3] They act instead of carefully weighing unimportant thoughts and words all their days. And they have the courage of their convictions, which is more than most penman and parlor reasoners have. I respect them. I wish, and have all along, that I might help in some decisive way.

Dreiser

And I read what Haywood said.[4] I like that man. Nothing to that Magazine Stuff.[5] Never heard of it. No time for editing right now.[6]

1. Karsner's article, "The Romance of Two Hoosier Brothers," *New York Call,* 5 December 1920, Magazine Section, 6–7, dealt with Dreiser and his brother Paul Dresser.

2. Karsner's "Suppose the Light Should Go Out," *New York Call,* 28 November 1920, Magazine Section, 1, deals positively with the socialist experiment in the Soviet Union.

3. In addition to the Russian revolutionaries, Dreiser refers to two English socialists, the novelist H. G. Wells and the journalist William E. Walling (1877–1936).

4. William D. (Big Bill) Haywood (1869–1928) was a militant labor leader who helped found the Industrial Workers of the World (IWW). His sedition conviction for opposing America's participation in World War I had recently been confirmed. It not certain what statement by Haywood Dreiser is referring to.

5. Unidentified.

6. The postscript is in Dreiser's hand.

1921

To Edward H. Smith [TCS-DPUP]

Dreiser was responding to Smith's gossipy letter of 19 March 1921.

P.O. Box 181
Los Angeles
Cal.
March 25, 1921.

Dear Smith:

No, I don't know Van Doren. Can't recall that I ever heard of him until I saw this article. He's a very good writer though, isn't he? As I said, however, I like your article better.[1] It is more all around and sounder. Mencken said he liked yours better.[2] I don't think he agrees with Van D in all his deductions.

Send on the victrola ere I lose the last of my few hairs.

If you come here in May I will be glad to put you up if you can sleep on a long wicker divan of handsome design. I will also show you various parts of this peculiar burg which grows like a weed. And I'll give you the house and phone number before you start.[3]

Thanks for your descent on Tyler. I should think N. Y. might stand for a few performances of that thing.[4] But I suppose old Sumner will be on hand. If only some one would bash him on the nut.

You should have told the young lady student that I never have less than five females on hand at once,—that I keep a herd.[5] And tell Luks that three persons have now sent copies of his drawing for me to sign.[6] Yea, and the Fine Arts Guild sent a copy for its walls. He made me look as though I were in the last stages of concupiscence, the swine. No doubt that explains the marked popularity.

Dreiser

You are to do me one more flavor, or have it done. Please have copies of the Bookman sent to these people.

1. Gaston Gallimard, 35–37 Rue Madam, (!) Paris, France. C/O Editions de la Nouvelle Revue Francaise.[7]

2. Rieder et Cie. 7, Place St. Sulpice, Paris, France.[8]

3. Curtis Brown, (Personal) C/O Curtis Brown, Ltd. 6 Henrietta St. Covent Garden, London, England.[9]

1. Both Smith and Carl Van Doren (1885–1950), literary editor of the *Nation* and a Columbia University professor, had recently published articles on Dreiser: Smith, "Dreiser—After Twenty Years," *Bookman* 53 (March 1921): 27–39; and Van Doren, "Contemporary American Novelists—Theodore Dreiser," *Nation* 112 (16 March 1921): 400–401; reprinted in Van Doren's *Contemporary American Novelists: 1900–1920* (1922).

2. Mencken, in fact, reported that Smith's article was "excellent" but that he also liked Van Doren's; see Mencken to Dreiser, 15 March 1921, in Riggio, *Dreiser-Mencken Letters*, II, 432.

3. Throughout his 1919–1922 Los Angeles stay, Dreiser used a postal address for his correspondence.

4. George C. Tyler (1867–1946), a prominent New York producer. Smith noted in his letter of 19 March that he had asked Tyler to consider producing *The Hand of the Potter* for a series of special matinees.

5. Smith reported in his letter that Van Doren had told his Columbia class that Dreiser was "decidedly polygamous," a remark which a "lady student" then passed on to Smith.

6. George Luks's full-page sketch of Dreiser had appeared in Smith's article (see note 1 above). A member of the Ashcan School of American artists, Luks (1867–1933) was a Greenwich Village friend of both Smith and Dreiser.

7. Gallimard (1881–1975), one of founders of the distinguished French literary review *Nouvelle Revue Française* and proprietor of the Librarie Gallimard publishing house.

8. Rieder et Cie was to publish the French translation of Dreiser's *Twelve Men* in 1923.

9. Dreiser's English agent.

To Edward H. Smith   [TS-DPUP]

P.O. Box 181
Los Angeles.
April 9th., 1921.

Dear Smith:

Just to clear things up I hereby report H. R.[1] is notified that the victrola awaits her order at the local express office. But consider her rage—which however has nothing to do with you. She is really very much obliged and asks me to tell you so. But the express charges from N. Y. to here on one victrola are $31.65. What do you know. That plus ten packing and shipping charges makes $41.65 on a machine the original cost of which was $90. How is that for taxing the humble consumer. Yet if you kick you're a bolshevist.

Mencken is not so bad, personally. If you ever meet him in a social way I think you'll like him. He makes me weary at times and I have dropped him more than once but somehow we drift together again.

Thanks for the word in regard to my books. I will kick. But I will never get a decent show until I get all my books under one roof and under one imprint.[2] My plan is to buy them all and then lease them on a twenty per cent basis, as does Shaw. I now own seven of them outright. One of these is Sister Carrie. My best wishes for your western trip. Sorry you find it useless to come this far.

Dreiser

1. Smith had arranged for the shipment of Helen Richardson's Victrola from New York to Los Angeles; see Elias, *Letters*, I, 353–54.
2. Dreiser's long-standing effort, from this period to his death, which he never accomplished.

To Ethel Kelley [TS-DPUP]

Kelley (1878–?), who worked for Dreiser on the staff of the Broadway Magazine *in 1906, had sent him her recently published novel* Beauty and Mary Blair. *Kelley published in various forms from 1915 to 1935 and achieved considerable success with her novel* Wings *(1924).*

P.O. BOX 181
Los Angeles.
May 17, 1921.

Dear Ethel Kelley:

I doubt whether I shall be able to make clear just how your novel does impress me. As realism, and in so far as it goes, it is pleasingly sound. To me the canvas appears to be not so very large and the tale not so very poignant,—a trait which seems to be much insisted on in these days. Yet as compared with the average triviality in the fiction realm it is leagues beyond what is done, of course, and from that point of view it would be little short of ignorant or malicious not to commend it highly. The thing has a noticeable conciseness and a directness in telling which, from a structural point of view would please any reader. The character delineations are most accurate and in several instances,—that of the young brother, for one, moving even.

Yet the family selected appears, to me at least, a most strawy aggregation,—almost soulless and with little import as material for drama. Its members neither move me to pity nor arouse even a feeling of whole-hearted contempt. They appear to be of such stuff as is hay and straw. Not that the picture does not show that. It does,—but rather unconsciously than otherwise. And Mary's discovery of what it is all about—at this day and date—well,—Mary was rather obtuse, wasn't she?—disturbingly conservative, anyhow.

Having said so much, I still think it an honest and creditable piece of work. The intention and the result are in the right direction. With one such thing so well done you ought to be able to find a theme which would truly appeal to you on the emotional side. If you ever do you will *astonied*, as the bible says, by the difference that will then show between this very fine handling of a somewhat unimportant theme and the lightning-lit picture which your heart has compelled.

Theodore Dreiser

To George A. Van Nosdall [TC-DPUP]

Van Nosdall, a rare book collector, wrote Dreiser on 3 May 1921 proposing that he prepare a limited edition bibliography of Dreiser's work that would also include some republication of early material. When Dreiser expressed interest, Van Nosdall promptly sent him a contract and a long list of queries. The bibliography was not published.

P.O. BOX 181
Los Angeles.
May 31, 1921.

Dear Mr. Van Nosdall:

Thanks very much, for the copies of the proposed contract which you would like me to sign. I am interested in the idea of a bibliography but cannot bring myself to sign the rather lengthy and complicated paper which you offer me. In the first place, I am not willing to sign a life time contract for any work with which my name is to be associated—not at present anyhow. The best I could bring myself to do would be to enter on such an arrangement for a period of ten years at which time, as I see it, it would probably be advisable to revise the work anyhow. If the limited edition which you propose were not sold by that time a rival or later form of it would not hurt it. It would be beyond the possibility of injury, anyhow.

Next, all the part referring to liability, in case of suit, would have to be expunged. I can see no possibility of anything in this work proving libelous. At any rate, since you are proposing to make the book it should be an easy matter for you to make it in such a way as to keep it from being libelous or infringing on anyone in any way. I am perfectly willing, in case the negotiations come to anything, to aid you to that end, but more than that I would not be willing to do.

In the next place—(pardon me for being as direct as possible)—I will not permit the use in this proposed work of any of the articles or poems so far mentioned. These that you list were, in the main, petty things done on order and with no literary merit, that I can see. There is one thing, published in Ainslees at about that time or earlier—an article relating to a week on a pilot boat, which, as I recall it now, was not bad.[1] At least I thought so at that time. If I could see that again I might not object to its use. Also, in Munsey's of about that time, are to be found several which might do. One of these—a sketch of Bayard Taylor, was not so poorly written.[2] Again, in McClure's, I think, I published an account of a trolley trip to Boston—the first of its kind, which was interesting and might be now.[3] In Harper's again, of near that same date—Harper's Weekly I mean—,I published a sketch called *Whence the Song* which was much quoted and praised.[4] I should think a thing like that would be more in keeping with what you have in mind. I would like to add that as yet you appear to have no data covering any of the things I did for The Cosmopolitan, McClure's, Harper's, Century, Harper's Weekly, Munsey's, The Booklovers, The Voice, Truth, Demorests, The (old) Broadway and some others. In the main they were better than the ones you list.

In the next place I will not agree that any of this unpublished material of mine shall not be used in any other book of mine during my life time. I am planning a book of pictures out of American life and a few of the best ones of those I have named will certainly be in it.[5] They will probably not appear, however, before your edition will have been disposed of.

Lastly, if at any time the remainder of the proposed edition should prove unsalable, I should like it offered to me at one third of the cost of the books and the plates at the then current market rates. The three months time suggested would be quite all right for me.

"With these few objections",—to quote the Hebrew in the story,[6] I think the proposed contract is all right—a conclusion with which you may not agree at all. Just the same, I am sincerely obliged to you for your interest in the matter and in me.

Theodore Dreiser

1. "The Log of an Ocean Pilot," *Ainslee's* 3 (July 1899): 683–92; reprinted in Dreiser's *The Color of a Great City* (1923).

2. "The Haunts of Bayard Taylor," *Munsey's* 18 (January 1898): 594–601.

3. "From New York to Boston by Trolley," *Ainslee's* 4 (August 1899): 74–84.

4. "Whence the Song," *Harper's Weekly* 44 (8 December 1900): 1165–66; reprinted in *The Color of a Great City*.

5. *The Color of a Great City*, published by Boni and Liveright in 1923, which, however, was limited to sketches set in New York.

6. An unidentified humorous story.

To Abraham Cahan [TS-AJA]

Cahan (1860–1951), in addition to founding the influential Yiddish-language Jewish Daily Forward in 1897, had published several well-received novels (in English) of New York Jewish immigrant life and was an active socialist.

P.O. BOX 181
Los Angeles,
Cal.
Dec. 23, 1921.

Dear Cahan:

   It certainly is nice of you to write and tell me how much you think of the *Hand of the Potter*.[1] And you can imagine how much I value the opinion, especially in this case, of the author of *The Rise of David Lavinsky*.[2] Cook writes me that with your aid he may be able to get the play staged at the Second Avenue Theatre.[3] That is more than kind on your part and I want to thank you most sincerely for your courtesy and interest. Since we all like to revert in thought to the really interesting and pleasant things in our lives my mind goes back to you, from time to time, and the days following the publication of Lavinsky. What became of the literary monthly or quarterly?[4] All of my very best wishes, always.

Dreiser

I shall journey to the Jewish Daily Times here with your clipping and see what they can do for me. Aren't you mean, not to send me your English version. Or do you write these things only in Yiddish.[5]

1. Dreiser's play, produced by the Provincetown Players at the Provincetown Playhouse in Greenwich Village, had opened on 5 December 1921. Cahan wrote on 14 December 1921 that he liked the play "immensely" and that he had written a three-column article, in Yiddish, about it. ("An Unusual Jewish Tragedy in an Unusual Theater," *Jewish Daily Forward*, 8 December 1921, p. 4.)

2. Dreiser means *The Rise of David Levinsky* (1917), Cahan's best-known novel.

3. George Cram Cook (1873–1924), a director and one of the founders of the Provincetown Players. The Second Avenue Theatre specialized in Yiddish plays.

4. Cahan had written Dreiser on 2 October 1918 that he was planning an English language literary magazine to be called *The Sheaf*.

5. Dreiser appears to mean the *Los Angeles Jewish Times*, which was in fact a weekly.

1922

To Frank C. Dodd [TS-DPUP]

Dreiser's London-based publisher John Lane was in the process of closing its New York office, which left Dreiser free to negotiate with a new publisher both for forthcoming works, such as The Bulwark, *and for the republication of* The "Genius." *The fact that Dodd, Mead & Co. had taken over the rights to Lane's American publications, including* The "Genius," *no doubt stimulated Dreiser to attempt to strike a deal with this firm in particular. His negotiations with both Dodd, Mead & Co. and Harper's were unfruitful, however, and in early 1923 he signed a contract with Boni and Liveright.*

P.O. BOX 181
Los Angeles,
Cal.
Feb. 9, 1922.

Dear Mr. Dodd:

Your letter reads like a very sincere and fair attempt to overcome the difficulties which lie in the way of a publishing arrangement between myself and your company. And I may as well say here that, other things being adjusted, the Dodd-Mead Company would be as acceptable to me as any other and more so than many another. However, as things stand, that is scarcely either here or there in the present situation. My suit against the Lane Company is nearing trial[1] and I have to take up this matter of dropping it with my attorney which is something which needs some correspondence at this end. Again you are in error as to The Bulwark. It is not finished. For various reasons it seemed best for me to drop it some while since. The arrangement I made with Boni and Liveright to publish it was satisfied in another way. They would like a novel from me but would offer no objection, I am sure, to my publishing it elsewhere if I deemed that worth while. The thing that has interested me for some time has been the possibility of finding some liberal minded American publisher, not too confined as to means, who would see in my collected works a future as well as a present source of revenue and who would be interested to assemble them with a *"set"* in view. The issuing of one more novel here or there is of no very great value to me. One can always find a publisher for a novel however commonplace its texture. And, divided as I am, among various publishers it does not appear to serve the interests of any of them to do very much for me or for my books as a whole. Your desire to discard The "Genius", to me one of my best books, rather casts a cloud on the one publisher idea to begin with,—at least in your case. I cannot see why I should not find a publisher at sometime or other who would like all of my books, if he could get them. As a matter of fact Harper and Brothers have made me what I look upon as in the nature of a standing offer to take over all of my books, under certain conditions, of course, if they can get them.

The thing however, has various angles. The novel, as I say, isn't done, and until it is neither you nor any other publisher would be anxious to enter upon a general arrangement, I am sure. In the next place the Harper arrangement, assuming that it is ever entered into, would include the publication of The Genius, which you do not want. They won against Mr. Sumner in the case of Madeline[2] and I presume that compared, they look upon The "Genius" as innocuous. I know that I do. My suit against the Lane Company is in it's way a crossing of swords with Mr. Sumner and may throw considerable light on the next step.

I may as well tell you, though, that I am not willing to accept fifteen per cent as a royalty. I know that the costs of making a book are high. On the other hand the prices (Retail) of books were not lifted until almost the last year of the war. And the costs of living had soared years before. Again I have not encountered any other publisher thus far who has quarreled with the royalty rate now being paid me.[3] Neither Harper, Lane, The Century Co. nor Liveright have ever mentioned it. I will not say that for a quid pro quo to come perhaps in the form of advertising and general press agent work I would not shade the present royalty rate but that need not be dwelt upon here.

Just now, as I say, the situation for both of us is rather unsatisfactory. For one thing I want to hear from my attorney. Also I would like to learn from Mr. Sumner exactly what changes, if any, will make the Genius acceptable to him.[4] Not that I will make them as he wishes but a compromise expurgation might be undertaken. How would you like to publish the book with all of the objected to paragraphs blackened out, Russian censorship style?[5] Again there is the question of a separate publisher for the Genius. Also for a four volume *History of Myself,* two volumes of which are already completed,[6] which is not, exactly, a pollyanish work. The Harper proposition looks to the publication of the latter volumes one a year, following the publication of the next volume. This latter is something which I would have to arrange for with you if you were to be my publisher.

But, as I say, the thing is complicated. I need to do some corresponding and to finish the novel in question or, at least, a novel. Pending a happy adjustment of all of these matters what do you expect to do about *A Hoosier Holiday.* The Century company considers *A Traveler at Forty* one of the very good things on its list.

When I have found out just about what I can do I will let you know. If you chance to be very much interested it is not impossible that a worth while arrangement might not be arrived at somehow.

Theodore Dreiser

N. B. Lane never advanced me any $2600. I had a general drawing account. Statements now in the hands of my lawyer, Mr. Hume, prove this clearly. I never signed a contract for The Bulwark. Filled in forms were presented me which I refused to sign. The enclosed letter to Lane, which please return, throws some little light on the quarrel.[7]

1. Dreiser had initially sued John Lane in 1916 to force them to offer for public sale *The "Genius,"* the novel they had published in 1915 and withdrawn in 1916 when the New York Society for the Suppression of Vice declared it obscene (see Dreiser to John Lane, 15 December 1916, n. 3). His second suit against John Lane, in early 1922, was for damages resulting from the firm's failure to reissue the novel.

2. The anonymous *Madeleine: An Autobiography,* which deals with prostitution, was published by Harper's in 1919 and prosecuted by the New York Society in January 1920; the case was dismissed by the New York Appellate Court in July 1920.

3. Dreiser usually received a 20 percent royalty.

4. With H. L. Mencken acting on Dreiser's behalf, Sumner and Dreiser reached agreement in May 1922 on what could be published in an expurgated edition of the novel. However, the new edition finally published by Boni and Liveright in August 1923 used the 1915 text unchanged.

5. Dreiser is probably referring not to Soviet censorship but rather to that of various Tsarist governments throughout the late nineteenth century.

6. By early 1919 Dreiser had completed the first two volumes of his autobiography, *Dawn* and *A Book About Myself;* see Dreiser to H. L. Mencken, 3 February 1919, in Riggio, *Dreiser-Mencken Letters,* II, 335.

7. The letter Dreiser refers to has not been identified.

To William C. Lengel [TS-DPUP]

Dreiser and Ray Long (1878–1935), a Hearst publications executive and coeditor of Hearst's International, had discussed in Los Angeles in February Dreiser's work on a series of portraits of women. Since Lengel frequently acted as Dreiser's agent and was also managing editor of Hearst's International, Dreiser sent him the first of these sketches, "Olive Brand," to pass on to Long.

P.O. BOX 181
Los Angeles.
March 21, 1922.

Dear Lengel:
Herewith the first of the series for Ray Long which please hand him, after you have scrutinized it, with my compliments. This is not the first paper to be used, merely the first one done. If he wants to use it first, well and good.

There will be others not so radical and one or two more poignant.[1] I expect to submit more than six from which he is welcome to make a choice of six. But, I would like them paid for as they arrive, so long as they are really up to the mark.

There is absent from this one a poem which is too long to be included here, I think. I plan to use it in the book version.[2] All names other than those of Moyer and Reitman are fictitious and those should be changed I suppose.[3] The cities, with the exception of N.Y. are fictitious. I am perfectly willing for anything that seems too much to be removed. Some of the other sketches will not be so radical. Others a little more so, maybe, but they can be toned down for your use. Let me hear from you.

Thanks for the telegram. The actor was Lionel Barrymore.[4] The thing is still in the air as it were. I hope you two like these sketches and I believe that you will.

Th. D.

1. "Olive Brand" is a portrait of Edith De Long Smith, a Greenwich Village woman who lived a bohemian life and died tragically young. Long turned down "Olive Brand" at this time as "too strong" (see Dreiser to David Karsner, 9 August 1922) but eventually did accept it for *Cosmopolitan*, where it appeared in the May 1928 issue.

2. In its book form in *A Gallery of Women* (1929), "Olive Brand" contains a ten-page poem.

3. Charles Moyer (1886–1929), head of the Western Federation of Miners, an IWW union, and Ben Reitman (1879–1942), an anarchist and the lover of Emma Goldman. Both figures are in fact named in the published magazine version of the sketch.

4. Lionel Barrymore (1878–1954), a leading stage actor of the 1920s, had wired Dreiser on 8 March 1922 to ask whether he would consider a theater version of *Sister Carrie*, since Barrymore was very interested in playing Hurstwood.

To Alfred E. Goldsmith [TS-HRHUT]

Goldsmith (1881–1947) was a New York rare manuscript and book dealer.

P.O. BOX 181
Los Angeles,
Cal.
June 8, 1922.

Dear Mr. Goldsmith:

I surely am obliged to you for the copy of An Island Cabin by Henry which you say you are sending me. I have been looking for it for a long time. Not that I think it so wonderful as that I knew Henry quite well at one time.[1] But I do think it most generous of you to let me have it.

Quite a few people wrote me about the articles in The Bookman. They were taken from a completed book and only within the last few days I have decided to let Liveright bring out that book this fall.[2] We are still in the midst of the details. He thinks it should sell and I hope it does. So you will see the new volume which you are kind enough to wish for.

Tell me. Do you feel that an expurgated edition of The "Genius" would sell? I have just received a somewhat modified demand from the New York Vice Society. They will pass the book with certain modifications. If I didn't think it had a chance for sale I wouldn't bother the publishers to make new plates.[3]

I met your brother here. He tells me he may enter upon movie work. Profitable if only one can get in right.

Once more, my sincere thanks.

Theodore Dreiser

1. *An Island Cabin* (1904), by Dreiser's former close friend Arthur Henry (see Dreiser to Richard Watson Gilder, 12 December 1899, n. 1), contains an unflattering fictional portrayal of Dreiser.

2. Dreiser's autobiographical sketches "Out of My Newspaper Days" had appeared in the *Bookman* (November 1921 and January–April 1922); Boni and Liveright published an expanded version of them in December 1922 under the title *A Book About Myself*.

3. In the end, *The "Genius"* was republished by Boni and Liveright in unexpurgated form in 1923; see also Dreiser to Frank C. Dodd, 9 February 1922.

To David Karsner [TS-DPUP]

For Karsner, see Dreiser to David Karsner, 26 July 1920.

P.O. BOX 181
Los Angeles.
Aug. 9, 1922.

Dear Karsner:

Thanks for the clipping about Debs[1] and various other things that drift along from time to time. It seems to me that you are growing not a little and getting a grip on the things that lie beyond the socialists' horizon. Not that I do not still believe that the socialization of many things is important. But even there best results are certain to flow from the presence of the individual and his ambitions.

Yet again, all this has little to do with this letter. I want to make a suggestion to you which may mean something and again nothing. However, it is in the nature of a business proposition. For years I have been dealing more or less through W. C. Lengel, formerly my secretary at the Butterick Company but for the last two years managing editor of Hearst's International and really managing editor of the Cosmopolitan. Nearly all of the stories and articles I have placed I have sold through him. Not that he ever needed the ten per cent I paid him but he wanted to do it and did do it. Even now he likes to have me send my things direct to him in order to let him see who he can interest. But of late he has become so burdened with work there that he can't do much and it is scarcely fair to unload things on him even though he would like to be so loaded.

There is another angle to this arrangement. He knows and I know that it is useless for me to attempt to deal through the average agent. He does not get me. And an agent cannot take much interest in anything he does not get and over which he is enthusiastic.[2] As editor I found that to be so. Whenever I have anything to sell my plan is either to address some publisher or editor whom I know and put the matter up direct. Or, where I do not know anyone, to get Lengel, who really cares a great deal about the sort of thing I do to approach some editor in person and put the matter before him in such a way as to make him see it. An article or a story or an idea of mine, talked over with some underling usually comes to nothing. Discussed with the editor or publisher by a man like Lengel, representing me and believing in the matter, in not a few cases the result is very different. It is the personal touch and the individual representation that does it.

With this as a preface, here is the idea. Quite recently I decided to do a number of studies of women somewhat after the fashion of Twelve Men. The trouble with this idea is that women are not men, not in any commercial or constructive fray and whatever is truly dramatic in their lives relates to love, marriage and sex. In these snowy days that makes the idea a little difficult. Even women themselves are likely to feel that their lives ought to be more than they are. Carmens, Du Barrys, De Staels, Emma Goldmans and such are not to be found at every corner. Still, taking this American world for what it is, and one individual's contacts, the situation yields some grist. I have come across a few interesting and illuminating characters. So much so that I see a few things to do and have done some of them. More will follow. They are studies of from ten to fifteen thousand words in length and if I should be able to do fifteen good ones I would consider that I had a good book.[3]

The point is this. Some of these sketches are not so broad as others. And some that are broad might be toned down sufficiently to permit a highly interested editor to publish them. If any magazine were interested it should buy five or six, announce them as a series, drum up a little interest and then publish them consecutively. I could submit to any highly interested editor four or five of those already done and if any of them were right, could fill in the series from others now in mind. I should have to know that at least five—preferably six were going to be used. A very fair price for five would be four thousand dollars. And that is modest. For six 4,800. Of that I would pay you four eighty, or ten per cent. To earn that you would have to see a few editors in chief, possibly only one, but anyhow, only one at a time, and try to interest that one,—sell him the idea first. My first suggestion would be Vance of the Pictorial Review.[4] Next Burton of McCalls.[5] There may be other editors. Apart from the business of selling the stuff to a magazine I should prefer you not to mention the fact that I am doing such a series. It is a good idea and some one might get into his head to do the thing in another way. After it is sold and the title of the series copyrighted I shall have no objection to the thing being talked about.

If this interests you at all and you think you would like to bother with it, I would be glad to have you try.[6] I should tell you that through Lengel I tried to interest Long of the Cosmopolitan, but he feels that the thing is too strong for him.[7] And he may be right. You want to remember in discussing this that these are not short stories and they have no short story quality. They are full length portraits, with much that is forthright, especially where morals come into play. At the same time they are not sexy,—just serious with, in most cases sex as a factor. Not always.

I will be glad to hear what you have to say. ·

Dreiser

The title of the new book is not The Book of Myself—rather comprehensive, that, but A Book About Myself. Very different. The latter only sets out to cover a three year period,—my newspaper experience plus interstitial matter.

1. Eugene Debs, the socialist leader; see Dreiser to David Karsner, 26 July 1920, n. 3.

2. Dreiser means "not enthusiastic."

3. In the end, A *Gallery of Women* (1929) contained fifteen sketches, of which six had appeared previously in magazines.

4. Arthur Vance (1872–1930), editor of *Pictorial Review*.

5. Harry P. Burton (1886–?), editor of *McCall's*.

6. Karsner, in his reply of 24 August 1922, agreed to a trial run as Dreiser's agent, with emphasis on placing his *Gallery of Women* sketches. He had no success, however, and the arrangement ended in late 1922.

7. See Dreiser to William C. Lengel, 21 March 1922.

To Eugene Debs [H-ISU][1]

A native of Terre Haute, Debs (1855–1926) had retired there after his release from a federal penitentiary in 1921 (he had been convicted of sedition in 1918 for opposing America's participation in World War I.) Debs had written Dreiser on 14 October 1922, noting that he had granted permission for his name to be used on a petition to Dreiser requesting that Dreiser consent to the removal of Paul Dresser's remains from Chicago to Terre Haute.

c/o Boni & Liveright
105 W. 40th St.
N.Y C.
Oct. 17—1922.

Dear Eugene Debs:

First let me say that I am one of the many who voted for Debs—on occasion[2] & who was gloomy because of the powers that could prosecute & lock him up. I admired your stand & I do now and I hope all good things for you. More I could not say to any man.

As to the matter of the ashes or bones of my late good brother—I am now placed in an odd position. The logical place for a monument is Terre Haute—and on the banks of the Wabash there. Paul liked Terre Haute. He liked to go back there. In the first days of your fame he knew of you & spoke of you to me. Several years ago a man by the name of Charles T. Jewett,[3] of 452 N. Center St. wrote me & wanted me to obtain the permission of the various members of the family for the transfer of the body there—in case a place & monument for it could be arranged. I consulted all those living & advised him that there was no objection. Then I heard nothing more except this—that it was probable that the body would be removed to Indianapolis. I undertook some publicity for the idea—outside the state but this seemed to meet with little favor from those in Terre Haute, so I dropped that. Not a word since.

Recently came a letter from the Indiana Society of Chicago, saything that it wanted to place a monument over the grave in Chicago. (St. Boniface R.C. Cemetary—North Side). It wanted the family consent. I explained about the Terre Haute idea & stated that there had been no objection then & would be none now, but that it might be best to see if the Terre Haute idea had fallen through. At the same time that your letter reached me yesterday (here) came one from Edward M. Halloway, Secy of the Chicago Indiana Society. He states that now the Indiana Society desires to co-operate with D. N. Foster, President of the Soldiers Home at Lafayette. That Governor McCray[4] favors placing the monument & body there—or, so I gather. That places me in an odd position. Personally I favored & do now, Terre Haute; as do the other members of the family. But if a quarrel is to develop which will mean no monument for a long time, I would rather see the Lafayette project go through. Actually, in the crisis I would like your sincere advice. I do not know Indiana very well & you do. What do you suggest. I am writing Mr. Halloway about your letter & stating that personally I prefer Terre Haute—as would Paul. He was born there & always liked it. But also I hope that no delaying quarrel arises. Perhaps you have influence with Gov. McCray—or the Chicago Indiana Society. Why not write them direct?[5] As to the consent of the family—I can get the written consent of those living I am sure. My compliments, my thanks & my sincere good wishes for yourself & your happiness.

Theodore Dreiser

1. Previously published in *Letters of Eugene V. Debs*, ed. J. Robert Constantine (Urbana: University of Illinois Press, 1990), III, 344–45.

2. Debs ran for president five times on the Socialist ticket between 1900 and 1920; Dreiser is on record as having voted for him at least once, in 1920.

3. Jewett was city editor of the *Terre Haute Star;* Dreiser is describing events of 1913. For an excellent account of Dreiser's involvement in the effort to build a Terre Haute memorial for Paul Dresser, see Richard W. Dowell, "Dreiser vs. Terre Haute, or Paul Dresser's Body Lies A-Moldering in the Grave," *Dreiser Studies* 20 (Fall 1989): 9–20.

4. Warren T. McCray (1841–1934), governor of Indiana (1921–24).

5. Debs replied on 20 October 1922 that though he too favored Terre Haute, he was unable to write Governor McCray because McCray had recently attacked him in a speech.

To Walter. W. Lange [H-DPUP]

Lange, a wealthy Milwaukee industrialist and Dreiser enthusiast, was seeking to acquire Dreiser manuscripts. As is apparent from Dreiser's later letter to James A. Ettinge (see Dreiser to James A. Ettinge, 7 November 1923), Dreiser, in response to Lange's interest, sought to increase the value of his manuscripts by enlisting the cooperation of various friends and dealers. Dreiser's plan was for him to initially provide Lange with the names of those who had supposedly purchased manuscripts from Dreiser. If Lange then asked one of these figures what he had paid for a specific manuscript, he was to name an amount cited by Dreiser; if Lange then offered to buy the manuscript at that price, Dreiser would provide the manuscript to the friend or dealer, who would then sell it to Lange with the deduction of an agent's fee.

Dreiser in His St. Luke's Place Greenwich Village Apartment, 1923.

16 St. Luke's Place[1]
New York City
Oct. 20—1922

Dear Mr. Lange:

Sorry to have missed you here—certainly am—and after you were good enough to wait as long as you did. My train missed connections at Chicago by five hours. Engine trouble. However, Chicago is not so far away & we may meet there soon.

Yes, I am planning to remain here for the winter, anyhow. I have just taken a place at the above address and unless I sublet it, will remain. New York after California is like rapids after comparatively still & clean waters. But I do not mind for the nonce—anyhow. I have some work to do here.

So you still think the price of the Jennie Gerhardt manuscript is high. The best answer to that will be any quotations you recieve from those who now own mss. These are:

1. Alfred Goldsmith—42 Lexington Ave. N.Y.—The Blue Sphere.

2. Henry L. Mencken—1524 Hollins St Baltimore—Sister Carrie.

3. William E. Lengel, Mgr. Editor Hearst Magazines—The Girl in the Coffin.

4. James A. Ettinge, Laurel House Hollywood, Cal—The Lost Phoebe.

5. George T. Keating—29 Broadway, N.Y. City—Free.[2]

All these were purchased direct from me & and I doubt if they will be willing to part with them. As for the others—I have them all—I think. Some have been stored so long that I am not sure—but I think all are available. It will be possible to get together those that I control. As for the others—I can't say.

But certainly I'll be glad to give you some unpublished mss—a group of poems—if you wish. As for the manuscripts I would like to talk to you sometime. We should be able to reach some understanding.

Thanks for the check for $1,350 which covers the original pen copy of Jennie Gerhardt and the only or original typescript of A Book About Myself. These two manuscripts I hold subject to your order. I will return them to storage. And I hope one of these days to come to Milwaukee & meet your wife & child. Your very direct & decisive actions interest me. You bring to mind a maxim credited to Julius Rosenwald of Chicago.[3] "I would rather be a beggar & spend money like a prince than be a prince & spend money like a beggar". I like that. And somehow it is like Chicago—its old time spirit.

Theodore Dreiser

It just comes to me that David Karsner Sunday Editor of *The Call*, N.Y. owns Laughing Gas—one of my one act plays.[4]

---

1. Dreiser had returned to New York in early October, after more than three years in the Los Angeles area, and had rented an apartment in Greenwich Village.

2. In addition to Mencken, Lengel, Goldsmith (see Dreiser to Alfred E. Goldsmith, 8 June 1922), and Ettinge (see Dreiser to James A. Ettinge, 7 November 1923), the list includes Keating (1892–?), a New York friend. It appears that Goldsmith and Ettinge played the principal roles in aiding Dreiser in the plan.

3. Rosenwald (1862–1932), who had been president of Sears, Roebuck, was famous for his generous philanthropy.

4. For Karsner, see Dreiser to David Karsner, 26 July 1920.

1923

To W. Wallace Ham [TCS—DPUP]

The Vitagraph Company, a major movie production company during the first two decades of the century, was about to release a film titled On the Banks of the Wabash, *directed by J. Stuart Blackton, one of the founders of the company. Ham, Vitagraph's publicity director, wrote Boni and Liveright on 14 September 1923 requesting permission to use excerpts from Dreiser's "My Brother Paul" in the company's press releases for the film.*

118 West 11th Street
New York City
Sept. 26th, 1923

Dear Sir:

Your letter to Boni and Liveright, my publishers, craving permission to use from one to three thousand words of the character picture entitled "My Brother Paul" from my book *Twelve Men* has been referred to me. From having perused that study you will have gathered, first, that I am the author of the first verse and chorus of that song "On the Banks of the Wabash", which as you explain inspired the Vitagraph photoplay of the same name; second, that my brother Paul Dresser was a man of a decidedly poetic and highly impractical turn, whose very generous and emotional disposition ill consorted with the appropriate necessity for looking after the interests either of himself or of those who during the last several years of his life, and because of the disposition before mentioned, were compelled to look after him. I refer in particular to his sister, Mrs. Emma Nelson, who, without expense to him, and in the face of inadequate means of her own, cared for him most lovingly during the last two years of his life; third, that because of his very generous and trusting disposition, but through no commercial fault of his own, the rights to his song "On the Banks of the Wabash", now being used by you as the basis of a photoplay, to say nothing of quite all of his other songs, passed from his control and netted him thereafter absolutely nothing. And in the face of this data, which as your letter shows, neither you nor the several officers of the Vitagraph Company, nor Mr. Edgar Selden of your company,[1] can fail to be aware of, that company without word or request for permission of any kind to any member of this family, proceeded to take over and capitalize after the fashion indicated in your letter, not only the rights to this song, but to the name and fame of Paul Dresser, a fame which I myself have done as much to strengthen and perpetuate as anyone writing of him since his death. And in reply to an inquiry on my part as to the source of your right to the use of this song title and its cost to your company, not a word.

And before me is another bit of interesting information quite recently come to hand. As Mr. Edgar Selden and the Vitagraph Company very well knows, the city of Terre Haute, Indiana, countenanced and aided by the state of Indiana, is seeking to gather money sufficient to erect a monument to the memory of the author of "On the Banks of the Wabash" at Terre Haute. And in pursuance of this wish the Paul Dresser Memorial Fund Committee of Terre Haute, Indiana, not so very long since addressed to Mr. Edgar Selden a letter, whose property this film production of yours is, I believe, suggesting that in view of his commercial as well as, presumably, his sentimental interest in the song and its author, he might like to make a contribution to the monument fund. And, although at the moment he was busily engaged in exploiting the name and the fame of the author of the same, as the poetic and sentimental basis for his film production, his contribution to the fund was exactly one dollar, a burdensome tax on him which was promptly returned to him by the committee. If I am in any way misinformed as to this, I would be glad to be advised.

Yet in the face of all this, Mr. Ham, and as the representative of the very practical Vitagraph Company and Mr. Selden, you have the insolence to address to me a request for permission to use my personal tribute to my brother as bait to catch audiences for your porch-climbers capitalization of my brother's property. And you would like to identify me as well as my brother with a piece of mushy sentimentality that is to net untaxed returns to yourselves only. And you will plaster the bill-boards and stuff the newspapers, in so far as possible, with tricky fox-like implications as to the whole-hearted and disinterested sentiment and romance which has inspired all this.

Pardon me if I fail to manifest any keen interest in your very liberal request. The sketch in question was intended for those who might possibly bring a disinterested and sympathetic viewpoint toward such a personality, not for those who like Mr. Selden and the Vitagraph Company seek to aggrandize themselves at the expense of all the generous and combined efforts that have made Paul Dresser the interesting tradition that he is today. I will thank you to ignore me and my comments on my brother entirely. Failure to do so will entail some interesting publicity in connection with all this which neither the Vitagraph nor Mr. Selden will relish.

Very truly yours,
Theodore Dreiser

1. On 28 September 1923, Albert E. Smith, the president of Vitagraph, wrote Dreiser that although Vitagraph had purchased the rights to Paul's song from Edgar Selden, Selden had nothing to do with the production of the film. Smith went on to note that Selden had not contributed to the Paul Dresser memorial fund and that Dreiser might be confusing him with Arthur Selwyn, a well-known actor, screenwriter, and producer who was employed by Vitagraph.

To James A. Ettinge [TS-DPUP]

Ettinge, a New York acquaintance, had aided Dreiser on several matters involving his New York apartment while Dreiser was in Los Angeles and had then himself moved to the West Coast. For the relationship of this letter to Dreiser's earlier maneuvering in his dealings with the manuscript collector W. W. Lange, see Dreiser to Lange, 20 October 1922.

118 West 11th St.
New York City.
November 7, 1923.[1]

My Dear Ettinge:

Thanks for your letter in regard to the Lange offer. As I wired you I think it is all right to close at $275. I sold *Free* (the original ms) several years ago for $200. And I really think $300 is little enough for that story. As a matter of fact I am told by Goldsmith[2] here that it is too low. However I think it best to close in this instance. Tell him to send on his check, extract ten percent for yourself with my blessing on it and send me the difference. As I wired you I am sending the original ms. of this registered. If the thing falls through return the ms to me. I have another goldbag on the line at this end. And if you see Newbegin again say hello for me.[3] Also that I said I wisht I could connect with his booze barrel. He has one.[4]

Theodore Dreiser

P.S. Here is a good tip. Get Newbegin to give the story of the sale of this ms. through you to the papers. Simply say that you bought the ms from me years ago at a lower figure and that you only sold it because you wanted to take over from me another manuscript which I had promised to sell you years ago. Don't forget the years ago. There is a hook to that string as you may see later. But don't say what the ms is. It may start Newbegin to trying to dispose of something and if it does, and should it result in anything I will count you in on the deal at ten per cent. I have offers now for quite a few of my ms.—The Girl in the Coffin for one, but want to bull the prices a little. I haven't so very many ms to sell and don't want to part with them for a song. Will you advise me promptly as to your thoughts and actions in this matter?

1. Dreiser's typist dated this letter 7 October 1923 but the date has been corrected to 7 November 1923. Ettinge had written Dreiser on 2 November 1923 that Lange had offered him $275 for the manuscript of "The Lost Phoebe." Dreiser's reply, though dated 7 October 1923, is postmarked 7 November 1923.

2. For Goldsmith, see Dreiser to Alfred E. Goldsmith, 8 June 1922.

3. John J. Newbegin, a San Francisco bookstore owner and rare book dealer.

4. Dreiser added this last sentence by hand.

1924

To Edward M. Dreiser [TS-EU]

The plan for a Paul Dresser memorial which Dreiser outlines took more than forty years to come to fruition; it was only in 1966 that Paul's birthplace was restored, moved to a site next to the Wabash, and became a museum in his honor. Since Dreiser's brother Edward (1873–1958) was an actor for many years, Dreiser turned to him for aid in locating Paul's songs.

118 West 11th St
N.Y.C.
Feb. 11, 1924.

Dear Ed:

You know, of course, that some years ago the state of Indiana made On the Banks of the Wabash the official state song of that state. More recently, as you may or may not know, a committee known as The Paul Dresser Memorial Committee was organized at Terre Haute, the purpose of which was to commemorate the memory of Paul in various ways. One of these is or was, for a part of this purpose has already been accomplished, to buy the old house in Third Street, Terre Haute in which Paul was born, remove it to the banks of the Wabash, place a small park around it, plant a grove of sycamores about the house and on the grounds somewhere prepare a tomb in which Paul's ashes are to be placed after being brought down from Chicago. As you may or may not know, I was instrumental in having Paul's grave in St. Boniface, Chicago properly marked with a large boulder brought from the Wabash and a bronze plate. I pulled the string which caused the Chicago Indiana society to do that.

In regard to the purposes of the Terre Haute Committee it has already done this much. The old house has been bought by it and plans are now afoot to get the money to move it, prepare the park and the like. Quite recently this committee wrote me and asked if I would not trouble to get together copies of every one of Paul's songs with a view to having them preserved in this house. As you may or may not know, I have Paul's old piano and am going to place it in this house when it is ready.[1] Also, a year ago I presented the Elks club of Terre Haute with a very large framed portrait of Paul that will be transferred to this house when it is ready. What I want now is some little help in getting together everything that Paul ever wrote with a view to having them preserved in this old home. I think, also, that photos of mother and father should be preserved there.

However, just now, I want to get together as many of Paul's songs as possible. If there are any unpublished manuscripts I want those too. Have you any,—any of the very old ones, I mean, The Letter That Never Came, say, or Mother Told Me So.[2] If you haven't any at all, do you know where there are any. I have already been to see Mr. Marks[3] and he has given me all that he has,—only a few. Paul wrote about seventy-five.[4] I have been to see Haviland.[5] He merely sent me to a man named Glaasmaker at Ditsons.[6] I have written him but have not, as yet, heard anything. Would Louise Dresser have any.[7] And do you know her well enough to ask her for them. Is there any person or friend of Paul's who would be likely to have a few,—here in N.Y. I mean. How about that cousin or something of Paul's from the west who once worked for you and Paul,—Myrtle something. Would she have any of the old ones. And do you know her well enough to write her and urge her to surrender them.

Along with the rest of us this should interest not only you but your wife for it will certainly tend to cast a little honor on your daughter and she will appreciate it in due time.[8] For the memorial is to be very beautiful. And Paul and it will be discussed for many a year.

What, if anything can you do for me in this respect.

Theodore

1. Dreiser had had the keyboard and strings removed from Paul's piano and was using it as a desk; after Dreiser's death, the desk was moved to Terre Haute and is now in the Dresser memorial.
2. Two of Paul's most famous songs; the correct title of the second is "My Mother Told Me So."
3. Edward B. Marks (1865–1945), a song composer and publisher.
4. When Boni and Liveright published *The Songs of Paul Dresser* in 1927, with an introduction by Dreiser, it contained fifty-eight songs.
5. Frederick B. Haviland (1868–1932), one of the partners in Paul's sheet music firm, Howley, Haviland, & Co.
6. The Oliver Ditson Co., a Boston-based music store with New York branches, which also published music; Glaasmaker has not been identified.
7. Louise Dresser (1882–1965), a protégé of Paul's; born Louise Kerlin, she took Paul's name early in her career as a music hall entertainer.
8. Ed's wife, Mai Skelly Dreiser, and his daughter, Vera Dreiser (1908–1998).

To Claude Bowers [TS-LLIU]

Bowers (1878–1958), who published several works on American history during the 1920s, was in 1924 a journalist at the New York World. *He and Dreiser often met and corresponded during the 1920s, in part because of their shared*

Terre Haute boyhoods. A strong supporter of Franklin D. Roosevelt, Bowers later served as American ambassador to Spain during the period of the Spanish Republic (1933–39).

118 West 11th St
N.Y.
May 22, 1924.

My Dear Bowers:

After leaving you and your wife yesterday I had a confab with Henry L. Mencken of The American Mercury.[1] I was telling him about you and your interest in politics and history and biography and the twists and turns of the American temperament. In fact I suggested you as the ideal person to do certain things for him which I know he is interested to do,—present certain political characters and certain aspects of our political and somewhat prejudiced life. He expressed a wish to meet you and I thought that maybe you may not be opposed to a confab yourself. If you are not, and some evening next week would be agreeable to you I would like to arrange for it. Mencken is a very brilliant and dynamic if somewhat prejudiced fellow and I think that a heart-to-heart talk between you might not be amiss. It may result in the general increase of knowledge. If you think well of it tell me what evenings, if any are best for you. Then I'll see what I can do with him.

Apart from that this is to acknowledge a delightful evening and to suggest that you and your wife come with me one of these evenings to one of these Greenwich Village cellars for dinner. I know several charming ones. If you two will express a willingness I will fix upon the date with you a little later.

My compliments to Mrs. Bowers.

Theodore Dreiser

And I never ate a better apple pie. Only my manners cheated me of a second slice.

1. Mencken and George Jean Nathan had published the first issue of the *American Mercury*, one of the most influential journals of the 1920s, in January 1924. Bowers, however, does not appear to have contributed to the magazine.

To Max Ehrmann [TS-DeP]

A poet and writer of fiction, Ehrmann (1872–1945) was born and raised in Terre Haute and was still a resident of the city. At this time he was playing an active role in the efforts of the Terre Haute Paul Dresser Memorial Association to raise money for a Dresser memorial in Terre Haute.

118 West 11th St
N.Y.
June 10, 1924.

Dear Mr. Ehrmann:

My efforts to discover the exact location of the house in which I was born have about come to nothing here. I have three sisters who ought to know. They agree now that I was born in a house on Ninth Street, near Walnut, but exactly where, memory saith not. One thing appears. A certain Mrs. Melony lived next door. That was in 1871. Also there is a certain Amelia Hartung,—now Mrs. Amelia Lang, supposedly still residing in Terre Haute at this time, who often came to the house in Ninth Street, knows where it is and could point it out. Also there is said to be in Terre Haute a certain Will Sobel, who knows the house, has been in it and can lay his hand on it as it were, any time. Do you know of any such persons. My sisters insist they are in Terre Haute at this time. Could you possibly find them.

Under the impression that I was born at Twelfth and Walnut, I, when passing through Terre Haute with Franklin Booth had him sketch the house at that corner. And it is shown in A Hoosier Holiday as my birth place.[1] All wrong, I hear now. So if you can do anything for me now, let me know.

I have the large package of cards concerning Paul which you sent me and am giving them to those whom I know like to have one.[2] I hear from Mr. Heinl in Washington that something like 35000 was raised in Terre Haute alone.[3] That strikes me as astonishing. Isn't that sum quite sufficient to remove the little house to the banks and fix it up. I should imagine so. If I had that much cash I could fix up four or five early birth places for myself I am sure. And Paul could do the same for himself.

My compliments, thanks and best wishes.

Theodore Dreiser

1. The sketch is in the prominent position of frontispiece to A *Hoosier Holiday* (1916).
2. Apparently cards announcing the activities of the Paul Dresser Memorial Association.
3. For Heinl, see Dreiser to Robert D. Heinl, 30 September 1924.

To Chauncey M. Depew [TS-BLYU]

Depew (1834–1928), former head of the New York Central Railroad and a U.S. senator from New York from 1899 to 1911, was a major public figure. During Dreiser's freelance journalist period, he had interviewed Depew, when he was still president of the New York Central, for his article "Life Stories of Successful

Men—No. 11, *Chauncey Mitchell Depew,*" *Success* 1 *(November 1898): 3–4.*
His letter to Depew follows his recent interview of him for the article "Chauncey
M. Depew," Hearst's International-Cosmopolitan *79 (July 1925): 86–87,*
183–85.

THEODORE DREISER[1]

Sept. 14, 1924.

Dear Mr. Depew:

In spite of the three hours consumed and your unfailing good nature I find three questions upon which I wanted light not touched upon. I suspect that a discreet uncertainty characterizes your speculations as to the hereafter but it would have interested me to ask your thoughts as to the visible scene,—the somewhat of chemic if mechanistic genius which seems to characterize it. In what mood and with what thoughts, at your best, do you stand before the spectacle of life,—its delights and its miseries? You have enjoyed or suffered ninety years,—as you will. Do you now incline toward a religious awe, a rapt and trusting admiration, a faith that man is used and guided for the best or used indifferently and without consideration for anything that he may desire. Your thoughts in connection with these will have value in connection with the picture I am about to try to present.

Again there is the mystery of love,—the chemic or psychic need of a man for a women,—or many women, as you will, and the need of a woman for a man. Do you consider it, as did the late Jacques Loeb,[2] and so many of the behaviorists of this day, the result of a blind and accidental physical and chemical formulae which had no beginning in any conscious mind anywhere, and that will pass as clouds pass, because of accidental chemical and physical changes in the universe over which nothing has any control. Or do you suspect or perhaps just hope, since to some it is beautiful, that it was preconceived by a higher intelligence and by that same preordained. In other words do you believe in a higher and governing intelligence that consciously intends human happiness or not. You need not answer of course, if you do not wish to. Lastly, among the arresting figures in any or all walks of life whom you have had the good or ill fortune to meet, did you ever encounter one or more than one whom you considered to be absolutely immune to the affections, sexual or romantic, paternal or maternal. And would you feel free to mention any particular individual? Did you ever know a strong man who was absolutely immune to the blandishments of women? And would you consider such immunity to be an advantage or a defect.

I hope you will pardon me for encroaching thus much further upon your very valuable time. And I want to thank you again for your very great courtesy to me.

Theodore Dreiser

If you would prefer that I should call and so permit you to reply verbally I will be very glad to do so.

1. Sometime in the fall of 1924 Dreiser began to use, and continued to use for many years, personal stationery with the heading "THEODORE DREISER."
2. Loeb had died in February 1924; for Dreiser and Loeb, see Dreiser to Jacques Loeb, 29 May 1919.

To Robert D. Heinl [TS-BLYU]

Heinl (1880–1950), a Washington, D.C., journalist and national chairman of the Paul Dresser Memorial Association, had reported to Dreiser that the campaign to raise the funds necessary for an imposing Dresser memorial had failed.

THEODORE DREISER

Sept. 30, 1924.

Dear Mr. Heinl:

I've been planning all this while, every few days, to write and thank you for one bit of information and another in connection with the monument and other matters. As I told you before I was not surprised by the outcome of the general campaign. Personally I never believed in it. For apart from Indiana, I do not know that the country has a very vital interest in this monument idea. They like the song but would only be satisfied to see a fitting memorial—not a very pretentious affair erected in connection with Paul. That was my thought all along and I still hold to it. If thirty or thirty-five thousand was raised there should be plenty to fix up the cottage and a small plot of ground on the Wabash and carry out Mr. Fortune's idea.[1] And if that is done it will be just what he thought,—fitting and beautiful. If you see him or write him at any time I wish you would thank him for his interest and efforts for me. I actually feel that had it not been for you getting him and his taking hold in the way that he did that the sum raised in Terre Haute would not have been raised. But perhaps this remark had better rest right here.

Incidentally I want to thank you for all that you did and assure you that I appreciate it very much. You certainly worked hard and solely because of the sentiment involved. A greater tribute to any cause cannot be paid.

My regards to your wife. And my best wishes for yourself and that delightful and amusing boy. When you are down this way let me know and I
will have you out to dinner.

Theodore Dreiser

These very long, lady-like envelopes were wasted on me. I don't like them
but am too frugal to throw them away.

1. Charles M. Fortune (?–1936), a Terre Haute politician with business interests
in Indianapolis who had accepted the chairmanship of the Paul Dresser memorial
campaign in January 1924.

To Upton Sinclair   [H-LLIU]

*Sinclair (see Dreiser to Upton Sinclair, 8 October 1914), who was working
on a study of turn-of-the-century radical American authors, had written H. L.
Mencken for information about the murder of the muckraking novelist David
Graham Phillips (1867–1911). Mencken pleaded ignorance but recommended
Dreiser as a source.*

THEODORE DREISER

Dec. 18—1924

My Dear Sinclair:

Mencken is wrong. I knew nothing of the Phillips shooting except what
I read in the papers at the time. As for your proposed visit—very glad to see
you. I am moving Jan. 1st from here (118 W. 11th St., N.Y.) to *1799 Bedford
Ave.*, Brooklyn—for a few months anyhow.[1] Can't give you a telephone
number, yet. But drop me a card a day or so beforehand.

Thanks for *Singing Jail Birds*.[2]

But don't forget that the brotherhood of man—(this entirely apart from
some of the co-operative phases of socialism) is mere moonshine to me. I see
the individual large or small—weak or strong as predatory & nothing less.[3]

My compliments and regards

Theodore Dreiser

1. Dreiser was moving to Brooklyn to have more time to work on *An American
Tragedy*.
2. *Singing Jailbirds, A Drama in Four Acts* (1924), by Sinclair and published by
him in pamphlet form. The play is based on a 1923 IWW-led strike in California.
3. No doubt written by Dreiser to provoke Sinclair, who was a committed
socialist.

1925

To Josephine Piercy [TS-LLIU]

The Indiana-born Piercy (1895–?), at this time a graduate assistant in the English Department of the University of Illinois and later a professor of English at Indiana University, had written Dreiser asking what advice he might offer to students in her composition classes. Although this letter is signed by Helen, in the role of Dreiser's secretary, the portions in quotes were undoubtedly dictated by Dreiser.

February 24, 1925.

Dear Miss Piercy:

I have presented your letter of February 10th to Mr. Dreiser and urged him to reply. All I have been able to obtain from him thus far is this: "Can it be that the Department of English of the University of Illinois is approaching so humble a source for advice on the composition of the English language? Has not Dr. Sherman sufficiently convinced the student body of the English Department of the University of Illinois of the fact that I cannot write and know nothing concerning the composition of the English language?"[1]

And he also added: "The fact is that technically this is true. I never took a course in English composition and I never consciously mastered the rules of grammar and do not to this day know what they are. Lacking the authority which such a technical course would have given me I still had the temerity to write but having since been properly shamed for it I now lack the temerity to advise in so grave a matter. I think that a more schooled source should be sought."

Concerning specimen passages of his best writing he would only say: "Have not the American critics in general sufficiently established the fact that there are none in my books? Therefore I can only bow and excusably waive any attempt to indicate one."

This is not what I personally hoped to have him write but it is the best that his present mood will furnish.

Sincerely,
Helen P. Richardson
Secretary to Mr. Dreiser.

1. Stuart P. Sherman (1881–1926), who was then a professor of English at the University of Illinois, had written a famous attack on Dreiser in "The Naturalism of Mr. Dreiser," *Nation* 101 (2 December 1915): 648–50.

1926

To T. R. Smith [H-CU]

Exhausted by the intensive labors required to see An American Tragedy *through the press, Dreiser, with Helen, was vacationing in south Florida, which was at that time experiencing a land boom. T. R. Smith (1880–1942) a Liveright editor, had played a major role in the editing of* An American Tragedy.

THEODORE DREISER

Ft. Lauderdale, Fla
Las Olas Inn
Feb. 14—1926¹

Dear T.R:

Thanks for your hearty wire. And I'm glad the reviews are justifying your own formost opinion.² I'll never forget your announcement after reading the end of Part II—that you *knew a manuscript when you saw one* & this was one. Its something to *really* know—isn't it.

As for plans I am thinking of returning to N.Y. for the time being. Since finishing the book I've been all but sick in bed—run down, principally. Worse yet this is a real estate mad house & nothing more. Signs, hot-dog stands, blaa and Tar-ah! at every road side turn. The middle west & hick south have decided to make a bigger & brighter & purer Riviera. They have all the names, architectural designs & prices. But as for the spirit—well that cant be made to order so easily. Its terrible—truly.

And cold! Its as cold as a November day right here & now—30 miles north of Miami & no stoves. The usual swill about nothing like this in 30 years—but I don't believe it. Others say its quite regular. If you ever come this way *don't fail* to bring your fur coat. I wish to Christ I had mine.

And some booze. Ah, that I could face you now & demand a bottle & swig it down. Would—would—that I could.

As soon as I recover my nerves I'll turn over the poems & a book of short stories for which I have a peach of a name.³ Then *A Gallery of Women*. I wish when I get back you'd give a party & let me get good & drunk. I need it after this Florida bunk.

Genuflections
Salaams
Dreiser

1. Although Dreiser dated this letter "Feb. 14—1926," the correct date is undoubtedly 14 January 1926; Dreiser left Florida on 24 January and on 14 January he wrote a similar letter from the Las Olas Inn, often with the same wording, to Frank Crowninshield.

2. *An American Tragedy* was published on 17 December 1925; the early newspaper reviews were almost all laudatory.

3. *Chains*, a collection of Dreiser's stories published by Boni and Liveright in 1927. Since this collection takes its title from one of its stories, it apparently was not given "the peach of a name" Dreiser refers to.

To Elmer Davis [H-LC]

Davis (1890–1958), one of the most well-known journalists of his generation, had worked for the New York Times *from 1914 to 1924 and was now freelancing. Davis wrote Dreiser on 6 January 1926 that he admired* An American Tragedy *greatly but he hoped that Dreiser, "as the dean of American realists," could "persuade people who are writing about life as it is to write, occasionally, a story in which fornication is not inevitably followed by pregnancy."*

Permanent address
61 W. 48th St
N.Y.C

THEODORE DREISER

Jan 15—1926
Ft. Lauderdale, Fla.

Dear Mr. Davis:

You misread the conception incident in an American Tragedy. I am far away & have no copy with me. There is a chapter in which Clyde Griffiths forces Roberta Alden to admit him to her room. The succeeding chapter—paragraph *one*, sketches a period of some three months in which the relationship was indulged before Roberta Alden came to him with her plaint.[1] What *would you* for two ignorant kids. Years! Even I would not prove so hopeful,—preventatives or no preventatives.[2]

As for the mysterious Miss X—in the real case—because of influence the love incident was excluded by agreement.[3] Since I created a seeming crime instead of a real one I was compelled to create a defense of my own. The district-attorneys of Brooklyn & White Plains as well as Arthur Carter Hume, attorney and J. G. Robin—legal sharp assured me that such a scheme as I suggested could be & *had been* put over.[4] One case that was cited was that of the young Philadelphia multi-millionaire accused of killing the chorus girl.[5] I may be wrong but I notice that the Catholic church can seal the mouths of not one but *all* American papers & reporters at one & the same time. My compliments. My kindest remembrances.

Theodore Dreiser

1. Dreiser himself is somewhat confused about the sequence of events he describes. Clyde and Roberta sleep together for the first time, as described at the close of Chapter XXI of Book Two of *An American Tragedy*, in the late summer. It is November at the opening of the next chapter, but Roberta does not become pregnant until late December and does not announce her pregnancy to Clyde until Chapter XXXIII, in February.

2. Dreiser wrote in the left-hand margin of this paragraph: "I offer in extenuation that most of my other heroines escape entirely. See The Titan, Genius, Financier. Even Jennie Gerhardt after first failure." Dreiser refers to the fact that Jennie is made pregnant by Senator Brander during a brief relationship but lives with Lester Kane for many years without a pregnancy. Strangely, Dreiser omits from this list Carrie, who lives with both Drouet and Hurstwood without becoming pregnant.

3. In his letter of 6 January, Davis also remarked, "Any good reporter would have discovered in two days that Sondra Finchley was the mysterious Miss X, and the efforts of her rich and influential family to keep her name out would have succeeded only in getting it into 96–point fullface caps. . ."

4. Arthur Carter Hume (1870–1942), Dreiser's personal attorney, and Joseph G. Robin (1876?–1929), a New York financier whom Dreiser portrayed in his sketch "Vanity, Vanity" in *Twelve Men* (1919).

5. This case has not been identified.

To Constable & Co. [H-TU]

Dreiser's one success story in the history of his otherwise acrimonious relationships with publishers was that of his lengthy association with the English firm of Constable and Co. from 1926 to his death. In October 1926 he met in London his Constable editor, Otto Kyllmann, with whom he established a warm friendship.

THEODORE DREISER

Feb. 19—1926

Gentlemen:

The suggested arrangement for issuing my various novels in England under your imprint has brought me no little pleasure.[1] It has been discussed by myself and Horace Liveright and he has already written you that with but one or two unimportant modifications the suggested terms are satisfactory. You understand, of course, that *all* foreign rights to my books rest in me and any contract drawn is between yourselves and myself. Next—in reprinting

Otto Kyllmann.

The Financier it is to be reset from a revised script which will be furnished you by me—unless, previously, as is now planned here, it is first reissued in book form here. In that case you will reprint from the new version.[2]

Apart from that there is nothing more to say except that I am very conscious of and most sincerely grateful to you for your very definite and direct expression of your critical approval of the various volumes and I can only hope with you that your future efforts in their behalf will confirm your practical as well as your critical judgement.

My acknowledgments
My very best wishes
Theodore Dreiser
61 W. 48th St.
New York City.

1. Constable and Company, in a letter of 2 February 1926, promised to publish a uniform edition of Dreiser's previously published work accompanied by an advertising campaign. The firm's "New Uniform Edition" of Dreiser's works began appearing in 1927 and within two years included all his previously published novels.

2. Dreiser refers to the revised edition of *The Financier*, which was published by Boni and Liveright in April 1927; Constable published the British edition of the novel that same year, using the revised American edition as the basis for its own resetting of the work.

To Jesse L. Lasky [TS-USoCar]

Lasky (1880–1958), head of Famous Players movie company, had been dealing with Dreiser and Horace Liveright for the film rights to An American Tragedy. *The three had met on 11 March 1926 at the dining room of the Ritz Hotel in New York to complete the deal.[1] When it became apparent that Dreiser and Liveright disagreed on the provisions of their previously discussed arrangement for Liveright's compensation, Dreiser became enraged, threw a cup of coffee in Liveright's face, and walked out. The incident was widely reported, but eventually Dreiser modified slightly the terms he spells out to Lasky to $80,000 for himself and $10,000 for Liveright, and the quarrel between the two was patched up. The film was delayed, however, until 1931, when it was made by Paramount Publix, the successor to Famous Players.*

THEODORE DREISER

March 14, 1926.

Dear Sir:—

My price for "The American Tragedy" is $90,000, from which I will pay Mr. Liveright a broker's commission of ten per cent.

If you wish to continue the negotiations interrupted at the Ritz, without Mr. Liveright present, you may write or call me at the Pasadena Hotel, 51st and Broadway.

Theodore Dreiser

1. There has been some confusion about the precise date of the incident. Both Swanberg, *Dreiser*, 305, and Tom Dardis, *Firebrand: The Life of Horace Liveright* (New York: Random House, 1995), 199, agree that Dreiser and Liveright met initially at Liveright's office on the morning of the Ritz date with Lasky to sign a contract giving Liveright the right to produce a play version of *An American Tragedy*. Dardis gives 19 March as the date of these events and Swanberg cites "mid-March." The contract (DPUP), however, is in fact dated 11 March, and Dreiser's letter to Lasky of 14 March confirms that the Ritz meeting had already occurred.

To Arthur Pell [TS-DPUP]

Pell was treasurer of Boni and Liveright. Dreiser's brother Rome (1860–1940) was a drifter and alcoholic; after he was located in the Chicago hotel, Dreiser continued to support him for many years. His initials were in fact "M. R.," for Marcus Romanus, not "R. M." It is not known when Rome began using Paul's stage name of Dresser.

N.Y., November 5th, 1926

Dear Mr. Pell:

I have a brother who goes by the name of R. M. Dresser. He should be in the neighborhood of 67 or 68 years of age. I have information that he is stopping at the Rufus F. Dawes Hotel, Chicago, Ill. The manager of that hotel is John Hansen.[1]

It is claimed that my brother is there and sick, without any means of support. I would like someone to go to this hotel and, if possible, identify this man as my brother, without telling him what the purpose is, and let me know by wire.

In addition, I would like to have this man explain or discover what, approximately, my brother's present standard of living is, and how much it would take to decently take care of him according to the standards which he now understands.

Very truly yours,
Theodore Dreiser

1. The correct name is Hanson.

1927

To J. B. Bindley [TC-DPUP]

Bindley, a Terre Haute druggist and head of the city's Paul Dresser Memorial Association, had written Dreiser to enlist his support for the grand and expensive memorial the association was planning. Dreiser, however, was committed to the far more modest plan he had outlined in his earlier letter to his brother Ed (see Dreiser to Edward M. Dreiser, 11 February 1924).

February Eighth, 1927.

My dear Mr. Bindley:[1]

I am very much obliged to you for the clipping from the Terre Haute Tribune, showing the progress of the Paul Dresser Memorial.

The truth is, however, that I am in no way emotionally interested in this particular scheme which this organization insisted on indulging in in connection with his memory. My suggestion, and that of Mr. Fortune of Indianapolis,[2] was that so little as $15,000.00 be secured wherewith the cottage in which Paul was born could have been purchased, one or two adjacent lots surrounding it to give it a small park form, and his body brought down from Chicago to be buried there. In addition, his musical effects which chance to be in my possession were to be transferred to the interior of the cottage. This inexpensive plan was vetoed by individuals who happen to be interested only in a crossroads monument.

It may be that this will be of greater advantage to Terre Haute as an up and growing American city. As a sensitive memorial to a man who added glamour and emotion to the name of Indiana, it is in my judgment nil.

I am sorry to be indifferent, but under the circumstances, the state is unavoidable.

Sincerely,

1. The typist's error of "Binley" is corrected here and below based on additional correspondence in the DPUP.
2. For Fortune, see Dreiser to Robert D. Heinl, 30 September 1924, n. 1.

To Mr. Kohl [TC-DPUP][1]

Dreiser and Helen met Kohl, who has otherwise not been identified, in Prague in August 1926, during their extended European trip. The New York production of An American Tragedy, *dramatized by Patrick Kearney and directed by Edward*

Goodman, opened on 11 October 1926 and was a great success. There is no evidence of a Prague production of the play.

February Eight, 1927

Dear Mr. Kohl:

I certainly recall with pleasure the bohemian dinner we attended in that most amusing of restaurants, and since leaving Prague, I have thought of you as perhaps the sanest and most sincerely artistic person that I met there.

It pleases me enormously that you are interested to do "An American Tragedy" in Prague, and because of your interest and the possibility that you may go further with the matter, I wish to advise you concerning some of the technical difficulties that were met with here in the first place that since the production of the play have been overcome. Let me first say, however, that under special cover I am sending you a working script of the play as it is being done now, and I feel that if that is followed carefully and adequately interpreted by individuals suited to the parts, that the play can be a success in Prague.

One of the difficult scenes in the play is that in which Clyde hears the voice of his darker self. As this was first done here, there was no mask used at all, and the impulse to murder and the justification of the mood was not artistically established. In fact, the lines as written were not sufficiently dramatic or important to carry this crucial point. To obviate that the mask, a plan of which I am herewith enclosing, was introduced. Technically this paper explains itself, but the very sombre, arresting effect is achieved not only by this mask, a duplicate of which will be forwarded to you on request, but by the very necessary addition of a sombre, sonorous and moving voice speaking in a low, slow monotone. I emphasize this because it is most important. This scene, as it has been done here, is absolutely ineffective without it. Furthermore, the optical effect which is so important in creating the right impression in the minds of the audience depends upon the manner with which the lighting of the mask is handled. As it is operated here, the voice begins with the word "Clyde" sonorously enunciated, and as it does so, the lights dim in and as the voice continues, the lights slowly come up until the mask is easily distinguishable from all parts of the house. At the conclusion of the voice, the lights slowly dim out, the cue for the lighting being marked in the script.

Another most important scene in the play relates to the trial. The lighting of Clyde's face in this scene should be done so that it has a waxy pallor, yet sufficiently strong for the audience to detect the emotions to which the vehemence of the legal attack subject him. The lawyers in assuming the audience to be the jury in this same scene should address them as though they were really twelve men, and they were entering into intimate confidence with them.

As I told you before, I do not know the financial conditions which govern such productions in Prague, but the usual terms will be satisfactory to me.

Sincerely,

1. Published in "Dreiser on *An American Tragedy* in Prague," *Dreiser Newsletter* 4 (Spring 1973): 21–22.

To Otto Kyllmann   [H-TU]

Dreiser had met Kyllmann (1869?–1959), his editor at Constable and Co., in London in October 1926, during his European tour. Constable was planning its "New Uniform Edition" of Dreiser's work, which was to include a new British edition of Sister Carrie.

200 West 57th St
N.Y.
Feb. 23rd 1927

Dear Kyllmann:

Under no circumstances publish the Heinemann—or cut form of *Sister Carrie*. The cuts were made under duress and protest.[1] The book was suppressed in America and Heinemann would not issue it over there unless it could be made to fit into his *Dollar* Series—which contained books of a given length. I hope it is not too much trouble to you.

Thanks for news of the Tragedy.[2] It is being done as I told you by Nordstedt in Stockholm and Gyldendal in Copenhagen.[3] I had a letter from Hegel[4] over a month ago & signed contracts.

Dreiser

It is also being done in Germany, Cezcho-Slovakia, Switzerland and Holland—so far.[5] I thought you might like to know.

1. Kyllmann had written Dreiser on 14 February 1927 that he had only recently discovered that the 1901 Heinemann British edition of *Sister Carrie* had been severely cut. These cuts were not made by Dreiser himself but rather by his close friend of that period, Arthur Henry.

2. Kyllmann had noted in his letter of 14 February that *An American Tragedy*, which had been published in late 1926, was being widely reviewed and that a second printing was being prepared.

3. The Swedish and Danish editions of *An American Tragedy*, published by these firms, appeared in 1927 and 1928 respectively.

4. F. Hegel, a Gyldendal editor.

5. Editions of the novel were published in Germany in 1927,Czechoslovakia in 1930, and the Netherlands in 1938. No Swiss edition has been identified.

To Sergei Dinamov [TC-DPUP]

Dinamov (1901–1939?), a Russian critic interested in American literature, worked for the state publishing house Gosidzat. He and Dreiser began corresponding in late 1926 and became friends during Dreiser's visit to Moscow in November 1927. Dinamov disappeared during the Stalin purges of the late 1930s.

March Fourteenth, 1927

My dear Dinamoff:

I was so happy to receive your letter and because of your sincere interest in my work, I shall try to make clear the genesis of the—shall we say inspiration, for lack of a better word. As I wrote you previously, Frank Norris was an unknown name to me until my contact with regard to "Sister Carrie" made us friends. It is true that he and Stephen Crane were then writing serious, courageous realism and there seemed to be a dawn of that sort of literature in America. I was twenty-eight, and rather ignorant of contemporary writers—I had read Hardy, of course, and Balzac and was greatly impressed—more, I think, because I was finding men who were writing about life as I saw it and wanted to write about it, than because I was influenced by them. For ever

Sergei Dinamov.

since I was a child I had brooded about life—its futility, its crassness, its cruelty—dark hours of depression descending upon me when I was so young as thirteen or fourteen. And now at twenty-eight when I felt so desperately the urge to express somehow this morbid viewpoint, I wrote "Sister Carrie". I had watched the then famous "breadline" in New York—the tragedies of the Bowery—the human wrecks who stood for hours in the snow and rain waiting for a bite of free food. And watching and speculating on what these derelicts might have been, there generated the idea of Hurstwood.[1] Whether or not there is some psychic influence—some mental wave which makes for an affinity between minds—I am not prepared to say definitely, but I am rather inclined to believe that would be a truer explanation of the so-called literary traditions in any land, than a conscious process of either imitation or conventional following along prescribed lines.

Now, as to my more immediate labors, I am at present working on a collection of studies of various types of women, which is to be called "A Gallery of Women". In form it is comparable to "Twelve Men". (Have you read that.) And I hope it will prove as interesting, if not more so. For added to character analysis—a clinic of temperaments, I might say—is the color of chemic attraction between the sexes—a striving to catch the elusiveness of the feminine temperament, which of course as all men know, is much more difficult, and therefore more interesting than a study of men by men. This work will probably occupy the rest of this year.

After that I am contemplating the third volume of the trilogy, volumes one and two of which are the Financier and The Titan, as you know. It is easy for me to understand your interest in Cowperwood. For he was not only a giant of finance, but a titan of living emotion, and his life of course gave me great scope for the huge canvas of America—not of today, with everything so well organized, so well-greased, but the pioneer America—the America of great development, when all that we have today was in process of procreation. This is why Cowperwood has always interested me and that is why he would interest the Russian temperament, I believe, for your country is now in that stage. And just here I want to say that I am eager for news of Russia—I wish you would tell me about it—just how successful the Soviet is—whether or not you believe conditions are better or worse than under the old regime—its future—in fact, an honest perspective of conditions, which I know you have. Russia interests me vastly. I understand it so little. When I read Dostoevksy I am held enraptured by the pictures he paints of the Russian temperament. With all its morbidity, it is so vivid, so flamboyant, that sometimes it seems almost unreal. It is surely antithetic to our own in America.

I am most interested by the experiment of Mrs. Astor and her English workman. You must know of it, of course—her offer to send an English laborer to Russia for six months, pay all his expenses, with the purpose of proving he would find conditions there intolerable as compared with England. The result, of course, was such great satisfaction with Russia that the man refused to return to his home land. That, of course, indicates a very flattering social condition there. Is it true?[2]

With reference to "An American Tragedy", I regret that I have no script of the play in my possession at this time. I shall have some copies made, however, and will at that time be glad to forward one to you. What do you think of the possibilities of making a production of this play in Russia? Perhaps you have connections, or are in touch with the theatrical situation there, and could tell me just how to go about arranging for its presentation in Russia. Somehow I feel that it would be interesting to your countrymen. I shall be glad to have your opinion.

Sincerely,

1. Dreiser refers to the nightly breadline at Fleischmann's Vienna Model Bakery which appears in chapter 47 of *Sister Carrie*. He also used this material in an earlier sketch, "Curious Shifts of the Poor," *Demorest's* 36 (November 1899): 22–26.

2. The story received front-page coverage in the *New York Times* of 29 December 1926. Dreiser is asking for verification of its truth because the account of the British workingman's satisfaction with Russia derives from a British labor leader who had visited the workingman.

To Otto Kyllmann [H-TU]

Constable published six books by Dreiser in its "New Uniform Edition" during 1927 and 1928, all novels except for the short story collection Chains. *Beginning in 1929, however, it did issue a number of Dreiser's nonfiction books.*

THEODORE DREISER

200 W. 57th St
June 4—1927

Dear Kyllmann:

Decidedly I would not issue more than two books a year. I find that one a year over here is ample and where a work is delayed the results are better. As for postponing the *Financier*—certainly—by all means.[1] I have always wished that you had decided to place one of the genre books between each two novels. For I consider *Twelve Men, Free, A Hoosier Holiday, A Traveler at Forty, A Book About Myself,* and *Plays of the Natural and the Supernatural* (there are ten of them in one volume) as among my best things. There are others—(Hey, Rub-a-Dub-Dub, The Color of a Great City, The Hand of the Potter) but the above would make a representative set of twelve. But I'm not urging this. It merely seems valuable to me.

Cant answer about coming over in this letter but maybe I will.[2] And I'd take a cottage of course. It would be fine to be near you *"and the wife"* as we say over here. But I'm sorry your not coming—very. Regards.

Thanks for the promise of the 6 vols of Am. Tragedy.

Dreiser

1. Kyllmann had written on 3 May 1927 that it might be wise to postpone a new edition of *The Financier* in order to proceed quickly with the publication of *Chains*. Since *The Financier* was published by Constable in 1927 and *Chains* in 1928, the plan seems to have been dropped.

2. Dreiser did in fact visit Kyllmann briefly when he stopped over in England in early February 1928 on his way back from Russia.

To Edward McDonald   [H-HRHUT]

Dreiser was on a three-month tour of Russia as a guest of the Soviet government. McDonald published several bibliographies of contemporary novelists in the late 1920s. His A Bibliography of the Writings of Theodore Dreiser, with a foreword by Dreiser, appeared in 1928, published by the Centaur Book Shop of Philadelphia.

Grand Hotel
Moscou, place du Revolution, No 1/2
Moscou, le, Nov. 25—1927

Dear Mr. McDonald:

As you can see I am here in Moscow and no doubt this information will come too late to aid you. I never published a volume of poems before 1900.[1] The Studies of Contemporary Celebrities—has a slightly different history. It was planned—and set up from magazine papers but never finally issued. I recalled it myself.[2] I cannot tell you about Jennie Gerhardt. I never even noticed the two forms Dreiser and Theodore Dreiser had been used on the back strip. I would be interested to know which is the genuine first edition.[3] Lastly I shall be very glad to have the cards recording the fifty articles written by me before Sister Carrie.[4] Thank you very much.

I am traveling in Russia & will not issue from it before Jan 10th probably at Odessa. Address anything to 200 W. 57th.

Sincerely
Theodore Dreiser

1. For Dreiser's planned but never published early book of poems, see Dreiser to Ellen M. Boult, after 9 June 1899, n. 3.

2. Another planned but never published early volume, in this instance of articles previously published in *Success* and other magazines. Dreiser's entry in the 1899 *Who's Who in America* lists both *Poems* and *Studies of Contemporary Celebrities* as works by him.

3. In his *Bibliography*, McDonald noted two states of the first printing of the 1911 Harper's *Jennie Gerhardt*, a first with Dreiser's full name on the spine and a rare second with only his last name. Since his bibliography was prepared with rare book collectors in mind, this was a significant distinction.

4. In fact, Dreiser made more than 100 contributions to magazines and newspapers between the beginning of his freelance career in the fall of 1897 and the publication of *Sister Carrie* in November 1900.

1928

To John Howard Lawson [H-SIU][1]

Hy Kraft (1899–1975), who was active in New York theatrical life, had suggested to Dreiser that Sister Carrie *would make a successful play and had recommended as an adaptor Lawson (1895–1977), a radical young dramatist whose avant-garde* Processional *(1925) had been well-received. When Lawson completed his version in 1929 Dreiser did not accept it. Lawson was later to become a highly successful Hollywood screenwriter.*

THEODORE DREISER

Aug 10—1928

My Dear Lawson:

I wished to answer your last note before this but had nothing to contribute.[2] Since then, though, I have thought to the following effect. One of the important things of the book—*the* important thing, really, is the mental and social decay of Hurstwood. This as you know can scarcely be more than hinted at in the last act—though it [word missing] the thing that moves all of us to which to dramatize the story. Now I have a way by which (I believe) Hurstwood's decay can be put over and the play itself strengthened by it. I offer you a choice of two prologues, one to be called A *Lodging for a Night.* This would present the Old Captain housing his company of bedless bums—as in the book—the hour in Madison Square, his solitary presence, the gathering of the bums, his appeal and their being marched off to the Bowery. But no suggestion of any connection with the play proper—just a picture inducing a proper psychic mood for the story that follows.

Or you may take A *Cycle of Decay,* another prologue. In six seven or eight or ten-ten-second scenes spotted against a black stage you could show the daily contest of a failure with life. He is dumped out of a full bed in a lodging house at 7 a.m. He walks the Bowery, eyes a restaurant, attempts an appeal here or there, rests wearily on a park bench or in doorway of a back street, but is driven off, tries a "mission" for warmth and a handout; does a turn in the work house, or begs a night in a police-station, or sleeps over a warm subway grating. There is also the bread line, a snow shoveling brigade—anything everything. The idea though is a quick series of scenes spotted—and over in three or four minutes—yet running a complete cycle. After such a prologue—but with no direct reference to the play, the play itself might end where Hurstwood stands in the vacant room & says "Left me; left me." The minds of all, I am sure would return to the prologue & so complete your effect. Let me know your reaction.

My compliments
My sincere good wishes
Theodore Dreiser
200 West 57th St
Circle 8795

1. This and the following letter to Lawson were published in "Dreiser Discusses *Sister Carrie*," *Masses and Mainstream* 8 (December 1955): 20–22.
2. Lawson had written to Dreiser on 19 July 1928 that he was thinking through his ideas for the final act of his dramatization of *Sister Carrie*.

To John Howard Lawson [TS-SIU]

THEODORE DREISER

New York City, October 10th, 1928.
My dear Lawson:—
    It does seem to me that you are getting much nearer the drama as well as the spirit of the book.[1] And after a fashion I like the idea of the bum or down-and-out as suggesting what I emphasized—the need of presenting clearly the drama of Hurstwood's decay. But I think you will not get this straight, or be able to present it to the best advantage, until you ask yourself, as I asked myself a long time ago, what was it exactly that brought about Hurstwood's decline? What psychic thing in himself? For most certainly it could not have been just the commonplace knocks and errors out of which most people take their rise. It is not enough to say that he is not a strong man, or that he lacked a first class brain. Granted. And it is obvious from the book. But there is something more. A distillation not only of his lack of strength and his mediocre brain, but of the day and the city and the circumstances of which, at say forty-odd, he found himself a part. And this is of a twofold character. First—a sense of folly or mistake in him because of his having taken the money of his employers and so having lost not only their friendship and confidence but the, for him, almost necessary milieu of Chicago—its significance as the center of his home, children, friends, connections—what you will. Next the ultimate folly of his hypnosis in regard to Carrie. For as the book shows her charm betrayed him. He erred, as he later saw it, in taking her, because she drifted from him—went her

own mental way—did not sustain him. These two things, once he was out of Chicago and so away from all he had known and prized, concentrated to form a deep and cancerous sense of mistake which ate into his energy and force. It was no doubt finally the worm at the heart of his life. And without the power to destroy it he was doomed. And it is that *conviction* which is the thing that is stalking him and that is necessary to symbolize in some way. But how? By your bum who becomes a detective and then a bum again? In part, yes, I am inclined to think so, although I think it might be better if the bum never became a detective.

On the other hand, by some words of Hurstwood here and there throughout the play—a Hamlet-like meditation, or phrase now and then—it is necessary to indicate the unchanging presence of this cancerous conviction of error—its almost psychic reality—a body and mind of defeat. For I do personally believe that in the super energies of all of us lie amazing powers. We can and do embody in the world without many things which fight or aid us. You, as you go along, will best see where and how the truth of this can be shadowed forth. But once it is in I think your listeners are likely to feel the essential awfulness of the man's fate. And so the real drama of the book. If so we are likely to have a successful play. I hope so. I like the spirit of your present outline very much and only wish that I might read the completed play.

Theodore Dreiser
200 West 57th St, N.Y.

1. On 28 September 1928 Lawson sent Dreiser an eight page "Working Plan" of his dramatization.

To Marianne Von Schön [TC-DPUP]

Beginning with The Titan *in 1928, Von Schön, a Vienna resident, translated several of Dreiser's novels into German for Dreiser's German publisher, Paul Zsolnay.*

New York City
October 22, 1928

Dear Miss von Schön:

Thank you very much for going to Zsolnay and straightening out the financial account for me.[1] I have received not only your letter but several from Zsolnay, one went to Brandt and Brandt[2] and one sent to me and the matter is now perfectly clear.

I note in your opening paragraph that you speak of "The Titan" as revised by Mr. Kramer. Exactly what is meant by this "revision"?[3] I did not know that "The Titan" was to be revised, and will object very much if without my consent it has been allowed. I would like to hear concerning this as soon as possible.

In regard to "A Book about Myself", which I am sending you, I wish to explain concerning it if I have not already done so. It is only Volume II in a series of books which is to be entitled "A History of Myself". Volume I of this series is entitled "Dawn" and is already finished. I can furnish it for inspection just as readily as I can "A Book about Myself". The latter was originally entitled "Newspaper Days" and the title was changed to what it is now without my consent. In view of the fact that it is only Volume II in a series of four or five volumes, I do not care to have it published separately now. I prefer to begin with Volume I, then issue "A Book about Myself" as Volume II under the title "Newspaper Days". Volume III will not be ready for some time but it is to be entitled "Literary Experiences", and may really be in two parts. As a matter of fact, I am sure they will make a set of at least four books, which will be a running history of myself and the America that I knew during the period covered. It has special value as I see it, because Volume I really pictures Middle West life from 1875 on to 1900, and I know of no other volume in this country that covers that in anything like the same way. Volume II ("A Book about Myself" or "Newspaper Days") is really an adequate picture of newspaper life in America for the 1880–1900 period, the formative and most dramatic period in all our newspaper history. Volume III will cover the really climacteric conclusion of the puritanical regime in American letters, and Volume IV will cover the break in literature as represented by the realistic school, really carrying American literature up to recent days.[4]

All in all, I look upon this series as perhaps the most individual and purely American and, because of its autobiographical character, the most vital of any of the works I have done so far. Therefore, if the thing is to be handled in Germany at all, I want it to be handled this way or allowed to lapse or rest until a later period, because I feel that the set requires and deserves to be presented in such a way as to bring its completeness and significance before the mind of the prospective reader.[5] I am sure that it will only get its just critical approval if that is done. I have always felt and still feel that the series in America has been greatly injured by the separate issuance of Volume II, and as soon as I can arrange it I propose to have the series done over, beginning with Volume I and "A Book about Myself" is-sued as "Newspaper Days" or Volume II.

I note that you mention the success of "The Hand of the Potter" in Ber-lin, but as yet I have heard absolutely nothing concerning it in America.[6]

If there is any data concerning it which you could furnish me, I wish you would do so, as it would aid in securing a proper presentation of it here.

In regard to the magazine publication in Germany of some of the sketches in "Twelve Men" and "A Gallery of Women", I am agreeable, and I would really like to see several from "Twelve Men" done at once. Concerning "A Gallery of Women", I shall be in a position very shortly now to send the entire set, which consists of fourteen sketches, upon which you and Mr. Zsolnay can pass, and if you feel that you wish to issue one or more of them in magazine form in Germany, you may let me know.[7]

In regard to "The Stoic", or Volume III of the financial trilogy, I expect to begin work on that before Christmas, and I figure that it will take possibly a year—maybe not more than nine or ten months—I cannot tell at this writing—but I am sure that it will not take more than a year.[8]

As for coming to Vienna, with all of the work I have in hand I question the advisability of it. It would be a pleasure, of course, if I could come there and meet the various people who have written me, but on the other hand, travel is a trying break in the ordinary run of my working life, and I am not as enthusiastic about it as some might be. If I should see a little later that I can do it quickly—that is, just a flying trip to Vienna and back—I may undertake it.

Will you take up this matter of the "History of Myself" very carefully with Mr. Zsolnay and let me know what your joint conclusions are?

Very truly yours,

1. Paul Zsolnay (1895–1961), Vienna-based publisher who published a large number of Dreiser's works in translation during the 1920s and early 1930s.

2. Dreiser's American agent for foreign rights.

3. Dreiser means Wilhelm Cremer (not Kramer), who, with von Schön, was translating *The Titan* into German. Von Schön assured Dreiser, in her reply of 19 November 1928, that the revision she had spoken of consisted of the polishing of the German translation.

4. Volumes III and IV were, of course, never written.

5. The two completed volumes of Dreiser's autobiography were, in fact, published by Zsolnay in 1932 as a set, with the second volume translated by von Schön.

6. *The Hand of the Potter* (in German translation) opened in Berlin in September 1928, had a successful run, and was then taken on tour.

7. It is not known whether any of the sketches from the two volumes appeared in German magazines; Zsolnay did publish *A Gallery of Women* in book form, translated by von Schön, in 1930.

8. Dreiser worked sporadically on *The Stoic* during 1928 and more fully in 1932, but did not complete the novel until 1945, shortly before his death.

To Horace Kallen   [TS-AJA]

*Kallen (1882–1974), a noted philosopher and Judaic scholar, was seeking Drei-
ser's support for the publication of the prison letters of Nicola Sacco and Bartolo-
meo Vanzetti, Italian-born anarchists who were executed in August 1927 for
murdering a payroll guard. Although the case attracted national and international
attention because it was widely believed that the two figures were convicted for
their beliefs, ballistics research in the early 1960s implicated Sacco as a probable
participant in the crime. The letters were published in late 1928 without the use
of Dreiser's name.*

THEODORE DREISER

[13 November 1928]

Dear Kallen:

I have been thinking over the Sacco-Vanzetti letters. I am willing to
sponsor them as letters, but it would be a misrepresentation of my actual
view in connection with their guilt or innocence if the public were able to
take the thought that I believed in their innocence.

In my case, it seems to me, asterisks should be inserted after my name
which would correlate with a short note to the effect that my sponsorship
stood for their interest as letters and not the merits or demerits of the trial
or execution. If this is not done the general conclusion will be that I am a
believer in their innocence. And I am absolutely unwilling to lay myself
open to that conclusion.[1]

Very sincerely,
Theodore Dreiser
200 West 57th Street
New York City
November thirteenth

1. In a 24 August 1927 letter to Dreiser, Horace Liveright wrote, "Patrick Kearney
tells me that he had dinner with you a few nights ago and that you believe Sacco &
Vanzetti to be guilty." (Kearney had dramatized *An American Tragedy* for its 1926
New York stage production.)

1929

To Otto Kyllmann [TS-TU]

Constable had been republishing Dreiser's novels in its "New Uniform Edition." During the 1930s it also undertook to republish many of his earlier books which were not novels.

THEODORE DREISER

200 West 57th Street,
New York City,
January 30, 1929.

My dear Kyllmann,

I certainly would like to have you not only re-publish some of my older books, but all of them. You are gradually issuing everything as it is anyhow and you might as well make a complete set. Liveright is planning a complete set to be sold for some fabulous sum one of these days and you might as well be in the position to duplicate it in England.

One thing in connection with all of this that I wish to take up with you is this:—as it is now, I pay Curtis Brown Ltd.[1] 10% of all that you earn for me, because he finally sold me to you. Last year, as you know, the English Government came along and placed a 20% income tax on top of that. Now I feel this way about it and I think that my feeling matches fairly closely with ordinary fair play. Either this Government Tax should be split proportionately three ways—between you, Curtis Brown and myself—or I should be given a higher percentage on my books to compensate me for the very large loss that goes with this general transaction. Don't you think so? If you think I am asking anything very unfair, I would be glad to hear your reasons.[2]

As for your publishing all of my books, I don't want any one else but you in England to ever publish them. You know how I feel about you personally and as I said over there, I am happy to have a publisher whom I can look upon as a friend.

As to when a certain book should be published, or the amount of time that should be allowed to elapse between this book and that—all of this rests with you and your judgment as a publisher. I have always followed your advice so far and, my best judgment permitting, will continue to do so.

Affectionately,
Dreiser

N. B. I am glad you like Moods so much. I sent you, I believe, the revised $3.00 trade edition which contains many more poems than were in the first edition and it is this second edition that I would like to have followed, with the illustrations as you suggested discarded, but since then I have written a few more—maybe so many as fifteen. Don't you think it would be advisable to include these in the English edition? I have never thought much of the idea of small volumes of poetry or moods which most poets issue from time to times. The Leaves of Grass idea of Walt Whitman has always appealed to me as much more sensible. Every time he re-printed it he included all he had written since the last printing.[3]

If I come over to England in the spring, will you go on another trip with me?

D

1. Dreiser's English agent.
2. Kyllmann replied on 13 February 1929 that it would be very difficult to avoid paying Curtis Brown its 10 percent but that Constable was willing to raise Dreiser's royalty to 20 percent on sales over 5,000.
3. Dreiser's poems, *Moods: Cadenced and Declaimed*, had been published in a limited edition by Boni and Liveright in 1926 and then republished, with twenty-nine additional poems, in a trade edition in 1928. Constable published its English edition in 1929, using the 1928 Boni and Liveright edition.

To Ralph T. Holmes [TS-UV]

Dreiser had admired the Bolshoi Ballet company during his visit to Moscow in November 1927. In February 1929, with the support of the financier Otto Kahn and the aid of Hy Kraft (see Dreiser to John Howard Lawson, 10 August 1928), he began a campaign to raise the funds necessary to underwrite the company's appearance in America. In the early summer of 1929 he withdrew from the campaign after realizing it would not succeed. Ralph T. Holmes was a Detroit newspaperman whom Dreiser had known from about 1918.

THEODORE DREISER

200 West 57th Street
New York City
February 21, 1929

Dear Holmes:

Since I talked to you about the All Russian Ballet, which I am bringing here, things have progressed quite rapidly. As I told you, although I do not care for any further publicity at this moment, Otto Kahn gave $25,000.[1]

Since then Conde Nast of the Conde Nast publications has subscribed for $10,000, Mr. Frank Crowninshield, the editor in chief of the Conde Nast Publications and Donald Freeman of Vanity Fair have joined with me to make the thing a success.[2] Nast, Crowninshield, and Kahn are going to sign the All American Committee of One Hundred or more which is going to issue an invitation to the official Soviet ballet to visit America.

Frank Crowninshield hopes to secure a contribution and the signature for this invitation from Mrs. Stotesbury of Philadelphia.[3] I have letters from Kahn, copies of several of which I enclose, which show that the individuals whose names he has given me will contribute liberally toward the guarantee fund which will take care of this company's visit, whether it succeeds or fails.

Among the people to whom he has committed the enterprise and who will certainly fall in with his suggestion of a contribution are Reeve Schley, Vice-president of the Chase National Bank here in New York, the president of the Bank of Italy of California and Fred F. French of the Fred F. French Realty Co. here.[4] Since I know Mr. French personally I know that he will gladly come in with a strong donation.

I am enclosing also a copy of the proposed corporation which is to control all the money and movements of the tour. It is suggested that I take the presidency of this but as a matter of fact, I have the intention to get Crowninshield or Nast or Fred F. French to take the presidency and maybe Crowninshield the secretaryship so as to leave me free since I get nothing out of it except the artistic satisfaction of seeing the thing a success.

Otto H. Kahn stated the other day here that one or all of the Fisher Brothers of the Fisher Bodies of Detroit[5] would be interested in this idea and if approached with my name and his would be glad to contribute say $25,000, which means to take 25 of the $1000 bonds of the All Russian Ballet in America.

I would like you to tell me whether you think that you personally could approach them in this matter or whether you have any friends with sufficient influence in Detroit who could do it or would get me the name of anyone besides the Fisher Brothers who would be likely to be interested. I do not want too many people from one city and if I take more than one or two or possibly three, I would really want less money from each; that is for instance if there are two or three people who would subscribe for $10,000 or $5,000 each, I would not ask the Fisher Brothers for more than $10,000 or $15,000. The total that I would require from Detroit would be $25,000. If you know anything about the situation in Cleveland and Buffalo in regard to this matter of contributions, please let me have the facts.

By all means say nothing editorially or in a publicity way concerning this because I have a direct request from the Russian government to say nothing until the contract is signed because it proposes to release by cable official information in regard to this entire transaction and I think that that will have more weight here than anything that can be said by me or anyone else on this side.

With best personal wishes, I am
Yours sincerely,
Theodore Dreiser

1. Kahn (1867–1934), an extremely wealthy banker, was a patron of the arts.
2. Nast (1873–1942), publisher of *House and Garden, Vogue,* and *Vanity Fair;* Crowninshield (1872–1947), editor of *Vanity Fair* from 1914 to 1936; Freeman, managing editor of *Vanity Fair.*
3. Lucretia (Eva) Stotesbury (1865–1946), a socialite and philanthropist.
4. Schley (1881–1960); A. P. Giannini (1870–1949); and French (1883–1936).
5. The Fisher brothers (Fred J., Albert, and Charles) had founded the Fisher Body Division of the General Motors Corporation.

To Otto Kyllmann   [TS-TU]

Dreiser was contemplating further work on The Stoic, *which deals with Cowperwood's financial career in England.*

THEODORE DREISER

200 West 57th Street,
New York City,
April 17, 1929.

Dear Kyllmann,

Are there any books in England that relate to finance? I mean any books that illustrate as a novel would the financial life of England?[1]

I recall Tono Bungay by Wells as having some minor financial references or aspects, and it seems to me that one of Arnold Bennett's books had some phases which illustrated in particular the British financial world, but I cannot recall the name.[2]

I have the feeling that you personally may know of either autobiographical or works of THE FINANCIER type, which would help me in catching the British financial color for the last volume of my trilogy, which, of course, in part is laid in London. Harold Frederic wrote one book, the name of which I have forgotten, but as I recall it now, it contained nothing of any real value.[3] I would think that if any recent British financier had written autobiographically and honestly of his experiences that might help a great deal. If you can pick up anything of the kind, please forward it at once and charge it to my account.

As ever,

Dreiser

P. S. I thought at first that I would write you concerning some phases of The Gallery of Women, the manuscript of which you have, but I have decided not to say anything at all in regard to it, but to await your opinion. You can tell me whether or not it has any meaning for your world over there or not.[4]

1. On 10 May 1929 Kyllmann sent Dreiser a list of seventeen books dealing with British finance.

2. None of Bennett's novels deals fully with British high finance, but *These Twain* (1916) depicts the successful rise of a businessman and the central figure of *Lord Raingo* (1928) is a millionaire.

3. *The Market-Place* (1899), the last novel by Frederic (1856–1898), an American novelist resident in England.

4. Constable published *A Gallery of Women* in 1930.

To Margaret Sanger [TC-DPUP]

Sanger (1883–1966), the leader of the birth control movement in America, was frequently under attack. By "pursued in this way," Dreiser appears to be referring to Sanger's having recently been prohibited by Boston authorities from speaking about birth control. On 18 April, both she and Dreiser had participated in an anti-censorship rally in Boston.

200 West 57th Street,

New York City,

April 20, 1929.

My dear Mrs. Sanger,

It is an outrage that you should be pursued in this way, but such is usually the fate of the person that brings a genuinely necessary reform to the world.

This idea may not triumph in your time, but it will or the world will pay a thousandfold in miseries that will involve war, starvation and disease.

As ever,

1930

To Theodore Kiendl [TC-DPUP]

Famous Players, after purchasing the film right to An American Tragedy *in 1926 (see Dreiser to Jesse L. Lasky, 14 March 1926), failed to produce the film. The basic issue Dreiser now sought advice on from Kiendl (1890?–1976), a New York lawyer, was whether Paramount Publix (the successor of Famous Players) still owned these rights, since Dreiser had signed a contract for a silent film and Paramount now wished to produce a talkie. Dreiser eventually did sign, in January 1931, a separate contract with Paramount Publix providing for additional compensation for the talkie rights.*

August 18th, 1930

Dear Mr. Kiendl:

The data enclosed in this envelope does not fully explain the Famous Players-Lasky situation.[1] The contract shows that I assigned all silent movie rights to Famous Players-Lasky, but it does not show that the original outline of the contract agreed upon by myself and Mr. Lasky and his attorneys, and as drawn by Famous Players-Lasky legal department, was finally presented to and signed by me.

What really happened was this: certain legal points having been raised, I decided to consult with Louis Levy, of Chadbourne, Stanchfield & Levy.[2] I did not know at the time that this firm had acted and was acting in various capacities for Famous Players-Lasky. Levy decided that the original down payment by Famous Players was to be much larger than I had thought necessary, also that the contract should be much shorter; in fact, as it is now; but in drawing it he wrote in what I did not want at all, and that was that Famous Players could change the title if necessary and do certain other things which were not in my original agreement with Lasky at all. When I protested, he said that Lasky and Zukor[3] and others were convinced that the title would not be changed but it was one of those precautions which was more that than an actual possible reality. In order not to have the whole situation go amiss as it had once before, I allowed the thing to go through, but now that the silent movie rights have lapsed as a financial possibility and only the talkie rights, on which Paramount has no real claim, remain, I feel that if the thing is to be done as a talkie, the contract must be revised in accordance with my original understanding. The title must not be changed, nor can the story be radically changed without my written consent.

Furthermore, I contend that because of the lapse of the silent movie rights and the appearance of the talkie, an entirely new contractual situation intervenes, and that because the talkie film rights—and the talkie film rights alone—are to be considered, I am now in a position legally whereby, in case Famous Players decide to proceed (in case I did not wish to surrender the talkie rights to them at their terms) to make the silent film of the book, I might enjoin them in equity on the ground that by now producing the silent film, (which for four years they refused to produce on the ground that it was immoral), they are destroying the material financial returns which lie in the talkie rights which now belong to me. In other words, having injured me in the first place by refusing to produce the silent film when it would have been of enormous advantage to me for them so to do, they now propose to injure me by the production of the film when it would be of enormous advantage to me for them *not* to do so.

For your information and consideration, I wish to state that neither the American play version by Patrick Kearney nor the German version to be staged by Piscator and Lina Goldschmidt in Berlin carry with them any film rights of any kind, either silent or talkie.[4]

As you will see from the letter and telegram of Horace Liveright,[5] (who is now in the employ of Paramount-Publix, of which Famous Players-Lasky is a subsidiary corporation) Famous Players is and is not interested in the production of the 'Tragedy' as a film. In his letter to me he endeavors to indicate that it will be a very difficult matter to convince Famous Players of the *wisdom* of producing the 'Tragedy' as a film. In the telegram, there is a very great interest and I am urged to cooperate, but without any return to me, and it is the talkie, and the talkie alone, that they are considering. In Mr. Liveright's letter you will also see a statement to the effect that a Mr. Hubman, of the American Play Company,[6] is ready to buy and Famous Players are willing to sell the film rights now possessed by them. This is some move to secure the talkie rights, and the talkie rights only, and the purpose of Famous Players-Lasky is obviously to avoid any censure which might arise from some such suit as I now contemplate.

Lastly, I wish to say this: in case Famous Players-Lasky, because of my refusal to surrender the talkie rights, refuse either to sell their film rights or to produce a talkie or a silent film and so block the production of the book as a film, I would like to know if it is not possible to bring suit for damages on this ground; i.e., that having refused to produce the picture on the ground that it is immoral, they have invariably stated that they have been prevented from so doing by the ruling of Mr. Will Hays, who is moral censor of the movies.[7] Yet when appealed to by me and others—for instance, George Bye, the literary agent[8]—for information as to the grounds for the ruling that the book is immoral, Mr. Hays has invariably stated that it was not himself who judged or decided that the book is immoral but some illusory, unnamed majority of the film producers, whose names or statements or rulings in this connection he refuses to divulge, on the ground that he is merely the secretary of the Motion Picture Producers Association and that it is not within his authority, without this, that and the other consultation, so to do.

For four years that situation has left me in the place where I could really not approach anyone with a proposition to either buy or produce "An American Tragedy", as I actually found on investigation, whenever I approached such agents or representatives of Metro-Goldwyn Mayer, Universal, Warner Bros., or R.K.O., that they invariably stated that in the first place the film was owned by Famous Players-Lasky and that it had been banned, and unless that ban was lifted and unless, in addition, Famous Players agreed to release it to someone else, they could not possibly move.

My feeling in the matter is that for personal reasons, both Hays and Lasky have determined from the beginning, first, to make me accept their terms in connection with not only "An American Tragedy" but all of my books, (which they once proposed to take over), and, second, to prevent, through Hays and his rulings, any other film company from interfering with whatever program they may have in connection with me.

It is on these several points that I desire your legal advice.[9]

1. Dreiser enclosed seven documents with his letter, ranging from his original contract with Famous Players to "Movie Morals as laid down by Will Hays" (holograph list accompanying the DPUP TC copy of his letter to Kiendl).

2. Louis S. Levy (1887–1952).

3. Adolph Zukor (1873–1976) founded Famous Players in 1912, which in 1916 merged with Jesse L. Lasky Features to become Famous Players–Lasky.

4. Patrick Kearney (1894–1933) adapted *An American Tragedy* for its profitable New York run in 1926; Erwin Piscator (1893–1966), an avant-garde director, and Lina Goldschmidt (1889–1935) sought unsuccessfully for some years to mount their version of *An American Tragedy* in Germany.

5. Two of the enclosed documents in Dreiser's letter to Kiendl (see note 1 above) were Liveright's 30 July 1930 letter and 14 August 1930 telegram to Dreiser.

6. Henry A. Hubman was head of the Motion Picture Department of the American Play Co., a firm which specialized in dramatic production rights.

7. Will Hays (1879–1954) was named head of the Motion Picture Producers and Distributors of America (the "Hays Office") in 1922 with the express assignment of imposing a moral code on film content.

8. George T. Bye (1887–1957), a New York literary agent who often handled Dreiser periodical publications during the 1920s and 1930s.

9. Kiendl replied on 17 August 1930 that Paramount probably did own the talkie rights to *An American Tragedy* and that a suit forcing Paramount to produce a silent version of the novel would probably fail.

To W. Randall Whitman [TC-DPUP]

Whitman had apparently addressed his letter about Dreiser's sources for An American Tragedy *to Donald (not Daniel) Friede because Friede, while working for Boni and Liveright, had, in a widely reported 1927 incident, been arrested in Boston for obscenity while selling a copy of the novel.*

200 West 57th Street,
New York City,
August 23, 1930.

Dear Mr. Whitman:

Your letter to Mr. Daniel Friede of Covici-Friede, Inc., has been referred to me.

Mr. Friede is not the publisher of The American Tragedy. The book is published by Horace Liveright, Inc., 61 West 48th Street, New York. I happen to be the author. You are mistaken in one or two points which I may as well correct here. I did not report the trial for any of the New York papers or the Associated Press.[1] I did not examine the data in the case until it was almost too late to get it—as late, for instance, as 1923. All the data I could find at the time was in the files of the New York World,—Several bundles of clippings which synopcized the trial.

You say you happen to know where the original letters now are. If you mean the pen written originals I would certainly like to know more about them. As a matter of fact, I have always wished that I could come into possession of the volumes which must have been printed for the Court of Appeals. I would be interested very much to possess those too.[2]

I will thank you very much for further information in regard to this.[3]

Very truly yours,

1. Whitman had stated in his 13 August letter that Dreiser had reported the trial for "one of the New York papers or Associated Press."
2. Dreiser is referring to the letters which Grace Brown wrote to Chester Gillette in the period before he killed her, a number of which he used almost verbatim in the novel. The letters were read out in court by the district attorney and then printed in the *New York World*. They were also published as a pamphlet, *Grace Brown's Love Letters* (Herkimer, N.Y., 1906), and in the trial record used by the Court of Appeal.
3. After some further correspondence, Whitman showed Dreiser the originals of Grace Brown's letters to Chester Gillette in June 1931.

To John Cowper Powys [TS-UV]

Dreiser met Powys (1872–1963), a Welsh-born novelist, in Chicago during the winter of 1912–13; they remained lifelong friends. Charles Fort (1874–1932), whom Mencken and many others considered a crackpot, collected bits of information and data and arranged them into apparent threads of meaning. Dreiser had met Fort in 1905 while editing Smith's and became an enthusiast of his work, especially The Book of the Damned *(1919). The Fortean Society was founded to preserve and promulgate Fort's work.*

THEODORE DREISER

200 West 57th Street
New York City
December 12th, 1930

Dear Jack:

The enthusiastic Forteans, as well as Mr. Fort himself, are delighted with your letter.[1] They are now, of course, anxious to include you as a "Fortean." The purpose of this Society, as I understand it, is to have Fort's books separated from the cranks in public library catalogues; supply Fort with data as it comes to the attention of its members; to attempt through publicity to force orthodox science at least to note and acknowledge the value or possible value of the gigantic quantity of data he has assembled; and to take over the data he has in his files for future work, in the event of his sudden death, to preserve it as a monument to his genius.

Whether or not you will want to be associated with all this is a matter for you to decide, and I have so told them, but I assure you that everyone connected with the movement is most appreciative of your interest. And whether or not you decide to go on record as a member of the Fortean Society, your letter will be a great help in the publicity work they have in mind.

Affectionately
Dreiser

1. In a letter of 3 December 1930 to Fort, Dreiser enclosed what he described as Powys's "fine tribute" to Fort and his work.

1931

To Ann North [TC-DPUP]

Ann North, the editor of Solidarity, *a journal of Workers International Relief, a radical organization, had written Dreiser on 12 January 1931 soliciting a contribution that "is understandable to workers, but nevertheless of artistic merit."*

> 200 West 57th Street
> New York City
> January 17th, 1931

Dear Miss North:

I am always being asked by one or another Communist organization or newspaper representing that system, for articles that will be beneficial to the development of the idea of the system in America. Though I know the Marxism theory thoroughly, and satisfied myself, by going there, of the experiment in Russia, I do not know the details of the lesser issues which confront the Communists here in America.

It seems to me that when you, or Mr. Engdahl, or Mr. Pass, or the John Reed Club, or The Masses, approach me for an article,[1] they, being closer to the movement than I am, would have some particular suggestions or perhaps a definite collection of data on a given topic which could be either selected from or re-cast by me so that I would not be outside the facts most interesting to the Party, and would be able to speak with the knowledge which it considers so necessary. If you have any subject with data which illuminates it clearly, I wish you could let me have it for consideration. If I can or cannot use it, I will be glad to eventually return it to you, and if anything comes of it, you will be entirely welcome to the article.

> Very truly yours,

1. John Louis Engdahl (1884–?), editor of the *American Socialist,* the official journal of the American Socialist Party; Joseph Pass (1887–1950), a Communist Party functionary; John Reed Clubs, established in various cities as a meeting place for communist writers; the *New Masses* (not *Masses*), began publication in 1926 as a left-wing successor of the *Masses,* which had been suppressed during the war.

To Samuel Hoffenstein [Tel-DPUP]

Paramount decided in December 1930 to proceed with a sound version of An American Tragedy *and Dreiser signed a new contract on 2 January 1931. The script was quickly adapted by Hoffenstein (1890–1947), a writer of comic verse who had recently arrived in Hollywood, and rushed into production, with Josef von Sternberg (1894–1969) as director. Although Dreiser's contract provided that he be shown the script, Hoffenstein had been unable to do so, since Dreiser was in Cuba during early February and could not be reached. Finally, on 17 February Hoffenstein wired Dreiser that it was too late for any consultation. After receiving Dreiser's return telegram of the 18th, Hoffenstein did send the script to New Orleans and then flew to the city prepared to meet Dreiser. On reading the script, however, Dreiser rejected it outright and left New Orleans without meeting Hoffenstein.*

COPY TELEGRAM

TAMPA FEB 18, 1931.

SAMUEL HOFFENSTEIN

PARAMOUNT PUBLIX CORPORATION

HOLLYWOOD CALIFORNIA

YOUR TELEGRAM OF THE SEVENTEENTH IS THE USUAL HOLLYWOOD SWILL AND BUNK SORRY TO SEE YOUR NAME ATTACHED STOP I WAITED IN NEW YORK UNTIL FEBRUARY FIRST THEN DEPARTED LEAVING WORD STOP YOUR TELEGRAM DID NOT ARRIVE HERE UNTIL FEBRUARY NINTH STOP PARAMOUNT PUBLIX DISTINCTLY AGREED TO SHOW ME SCRIPT AND CONSIDER MY ADVISE STOP IF THEY ARE HONEST AND SINCERELY WISH TO WORK WITH ME IN THIS YOU CAN CONSULT WITH ME YET HERE OR ANYWHERE ELSE SINCE I AM GOING WEST SUGGEST YOU MEET ME NEW ORLEANS FEBRUARY TWENTY THIRD STOP IF YOU ARE READY TO DO THIS AND WE CAN TALK AMICABLY WIRE ME GENERAL DELIVERY NEW ORLEANS OTHERWISE MAIL SCRIPT TO SAME PLACE NOW

THEODORE DREISER

To Mrs. Clinton Pinckney Farrell [TC-DPUP]

Mrs. Farrell was president of the New York City–based Vivisection Investigation League, an anti-vivisection organization.

200 West 57th Street
New York City
February 25, 1931

My dear Mrs. Farrell:

I am sorry for my delay in answering your recent letter relating to the bill to prohibit experiment upon living dogs,[1] but because of my interest in the matter, I have taken the time to make certain investigations which I hoped would enable me to arrive at a fair and intelligent conclusion. I have always been inclined to view with horror these experimental operations on living animals, and before I made the investigations to which I refer would have put myself on record as being heartily in favor of a bill to prevent them. But now, after going into the subject most thoroughly with experimenting surgeons of the highest repute, I am convinced that there is much to be said in favor of animal experimentation.

In the first place, it would seem that the dog itself is benefited by the scientific knowledge that necessarily follows on vivisection operations. In fact, there is evidence to prove that such diseases as distemper and hookworm can now be relieved because of knowledge based on these experiments.

There is also the matter of the discovery of insulin. The whole history of this triumph of science rests on studies made on the dog.

Also I want to cite the work of Dr. Whipple[2] in tracing the formation, transformation and regeneration of pigments in the body. By experimenting with the effects of food in dogs' stomachs, he discovered that liver feeding was far more effective than muscle or meat feeding. This clue was then taken up by Dr. Minot,[3] a blood disease specialist, and led finally to a method of preventing that previously baffling disease, pernicious anemia.

I might go on to include many other instances of benefit to mankind resulting from experimental operations on living dogs, not the least of which is our present knowledge as how to take blood pressure, but I feel that those I have outlined are sufficient. They are sufficient for me, at least, to arrive at the belief that distressing as these experiments are to think about, they lead to too much useful information to allow me to vote in favor of their abolishment.

Thanks for the opportunity of expressing myself on this subject, and also for your commendatory personal interest.

Very truly yours,

1. Mrs. Farrell in a letter of 6 January 1931 had asked Dreiser to support a bill before Congress prohibiting experiments upon living dogs in the District of Columbia.
2. Dr. George H. Whipple (1878–1971), who was to be awarded a Nobel Prize in 1934 for his research on bile production in the liver.
3. Dr. George R. Minot (1885–1950), a Harvard blood disease specialist who shared the 1934 Nobel Prize in Medicine with Whipple.

To Burton Rascoe [TS-BRUP]

Rascoe (1892–1957) was a prominent newspaper columnist and literary critic, initially in Chicago and then in New York. A longtime supporter of Dreiser, he published in 1925 Theodore Dreiser, *a brief laudatory account of his life and work. In an attempt to correct Rascoe's recent retelling of the* Sister Carrie *suppression story, Dreiser here concentrates on the issue of the distribution and sale of the first edition.*

THEODORE DREISER[1]

200 West 57th Street,
New York City,
April 13, 1931.

Dear Burton:

I have just read a clipping of your comment in the American of March 21st.[2] The account in the Colophon is correct.[3] Doubleday Page & Co. never sold any copies or, if they did, I never received any check or money of any kind from them.[4] The exact truth is that six years after they suppressed the book, I encountered their lawyer of the time, Thomas F. McKee,[5] who may still be selling legal advice somewhere in New York. He told me that at the time that they decided to suppress the book, they called him in and asked him, in case they did not distribute any of the books but merely held them, whether I would have cause for legal action, and he advised them that I would.

However, being very young and timid at the time, I knew nothing of this, and thought nothing of any legal action. It seemed to me as though the decision of a publishing firm such as Doubleday Page & Co. was final in my case. It was only some four years later when I had begun to work for Street and Smith as one of the editors of their boys libraries, that I managed to save enough money to buy from J. F. Taylor & Co., to whom they had sold the plates, etc., such books and sheets as were still remaining at the moment. I do not recall the number. I think that altogether there may have been a hundred or so bound copies of SISTER CARRIE which I gave away to relatives and friends. The remaining sheets, I forget how many, were bound, not re-bound, by B. W. Dodge & Co. and constituted a part of the second edition of the work.[6]

If Doubleday Page & Co. sent me a check there should be some record of it in their office. If this is of any interest to you, you might persuade them to produce it.

Dreiser

1. Dreiser wrote by hand on the upper left corner of this letter: "Confidential—not for publication until after the check question is investigated & settled."
2. Rascoe, "Book Notes," *New York American*, 21 March 1931, 17.
3. Dreiser's "The Early Adventures of *Sister Carrie*," *Colophon* Part 5 (March 1931), n.p.; reprinted as an introduction to the 1932 Modern Library edition of *Sister Carrie*.

4. In his column, Rascoe had referred to Vrest Orton's *Dreiserana* (1929), in which Orton claimed that Doubleday's records indicated sales of more than 400 copies, from which Rascoe inferred that Dreiser must have received some royalties. Doubleday, Page & Co.'s several statements to Dreiser (at DPUP) reveal a total sale of 456 copies of the first edition and a total royalty of $68.40.

5. Thomas H. McKee (not Thomas F.) told Dreiser about Doubleday's actions in 1907 when McKee was involved in the management of the *Broadway* magazine and Dreiser was its editor.

6. In fact, Charles A. MacLean, Dreiser's friend at Street & Smith, bought the plates from Taylor in 1904; Dreiser then bought them from McLean in 1906. The Dodge edition of the novel appeared in 1907.

To Anna Strunsky Walling [TS-Hun]

During May 1931 Dreiser wrote a number of letters to prominent writers and public figures (in addition to Walling these included O. G. Villard, Elmer Adler, and Carl Sandburg) enlisting their support in defense of the Scottsboro Boys, a group of eight young African Americans sentenced to death for the rape of two white women in Scottsboro, Alabama. Walling (1879–1964), who had coauthored The Kempton-Wace Letters *(1903) with Jack London, was married to the prominent English socialist William English Walling and was herself politically active. After the case gained national attention, the men were granted a stay of execution and in 1932 the Supreme Court reversed their convictions. Both the National Committee for the Defense of Political Prisoners and the International Labor Defense were Communist-front organizations.*

THEODORE DREISER

May, 1931.

Dear Friend:

May I write you concerning a National emergency?

The state of Alabama has set July 10th as the date for the judicial massacre of eight children. It took three days in all for a Scottsboro, Alabama court to try, convict and sentence these eight boys to death in the electric chair—lynching sublimated by legality.

The charge was rape. But the charge was an afterthought. The boys— Negroes, fourteen to twenty years of age—were arrested for stealing a ride on a freight train. Two white girls, in overalls, were also found "hoboing" on this train. The Sheriff asked the girls if the Negro lads had molested them. They said no. But, after a short stay in the Sheriff's custody, the girls made the charge. No time was allowed for an investigation or the gathering of evidence. The Court would not permit any questioning by the defense to prove what is a matter of record,—that the girls are notorious prostitutes and irresponsible,-yet the eight boys were sentenced to be executed solely on the conflicting and unsubstantiated testimony of these two prostitutes, to the cheers of a mob of 10,000 and the music of a brass band.

Time is short. Eight lives are in imminent danger. We are organizing a committee to halt this judicial lynching. We are asking for funds to secure a new trial for the boys—and give them their chance to prove their inno-cence. Our Committee is working in cooperation with the International Labor Defense which is defending the case; money is urgently needed for lawyers, investigators, minutes, and the other inescapable expenses.

Won't you please contribute what you can, today? I am enclosing a slip to fill out and a return envelope.

Very sincerely yours,

Theodore Dreiser

P.S. This is the first step of the National Committee for the Defense of Political Prisoners, now in formation. The Scottsboro case is our imme-diate issue in our fight against the present epidemic of racial, industrial, and political persecutions in our country. The Committee already includes Lincoln Steffens, Burton Rascoe, John Dos Passos, Suzanne La Follette,[1] and many others.

1. La Follette (1893–1983), a cousin of Senator Robert M. La Follette, was a feminist journalist and reformer.

To Ernest Boyd [TS-BLYU]

The Irish-born Boyd (1887–1946) had moved to New York in the early 1920s and had quickly achieved success as a literary critic and journalist. (He and Dreiser were soon to be two of the coeditors of The American Spectator.*) Dreiser's outburst about Jews in the entertainment world may have arisen because of his difficulties with Horace Liveright, Jesse Lasky, and Joseph von Sternberg—all Jews—over the film version of* An American Tragedy.

THEODORE DREISER

200 W. 57th Street,
New York City,
May 1, 1931.

Dear Boyd:

I was sorry the other night about the sudden injection of the criticism of the Jew as an American producer or writer of purely individual musical comedies. As you know, no sane man, even those who entertain positive racial prejudices, deliberately maligns the individuals of the race. Among my personal friends are many Jews whom I enormously admire. One of these chances to be Dr. A. A. Brill; another Abraham Cahan of the Jewish Daily Forward.[1] One of my greatest philosophic admirations is for the mind and viewpoint of Spinoza.

Nevertheless, I reserve the right to pass criticism on the actions of any portion of any race that I consider detrimental or offensive to me.

I had no idea that Madeleine Davidson was a Jewess.[2] As a matter of fact, I think she may be mistaken. Such things have happened before. She certainly doesn't look the part and would have to bring in testimony, but just the same, I want to explain this to you personally, so that you will understand that no personal affront was contemplated and that no feeling on my part could possibly attach to any expression of opinion from either myself or anyone else.

The dinner was enjoyable up to the moment of the TNT. It might have been called ideal.

Have you forgotten about the letter from L'Ordre? As I understood it, you were going to either glorify or demolish France in 500 words.[3] When you explode after your characteristic fashion, let me see the result.

All my love
Dreiser

1. For Brill, see Dreiser to A. A. Brill, 20 January 1919; for Cahan, see Dreiser to Abraham Cahan, 23 December 1921.
2. Madeleine Davidson has not been further identified.
3. The Paris magazine *L'Ordre* wrote Dreiser on 17 April 1931 requesting his opinion about contemporary French life and culture. Dreiser apparently passed the request on to Boyd, who had lived for many years in Europe.

To Frank Crowninshield [TC-DPUP]

Dreiser's response to Paramount's imminent release of a film version of An American Tragedy *which he strongly objected to was to enlist the support of the literary community in defense of the freedom and integrity of artists and their work. (This was a tactic he and H. L. Mencken had employed earlier during the struggle over the banning of* The "Genius." *) In late April, he wrote to almost two dozen New York literary figures outlining his objections to the adaptation and inviting them to participate in a committee which would view the film and determine whether or not it violated the thematic and artistic integrity of the novel. (For an example of this letter, see Dreiser to Harrison Smith, 25 April 1931, in Elias,* Letters, *II, 526–30.) Dreiser, in his 6 May letter to Crowninshield (1872–1947), the prominent editor of* Vanity Fair, *is replying to several issues raised by Crowninshield in response to Dreiser's invitation.*

200 West 57th Street,
New York City,
May 6, 1931.

Dear Crowninshield:

Despite the fact that one paragraph in this contract permits additions and subtractions, Paragraph 10, as well as preliminary verbal understandings with the attorneys for Paramount-Publix covered the fact fully that the ideographic structure of the book was not to be altered. True, it was to be filmed in such a fashion as would meet whatever censorship limitations there are governing the movies, but in regard to that and to the ultimate complete plan for the movie, I was to be consulted.

The completed plan or script from which Mr. von Sternberg[1] constructed his play was never really shown me. I saw rushes of things which were not in the script as furnished to me at all. Furthermore, it was actually admitted in Hollywood by von Sternberg and others, that the ideography of the thing which I presented was stronger and better for the movie purposes than the one in hand and would require but a reel or two further to bring the whole idea of the book into focus, but he also stated in the presence of the attorneys that the Company itself, in other words, Mr. Schulberg,[2] would not permit of changes owing to brevity of time in which the film was done and the reel limitations which had been set.

If you will re-read my letter carefully, you will see that I am claiming that the underlying idea of the book cannot reasonably, in equity, be distorted. There is nothing in the contract which says that it can be and my personal understanding with these people was that it was not to be altered. As a matter of fact, I was assured that Mr. von Sternberg as well as Mr. Hoffenstein[3] were very enthusiastic about the idea of the book as it was, and in their work would approximate it as nearly as possible. It is for this reason and for this reason only that I have entered into this argument.

That it is a sound one is proved by the fact that it has already borne fruit. Eugene O'Neill and Sinclair Lewis are now to be allowed to supervise their productions.[4] Before this argument began, no such thing was possible. There isn't an author on record who was ever permitted to do the same.

1. For Josef von Sternberg, see Dreiser to Samuel Hoffenstein, 18 February 1931.
2. B. P. Schulberg (1892–1957), general manager of Paramount productions.
3. For Samuel Hoffenstein, see Dreiser to Samuel Hoffenstein, 18 February 1931.
4. O'Neill's play *Strange Interlude* (1928) and Lewis's novel *Arrowsmith* (1925) had recently been acquired by film companies, but since O'Neill was later deeply disappointed by MGM's film version of his play, Dreiser's statement may not be entirely accurate.

To Arthur Pell [TC-DPUP]

Pell, who had been treasurer of Horace Liveright, Inc., Dreiser's publisher, became head of the firm when Liveright was forced out in early 1930. Clarence Darrow (1857–1938), one of the nation's most famous defense lawyers (he had defended the radical Big Bill Haywood, the murderers Leopold and Loeb, and the biology teacher J. T. Scopes), was also noted for his iconoclastic views on many issues. No such book as proposed by Dreiser appeared.

200 West 57th Street,
New York City,
May 25, 1931.

Dear Pell:

This is a memorandum of the Darrow idea.

I think really one of the most readable and effective thought or philosophy books of this time could be gotten up out of the lectures, the interviews, the debates, and the public statements of Clarence Darrow,—the matter he has spoken of over the country and written for magazines, newspapers, etc. etc.

I have never yet read a statement of Darrow's that was not arresting and thought-provoking in the particular field in which he was mentally moving.

A series of heads could be laid down, things such as Religion, Philosophy, Law, Taxation, Economics, and others, and under these heads or related ones, could be put down in the same extended form in which he presents them, the different things he has said. I can't imagine a book that would be more readable or more salable, because he has not only absolutely matchless courage, but brilliance and wide knowledge of what he is talking about, as well as an iron and driving style which makes for delightful reading and I think, too, it would make for wide mental development in this country, if properly distributed.

I would like to see such a book gotten up and would really like to direct the nature of it. The simplest way would be to prepare the data and arrange the whole thing without annoying Darrow too much, and then just show it to him.

If an introduction were needed, almost anyone would be glad to write such an introduction. I don't think one would be.

To Carl Van Doren [TS-PU]

After some delay, Paramount's version of An American Tragedy *was shown to the eighteen members of the* An American Tragedy Review *Committee (see Dreiser to Frank Crowninshield, 6 May 1931) on 15 June. Van Doren (1885–1950), a member of the committee, had taught at Columbia University and was a well-known literary historian and critic as well as editor of* The Literary Guild, *a book club. The committee found the film far inferior to the novel, but Dreiser's suit to enjoin Paramount against showing the film was dismissed on 22 July.*

THEODORE DREISER

200 West 57th Street,
New York City,
June 1, 1931.

My dear Van Doren:

Mr. Lasky[1] has written me that the film of AN AMERICAN TRAGEDY, Hollywood form, will be ready for a private showing not later than the 15th of June. He suggests that that date would be acceptable to him. The place would be in the large projection room in the Paramount-Publix Theatre Building.

I wish to know now if it will be convenient for you to meet with the other members of this Committee, a list of whom is enclosed, on June 15th, at 3.30 p.m. Will you be good enough to let me know as soon as possible in order that I may arrange with Mr. Lasky?

After the film is shown, I would consider it a great advantage, as well as a pleasure, if I could personally confer with the Committee for a few minutes, either in the theatre or at my studio here. Such a meeting following upon the showing of the picture would be over, I should think, by 5.30 p.m. If this is acceptable to you, you might signify your decision as to that also.

Again, my thanks for your co-operation.

Theodore Dreiser

1. For Lasky, the head of Paramount, see Dreiser to Jesse L. Lasky, 14 March 1926.

To Herbert Hoover [TC-DPUP]

The government had been deporting alien anarchists and other radicals since the turn of the century, a practice which it continued against alien communists in the 1920s and 1930s. The International Labor Defense, the organization that had helped found the National Committee for the Defense of Political Prisoners (see Dreiser to Anna Strunsky Walling, May 1931), had taken up the cause of the two figures Dreiser names in his letter. It is not known whether President Hoover saw this letter, since his files reveal that it was routed by his secretary to the secretary of labor, who acknowledged its receipt to Dreiser.

200 West 57th Street,
New York City,
June 2, 1931.

My dear Mr. President:

For sometime, I have been reading of attempts to deport to their native lands aliens who are considered undesirable by the Government of the United States. In several cases, because of political conditions in the foreign countries involved, these aliens will, without doubt, be executed upon arrival.

There is, for instance, Guido Serio, anti-Fascist refugee, who is to be deported to Italy. He has a visa for the Soviet Union, and is willing to go there at his own expense.[1] Press reports indicate that he will be executed if he is handed over to the Fascist militia. There is Tao Hsuan Li, Boxer Indemnity Scholarship student, who is to be deported to China, where, I read, he faces certain death for his revolutionary activities. He, too, is to be denied "voluntary departure" for the Soviet Union.[2] And there are other cases.

I am wondering if there isn't some remedy which can save people from this unreasonable deportation. This country, which fought a war for mental independence, is now sending men to death for their opinions. It seems to me that this is the same form of Czaristic tyranny which produced the exile system in Russia, and the reprisals of the Nihilists,[3] and all that has followed since.

Is there not, Mr. President, some actions which you can take, or cause to be taken, which will prevent this inhuman and unreasoning application of the anti-anarchist laws?

I am

Respectfully yours,

1. In October 1931, a U.S. district court judge for New York ordered that Serio, if he so desired, be deported to the Soviet Union as an alternative to Italy.
2. In September 1931, the U.S. Department of Immigration agreed that Li be permitted to accept deportation to the Soviet Union rather than China.
3. Nihilism, a late nineteenth-century Russian revolutionary movement, included a belief in the necessity of violent acts against the state. The movement was ruthlessly suppressed by successive Tsarist governments.

To Anna Mooney [TS-BLUC]

Tom Mooney (1882–1942), a San Francisco labor leader, had been sentenced to death in 1916 for participating in the bombing of a San Francisco pro-war rally. After considerable outcry against the sentence, it was commuted to life imprisonment in 1918. His cause was taken up by the international left during the 1920s, and Dreiser himself became interested in it in 1928. In May 1930, he visited Mooney at San Quentin prison and within the next few days pleaded Mooney's case to Governor C. C. Young; Fremont Older, editor of the San Francisco Call-Bulletin; and the publishing magnate William Randolph Hearst. In November 1932 he was a speaker at a Free Tom Mooney rally in San Francisco. Anna Mooney, Tom Mooney's sister, was active in the various organizations fighting for his release, which did not occur until 1938.

THEODORE DREISER

200 West 57th Street,
New York City,
July 6, 1931.

Dear Miss Mooney:

I have been as active in the behalf of Mooney as anybody, perhaps more so than many. I have published articles; I was the one who really forced Governor Young, when he was in office, to read the testimony in connection with Mooney, and at least offer some excuse for his inaction. I personally visited different individuals in power in California in order to induce them to work in Mooney's behalf. One of these appealed to and personally visited was William Randolph Hearst who appeared to be anxious to do what he could, but it seems that the American corporation attitude toward Mooney and, in fact, any defender of labor, is sufficient to overpower all opposition. It silences judges and their courts, legislators and every other form of public official.

It is not necessary for anybody today to say that Mooney is not guilty or that he was fraudulently convicted. It is plenty to say that being innocently and fraudulently committed, after fifteen years in prison, he is still there, and that in the face of the fact that quite all of the fair-minded sentiment of the world has already appealed for his release. I wish that this letter might accomplish it.

Very truly yours,
Theodore Dreiser

To Dear Sir [TC-DPUP]

The National Committee for the Defense of Political Prisoners, of which Dreiser was chairman (see Dreiser to Anna Strunsky Walling, May 1931), determined in October 1932 to mount a campaign to make known the plight of the miners of Harlan County, Kentucky, by organizing a committee of prominent citizens to visit the area and investigate its conditions. Dreiser's letter of 14 October was sent to such figures as Senators George W. Norris of Nebraska and Robert M. La Follette of Wisconsin, the newspaper publishers Roy Howard and William Allen White, and Felix Frankfurter, then a professor of law at Harvard.

NATIONAL COMMITTEE FOR THE DEFENSE OF POLITICAL PRISONERS
80 EAST 11TH STREET, ROOM 430, NEW YORK, N. Y.
MINERS DEFENSE[1]

October 14, 1931

Dear Sir:

As chairman of the committee for the Defense of Political Prisoners, I ask you to join a group of statesmen, educators, clergymen and writers who are going to enter the Harlan, Ky. coal fields and investigate the Harlan reign of terror. A complete summary of the terror would require volumes. Some of the typical outrages are as follows:

March 2: Two hundred men lose their jobs because they attend a meeting of the United Mine Workers of America. (American Federation of Labor)

162 • *Theodore Dreiser*

Dreiser at Harlan, November 1931.

April: Wholesale evictions, in some cases with only thirty minutes' notice. The law requires several days' notice. One miner not allowed to cross bridge when evicted, but forced to ford river with his household effects.

April: Deputies instituting terror interfere with due delivery of United States mails by forbidding miners access to post offices located in company stores. Miners attempting to get mail jabbed in ribs with guns and otherwise threatened.

April 18: Bill Burnett wounded three times by posse of deputies, and indicted for murder when he shot back in self-defense.

May 5: The Battle of Evarts. Miners raked by machine gun fire. Deputies and miners killed. Terror increased.

May 6: Circuit Court Judge Jones calls handpicked Grand Jury and institutes judicial terror against miners. Family of Judge Jones interested in mine properties. In selecting Grand Jury, Judge Jones actually refused to read off names unsatisfactory to him. Hand-picked Grand Jury returned thirty triple murder indictments, thirty indictments for "banding and confederating" and one for criminal syndicalism.

There were no indictments returned against those who had killed miners and perpetrated other outrages against them.

June: Deputy Bill Randolph kills Chasteen, a restaurant man in sympathy with the miners. Randolph's arrest insisted upon by the National

Guard. Randolph jailed, allowed a private room, a radio and other unusual privileges.

Randolph later acquitted.

This case is an example of the manner in which the terror is aided and sustained by the courts. Sympathizers who are not killed are framed, indicted, jailed and intimidated—until they promise to leave the county. Whenever able to make a deal that will take sympathizers out of Harlan, authorities drop trumped-up charges.

July 11: Allan Keedy, theological student and preacher in the Evarts church, arrested and charged with obstructing justice—because he tried to bring certain facts to light. Framed evidence presented against Keedy—who was released when he promised to leave county.

July 23: Jessie Wakefield's car dynamited. Mrs. Wakefield brought relief to starving prisoners' families. No arrests followed the dynamiting of her car—and no investigation.

July 25: Twenty-eight additional thugs imported to augment sheriff's staff sustaining "law and order". Among these thugs were gunmen from Breathitt County who were known to be fifty dollar killers—that is, they would kill a man for fifty dollars. At least two of these thugs were pardoned from the West Virginia penitentiary on condition that they join the "deputies" terrorizing the mine community.

Prosecuting Attorney Will Brock of Harlan told the above to Arnold Johnson, theological student and field worker for the American Civil Liberties Union—and that criminal dockets were closely watched and deals made to release notorious murderers if they would join the Sheriff's group of terrorists.

(yes, Harlan is in Kentucky, and Kentucky is in the United States of America)

July 28: Bruce Crawford, Norton, Virginia, editor—shot. Arnold Johnson told he would be killed the next time he crossed the bridge leading to his home, and his home dynamited if he remained.

July 29: Dynamite exploded in yard of Jason Alford's home. Reason—Alford an organizer for the National Miners Union.

July 30: Wholesale raids on homes in Wallins Creek, cars stopped, all passengers subjected to illegal searching. These raids continued for four days in a wave of increased terror. Property and homes destroyed, men, women and children bullied and brutalized—all this by way of attempting to halt the miners' convention.

Aug. 7: Charles Walker of Evarts arrested and jailed because he said: "You couldn't get justice in Harlan County, and that's why I've been careful of what I say and do."

Aug. 8: Henry Thornton, Negro organizer of National Miners Union, taken from his home by four Deputy Sheriffs, threatened with death, severely beaten and slugged with guns on lonely mountain road—then brought into jail with gaping scalp wounds, charged with drunkenness, held in jail for fourteen days, tried by a jury which included Deputies—found guilty and fined.

Aug. 9: McKinley Baldwin taken from home by night, carted away by deputies, chained to a tree and beaten. Cause: Activity on behalf of miners.

Aug. 10: Strikers' soup kitchen dynamited and completely demolished. This kitchen had been feeding four hundred women and children every day.

First we have the terrors of feudal industrialism—starvation wages, inhuman conditions, cheating checkweighmen, company shacks and profiteering company stores—all making for strife.

Second we have the terrors of modern industrial strife, the suspension of civil and human rights, the due process of law being perverted and subverted in an attempt to kill and coerce striking miners.

Third we have a sustained terror of starvation directed not only against the miners, but against their women and children. Soup kitchen atrocities culminate in:

Aug. 30: Deputy Sheriff Lee Fleener makes night attack on soup kitchen, driving up without warning, turning his headlights into the faces of three men at the kitchen, immediately opening fire—killing Joe Moore and Julius Baldwin, and shooting Jeff Baldwin in the back.

Fleener never indicted, now at liberty.

There are many more actual instances of the terror. But these will suffice. Now as the manner in which the terror is sustained. Upon his own admission, Judge Jones kept the jury wheel in his office all summer. The wheel contains the names from which members of all juries are chosen—and for a judge to have it in his office is a direct violation of both the letter and spirit of the law.

The judicial terror has used three other means of attack: First, insisting upon extraordinary bonding requirements. Second, ordering changes of venue which give distant courts jurisdiction, making it practically impossible for starving miners to transport their witnesses. Third, requiring defendants to make promises of leaving the county before being released.

The facts themselves form a terrific indictment, an indictment of those who own and operate the mines, indictment of the Harlan authorities who sustain this bloody travesty of "law and order".

A Grand Jury of prominent Americans is going into Harlan to investigate the details of this indictment. Will you come along?

Our party will meet in Lexington, Kentucky, on November fifth, and will proceed to Harlan on the sixth.

May I request your immediate reply.

Most sincerely yours
Chairman

1. The left margin of this letterhead contains the names of the fifty-one members of the National Committee for the Defense of Political Prisoners.

To Roy W. Howard [TC-LC]

Despite showing some interest in joining the delegation, Howard (1883–1964), chairman of the Scripps-Howard chain of newspapers (which included the New York World), chose not to participate. Indeed, all the other prominent figures Dreiser had contacted also declined, and in the end the group consisted entirely of NCDPP members and other radicals.

Hotel Ansonia,[1]
New York City,
Oct. 29, 1931.

Dear Roy:

I was very glad indeed to learn from you today that there was a possibility of your joining the delegation to investigate conditions in Harlan, Kentucky, and you may be sure that any person you select to accompany us will be equally welcome.

Assuming that you may be interested to go, I am putting before you the detailed plans of the delegation, so that you may have an idea of just what will be done.

At present, the delegation consists of John Dos Passos, Bruce Crawford, editor of Crawford's Weekly at Norton, Virginia, Charles Rumford Walker, who is well known for his writings in connection with the steel industry, Anna Rochester, author of Labor and Coal, Lester Cohen, author of Sweepings, Samuel Ornitz, author of Haunch, Paunch and Jowl, and Josephine Herbst, a novelist.[2]

It has been found more convenient for the delegation to meet at Pineville, Kentucky, than at Lexington, as this latter town is only thirty miles from Harlan. There is a fast train leaving Pennsylvania Station on Wednesday, November 4th, at 2.30 p. m., which arrives in Cincinnati at 7.45 the next morning. A Louisville & Nashville train leaving Cincinnati at 9.00 a.m. reaches Pineville that afternoon at 2.15. I understand that there is a very nice hotel at Pineville—the Continental.[3]

The National Miners Union is arranging for a mass meeting of miners to welcome the delegation at Pineville, and this meeting will be more or less a test of the rights of the miners to free speech and assemblage. It may not be permitted.

However that may be, on Friday morning the delegation will proceed to Harlan by automobile, to the Lewallen Hotel. From there will issue trips to Evarts, scene of some of the shootings, and to Straight Creek, where 6,000 miners are now out on strike. Possibly others, also. Miners, operators, Sheriff Blair and Judge Jones will be interviewed.[4] It is planned to remain until Monday, the 9th.

In order to get all the necessary data, it will probably be necessary to divide the delegation into groups of two or three, one going here and another there. Stenographers, a managerial guide, etc., are already arranged for. It occurs to me that while you might not be inclined to undertake any of this work, you might find it valuable to be there as an observer. Such deductions as you might make should serve as a guide in this changing political scene of ours.

I hope sincerely that you and anyone you may select will find it possible to make this trip.

Dreiser

1. In late September 1931 Dreiser had given up his Fifty-seventh Street apartment and moved to a suite in the Hotel Ansonia, on Broadway and Seventy-third Street. The Ansonia was to remain his New York City address until February 1935.

2. Dos Passos (1896–1970), whose *Nineteen-Nineteen*, the second volume in his *U.S.A.* trilogy, had recently appeared; Walker (1893–1974); Rochester (1880–1966); Lester Cohen (1901–1957); Ornitz (1890–1957); and Herbst (1897–1969). Dos Passos, Cohen, and Ornitz were members of the NCDPP. In the end, Anna Rochester and Josephine Herbst did not make the trip.

3. The group reached Pineville on 5 November and departed on the morning of the 9th.

4. A stenographer recorded the various interview sessions, which were published in March 1932 as *Harlan Miners Speak: Report on Terrorism in The Kentucky Coal Fields* . . . with an introduction by Dreiser. Sheriff John H. Blair and Judge David C. Jones were Harlan County officials controlled by the mine owners.

To Editors [Tel-UI]

Dreiser was accompanied on the Harlan journey by a young woman whom he introduced as Marie Pergain. On the night of 6 November, she was observed entering his Pineville hotel room; when toothpicks then placed at the foot of the door of his room were discovered undisturbed the following morning, a grand jury was quickly convened and a charge of adultery was brought against Dreiser. Dreiser learned of the charge while on a train returning to New York and had Bruce

Crawford issue a statement to the press on the incident. The story of the charge against Dreiser and his riposte received national attention.

NOTE TO EDITORS

BRISTOL, VA.—TENN., NOV. 9—FOR YOUR INFORMATION THE COMPLETE TEXT OF THE STATEMENT WHICH THEODORE DREISER GAVE OUT TONIGHT THROUGH BRUCE CRAWFORD IS AS FOLLOWS:

"YOU MAY SAY THAT IT IS USELESS FOR BELL COUNTY TO SPEND MUCH NEEDED MONEY IN INVESTIGATING ME. I AM IMPOTENT, AND I DON'T BE-LIEVE THE NOTORIOUS AND ALL-POWERFUL LAW OF KENTUCKY CAN COMPEL AN IMPOTENT MAN TO COMMIT ADULTERY. I DO ENJOY THE COMPANIONSHIP OF LADIES. I AM FOND OF THEIR CONVERSATION. BUT I AM IMPOTENT AND THE PERJURED EVIDENCE OF JUDGE JONES COURT WOULD BE POWERLESS TO PROVE OTHERWISE."

THE A.P.

To Max Eastman [TS-LLIU]

On 13 November 1931, Eastman (1883–1969), a well-known radical journalist, wrote Dreiser complimenting him on his response to the editorial charge. "I have no adjective to describe it," Eastman wrote, "for it is both funny and sublime—an event in the cultural history of man."

THEODORE DREISER

Hotel Ansonia,
New York City,
Nov. 20, 1931.

Dear Eastman:

Thanks for your letter. You are the first, of all those I know, to get the real point I was trying to make.

Regards—
Dreiser1

1. Added to the letter in Eastman's hand is the note: "I expressed my pleasure in his telling the reporters, when he was arrested in Harlan for sleeping with a girl, that he couldn't have, he was impotent. It was in all the papers—look it up. I know upon the most intimate possible authority that he was *not* at the time impotent." The "intimate authority" Eastman cites was no doubt Yvette Szekely (1913–). Szekely and Dreiser had had become lovers in February 1930; when she and Eastman also became lovers, in January 1931, she appears to have informed Eastman of her ongoing relationship with Dreiser.

To Nazife Osman Pasha [TC-DPUP]

Pasha, the American correspondent of a Turkish newspaper, wrote Dreiser on 16 November 1931 from Los Angeles requesting his reply to a number of questions.

Hotel Ansonia,
New York City,
November 21, 1931.

Dear Madam,

The following is my reply to your questions for your interview with me.

What do I think respecting differences of the intelligence of men and women, their contributions to civilization and the possibilities of achievements in the future?

I believe there is no difference between the intelligence of men and women. To date, psychologists have offered no convincing data that women are less brilliant than men and vice versa. Of course, it is true that in the large, women have not accomplished as great achievements as men. However, women's part is not all on the surface. Many women of unusual mental gifts have influenced history vastly more than is realized by reading the usual summaries of it. The woman is naturally to be protected because she is the one who bears children. Her role as mother naturally puts her in the position of a comforter and aide to man rather than the one who takes the initiative or who puts the project through. This naturally brings it about that the man accomplishes the ideals and sees them through. There have, however, been notable instances of women geniuses. I cannot think of a field in which they would not accomplish as much as men. However, whether they ever will be equal with men in this sense, I question. Firstly, the ingrown prejudices of centuries would have to be overcome. Secondly, women seem happier in the subordinate role which they almost naturally pick out for themselves. I think it is perfectly true that more and more women are likely to take a hand in ruling the world. This is because silly prejudices and silly tripe are being overcome.

Do I believe that if women had ruled the world, we would have a better civilization without war and misery?

My answer is no. I consider that some of the most vicious, selfish, ruthless characters in all history have been women. I think it is these strong individualists who with their domination over the masses have caused war and misery that could be mitigated not in my opinion by the supremacy of women. Rather, I feel that both men and women in the masses of society are on the whole opposed to war from a humanitarian point of view, yet war enriches the few at the top who inspire the masses to carry it out. In carrying it out, both men and women strive with nearly equal spirit. Although men do the actual fighting, women become animated and inspired with vast organization and relief work in war.

As I view present civilization, it is on the whole unworthy of the name.

You ask if principles of civilization are based upon selfishness and hardship?

They most certainly are. The world is so organized that everywhere, except in Soviet Russia, the masses are preyed upon by the so called constructive geniuses at the top. The rich can erect monuments, build palaces, buy yachts, etc., while the masses in agony and human misery flock right around these riches and display. What is more, civilization does not seem to be working toward mitigating these outrages. On the other hand, they are even extending them not only by gaining control through industrial employment of so called uncivilized races, but also making that control limited more and more to a few enormous trusts and cartels.

I do not consider that the World War had a noble inspiration. Rather, I look upon it as an outrageous slaughter for the enrichment of a few great corporations which supplied the vast quantities of oils, ships, uniforms, ammunition, and all sorts of equipment needed to carry it out.

Now, do I consider a civilization really complete without a universal peace?

I do not. But I do consider that a universal peace would be one of the most difficult achievements of mankind. It could never come about without equity among all men. It is difficult to conceive the high state of teaching and improvement necessary to bring this about. Without a high state of development, one race or group is bound to be oppressed and until no race is oppressed is universal peace possible.

You ask if I consider that women's equal participation with men in handling the World's affairs may lead the world to a better humanized civilization.

I think that women should participate in World affairs as much as they want to, but I dont necessarily think that it is their participation which is going to humanize the world. Rather, I think this equity can come about only by the vigilance of the common people and the supremacy of their interests over the selfish few who control the laws.

Yours truly,

1932

To Hector Audino   [TC-DPUP]

Audino had written Dreiser on 4 April 1932 suggesting that he follow up his Tragic America *(published in December 1931) with a book examining the proposition that all men are created equal. "This early American declaration," Audino wrote, "has been ridiculed from so many quarters that it stands discredited the world over outside of Russia. Yet to-day, we have a much more scientific basis for believing such a theory than our forefathers had in 1776."*

Hotel Ansonia,
New York City,
April 11, 1932.

Dear Mr. Audino:

It is absolutely true that science and even economic development itself has proved that although all men are not created with equal ability, at least they are created equal in the opportunities which should be afforded them to further their abilities, whether small or great. As Marx put it succinctly: "From each according to his abilities to each according to his needs."

As for writing another book, now is not the time. I have already written one book which, if carefully considered, is sufficient to accomplish, really, all such changes as would bring about an equitable arrangement here or anywhere. What is actually needed is organization and intelligent and sympathetic co-operation with a view to conferring not only as to ways but means as well, and with these in hand, action, action to achieve a better social arrangement about which so many are now thinking. If when you say "I stand ready to assist you in your courageous work" you mean that you are practically interested in developing such an organization, I would be very glad to know it.

My thanks for your letter.

To Carl Van Vechten   [TS-BLYU]

Van Vechten (1880–1964), a well-known novelist and photographer, had played a major role during the 1920s in encouraging and popularizing black artists of the Harlem Renaissance. For Dreiser's earlier efforts on behalf of the Scottsboro Boys, see Dreiser to Anna Strunsky Walling, May 1931.

THEODORE DREISER

Hotel Ansonia,
New York City,
April 14, 1932.

Dear Van Vechten:

Because of your interest in the Negro, I am seeking a little help from you.

You know all about the Scottsboro case or, if you don't, the enclosed data will explain it. Anyhow, with no reasonable provocation, the death sentence for seven of them has been confirmed by the Alabama Supreme Court, and the execution date set for May 13th. The National Committee for the Defense of Political Prisoners is staging a big demonstration at the Bronx Coliseum on May 8th, to raise funds for the further defense of these boys in an appeal to the United States Supreme Court.

In this connection, they have asked me to interest, if possible, Paul Robeson to come and sing, and also, if possible, Roland Hayes and, should these fail, Hall Johnson and his group.[1] So far, I have been unable to find out where either Robeson or Hayes is. I wrote Hayes, in care of his agent in Boston, several days ago, but evidently my letter hasn't reached him. I wonder if you know where they are, and also I would like to know if your interest in the Negro would permit you to urge Robeson or Hayes or both, and the Hall Johnson group, to evince, through their art, their sympathy and their protest against the injustices heaped upon their race.

Personally, I have cabled Shaw[2] asking him to speak over the telephone to the audience, since his speech could be amplified at the hall. Melvin Levy, secretary of the N. C. D. P. P. has suggested, since he has information that Paul Robeson is in Europe, that he might sing from there over such a hook-up, unless he intends to return before the date of the meeting.

The time is very short, and those who are arranging the meeting are anxious and worried. Let me know if you can do anything for them.

Regards—
Dreiser

1. Paul Robeson (1898–1976), a famous African American actor and singer; Roland Hayes (1887–1976), an African American tenor; and the Hall Johnson Choir, an African American group led by Francis Hall Johnson (1888–1970).
2. George Bernard Shaw (1856–1950) often supported left-wing causes.

To George Jean Nathan [H-Cor]

Dreiser had known Nathan (1882–1958), a well-known editor and a prolific writer on drama, since 1916 through Nathan's association with H. L. Mencken in the editing of the Smart Set *and the* American Mercury. *Within a month of his letter to Nathan, Dreiser, Nathan, and several other literary figures were to be engaged in plans for a new journal, the* American Spectator. *Dreiser and Mencken had quarreled in 1926 and were not to resume their relationship until 1934.*

Hotel Ansonia
Broadway 73rd and 74th Streets
New York
April 27—1932

Dear George:

Unquestionably some of the slams dealt by Mencken are deserved. They are true. On the other hand his strictures are so wholly based on an almost idolatrous devotion to the Kaiser or super-man idea:—Everything for the strong nothing for the individual who is not a superman that at times he borders on the ridiculous.[1] Strength does not go without weakness. The superman is not even imaginable without the individual who is not superman. He rises by reason of his presence. The individual is not concievable without the mass from which he takes his rise and against which as a background—and so only—he can shine. I would have more respect for the ramping trumpeting individualist if only he had the brains to get this. I would have more respect for him if the moment strength fails him he did not always fall back upon the courtesy or the charity of the weak.

The individualist who holds himself separate and independent is to me, a fool. He is a part of organized society (which means everybody) [word missing] uses it—all of its equipment—machinery, laws, libraries, restaurants, farms—in short the labor of all & then poses as independent. For my part I hold him a debtor to the society he flouts & and the working weakling whom he so grandly chooses to spit upon. Noblesse oblige would suggest and equitable break for the millions who make life bearable for him. We are all needed a little—no one much.[2] Emerson said that[3] but its true just the same.

Regards
D

1. Dreiser appears to be alluding not to a specific work by Mencken but rather to his early favorable estimation of Friedrich Nietzsche's philosophy of the superman and to the more recent hardening of his anti-democratic beliefs during the late 1920s. Of course, Dreiser himself, some twenty years earlier, had sympathetically depicted a Nietzschean protagonist in *The Financier* and *The Titan*.

2. Dreiser in these remarks attempts a reconciliation between his earlier belief in the inevitable presence of both the powerful and the weak in social life and his 1930s emphasis on the need to provide an "equitable break" for the latter.

3. I have not been able to find this comment in Emerson's works.

To Bennett A. Cerf [TC-DPUP]

Cerf (1898–1976), the founder and head of Random House, and Morris Ernst (1888–1976), a well-known civil liberties lawyer, were seeking to gain testimonials from major writers on the literary qualities of Joyce's Ulysses *before challenging the United States Customs ruling that the work was obscene. The American ban on importing or publishing the novel was successfully overthrown in a landmark case of 1933.*

Room 709,
1860 Broadway,
New York City,
May 13, 1932.

Dear Mr. Cerf:

As you and Morris Ernst know, I have always regarded the attempted censorship of any book as one of the most absurd of all unintelligent human actions. I do not need to mention its futility. Books, banned or boosted, are read by those who wish to read them.

But, of course, I despise and deplore the attitude which prompts the censorship of any book, as well as the wholly unnecessary inconvenience and annoyance to which it puts those connected with it.

ULYSSES is, of course, a highly intellectual work. To read it is to spend a day inside a seeking and profoundly observant human mind, to learn its mysterious wanderings and secret paths. And because it is what it is, some things enter into it which are not generally recorded. But, and for precisely that reason, these things add to its value as an amazing, if not unique, social and literary document.

Naturally, I hope that you are victorious, and promptly, in getting by with it.

Very truly,

To Edmund Wilson [TS-BLYU]

Although Wilson (1895–1972), a significant voice in American literary and intellectual life for almost all his career, was soon to withdraw from support of left-wing positions, he was still active in radical causes when he sought Dreiser's endorsement of his manifesto.

THEODORE DREISER

En route
San Antonio
Texas
June 4, 1932

Dear Mr. Wilson:

I must ask you to excuse the long delay in replying to your letter.[1] As you probably know, I left New York some time ago on an extended vacation. Your letter, (I never received the first which you say you sent) enclosing a manifesto which you asked me to sign, was received while I was in process of leaving. And because of travel, mail delays, and the like, I have found it simply impossible to keep up with correspondence.

I have read and considered your manifesto with the greatest interest. It expresses an attitude as well as a method which I have maintained and expounded for years.[2] In fact for the last ten years I have constantly emphasized and argued the responsibility as well as the obligations of the individual to organized society from which he derives and whose benefits he shares. I have held that he personally is responsible for its equitable functioning and for its constant improvement. More, I personally have urged intellectuals in America as well as the world over, to unite and labor in order to bring about a social state such as your manifesto emphasizes. As a matter of fact, I. W. L.,[3] an organization whose proclamation I requested be sent you, took its rise from criticism as well as advice which I offered to the group which made up The National League For The Defense Of Political Prisoners.[4] Sometime before your manifesto reached me, the proclamation of I. W. L. was brought me for endorsement. I then endorsed it. Also I pledged it my undivided support.

Feeling that the multiplication of organizations of the same ideals and principles can only weaken a struggle which requires the undivided support of all who agree with those ideals and principles I see only harm, not good, in joining your group. If you had been the first to come to me instead of the second I would have joined with you. As it is I must stand by I. W. L. until it becomes plain that it as an effort is a failure.

Regretfully, and cordially yours,
Theodore Dreiser

1. Wilson's letter, with its enclosed manifesto, is dated 2 May 1932. Both the letter and the manifesto were published in Wilson's *Letters on Literature and Politics, 1912–1972*, ed. Elena Wilson (New York: Farrar, Straus and Giroux, 1977), 222–23.

2. The manifesto, after noting the world economic crisis, called upon all intellectuals "to identify their cause with that of the workers" in order to achieve a
"social-economic revolution . . . based on common material possessions." John Dos
Passos, whom Wilson had also asked to sign the manifesto, raised questions about
its wording, and publication of the document was delayed and then shelved.

3. The Intellectual Workers League, a short-lived Communist-front organization.
For Dreiser's qualified endorsement of the aims of the I. W. L. during this period,
see Elias, *Letters*, II, 586–89.

4. For Dreiser and the National Committee (not League) for the Defense of
Political Prisoners, see Dreiser to Anna Strunsky Walling, May 1931.

To Otto Kyllmann [TS-TU]

*Dreiser's appeal to Kyllmann, his English editor, for information about English
life reflects one of the difficulties he faced in his efforts to complete* The Stoic.
*(He was not to do so until shortly before his death in late 1945.) For Dreiser's
earlier effort to enlist Kyllmann's aid in authenticating the British background of*
The Stoic, *see Dreiser to Otto Kyllmann, 17 April 1929.*

THEODORE DREISER

El Paso, Texas
June 15th. 1932

Dear Kyllmann:

I am out here on the Mexican border, the country where men are men
. . . working on THE STOIC, which you are presently to publish. Really
this territory belongs to two of your favorite novelists, Harold Bell Wright
and Zane Grey.[1] But I have invaded their preserve in order to catch a
little inspiration, so far, however, without any great success. Just the same,
however, right over the Rio Grande, which is only about five minutes from
where I am writing, is Mexico and the city of Juarez where I can get all the
liquor I can pay for. And I am looking to that for help.

It was awfully nice of you to send me that picture of, was it Egdon Heath?
Anyhow, the Heath which you and I walked over and which I enjoyed so
much.[2] The rain, the rainbow, the English hunters, the ginger beer, that
little sea town in which we spent the night. . . . It is all as fresh as though
it were yesterday and I wish I might come over. As a matter of fact, if it
were not for a pending law suit in New York, I would. But until I know
positively whether I am to be let out of that for the summer, I cannot tell.[3]
If I should hear favorable news at any time, I will cable you. Meanwhile
here is something with which you must help me if you will.

As you know, quite a little of THE STOIC, perhaps as much as one-half, takes place in London with side excursions to the Continent and New York. The London part is so important that I want all that is done so far, which is forty chapters, about one-half of the book, gone over by someone who is thoroughly familiar with English law, English social, financial, political ways and states, as well as the Continent, Paris, Monte Carlo, and the various sea and health resorts, for the period in which this book is laid, 1900 to 1908 inclusive. What your reader should do is to catch all of the errors and anachronisms which occur in the worlds which I am trying to describe. Whoever does the reading is going to find a lot of misapprehensions and mistakes on my part in regard to British law, British financial methods, British social and class distinctions, errors, possibly, in connection with contacts that could never come about, errors in regard to expressions used by the English in contrast to those customary to Americans at that time, and so on. No doubt I am making all my Englishmen talk like Americans which is exactly what I don't want. And equally, no doubt, I am putting lawyers and financiers and perhaps even society people in streets, places, clubs, and the like where they would never be. But if so, whoever it is who reads this script for me, will be able to bawl me out and at the same time substitute the right things. Would that it were your genial self.

I am willing to pay for the work, of course. I remember with pleasure that lawyer who edited your magazine, THE NINETEENTH CENTURY, who took me over The Inns Of Court and to Cambridge. He would be the one, I should think, to look at the law and financial portions, unless you have someone else in mind.[4] Anyhow, here is what I want to do. By the time you get this letter, I shall have ready to send you as I said, the first forty chapters, typewritten. I would like it if you would cable me c/o Evelyn Light, Secretary, Room 709, 1860 Broadway, New York, and simply say O.K. If you do Miss Light will immediately forward from New York the copy she has. And then if you will have the work of severe criticism, plus all necessary corrections or substitutions rushed and the forty chapters sent back quickly to Miss Light, I will use that first half as a guide in revising the second. That is, the mistakes which are found in the first half will not be found in the second.

My friend Arthur Pell, of Liveright, Inc.[5] is scheduling this book for August first. But I am sure it will have to be a little later than that. And I am writing him to that effect. Just the same the novel should be completed by August first and after that it will be all a question of how much time is required to print and distribute it. Pell always insists, to me at least, that it takes about six weeks to set up, print, and distribute a book, one of mine, anyhow. That would make the publishing date about September 15th. But this time I propose to avoid corrections on any of the galleys which should hasten the day of publication not a little.

Anyhow, please cable me at once as to this. When I get to England, if I do, I'm going to try to persuade you to come back here to the West Coast, where with your name and a pocket machine gun, you should be able to shine as one of your own Zane Grey's heroes.

Affectionately,

Dreiser

1. Dreiser may be facetious; Wright (1872–1944) and Grey (1875–1939) wrote bestselling westerns.

2. Dreiser is recalling his stay with the Kyllmann family during his visit to England in October 1926. In his letter to Dreiser on 19 August 1932, Kyllmann noted that they had walked on Exmoor, in Somerset, not on Egdon Heath, which is in Dorsetshire.

3. Dreiser is probably referring to a threatened lawsuit by William Reswick arising out of Dreiser's involvement in the aborted Bolshoi Ballet tour in 1929 (see Dreiser to Ralph T. Holmes, 21 February 1929, and Swanberg, *Dreiser*, 394).

4. This figure has not been identified.

5. Pell (see Dreiser to Arthur Pell, 25 May 1931) had for the most part been running the Liveright firm while Horace Liveright was in Hollywood.

To Ernest Boyd [H-BLYU]

The American Spectator *was planned as a literary monthly, in large-page format, which would publish short, provocative pieces by prominent writers. Since the journal would contain no advertising, it would pay very low rates to contributors. George Jean Nathan (see Dreiser to George Jean Nathan, 27 April 1932) and Ernest Boyd (see Dreiser to Ernest Boyd, 1 May 1931), both of whom had considerable editorial experience, were the managing editors, and Dreiser, Eugene O'Neill (see Dreiser to Eugene O'Neill, 7 May 1919) and the novelist James Branch Cabell (1879–1958) added literary prestige to the editorial board. In fact, Dreiser devoted a great deal of time and energy to the journal during the period he was connected with it, from the summer of 1932 to January 1934, principally in soliciting and reading contributions.*

THEODORE DREISER

June 27—1932

Dear Boyd:

The business of The American Spectator was never settled. Nathan spoke of arranging the details but what are they. Who owns the thing? Who directs it? What am I?—a kindly contrib. Or what? What is its policy and when and where was it fixed upon. I note that it is to omit "all *social* and political references."[1] I can understand the political. But the social: How does one escape that? Is it to be like the last paper you worked on?[2] I see only reportorial reports, imaginative flights, ala Irving and philosophical comments ala Voltaire (if only one could achieve them). When I understand all I will report.

Sorry I cant give you a direct address. Am working on The Stoic and gypsying. But a letter address care E. Light, Secretary, Room 610, 1860 Broadway will duly reach me. Had to get out of N.Y. to work. Regards and always my affection.

Dreiser

You can also address Iroki, R.F.D.-3, Mt. Kisco.

1. Dreiser is quoting from a joint letter by Boyd and Nathan on 17 June 1932, in which they noted their expectation that he would "be able to let us have something for the first issue which will be, of course, in your characteristic vein but omitting all social and political references, inasmuch as we have decided that the review will ignore that side of things." Dreiser's difficulty in convincing the other editors that the *American Spectator* should address contemporary social issues was to be a sore point throughout his relationship with the journal and led ultimately to his resignation from its editorial board.

2. Boyd had edited *The New Freeman* the previous two years.

To Thomas Burke [H-HRHUT]

A characteristic Dreiser letter soliciting a contribution to the American Specta-tor. *Burke (1886–1945), an English author, was best known for his* Limehouse Nights: Tales of Chinatown (1916). *Dreiser had met him during his 1926 visit to England.*

THE AMERICAN SPECTATOR

A LITERARY NEWSPAPER

Mt. Kisco, N.Y.

Sept 3—1932

Dear Burke:

Here is something that should interest you,—a literary newspaper that involves no trace of cowardice and that prints as it is written. Naturally though in view of its mental determination all contributors are by invita-tions. And we sit in judgement not on morals or conventions but on mental force and appeal. Since it is international I personally want to see something by you—the color & thoughts of London or England or Burke on the world in general.

The reward is really—good company. The actual cash is 1 cent a word and the space limit from 500 to 2500 words. No more. Would you suggest something. This is not only a personal but an editorial invitation—all five concurring. And if only you would suggest some other stirring mind. I cannot tell you how much *personally* I would prize 2000 last ironic & salty words from George Moore. If only that were possible.[1]

Anyhow write me a word.[2] When the first issue appears—and you should be in it—you will see how interesting, varied & internationally far flung are the minds & viewpoints.

Theodore Dreiser

1. The elderly English novelist and memoirist Moore (1852–1933) was seriously ill.
2. Burke contributed the essay "This Bibliography Nonsense" to the *American Spectator* 1 (May 1933): 3.

To Ernest Boyd [H-DPUP]

Wednesday
[After 9 September 1932][1]

Dear Boyd:

I sent you two articles by *Bruce Crawford*—one on the possibility of *dictatorship* in America—the other a Virginia neighborhood description cut by me [word missing] the Virginia Quarterly Review.[2] No comment on either article has been made either to me or apparently to Crawford. Since I desire the Virginia quarterly article for myself and to say something to Crawford about the other, I find it necessary to ask you & Nathan to act on the matter. I am fearful of one thing & that is that a very narrow & highly literary & above all severely specialized critical range is likely to be sought by you and Nathan—as opposed to the larger and easier range of human comment and color which appeals to me. Since in the first category we have had The Nation, The New Republic, The Freeman, The Dial and God knows what also. All narrow ranged & and more or less profitless ventures. I personally am opposed to this possible viewpoint—so much so that it is fatal & final with me. I propose a broader field in which I can take a lively mental interest. Less than that will cause me to cease effort & retire. Nonetheless—

Affectionately
Dreiser

1. Although undated, the letter was written after 9 September 1932, the date on which Boyd thanked Dreiser for sending him Crawford's articles, and before 22 September 1932, when Boyd returned the article on dictatorship in America to Crawford.

2. Crawford, a radical Virginia newspaperman, had accompanied Dreiser on his investigation of conditions at the Harlan coal mines (see Dreiser to Roy W. Howard, 29 October 1931). Crawford's Virginia article, "Piney Ridge, Virginia," appeared in the *Virginia Quarterly Review* 8 (July 1932): 371–84. In a letter to Dreiser on 29 September 1932, Boyd reported that Crawford's article on dictatorship in America was too long for the *Spectator*.

To Marion Foster Wotherspoon [TC-DPUP]

In the course of a visit to Los Angeles in early November, Dreiser attacked in an interview the activities of the Red Squad, a special unit of the Los Angeles Police Department, headed by Captain William F. Hynes (1896?–1952) and devoted to disrupting left-wing meetings and demonstrations. Mrs. Wotherspoon (1863–1944), a journalist, was a member of the Pasadena branch of the American Civil Liberties Union.

c/o The American Spectator,
12 East 41st Street,
New York City.
Nov. 22, 1932.

Dear Mrs. Wotherspoon:

It was very courteous of you to call me up in connection with the civil rights war in Los Angeles. I was very busy at the time, so busy that I really could not give any more than a few minutes to anything.

Nevertheless, as I told you, I was very much interested in your desire for a conference with me in regard to the activity of Captain Hynes in Los Angeles. I would have been glad to talk with you as I would have been to talk with the Secretary of the Civil Liberties Union who also called me up, but it was impossible for me to arrange it.

However, I wish, if possible to interest you in the program in connection with Captain Hynes which is being looked after by Samuel Ornitz, c/o R. K. O. Studios, phone, Ho:5911, (home, 1632 N. Martell, Hollywood, Phone, Grant:0823). Mr. Ornitz, who is a writer of position and who has valuable connections with R. K. O., was with me in Kentucky, one of the most valuable advisors and assistants that I had there.[1] He is not a Communist; he cannot even be called a radical, but he is sincerely interested in the social and economic rights of the public, the masses as well as the classes everywhere. Solely for the purpose of constructive effort, he has aided financially, not only through his own purse but those of others, the efforts of the International Labor Defense in Los Angeles. Along with Lincoln Steffens and some others, he came to San Francisco to help with the monster Mooney demonstration at which I spoke while I was there.[2]

He is sincerely interested in building up or strengthening any effort that looks to the ending of such social abuses as Los Angeles has suffered from Captain Hynes and others.

The one night that I could give to this work, he managed, through his friends and my presence, to raise fifteen or sixteen hundred dollars for work in connection with some local social-abuse causes.

He is very much interested to organize a public attack on the methods of Mr. Hynes which he is satisfied will bring results. These plans he laid before me, and he would be only too glad to do the same for you or the Civil Liberties Union or any other person or organization who is interested in this very unsatisfactory situation.

I write this letter asking you to co-operate with him and help organize this thing because I believe the plan he had in mind is the one. It could result in very arresting publicity and probably in quieting Captain Hynes as well as abuses of the kind which he represents. I told him to call you up and try to get in touch with you and also with the Civil Liberties Union man who had previously telephoned me. If you see any way in which the various public-spirited people there could be joined up on this contest, I wish you would let him know and, furthermore, I wish, if you are sufficiently interested, that you would communicate with me in connection with it.

Very truly,

1. Ornitz (1890–1957), who had made a great success with *Haunch, Paunch and Jowl* (1923), a novel of New York Jewish life, moved to Hollywood in 1928 to become a screenwriter. He had accompanied Dreiser to the Harlan coal fields in November 1931 (see Dreiser to Roy W. Howard, 29 October 1931).

2. Dreiser spoke at the San Francisco Mooney rally on 6 November 1932; for Dreiser and Mooney, see Dreiser to Anna Mooney, 6 July 1931. Steffens (1866–1936), the famous turn-of-the-century muckraking journalist, supported many radical causes during the 1930s.

To S. Anargyros [TC-DPUP]

During the winter of 1932–33, Dreiser was planning a film, in collaboration with the dramatist Hy Kraft (see Dreiser to John Howard Lawson, 10 August 1928), on the 1907 revolt of Kentucky and Tennessee tobacco farmers against the Duke tobacco trust. After quarreling with Kraft in the spring of 1933, Dreiser continued to work on the script independently but never completed it. S. Anargyros, a P. Lorillard executive, replied on 7 January 1933 that it was against company policy to permit factory visitors.

care The American Spectator,
12 East 41st Street,
New York City.
December 30, 1932.

Dear Sir:

I am investigating the possibilities of writing a novel based on the tobacco industry, and I address you to ask if you would be good enough to allow me to make a tour of your factory, so that I may acquaint myself with the general process of cigarette manufacture.

I shall be very grateful for any courtesies you may extend.

Very truly,

1933

To Francis H. Bangs [TS-BLYU]

Bangs was preparing a biography of his father, the turn-of-the-century popular humorist John Kendrick Bangs (1862–1922), whom Dreiser had known early in their careers when Bangs was the editor of Harper's Weekly.

THEODORE DREISER

The American Spectator,
January 9, 1933.

Dear Mr. Bangs:

Yes, your father and I were on very good terms. I think that it was in 1901 I met him.[1]

Originally, WHENCE THE SONG was sold to Harper's Magazine, and then, for some reason, transferred to Harper's Weekly,[2] but THE COLOR OF LIFE, 1901, was submitted, if I recall correctly, to Harper's Weekly, and Bangs sent for me, praised it, and said that he wanted other material from me if he could get it.[3] I did one thing more, CHRISTMAS IN THE TENEMENTS,[4] but after that my general state was such that I really could not attempt the kind of work that would have been acceptable to him.

We became very friendly. He was exceedingly cordial and, later, when I took charge of the Broadway magazine, came in, I believe at my request, to see me about THE IDIOT ON BROADWAY.[5] Just what followed then I cannot now recall. I know that shortly after I put the Broadway in editorial shape for success in that field, Hampton[6] decided that he wanted to run a more serious and economically critical magazine, on the lines of McClure's, if possible.

We were still working on that idea when I left to take charge of the Butterick publications. Later, around 1907 or 1908, when I became connected with the B. W. Dodge Co., I suggested to Dodge that he get Bangs to submit a book, which he did,[7] and I recall meeting him in the office of B. W. Dodge, which was then on 27th street.

Altogether, he was always cordial to and appreciative of everything that I did and, needless to say, his work, especially THE BICYCLERS and THE HOUSEBOAT ON THE STYX[8] appealed to me as delightfully humorous compilations.

Very truly,
Theodore Dreiser

1. Bangs, in his letter to Dreiser on 29 December 1933, asked a number of specific questions about Dreiser's relationship to Bangs's father, beginning with the sketches Dreiser contributed to the Christmas number of *Harper's Weekly* from 1900 through 1902.

2. "Whence the Song," *Harper's Weekly* 44 (8 December 1900): 1165–66a; reprinted in *The Color of a Great City* (1923). Bangs was on the editorial staff of *Harper's Monthly* until November 1899, when he became editor of *Harper's Weekly*.

3. Dreiser means "The Color of To-Day," *Harper's Weekly* 45 (14 December 1901): 1272–73; reprinted in *Twelve Men* (1919) as "W. L. S."

4. "Christmas in the Tenements," *Harper's Weekly* 46 (6 December 1902): 52–53; reprinted in *The Color of a Great City* (1923).

5. Dreiser edited *The Broadway Magazine* from April 1906 to June 1907. There does not appear to be any Bangs work with this title; Dreiser probably means Bangs's book of sketches *The Idiot* (1895) or its sequel, *The Idiot at Home* (1900).

6. Benjamin B. Hampton (1875–1932), the publisher of *The Broadway Magazine*.

7. Bangs's *The Autobiography of Methuselah* was published by B. W. Dodge in 1909.

8. Two of Bangs's most popular works, both published in 1896.

To Peter A. Bogdanov   [TC-DPUP]

Bogdanov was chairman of Amtorg Trading Corporation, an organization established in New York by the Soviet Union in 1924 to further trade between the United States and Russia.

January 13, 1933.
Peter A. Bogdanov,

Dear [word missing]

As you probably know, I am connected, as one of the five editors, with The American Spectator, a literary newspaper now in its fourth month. A copy of the latest issue is being sent you, and I feel sure that I do not need to point out that the paper is not commercial in intent, but offers itself as a world forum for distinguished viewpoints, aesthetic, economic, humane.

Since the paper started, I have been endeavoring to get the names and addresses of Russians who might be asked to contribute to it. Not only that, but I would like a five or six or seven hundred word signed statement from Stalin on anything he chooses to talk about. For instance, if he would like to deny that he lives richly and is guarded by machine guns, and explain that the truth is that he lives very simply and is not guarded, such a statement would be really priceless for this paper.

Another thing I would like is a sketch—several sketches—not on the theory and practice of Communism, or anything relating to the five year plan or to the completion of any great work, but some human interest sketches, little pictures of how the farmer and the worker actually live, but without Communist dogma being brought in in any form.

Another brief sketch might relate to the Russian medical system as it now functions, not so much in the clinic as with the visiting doctor—the man who goes to see the patient too sick to come to him. Further, I would like someone to present in light, gay and very human colors the way the Russian educational system is applied, for instance, to the people in the extreme north of Siberia, the wandering tribes that inhabit that region.

Also, I have been told about Professor Koltzoff,[1] who has been experimenting with a new rejuvenation treatment, and I would like a thousand-word article by him on his discoveries, methods, etc.

The reason I go into these details is to indicate the type of material we seek and how valuable we believe just this sort of thing to be, and what I need and want are the names and addresses of really clever Russian writers, poets, critics, humorists, who can be told about this paper and asked to contribute to it.

As you know, I am constantly being asked by the editors of Russian publications for statements on various matters. Within the month, I have sent such a statement to the paper SMENA. On my desk there are requests for contributions from PRAVDA and from ZA RUBEZHOM. To such requests, in past years, I have responded and responded; my books are translated and printed in the U. S. S. R., sold to the profit of the Russian Government, but not to me; I am constantly doing this and that to assist Communist issues here in America, making or soliciting contributions to them in one form or another, and yet when I ask for connections of the sort mentioned above, I get nowhere. I have written Dinamov[2] several letters on this matter, but have received no assistance.

To the two papers above mentioned, I am replying that I would like to respond, but that until I receive some recognition of my services and needs, I scarcely feel inclined to continue this work of writing articles, sending cables, etc. at my own expense. And I cannot see that this reply is anything but equitable.

Certainly there can be nothing but advantage to the U.S.S.R. in having an outlet through a medium like The American Spectator, and I cannot understand why it is necessary for me to struggle so to get this really simple and only courteous assistance.

May I not ask that you be good enough to put me in touch with the people who can be notified about this paper and asked to contribute to it? Possibly you could give me a letter of introduction of some sort, or, if not that, just a list of names and addresses and your permission to say that you supplied them?[3]

With best regards,

1. Probably Nikolai Koltsov (1872–1940), a prominent Russian geneticist.
2. For the Russian editor Sergei Dinamov, see Dreiser to Sergei Dinamov, 14 March 1927.
3. Bogdanov replied on 20 February 1933 that he had forwarded Dreiser's request to Karl Radek, an editor of the Russian journal *Izvestia*.

To William Aspenwall Bradley [TS-HRHUT]

Bradley (1878–1939), the major American literary agent in Paris during the 1920s and 1930s, had been asked by Dreiser to consider the American Spectator *as an outlet for his clients. Dreiser's letter contains an outline of the often complex editorial relationship between Nathan, Boyd, and himself, the three editors largely responsible for the contents of the journal.*

THE AMERICAN SPECTATOR

A LITERARY NEWSPAPER

January 28, 1933

Dear Mr. Bradley:

I have your letter of the 12th. First, let me thank you very much for your courteous and sympathetic reception of my request. It is much appreciated, and I feel sure that your interest will prove a valuable asset to us.

As to the editorial policy,[1] it may seem a little exclusive to your foreign authors, but I might explain that we have found it best to ask prospective contributors to send us suggestions for possible articles—one, two, six, a dozen. These are then discussed here, and we, in turn, indicate the items which seem most likely to get under the mark. Or, on the other hand, their suggestions may inspire counter-suggestions on our part. If we all agree here on the value of one or more suggestions, the finished article will, as you can understand, very likely be accepted and used. If the opinion is not unanimous, but appeals strongly to one or two, then these latter may be depended on to do whatever they can to persuade the others. As for myself, you may be sure that I will do my utmost to have accepted those things which seem important to me. But I, as one editor, cannot, of course, say that this will always be possible, because the viewpoints here are so individual and varied.

I feel sure that if you present the case in this way, the conditions will not appear as stringent as otherwise they might.

As to the article AN INVITATION TO AMERICAN HISTORIANS by Bernard Fay,[2] I haven't seen it, but I assume you understand that we would not want to use anything which has been widely publicized before. Possibly you refer to a method rather than to material, and if that is so, of course, we should like to know more about it. And about the other authors you mention, and any suggestions they may have.

As to Ford Madox Ford,[3] I wrote him sometime ago, but the letter was returned. Now I am writing him in your care, and I hope you will add your efforts to mine, so that he may be persuaded of the importance of this paper's purposes.

Again, my thanks for your interest.

Very truly,
Theodore Dreiser

1. In his letter of 12 January, Bradley had noted that both the editorial procedure and the level of payment of the *American Spectator* constituted problems for most European-based authors.

2. The historian Fay (1893–1979), a friend of Gertrude Stein (also one of Bradley's clients), was a prominent French commentator on American subjects. Fay's article "An Invitation to American Historians" appeared in the December 1932 *Harper's*.

3. Bradley had also suggested as a prospect the English novelist Ford (1873–1939) who was at that time living in France.

To Clyde Beck [TC-DPUP]

Beck (1884–?), was literary editor of the Detroit News. *For John Maxwell's book on the authorship of Shakespeare's plays, see Dreiser to Benjamin W. Huebsch, 21 June 1920.*

The American Spectator,
February 17, 1933.

Dear Mr. Beck:

I recall with pleasure our meeting in the office of the STAR in Indianapolis, about 1915, I think.[1]

Poor old Maxwell! I wanted so much to get his book on Shakespeare edited and published, but he would never permit its being cut and I never could find a publisher who would invest the money necessary to publish so long a work, particularly since the size of its sale was such an uncertain quantity.

Nevertheless, I still feel that the book should be published, but somehow it seems more hopeless than ever, because now his son has it, and apparently has a complex in regard to letting any publisher or anyone else have possession of the copy even long enough to examine it. The whole thing is fantastic because the book contains very important material and, true or false, should certainly be added to the Shakespearean controversy.

In regard to SISTER CARRIE: There are copies occasionally offered.[2] I saw one advertised in, I believe, The Publishers' Weekly, a year or so ago. The price was over $300. I think there was one auctioned by Silo which brought $750. I would not know what to suggest in regard to this, but in so far as first editions of the others are concerned, they are easy. For instance, a person should be able, to this day, to pick up a first edition of JENNIE GERHARDT for two or three, at the most, four, dollars. I think copies of the second edition of SISTER CARRIE which was the first distributed edition, can be purchased for as low as $4.50.[3] In fact, I have seen them. I should think dealers could advise you as to all that.

Stuart P. Sherman! I recall your telling me the story of your fateful quarrel with him over my books. I also recall, with a sense of something mystical, his death by drowning in the boat with that girl he took out on a lake in the summertime. He must have been obsessed by the TRAGEDY.[4]

Regards.

1. The meeting Dreiser refers to probably occurred in July 1919, when Dreiser was in Indianapolis to visit Maxwell, then a reporter on the *Star*.
2. In his 26 January 1933 letter to Dreiser recalling their meeting, Beck also enlisted his aid in acquiring a first edition of *Sister Carrie*.
3. The 1900 first edition of *Sister Carrie* was in fact "distributed" (that is, offered for sale) by Doubleday, Page but was not advertised or otherwise pushed; the 1907 second edition was published by B. W. Dodge.
4. Stuart P. Sherman (1881–1926) had written a powerful and widely known negative critique of Dreiser's work—"The Naturalism of Mr. Dreiser," *Nation* 101 (2 December 1915): 648–50—but reversed his position in a review of *An American Tragedy*—"Mr. Dreiser in Tragic Realism," *New York Herald Tribune Books*, 3 January 1926, 1–3. After Sherman died while canoeing in August 1926, Dreiser came to believe that Sherman was accompanied by a girl he was having an affair with, who also died, and that both the reversal of his critical opinion of Dreiser and the circumstances of his death were in some way related to the illicit love affair and tragic boat accident in *An American Tragedy*. In fact, Sherman was accompanied in the canoe by his wife, and he died of a heart attack while swimming ashore after it overturned.

To Llewelyn Powys [TC-DPUP]

Dreiser met Llewelyn (1884–1939), the youngest of the three Welsh-born and literary Powys brothers, in San Francisco in 1921. Dreiser had written him, along with many other literary friends, soliciting contributions to the American Spectator.

Iroki, Dreiser's Mt. Kisco Estate.

March 11, 1933.

Dear Llewelyn:

The four papers you sent created not a little enthusiasm around the house at Mt. Kisco. Everybody who read them applauded heartily.

Down at the office of The Spectator, the question of a series came up, and they are almost unanimously against a series, but we are taking the last two, and I am returning the first two.[1]

You say something about The Spectator paying so little. It actually does not make a penny. It sells for ten cents, as you know, and there is just enough out of the general cost to cover the contents at one cent a word. All of the editors give their services free, and if anything more were paid, they would have to contribute to a pool out of which larger prices would be paid. The feeling of all of them, because of the free service rendered and the advertising import which the combination naturally achieves, is that expenses should not be charged to them. As you know, it does make a rather remarkable medium and one which is freely commented on here. Actually, I think it ranks higher critically than any other paper in America. At least, all of the writers and editors of the country appear to think so. They give it special space and comment. It does not need to advertise, because it gets a much more valuable type of advertising in the form of discussion. That is why all of the editors feel that writers should be content with one cent a word for the present, at least. If it ever pays, I think that the rate would probably be raised to two cents.

Personally, though, I wish you would write me and tell me what your actual condition is; how you are getting along, what the state of your health is, and all.[2] As you know, I feel keenly about you and Jack,[3] and I would not want to feel that you were in serious straits which might be helped a little.

Regards.

1. The two which appeared in the *American Spectator* were "Morality," 1 (August 1933): 4; and "Reformation," 2 (August 1934): 13, 15.
2. Llewelyn suffered from tuberculosis for much of his life.
3. John Cowper Powys (see Dreiser to John Cowper Powys, 13 April 1931), Llewelyn's brother.

To Sherwood Anderson [TS-NL]

Dreiser's warning to Anderson about sharp dealing by Hollywood studios appears to stem both from his own recent difficult relationship with Paramount over the filming of An American Tragedy *(see Dreiser to Samuel Hoffenstein, 18 February 1931) and the fact that Horace Liveright, whom he had come to mistrust, had worked for Paramount during the early 1930s. Both Jesse Lasky, head of Paramount, and Liveright were Jews.*

THEODORE DREISER

The American Spectator,
May 12, 1933.

Dear Anderson:

Whatever else you do in connection with Paramount or anyone representing them or any other picture business, for Heaven's sake, do this:

Do not accept conversation in lieu of written data covering all that was said. If something is discussed conversationally, or decided conversationally, ask that it be written out and signed and put in your possession.

Next, in connection with any contract offered you, in the first place avoid signing it until you have had a chance to study it and, furthermore, to have an American lawyer, not a Jewish one, examine the contract for you. Do not take the statement or the paper of any lawyer representing any Hollywood proposition without first turning it over to your own lawyer—always an American—with a view to getting yourself straight.

If you do not do these things, you will probably find that you have let yourself in for complete defeat in whatever it is you wish to do.

Best wishes.
Dreiser

To George Jean Nathan   [TC-DPUP]

In May 1933, Dreiser and the four other editors of the American Spectator *engaged in an "Editorial Conference" on the Jews, which was scheduled to appear in the September 1933 issue of the journal. Dreiser had been the most outspoken figure in the discussion. For Dreiser's anti-Semitism during the 1920s and 1930s, see the introduction, pp. xxvii–xxix.*

26 May 1933.

Nathan:

This editorial conference article cannot go through without a final o. k. from me, as well as an o. k., of course, from the other editors. It involves statements and a point of view which, coming from me, are sure to have national reactions and we will have to be careful of the language.[1] I want to o. k. all my remarks in specific detail.

Dreiser.

1. Dreiser's concern over the "national reactions" to his remarks are also apparent in a later undated letter to Nathan (Cor), in which he asks that all statements made by the *American Spectator* regarding the interview be attributed to the editors in general rather than to him alone.

To Walt Carmon   [TC-DPUP]

Carmon, a communist journalist, had been managing editor of The New Masses *before moving in early 1932 to Moscow to edit* International Literature, *a journal devoted to the worldwide communist movement. Dreiser had contributed the short article "War and America" to the journal's second issue (April–June 1932) and was to make several other contributions as well.*

The American Spectator,
July 4, 1933.

Dear Mr. Carmon:

Needless to tell you, I like INTERNATIONAL LITERATURE very much.[1] I think that from a foreign propaganda point of view, it is the most useful and effective thing that comes out of Russia, and the most interesting.

It does seem to me, though, that you editors might more carefully scan the world press for comments not so much uncritically enthusiastic about Russia but, on the other hand, comments which show plainly and most often unthinkingly the inroads which Communistic ideas are making on the world at large. Summaries of that kind coming out of Russia and being distributed all over the world would not only hearten the believers in Communism but suggest ways and means of furthering the inroads commented upon.

I have recently seen here, in THE NEW YORK TIMES, an account of an address by A. P. M. Fleming of the Metropolitan-Vickers Company of Manchester, England, at the Chicago World's Fair.[2] In this address, he called upon the capitalistic world to unite all its intellectual and inventive and creative force in order to offset the admitted force and effect of united Russia. He said, "Why is it that Russia can do so much more than any capitalistic country, or all of them together, disunited?" and while he is not interested to do anything for the mass, he is anxious to do something for the class by uniting all class genius to this end. That, and related things, are what should appear in INTERNATIONAL LITERATURE.

More and more, as I observe the world, I am satisfied that the Russian revolution is the one and only thing that has opened the door to a better and more equitable, more creative and more humane social order.

Very truly,

1. Carmon had written Dreiser on 10 June 1933 requesting a comment on the first two issues of *International Literature*.
2. William L. Lawrence's "Two 'World Brains' Held in Death Duel," *New York Times*, 1 July 1933, p. 7, reports Fleming's speech. It was delivered, however, not at a World's Fair but at a meeting of the American Society for the Advancement of Science.

To Ludwig Lewisohn [TS-HRHUT]

Lewisohn (1883–1955) was a prominent critic of American literature and novelist of Jewish-American life whom Dreiser had come to know in Greenwich Village in the late 1910s; he had been living in Europe since 1924.

THEODORE DREISER

The American Spectator,
July 5, 1933.

Dear Lewisohn:

In regard to the excerpts for your anthology, o. k. I include one condition, and that is that you indicate the four excerpts.[1]

I fancy that as things are, you must have your problems and plenty, as everyone else seems to be having them, myself included.

How are things in Paris, and how are things in the Palestinian republic, if such it is?[2] For the life of me, I never can understand why the Jews
who, in one place and another, find themselves scored by local or national
prejudices, do not wish really to establish a nation of their own, therein to
exercise their great genius for all phases of life, and to present the world
with an example of an equitable and creative nation sufficient to inspire the
rest of the world to follow its example and leadership.[3] The world certainly
needs that.

Dreiser

1. Lewisohn was preparing the anthology *Creative America* (New York: Harper's,
1933), which includes several excerpts from Dreiser's work.

2. Lewisohn had become an ardent Zionist and had visited the Jewish settlements
in what was then the British Palestine mandate.

3. Although Zionism had a considerable following among European and American Jews during the 1920s and 1930s, many Jews on the left followed the party-line
position that Zionism was a threat to the larger goal of proletarian unity whatever
one's ethnic background.

1934

To Sherwood Anderson [TS-NL]

Since Dreiser had in late 1933 encouraged Anderson to become the sixth member of the American Spectator *editorial board, he felt the need to write him personally about his resignation.*

THE AMERICAN SPECTATOR

A LITERARY NEWSPAPER

January 4th, 1934.[1]

Dear Anderson:

I enclose a copy of a letter just mailed to Nathan, the contents of which he will present to you. My reason for doing this is rather clearly outlined in the earlier letter indicated.[2]

My hope always was that I could at least tinge THE SPECTATOR with a humanitarian and social point of view that would be as forceful as I thought it should be. To a certain extent, it has achieved that, but not without a great deal of difficulty and argument.

Another reason for my wish to withdraw, though, is that the quantity of my present work is so great that I cannot really longer give the time to seeking out and inspiriting the type of material that really interests me, and to do less than that would mean that the policy would be left to the others and that I would be underwriting that as more or less representative of and adequate to my personal mental reactions. Not being willing to do that, I feel that the next best and really only thing for me to do is to sever my connection with the paper.

I remember you asked me whether I intended to remain with THE SPECTATOR, and I told you that I did, and I would be glad to do so if I were not satisfied that temperamentally and intellectually I cannot really align myself with the general program of the paper.

Just the same, I hope that this will not influence you or cause you to withdraw, because I feel that the paper needs very much what you have to give it.

Dreiser

1. The typist's incorrect dating of this letter as 4 January 1933 has been corrected.

2. Dreiser's letter to Nathan of 4 January 1934 is a brief letter of resignation; in it, Dreiser refers Nathan to his letter to him of 7 October 1933, in which he spelled out at great length his disagreement with an editorial policy which appeared to Dreiser to favor the light and trivial over the serious-minded and socially responsive. The 7 October 1933 letter to Nathan is in Elias, *Letters*, II: 642–47.

To William C. Bullitt [TC-DPUP]

Bullitt (1891–1967), a career diplomat, had unsuccessfully argued in 1919 for the recognition of the new Soviet government by the United States; when recognition finally occurred in 1933, after the inauguration of Franklin D. Roosevelt, Bullitt was named ambassador to the Soviet Union. Dreiser sought unsuccessfully for many years to obtain from Russian publishers the royalties promised by his contracts, a failure which especially irritated him given his frequent support of the Soviet Union.

Hotel Ansonia,
New York City.
Feb. 27, 1934.

My dear Mr. Bullitt:

I should like to present to you a circumstance which has, for some years, been a matter of great dissatisfaction to me, and to inquire if you could not have directed to it the attention of some source which might bring it to an equitable conclusion and an equitable continuance in the future. I refer to the publication of my books in Russia, and the small and very irregular returns in royalties.

I know that, in the main, authors have received no return whatever for such publication, or have been entitled only to a return in Russia in roubles, but this instance, by reason of several phases, is somewhat different.

First, there is a contract, copy enclosed, which, on Jan. 17, 1928, I signed with Gosizdat, the State Publishing House, and which calls for the payment of certain lump sums, as well as regular statements, and remittances of earned royalties. Against this agreement, I received only the sum of $486.52; no statements whatever, although these were requested.

In August, 1929, I had a letter from Zimlia i Frabrika which read, in part, as follows:

"We certainly cannot allow our attention to pass over a famous writer such as you are. I know that you have had a contract with Gosizdat for the publication of your works, which was not consummated. Land and Factory is related to Gosizdat and the latter will not publish your books because the contract has been turned over to us. We, of course, are quite free from any obligations in relations with the foreign authors, because of the absence of a literary convention. Nevertheless, in several instances, we are finding it necessary to meet certain authors half-way, with reference to payment for their labors, especially those who have some importance in the cultural world and exert an influence upon the development of mankind in general. In such a category of writers we include you. And we have considered that your labor as a writer naturally has to be paid for. The difficulty arising is that for one book we are compelled to pay both the author and the transla-tor. This, of course, increases the price of the book to a great extent and we are aiming at publishing books as cheaply as possible. This you can see by the cost of your books published in America and in Soviet Russia. Here they can be done for half. Taking the above into consideration and in the absence of certain rules, we can offer for each book which we shall publish $350.00 beginning with October 1, which is the beginning of our fiscal year. On such a basis, we can immediately make an accounting with you for the first book to be published—JENNIE GERHARDT. All the re-editions of what has already been published by Land and Factory will also be paid for at the rate of $350.00 based upon an edition of 6,000 for each book."

To this I replied that I regretted the ignoring of my contract with Go-sizdat, but that I would accept the terms offered by Zimlia i Fabrika. After that, I received from Zimlia i Fabrika two remittances of $350. each, without explanation. I assume that the first was for JENNIE GERHARDT.

More recently, I had a letter dated June 4, 1933, from the State Pub-lishing House of Fiction & Poetry, of which copy is attached. From this establishment, Ogiz, I have had two remittances, one on July 11, 1933 for $645.41; another on Jan 13th of this year for $321.31. To Ogiz, I replied that since their offer represented a considerable reduction from the original contract, and since I had had nothing approaching fulfillment of two previ-ous contracts, I would accept their offer only pending an eventual agreement upon something approximating the original terms, the most important of which, of course, is a continuous 10% royalty on copies sold which should, for some years past, have been reaching me regularly.

To indicate in part the extent to which publication of my books has been carried on, I should like to quote a short passage from an article recently written by a prominent Russian critic, author and editor who, in comment-ing on American literature in Soviet Russia, says, "I remember how they were afraid to publish the collected works of Theodore Dreiser. They were afraid that there would be no sale for his great works. These fears turned out to be unfounded—Dreiser's books disappeared from the bookstores as soon as they appeared, and he rapidly became one of the favourite writers among our Russian readers . . . I will mention the fact that Theodore Dreiser was well known in the Soviet Union long before he began to write about it." (1928.) My book on Russia appeared in the United States in 1928, after I had made a tour of Russia by invitation of the government, so you will see that a considerable number of years is involved. Also, that there has evidently been large publication of my books without my consent, by numerous houses, and without any return to me.

There is another phase in the balance of all this which I feel should not be unimportant in any consideration given this matter by Russian officials, and that is the fact that for years I have given not only my time but my work and money to the end that there might be, not only in this country but universally, a more sympathetic understanding of the ideals of government, to my mind so equitable, enlightened and enlightening, which Russia has set itself. Being sensitive to a high degree of the inspiring example Russia has fixed, and the contrasts elsewhere which, in so many instances are, to my mind, so unfavorable, this has been not only a matter of voluntary expression on my part, but, in numerous and specific instances, it has been indirect response to requests from Russia or from her sympathizers here.

I cannot see, therefore, that it is anything but equitable to request a fulfillment of the spirit if not the letter of the contract into which I originally entered. It is obvious that the sales of my book have reached great proportions, and that an accounting now of the 10% royalty originally intended would represent a considerable sum. However, since I assume, from the fact that regular statements have never been forthcoming, that it is almost useless to request these, I wonder if it would not be possible for you to have proposed to the official sources in charge of these matters that there might now be a lump sum return to me, retroactively representative of the proportion certainly due me from the returns which they, for years, have been collecting.

I am sure that both you and they cannot but see the fairness and justice of this, and I should be most grateful if you could have some such conclusion brought about.[1]

Permit me, in closing, to offer you my best regards, and to express the really great pleasure it gives me to address not alone an American Ambassador to the U.S.S.R., but yourself in particular as that representative.

I am,

Very truly,

1. Bullitt replied initially on 28 March 1934 that the embassy would take up Dreiser's complaint with the appropriate authorities. He wrote again on 14 May 1934, enclosing a letter from Gosizdat which maintained that Dreiser had been paid in full for all he was contractually owed.

To Donald Friede [TC-DPUP]

Friede (1901–65) had been a member of the Horace Liveright publishing firm before he started his own house, Covici, Friede. The issue of how much Dreiser should pay the reorganized Liveright company for his plates, books, and unbound sheets was placed in arbitration and not settled until September 1934.

Hotel Ansonia,
New York City.
Mar. 22, 1934.

Dear Friede:

For your information,[1] I should like to say this:

I had a contract with Liveright, Inc. at the time that Horace Liveright was in charge, and that contract covered the use of all of my past and future works for a period of five years.[2] It did not, however, include any of my copyrights, since I resumed all these at the time when I made this five year contract. I even owned the plates of SISTER CARRIE and at the end of the contract, was planning to purchase all of the plates.

However, the failure of Liveright, Inc. about May, 1933, automatically, because of a clause in my contract, terminated the contract, the only things to be adjusted being any sum of money which I might owe Liveright, or Liveright might owe me, plus the cost of the books and the plates which automatically, under the lapse of the contract, had to be surrendered to me at a reasonable cost.

Immediately upon the failure of Liveright, I sought to obtain possession of my books and plates, but was confronted by the fact that the business, although it was distinctly stated that my books could not be transferred to anyone without my consent, had to be sold as a whole. It was so sold under foreclosure to the highest bidder, and was knocked down to an entirely new group of people. The price paid by these people was $22,000. But once this price was paid by them for all of the stock, copyrights of the authors, etc. of Liveright, Inc. they asked of me personally $28,000. for my plates and $10,000 for my books. This, of course, I refused, because I was not buying either my copyrights or my publishing rights from this organization, but simply my plates in order that I might allow some other publisher to use them.

Automatically, under the contract, this compelled the appointment of three arbitrators, and even this was fought on the ground that the arbitration should arbitrate not only the question of the price of the plates and the remaining bound books in the possession of Liveright, but also the question of some money which I was supposed to owe them, but to which I objected on the ground that under the contract they owed me much more. When this matter was finally settled in the courts, they were compelled to drop the question of any money which I might owe them, and arbitrate solely the question of the value of the plates of 22 books and of 12,680 bound books and 2271 sheets. For the plates, after consulting with various publishers as to what was fair, and considering that nothing except the metal of the plates was involved, since they could neither sell them nor use them, $2,000. was offered by me, and, for the books, 25 cents a copy. They countered with a demand for $8,000. for the plates and, originally, $1.00 a copy for the books. What their demand now is, I do not know.

Just these two prices and nothing else is what will come before the three arbitrators. I am told that $2,000 for the plates, since they cannot be used by anyone but me, is liberal, and that the 25 cents a copy for the books is satisfactory. I have been told this by Bennett Cerf of Modern Library, by Richard R. Smith of Stokes, by Tom Coward of Coward McCann and by A. H. Gross, formerly manufacturing man for Liveright and present manufacturing man for Coward McCann.

Of course, I do not wish to force this conclusion on any of the people whom I am asking to appear and give an opinion, but I am offering the evidence so far with the request that after hearing the other side as well as my side, they independently decide what they think is fair.

Mr. Hume, my attorney,[3] is to be here at the Ansonia tomorrow, Friday, at 4.00 o'clock, to confer about this matter, and while I understand that you were a little doubtful about being able to meet this time, I hope that you can, and I shall be most happy to see you.

My regards.

1. Friede had agreed to appear as an expert witness in the arbitration hearing scheduled for 11 April 1934.
2. Dreiser appears to be referring to his February 1929 contract with Horace Liveright.
3. Arthur Carter Hume, Dreiser's personal attorney for many years.

To Burton Rascoe [TS-BRUP]

Rascoe (see Dreiser to Burton Rascoe, 13 April 1931), a longtime friend and supporter, had included a chapter on Dreiser in his essay collection Prometheans, Ancient and Modern *(1933).*

May 4th, 1934.

Dear Burton,

I finished "Prometheans" practically at one sitting. All in all, I think very highly of it, and for the following reasons:

In the first place whatever the sources of your material, the treatment of it is so modern and engagingly intimate, that I found it delightful. So much so, that I wish it were possible for you to re-survey a great deal of history in just this way. You eliminate all the tedium that goes with stilted, or shall I say carefully phrased scholasticism. Of all the papers in the book, I'm sure I like "St. Mark" the best. The style is, as I say, and the material immensely illuminating to me. At last I have an intelligent line on the origins of Christianity, and I am grateful for that. The next best paper to me, is, "Lucian", with its picture of the Roman world of his day. And after that, I think I like "Petronius" and "Apuleius", and then "Aretino." Personally, I feel that you are a little short of an adequate grasp of D.H. Lawrence's solar plexus theory.[1] However, my reasons for saying this, are too complicated and personal to be presented here. When I next see you, I will tell you all about it. Meantime, have you by any chance the book or pamphlet in which he presents this doctrine? If not, tell me where I can get it.

I think the study of myself is excellent, and sound, but some of your data is a little off. I never wrote anything on a typewriter although in my time I have owned three good ones and gave them all away. Next, I was married almost ten years, and not twelve. And I did not go to Doubleday with a lawyer, for I did not have the money to hire a lawyer. What really happened was that Frank Norris, who was greatly interested to see the book published, urged me to stand on my contract which, as he said, would automatically compel Doubleday to publish it, or lay himself open to damages of some kind. But at that, I never threatened to sue Doubleday. At Norris' suggestion, I talked to him, and asked him if he wouldn't publish it, and he said that if I insisted on it, he would so do, but that was all he would do. He would not advertise or distribute it. At that I wanted to take the thing away, but Norris said, no; that it was really not Doubleday, but his wife who was causing the trouble. And that once the book was in print, and he saw how the critics received it, he would change his mind. Also, he said that he would see that all the principal critics got copies, and that their reaction would certainly move Doubleday to favor the book. But Norris was wrong. For my part, I came to feel afterward that I was wrong also. But I was young and inexperienced, and accordingly left the matter in Norris' hand. True enough, the book was published, but nothing was done for it. It was not even distributed, except to critics by Frank Norris. And consequently, it died, because no copies were furnished to the trade.[2] However, that is an old story, and need not be rehashed by you or anyone.[3]

What troubles me is you yourself. From my talk with you, I gathered that you were for some reason despondent and disheartened, and a little too indifferent to your own very great ability.[4] For a person who can do a piece of work like "St. Mark", can do a lot of very important things. So much am I troubled by this thought, that I am proceeding to lecture you. You have too much to give to think of letting down at this point. You are too young and too gifted. I think you should take yourself sharply in hand, seize on that proposition for instance to re-establish "The Bookman", and when you do, push it vigorously.⁵ I know from reading this book of yours that now you are mentally equipped to make a brilliant success of that, or any thing of that kind. And if you can get a contract, that will safe-guard your returns on the work that you do, it wont be long before you will be free of any financial troubles or complications which now may trouble you. Besides, it would pull you out of the doldrums, if you are suffering from the doldrums. Are you listening? For what I am saying is being said in great sincerity. And I am hoping that you will take it all to heart, and do something about it as swiftly as possible.

Anyhow, let me hear from you, and if you have the D.H. Lawrence book, lend it to me for a week or so. I promise to swipe it permanently.⁶

Affectionately,

T. D.

Hotel Ansonia,

New York, N. Y.

1. Lawrence explains what Dreiser calls his "solar plexus" theory in his *Psychoanalysis and the Unconscious* (1921), in which he argues that man's best impulses and acts arise from the instinctive knowledge centered in his ganglia and plexuses.

2. See Dreiser to Burton Rascoe, 13 April 1931, for Dreiser and Rascoe's earlier exchange on the issue of whether Doubleday sold any copies of *Sister Carrie*.

3. Dreiser had indeed been retelling more or less the same account in letters, interviews, and articles for almost thirty years. See, for example, Elias, *Letters*, II: 417–21; *Theodore Dreiser: Interviews*, ed. Frederic E. Rusch and Donald Pizer (Urbana: University of Illinois Press, 2004), 1–3; and "The Early Adventures of *Sister Carrie*," *Colophon*, Part 5 (1931), reprinted as the introduction to the 1932 Modern Library edition of *Sister Carrie*.

4. Although busy with a number of writing jobs, Rascoe during the early 1930s was in financial difficulties and also often in poor health.

5. The *Bookman*, a literary journal which Rascoe had edited in the late 1920s, had recently ceased publication after many years of pre-eminence in the field.

6. Rascoe replied on 8 May 1934 that someone had already borrowed and not returned his copy of Lawrence's book. Dreiser appears to have acquired a copy elsewhere, since his library, preserved at DPUP, contains Lawrence's *Psychoanalysis and the Unconscious* (London, 1931) (see note 1 above) with marginalia by Dreiser.

To Albert H. Ledoux [TC-DPUP]

*Ledoux had written Dreiser several times in early 1934 about his personal prob-
lems.*

Hotel Ansonia,
New York City,
May 21, 1934.

Dear Mr. Ledoux:

Writing you is by no means an easy matter.

For, as you present yourself, you are burdened with unseen urges, shadowy
apprehensions, lacks which you assume, I gather that, I can dissolve, or
blow away. And in substantiation of your belief, you proceed to endow me
gifts, showered, as you indicate, by bounteous fortune. Reading your letter,
I might—if I were not the subject of the alleged gifts—look on myself as
Fortune's favored child. Alas, it is I who must deal with my own temperament, and that makes a different picture.

If it were only frank, easy, mutually compensating friendship that you
required, and not aid in connection with some mysterious girl—your aesthetic half, or better half, whom I am to help you find. And at a time when
aesthetic counterparts in the forms of women weigh dully on my imagination. In fact, the mere thought evokes doubt as to the downright wisdom
of it all, and leave me a little cool if not frozen. Is not some form of contact—minus this illusive, aesthetic counterpart—possible. I know they are
real enough at times—Dante and Beatrice, Poe and his lost Lenore, Romeo
and his Juliet, but the difficulties are so very great—and so very deluding.

I am not cynical. Yet I have lived through a Juliet or two, and lain
beached and all but destroyed. Yet all one can do is to live—or die—alone.
And there friendships cannot aid—not even charity can reach to one.
Would not merely friendly conversations do?

To William E. Borah [TS-LC]

*Dreiser was increasingly irked during the 1930s by unauthorized translations
of his works, a condition permitted by the failure of the United States to ratify
the Berne Convention of 1886 (extended by the Rome Pact of 1928) which
provided international copyright protection to authors of member states. Borah
(1865–1940) was a Republican senator from Idaho. Dreiser wrote similar letters
to each member of the Senate Committee on Foreign Relations, which had begun
hearings on the issue in March 1934.*

THEODORE DREISER

Hotel Ansonia,
New York City,
May 26, 1934.

Dear Senator Borah:

Recently I sent a telegram to the Chairman of your Committee and to the three members of the sub-committee, in which I urged prompt adherence to the Rome Copyright Pact of 1928, the proposed copyright legislation to be allowed to go over until next session. I wish to repeat this message to you, and to call your attention to President Roosevelt's statement that he hopes to be empowered to make this country a party to this convention. May I not urge you strongly to make this possible?

Only a few days ago, I received a copy of a Japanese translation of my novel JENNIE GERHARDT. For years, I had been told that my books were being translated and published there, and the familiarity with them of various Japanese bore this out, but this is the first concrete instance I have been able to obtain. It is extremely distasteful to me to realize that this publication of my books, unknown to me, and certainly unauthorized, is taking place. I am informed that as Japan is a member of the Rome 1928 Pact, but that as the U.S. is not, there is absolutely no means of obtaining any return from the translation and sale of my books in Japan, nor—and this is of equal importance—any means of protecting myself against aesthetic misinterpretation if this has taken place.

Let me add my name to the long list of persons and organizations who are seriously interested in this matter, and who consider that adherence to the 1928 Treaty would work importantly to the ends of international justice and good will.

Very truly,
Theodore Dreiser

To Albert H. Gross   [TC-DPUP]

Gross (1895?–1948), who worked for the Coward-McCann publishing company, had sent Dreiser a galley proof copy of the chapters on Dreiser in Grant Richards's Author Hunting by an Old Literary Sports Man, *the American edition of which Coward-McCann was about to publish. Except where noted, the published work does not contain the errors Dreiser points out in this letter. For Dreiser and Richards, see Dreiser to Grant Richards, 27 May 1910.*

Hotel Ansonia,
New York, N.Y.
June 26, 1934

Dear Gross:

In regard to Grant Richards's book and his chapter on me, it is very good, only he is mistaken in regard to several minor matters.

In galley two (I checked the spot with an arrow), he says that Frank Norris said, "I had him (Dreiser) come through from Chicago." I was not in Chicago at the time. I was living in New York here at 102nd St. and Central Park West, but I had gone to Missouri for the summer and he asked me to come back, which I did.

In note 1 of this same galley, I see he quotes an interview printed in the New York Evening Post to the effect that I had read Will Irwin's Story of Eva. It was not Will Irwin, it was Will Payne who wrote that one good book and afterwards nothing but Saturday Evening Post articles.[1]

Further on in this note 1, he says I wrote Sister Carrie and left the first part of it with the publishers. I left a complete manuscript, not only part.

In the third galley, in the second paragraph, Richards discusses the reception of Sister Carrie here and in England and gives the impression that it died completely and that only the praise of Bennett and Frank Harris revived it. As a matter of fact, the book was never really out of discussion in America from 1900 on. One of the men who took up the cudgels for it and occasionally referred to it was James Huneker, then the first critic in America.[2] Along around 1906 it was Henry L. Mencken who began in Baltimore, and from then on it was really more or less constantly commented upon, which culminated with the publication of Jennie Gerhardt, and the comparison of the two books of course.

In the same galley, Richards quotes a letter from me, the last paragraph of which I have lined and questioned. It reads, "I hope if you are interviewed you will say something definite about me and Jennie." Also a little later in this letter he adds, "Once there I will get at least an equal run with Robert Hichens and Arnold Bennett over here."[3]

I don't recall that. I am dubious as to the reality of the paragraph although I do not want you to say this to Grant Richards, but if the paragraph is going to be used, I would like to see the original of the letter from which it is taken.[4]

All the rest is just as he says, except in the last galley. He states that I was to determine to return on the Titanic. It was his idea not mine, because he thought that it would be an ideal way to finish the book with the first trip of this very important boat. Fortunately I missed it and furthermore, by that time, as Richards will remember, my funds were so low that the difference in passage money required to cross on the Titanic would have been beyond me. If he does not want to make the correction that is as you please. It is not a very great matter, only I think he would prefer to be correct. The chapter is very good.

Tell me, is he in the United States, and if not, is he coming here? I would like to invite him to have dinner with me.

1. Will Payne (1865–1954), *The Story of Eva* (1901).
2. Huneker (1860–1921), a prominent man of letters, may have spoken about *Sister Carrie* to others, but his first recorded publication on any of Dreiser's works did not occur until his review of *The Titan* in 1914.
3. Hichens (1884–1950), author of *The Green Carnation* (1894), and Bennett (1867–1931) were widely read English novelists of the period.
4. Richards kept this paragraph intact in *Author Hunting* (175–76), since he apparently had Dreiser's original holograph letter to hand, which does contain these remarks. The letter appears in Elias, *Letters*, I, 125, with its date corrected by Elias to 4 November 1911.

To John Cowper Powys [TS-DPUP]

Several members of the Powys clan had settled in Dorset in June 1934, from where Powys wrote Dreiser on 3 August 1934. For John Cowper Powys, see Dreiser to John Cowper Powys, 12 December 1930; for Llewelyn Powys, see Dreiser to Llewelyn Powys, 11 March 1933.

THEODORE DREISER

Hotel Ansonia,
New York City,
Sept. 4, 1934.

Dear Jack:

Thanks for your bulletin concerning the estate of the Powys family in England. Do you know by any chance that you are the most economical user of paper that the world has seen up to this date? You write lengthwise and then you write crosswise and then to get still more use of the paper you write at an angle of fifty degrees across both the other pencilings. But I am glad you are settled down in "Down Barn"—if you are—and that Phyllis[1] has someplace to go for dinner and that above all Llewelyn[2] is getting the advantage of your magic temperament. You know, for all your "kidding" I believe in your witchcraft. I believe that you are one of those diabolic and shameless magicians of the nether world and that you work both evil and good at will.[3] In the case of Llewelyn I know, since you love him so much, that you will work only good and that he will live to write many more books and to flood the world with his beautiful irony.[4] As for myself I stand, as you know, in awe of your evil powers and always in every way seek to placate you, to make your mood toward me kinder, else I know what legions of devils would descend upon me through the air from England.

You need not say to Llewelyn how much I wish him to get well because he knows that. He is always in my thoughts. But tell your brother Theodore[5] to exercise his realistic powers to the fullest extent in connection with the two of you in order that you may both be brought down to the grim realness which he seems never to cease contemplating. And say to Phyllis to be true to Kansas—drought or no drought—England can never do for her what Kansas did and ever will.

Lovingly,
T. D.

1. Phyllis Playter, an American whom John Cowper Powys had met in 1921 and with whom he lived for the remainder of his life. Although Dreiser later in this letter appears to claim that she was from Kansas, she was born and raised in Missouri.

2. Throughout this letter, the typist's misspelling of Llewelyn has been corrected.

3. An allusion to the mystical element in John Cowper Powys's work.

4. Llewelyn had suffered a major recurrence of tuberculosis in August 1933.

5. A third Powys brother, Theodore Francis (1875–1953), a novelist of Dorset life.

1935

To Henry S. Canby [TS-BLYU]

Under the conservative leadership of its longtime secretary Robert Underwood Johnson, the National Institute of Arts and Letters had resisted offering membership to many of the writers who had come into prominence since the World War. In late 1934, however, the nominating committee of the institute, chaired by Canby, reversed this policy and voted to ask Dreiser, H. L. Mencken, Ernest Hemingway, and Sinclair Lewis if they would stand for election. Of these, only Lewis assented and was duly elected. Canby (1878–1961) had been a professor at Yale before helping found the Saturday Review of Literature *in 1924.*

THEODORE DREISER

Hotel Ansonia,
New York City
Jan. 14, 1935.

Dear Mr. Canby:

I had left town before your last letter appeared and find it now upon my return.[1]

I am not unappreciative of your apparent wish to enlarge and make more representative The National Institute of Arts and Letters. Nonetheless, without prejudice to any of the members of this Organization I am opposed to joining. This opposition has an aesthetic root, the significance of which is not easily set forth in a letter. At some time or another I would not be opposed to discussing this antipathy, but not at present, especially in view of the request. It may be that such an organization has value and importance, but that subject again is something which I will have to defer to a later date, that is, when the question of my joining this or any other Institute is no longer before me.

Thank you very much for your wishes in behalf of the organization and in regard to me.

Theodore Dreiser

1. Canby's initial letter to Dreiser, on 2 January 1935, noted that the nominating committee had unanimously endorsed him and requested permission to place his name on the final ballot. Dreiser then wrote to H. L. Mencken on 3 January 1935, asking Mencken's opinion about the invitation, and on 4 January Mencken replied, advising against acceptance. (See Riggio, *Dreiser-Mencken Letters,* II, 570–71.)

Dreiser then wrote to Canby on 7 January declining the opportunity to "apply for membership." Canby's reply on 8 January reminded Dreiser that he had been nominated, not asked to apply, and requested that Dreiser reconsider. Dreiser's letter of 14 January is therefore a reply to Canby's letter of 8 January.

To George Douglas [H-Cor]

Dreiser had met the Australian-born newspaperman Douglas (?–1936) in San Francisco in 1920, and they soon established a warm personal bond based in part on their philosophical rapport. Since Douglas had moved to Los Angeles in 1929 to work on the Los Angeles Examiner, *Dreiser planned to stay with him from late April to October while preparing his philosophical study* The Formula Called Man.

Friday, Feb. 15—1935

Dear George:

   I am going to wind up my affairs here & come out there. Will be with you shortly. Save the room. Incidentally, can you find there the several works by Jacques Loeb—Heliotropism,[1] Stereotropism[2] and a book the Physiology of the Brain[3]—also by Loeb. It was published by Putnam in 1900. If so look

Dreiser and George Douglas.

them over. They relate clearly to the entire substance of this book of mine. If you read them I will talk to you about them when I get there. There is another book. Wells & Huxley Biology.[4] I want the illustrative data of these. I will send my car I think. I know leading people over at the Institute of Technology and we will use them—have them in for discussions & helpful thought.[5] Will write or wire more.

Regards

D

I am really sick but I'll [word missing] better when I get there I'm sure.

1. Probably Loeb's *Further Proof of the Identity of Heliotropism in Animals and Plants* (1910). For Dreiser and Loeb, see Dreiser to Jacques Loeb, 29 May 1919.

2. Not a complete work but rather the title of a chapter in Loeb's *The Dynamics of Living Matter* (1906).

3. *Comparative Physiology of the Brain and Comparative Psychology* (1900).

4. Dreiser is referring either to *The Human Mind and the Behavior of Man* (1932) by H. G. Wells, Julian Huxley, and G. P. Wells or the same authors' *The Science of Life* (1931).

5. Both Calvin Bridges (1889–1938), a distinguished geneticist, and Robert A. Millikan (1868–1953), a Nobel Prize–winning physicist, were at the California Institute of Technology and were interested in the relationship between science and religion.

To Hereward Carrington [TC-DPUP]

The British-born Carrington (1880–1958), who had founded the American Psychical Institute and Laboratory in 1921, wrote prolifically on psychical subjects.

Mt. Kisco. N. Y.
April 3, 1935

Dear Carrington:

I know that the work of the American Psychical Institute is important and I wish I could give some little time to it now because I am interested to see where the workers in that field are getting.[1] However, I am going West very shortly and I do not expect to be back before fall. When I do return, I will get in touch with you. So far in my life I have never been able to connect data of physical science with that of psychic research but I am by no means sure that there is not a connection which cannot be definitely established. The physical laboratories as yet have never been able to present either the mechanics of protoplasm or the nature of the force behind the mechanics and yet out of the two come human life.

I hope your society has money enough and energy enough to extract something irrefutable in connection with its research and yet like to have that happen before I die.

Cordially

1. Carrington had sent Dreiser a printed invitation to join the Institute.

To Walter Landauer [TS-UConn]

Landauer (1896–1935), a professor at Connecticut State College, had written Dreiser on 20 May 1935 that in response to the participation of Connecticut State students in a nationwide demonstration for peace on 12 April 1935, the trustees of the college had passed resolutions restricting student meetings on campus and prohibiting protests against military training at the college.

THEODORE DREISER

232 S. Westmoreland Ave.,
Los Angeles, May 30, 1935

Dear Mr. Landauer:

Unquestionably, there is a movement on foot in the United States, looking to the suppression of the individual, not only in the matter of speech but in the matter of freedom of action. Here in California, they are at the labor of passing a law, preventing citizens without visible means of support, from entering the State of California.[1] I do not need, I think, to indicate to you, how simple it will be to find a lack of satisfactory means of support in all selected cases. Furthermore, I am satisfied that this law, if made effective here, will be immediately imitated by a majority of other States in America, and particularly those dominated by aggressive and oppressive financial powers.

As for the suppression of speech in Storrs college, of which you complain: it seems to be in line with the policy of the commercial interests throughout the Country. Their power through their propaganda, their legislators, their newspapers, courts and judges, to emphasize their objection to free speech, is obvious. I think the students of Storrs College are right in objecting, and I certainly wish them victory.

In regard to the second resolution, covering establishment of military training in Storrs College: I so strongly object to military training in an educational institution, that I condemn the action establishing military training, and consider the resolution adopted by the Board of Trustees, as nothing more than a Red Herring drawn across an evil trail. There should not be military training in Storrs College, and there should be freedom of speech.

> Yours very truly,
>
> Theodore Dreiser

1. An allusion to the effort to prevent refugees from the southwestern dust bowl ("Okies") from immigrating to California.

To Joseph Fischler [TS-LLIU]

Fischler (1886–1950) had begun corresponding with Dreiser in 1916 while serving a prison term at San Quentin for fraud. After his release, he moved to New York where he and Dreiser became friends. For many years Fischler was an executive of the General Motors Company and often advised Dreiser on financial matters.

THEODORE DREISER

> 232 S. Westmoreland Ave.,
> Los Angeles, May 30, 1935.

Dear Fischler,—

It is nice to hear from you, and indirectly, from Mooney.[1] I intended before this, to send you my present address, but have been rushed with work. Besides, I knew that a letter addressed to Mt. Kisco would be forwarded.

What you tell me about Mooney, is interesting. He seems to be always wavering between his personal activities as a big business man, and his reflections on the ethics of commerce. I have not read the document by him which you enclosed, but I will. I judge the charts included, are yours.

By all means, if you come out this way, look me up. In spite of my alleged anti-semitism, I still pick and choose, as you know, and I would not trade one of my selection, for some ten thousand of another kind.[2]

Give Mooney my address, and if he blows out this way, we will sit down and talk things over. I have always wished that he could become a directing force in some social program, but those things happen, or they don't.

Incidentally, I ran into H. S. Kraft,[3] in Hollywood. If his sartorial appearance means anything, he must be prospering greatly. He was infuriated when I refused to shake hands or to discuss any matter whatsoever. What form his revenge for this will take, I can only guess.

Let me hear from you whenever the mood impels you.

> Regards,
> Dreiser

1. James D. Mooney (1884–1957), executive vice president of General Motors and a frequent writer on economic issues. In a letter to Dreiser on 22 May 1935, Fischler enclosed a pamphlet by Mooney on the tariff issue. See also Dreiser's letter to Mooney himself, 14 March 1931, in Elias, *Letters*, II, 513–16.

2. Hutchins Hapgood had published in the May 1935 *Nation* his late 1933 exchange of letters with Dreiser dealing with Dreiser's attitude toward the Jews as displayed in the *American Spectator* "Editorial Conference" of September 1933 (see Dreiser to George Jean Nathan, 26 May 1933). Since Dreiser endorsed in his letters, with even greater vehemence, the comments he made in the conference, Hapgood's article received much attention. Fischler himself was Jewish.

3. Dreiser had turned against Hy Kraft, whom he had worked with on a dramatic adaptation of *Sister Carrie* (see Dreiser to John Howard Lawson, 10 August 1928) and a film version of *Tobacco* (see Dreiser to S. Anargyros, 30 December 1932), because he believed Kraft was acting in Hollywood as his agent without his authorization.

To Olin Downes [H-UG]

A well-known writer on music, Downes (1886–1955) was music critic of the New York Times from 1924 to his death.

232 Westmoreland Ave
Los Angeles, Calif.
[After 1 August 1935][1]

Dear Downs:[2]

You must know that I am hard put to it to wisely—if not sympathetically—comment on a nature as rich and sensitive and colorful as yours.[3] You bubble like the crater of a giant volcano. You mourn like a stormy, expiring November day. There is sorrow and pain and regret and dispair in so much that you voice—but also a giant courage. The times when you have descended on me and erupted your volcanic moods and reactions to life—I have listened as to a symphony—Trist,[4] Pathetique, Eroica. And half wished to cry—and did in the depths of me. But to what end? Life is life. Is it a dream? Is it a giant jest? Is it a cruel, meaningless accident?—or a planned tragedy-comedy? Regardless of what you think of me I react nervously and affectionately as well appreciatively to all that you pour forth. But I cannot properly respond. If I could I would write you just such letters as you write me. And hope to get more such letters as yours in return. At present I am sharing the home of George Douglas the distinguished West Coast critic—(of San Francisco and here).[5] We spend hours and hours going over and over the inexplicables that make life and Shakespeare and the Bible and Shelley and Olin Downs and the rest of us—and getting no where. When I finished your letter—and since he was sitting near me,—I gave it to him. "Beautiful! Beautiful! Beautiful," was one thing he said. "Now isn't that lovliness itself. And how fully it reveals the richness of the man writing. He talks of writing. But see how exquisitely he writes here." And then he told of listening to you over the radio.

Downs there is nothing to say. I am here. I am working. I am mostly—at heart—as sad as death. If you were here you could come & live with us. And talk & talk. It is beautiful just here. I work looking out on a flower box of a patio—with a fish pool & birds. But somehow I am as sad and restless and shaken as your letter. By what? *Life!* The thing of which I can make nothing. When I return to New York I will let you know. And write me when & how you will. I respect & admire you so much.

Dreiser

1. Dreiser's undated letter is a reply to Downes's letter postmarked 1 August 1935.

2. Dreiser frequently misspelled Downes's name.

3. In his letter of 1 August 1935, Downes relied on Carrie's longings at the conclusion of *Sister Carrie* to expand on his intense desire to write truthfully about life and art.

4. In addition to Tchaikovsky's *Pathetique* and Beethoven's *Eroica* symphonies, Dreiser appears to be citing Jean Sibelius's "Valse Triste."

5. For Douglas, see Dreiser to George Douglas, 15 February 1935.

To M. Lincoln Schuster   [TC-DPUP]

Schuster (1897–1970) and his partner Richard L. Simon (1899–1960) founded their publishing firm in 1924 and achieved almost immediate success. Dreiser had signed a contract with Simon & Schuster in September 1934 for the publication of all his forthcoming and past works. Dreiser's appeal to Schuster for aid in handling his foreign publications represents his frustrations over at least a decade in this area.

232 So. Westmoreland
Los Angeles
August 7, 1935.

My dear Schuster:

I am in some little trouble in connection with the International Literary Bureau of which Sanford Greenburger is the head.[1] My connection with the agency started with Eric Posselt as you know and with the transfer of my works to your house. Since then I have had considerable trouble and it seems to grow more complicated. In the first place, Posselt collected $150.00 for placing the 'Genius' with Nordstedt & Son of Sweden and then disappeared with the money.[2] It is true that Greenburger finally agreed to make good the money out of any royalties accruing to him through works of mine placed by him but as yet nothing has come of that, and the Nordstedt affair is still in the balance. The next thing that happened was that in connection with straightening out my affairs with Zsolnay of Vienna[3] $184.50 disappeared and was never even clarified until Thomas White, the head of the Vienna branch of the International Literary Bureau wrote me just how it had been sent, and assured me that unless Greenburger paid it, he would. In that connection I have received a long explanation of some long accounting by some accountant employed by Greenburger. Now it may be all right but it is too complicated for me to understand and it unloads a lot of expenses for cables, books, etc., which seem excessive to me, particularly in view of the fact that Greenburger and White are collecting 10 percent and handling my affairs in the first place.

I do not want to be unduly suspicious or quarrelsome but it is very hard to work and at the same time have to worry over a lot of financial complications which a competent and honest agent is supposed to take off your hands. In this connection what I want to know is this, can I send you this general correspondence and will you have your business manager look over it and tell me what he thinks? Whether it is right or wrong, and how and why? A great deal of my time is being wasted over a series of letters out of which I get nothing except further complications. To make clear what I say, I am sending you a copy of a letter I am mailing to Greenburger today.

At the same time until further notice [word missing] and until you decide whether you are willing to bother with it, and if you do, what you think of the whole business? I wish you would treat the matter confidentially. I do not wish to be unfair to Greenburger or to quarrel with him any more than I have to, but I did not with-hold the $184.50. Mr. White said that he (Greenburger) did.

Will you let me know by return mail whether I may send the matter to you, and oblige

Very truly yours,

1. Sanford J. Greenburger (1903–1971), whose firm was headquartered in New York. Erich (not "Eric") Posselt worked for Greenburger in New York, while Thomas White was his Vienna agent.

2. The Nordstedt firm published an edition of *Jennie Gerhardt* in 1930, but no Swedish edition of *The "Genius"* seems to have appeared.

3. Paul Zsolnay (1895–1961), with whom Dreiser had signed a contract in 1933 giving Zsolnay's publishing firm exclusive rights to his publications in German.

To Carl Laemmle, Jr. [TCopy-DPUP]

Carl Laemmle, Jr. (1908–1979) was the son of the founder of Universal Studios, Carl Laemmle (1867–1939), who had semi-retired in 1929 and named his young son production head of the studio. Dreiser continued for some years to maintain that Universal had plagiarized from Jennie Gerhardt *in its film version of Fannie Hurst's* Back Street.

COPY
An unanswered letter addressed to Carl Laemmle, Jr., Universal City, Los Angeles, California.[1]

August 23, 1935.

Mr. Laemmle:

As you will recall, in 1930, you paid me in advance for a conference in regard to An American Tragedy, which, as I anticipated it would, came to nothing.[2]

But that is not what I am writing about. In 1932, without either my knowledge or consent, your organization, while ostensibly purchasing and producing a novel by Fannie Hurst entitled Back Street,[3] used that novel which had a few plot and character points in common with my novel, Jennie Gerhardt, to practically steal and produce as a moving picture, the entire drama of Jennie Gerhardt in toto—the entire drama but not the exact text because in your version of Back Street you changed the German gentile Gerhardt family into a Jewish one.

But apart from that—and despite your legal possession of Back Street, which you might have interpreted accurately, and without injury to me, you, or Universal, which is your corporation, proceeded to borrow (steal is the correct word) from my novel all of its actual drama in order to get the benefit of picturizing my novel without paying for it.

Unfortunately I never heard of Back Street at the time, and therefore did not see it. Otherwise I would have interposed legal objections to its presentation.

When in 1934, having at last heard of and seen it, I had my lawyer write Fannie Hurst, her reply was that she had nothing to do with the theft of my drama which was in Jennie Gerhardt. That what she did was to sell her book Back Street to you, or Universal, and that it was Universal which made these changes without her knowledge or consent. That she had nothing to do with the picturizing. When Mr. Hume, my lawyer, wrote you, or Universal, your lawyer's reply was that Universal had bought Back Street from Fannie Hurst and had produced it in good faith—did not acknowledge any theft and was prepared to battle the matter legally. By that time all the profit that could be extracted from it had been extracted by you.

Yet, because of this theft, I had to take less for a novel (Jennie Gerhardt) that would otherwise have brought much more. And though you knew of Jennie Gerhardt, you preferred to pay Miss Hurst $35,000 and steal my book rather than pay me the price of my book and give me proper credit. Not only that, but after selling Jennie Gerhardt to Mr. Schulberg of Paramount,[4] I had the amazing experience of seeing those honorable producers transfer a part of the technique of Back Street to their interpretation of Jennie Gerhardt, in order, I presume, to avoid the trouble and expense of doing the whole thing de novo. I call your attention to the death bed scenes of Jennie Gerhardt and Back Street by Paramount and Universal.

Mr. Laemmle, either you are a common thief, or Universal is, or both are, operating as so called distinguished picture producers.

The reason that I am writing you now is because I am here in Los Angeles where you are, and where I can be reached—by suit for slander, if you choose, in which case I can publicly and legally air my grievance. Or, if you have a satisfactory explanation—one which would naturally and honorably extract an apology from me, I am here to receive it, and, if necessary make such apology.

Or, perhaps, you will sufficiently resent this imputation to personally seek me out with a demand that I retract it. In which case, you will find me here and at your service at any time.

I am—

Very truly indeed,

(Signed) Theodore Dreiser

P. S. For your information I am now keeping informed as to current pictures and any further stealing of my books will be met by legal action at the right time.

1. Dreiser apparently had his secretary prepare copies of his unanswered letter to Laemmle, heading each with this announcement. Robert H. Cochrane, a Universal executive, eventually did answer Dreiser's letter to Laemmle; see Dreiser to Robert H. Cochrane, 1 October 1935.

2. See Dreiser to Robert H. Cochrane, 1 October 1935.

3. *Back Street* (1931), a bestselling novel by Hurst (1889–1968).

4. B. P. Schulberg (1892–1957), then head of production for Paramount, bought the film rights of *Jennie Gerhardt* from Dreiser in November 1932.

To M. Lincoln Schuster

Schuster had written Dreiser on 20 August 1935 asking about his progress on The Stoic, *since Simon & Schuster hoped to publish the novel in the fall. Dreiser's reply deals entirely with his book of philosophy.*

4922 Rosewood Avenue[1]
Los Angeles
August 27, 1935.

Dear Schuster:

In the first place thanks for your birthday telegram.

In regard to your inquiry as to the success of the book, I can present it best this way. There are some 30 topics or chapters that have to be dealt with. The data for each chapter has represented a special field of investigation. The investigations are about completed. The data type written and ready for condensation. Some 8 or 9 of the chapters are written. Once the data under each chapter-head is thoroughly digested the writing is nothing. I really hope to finish this book late this fall; but I do not believe it is advisable for you to publicize the subject. If you do, you will take away from the element of originality and surprise which I feel is inherent in the book. If anything is said, it should be said quickly and emphatically at the time you are sure of the publishing date.

Thanks also for your interest in the Greenburger matter.[2] His relations with me bids fair to be straightened out. But the actions of Thomas White who controls the Vienna branch of the concern is causing me a great deal of worry. And if you would be so good I wish you would have Shimkin[3] inquire of Greenburger as to the Vienna situation, and what, if anything he can do to cause White to carry out his agreement with me. After all they are partners and Greenburger must have some influence with him.

Regards,

1. Dreiser had been living with George Douglas on Westmoreland Ave., but moved in mid-August to an apartment on nearby Rosewood Ave., where he would remain until his return to New York in October.

2. See Dreiser to M. Lincoln Schuster, 7 August 1935.

3. Leon Shimkin (1907–1988), a partner in Simon & Schuster and later its president.

To Otto Kyllmann [TS-TU]

Although the Hays Office (see Dreiser to Theodore Kiendl, 18 August 1930, n. 7) had been established by the Hollywood film industry in 1922 to enforce a code of propriety in film contents, its efforts were sporadic and often ineffective. In 1934, however, Joseph Breen (1890–1965), Hays's assistant, bolstered by the support of various Catholic organizations, began to vigorously enforce the code.

THEODORE DREISER

4922 Rosewood Avenue
Los Angeles
September 9, 1935.

Dear Kyllmann:

This is a letter about the Gaumont British Corporation, my books and yourself. As you know the comparatively recent attack of the Catholic Church on the morals and ethics of all Hollywood Picture Products has tightened up the Censorship here not a little. Gangster pictures are "*out*". The purely sex picture of the Jean Harlow-Clara Bow type is out (Clara Bow—The IT Girl).[1] They have reduced the speed of Mae West by about 40%.[2] No man or woman can be indicated as living together out of wedlock and, where illicit relations are indicated as having existed in the past, they must, if they refer to principals, wind up at the altar or before a magistrate at least. In short all American pictures are now sharply scrutinized by the Church and the State, to say nothing of the 48 separate states. So such books of mine as 'Sister Carrie', 'The Financier' and 'The Genius', to say nothing of the number of my short stories are temporarily at least, in the discard.

However, I notice this, that such Gaumont Pictures as come over here— Henry the Eighth, Payment Deferred, The Scarlet Pimpernel, and some others are not only sanely liberal but sanely dramatic, most of the purely American exaggeration and eccentricities being eliminated. Besides they are not only pleasingly but at times impressively interpreted by competent actors. For these reasons, I have been thinking that if I could interest Gaumont in one of my books, preferably 'Sister Carrie' (which most certainly should be done as a picture) it would prove a mutually advantageous arrangement. For all of our hoopla nationalism America still has a sincere respect for English reserve, love of order, responsibility and the conventions in general and for that reason is beginning to esteem these Gaumont productions as a relief from so many of our utterly meaningless and unbelievably bad box office trivialities. In so far as my books are concerned, while they are so purely

American (and perhaps because of that), I have the feeling that they might be done with more care for, and respect of, American eccentricities and characteristics than they would here. Furthermore the fact that so purely an American novel as 'Sister Carrie' had been impressively done in England would give it not only added acclaim here but throughout the British Empire, thus adding to its financial import and success.

As you know, I sold the silent rights of 'An American Tragedy' to Paramount in 1927 for $100,000. They allowed those to lapse. But in 1930 they purchased the talking rights for $68,000. In 1932 I again sold Paramount 'Jennie Gerhardt' for a total of cash and royalties of $50,000.[3] At this present time, there is talk here of buying 'Sister Carrie' for 50,000, but the actress proposed, and the moral modifications required pain me greatly.[4] I would very much prefer if I could sell it to Gaumont and have it done in England. Could you by any possibility act for me in this? I would have to get something more than $50,000 for as you know the British income tax takes twenty percent, and all agents take ten. So I would like to sell it for a net of 50,000 to me. For over here, I would have to pay still another heavy tax. Of course the sum paid might be divided and part paid in one year and part in another. But even so,—

Cant I induce you to act for me as my agent for a commission of 10%? I would so much like to work through you. Incidentally, if any advance publicity concerning even the possibility of such a transaction between myself and Gaumont and concerning '*Sister Carrie*' were to be achieved it would help not a little in the matter of negotiation and might bring about a favorable Gaumont reaction.[5]

If this comes to anything most certainly I will visit England.

Never doubt that I continue to think of you as a rare and engaging spirit, never as a mere publisher.

Dreiser

Note the address,—4922 Rosewood Ave. Los Angeles. I'm out here until Oct. 15 so you'll have time to address me here.[6]

1. Two major Hollywood sex symbols, Harlow (1911–37) in the 1930s and Bow (1905–65) in the 1920s. Bow starred in the sexually provocative film *It* (1927) and was thereafter frequently called the "It Girl."

2. West came to Hollywood in 1930 after starring in various Broadway sex comedies; her movies continued to be popular throughout the late 1930s.

3. The correct figures for these sales appear to be $90,000 for *An American Tragedy* in 1926 (not 1927) (see Dreiser to Jesse Lasky, 14 March 1926) and $55,000 for the sound rights to the novel in 1930 (see Swanberg, *Dreiser*, 369). Dreiser received $25,000 for the film rights to *Jennie Gerhardt* in 1932, but this sum was later augmented by his share of the royalties.

4. No deal for an American film version of *Sister Carrie* was made at this time; the novel was finally sold to RKO in 1940 and was filmed in 1952. See also Dreiser to Otto Kyllmann, 15 April 1936.

5. Kyllmann replied on 11 October 1935 that he had discussed a film version of *Sister Carrie* with Gaumont and that the company found Dreiser's asking price too high.

6. Dreiser added the postscript by hand.

To Robert H. Cochrane [TC-DPUP]

For Dreiser's earlier letter dealing with his belief that Universal Studios had pla-giarized Jennie Gerhardt, *see Dreiser to Carl Laemmle, Jr., 23 August 1935. Cochrane (1879–?), a vice president of Universal, had engaged in an equally contentious correspondence with Dreiser in 1932 over Universal's alleged fir-ing of the dramatist Patrick Kearney for his political activities; see Swanberg, Dreiser, 396.*

4922 Rosewood Avenue
Los Angeles
October 1, 1935.

Mr. Cochrane:—

Your attempt at nonchalance and persiflage in connection with my let-ter addressed to Carl Laemmle, Jr. joins up well with the original actions of Universal or Carl Laemmle, Jr., or both, which I castigated. Accordingly I do not mind your giving my first letter and your evasive reply, and this my final communication to the public, assuming that all three are joined together unaltered.[1] But first I must explode your unverified and therefore malicious charges.

For instance, in so far as my statement that Mr. Laemmle, Jr. paid ($500.00) for an interview with me, it is true. The time was July, 1930. The intermediary representing Mr. Laemmle, Jr. was Paul Fejos, the Hungarian director, now of Budapest, but then of Universal. At least he had recently completed as director for Universal, three pictures: *Lonesome*, *Broadway* and *La Marseilles*.[2] I was passing through Los Angeles at the time and hearing of my presence, he came to the Ambassador with word that Mr. Laemmle was desirous of discussing my works with me, particularly An American Tragedy, which was at that time being held back by Paramount. I explained that I was leaving and that if it was to be it must be quickly. For some reason there was a delay of two days and I departed for San Francisco, leaving my itinerary. At Portland—the Roosevelt Hotel—some days later, I received a wire asking if I would return. It was from Mr. Fejos. My reply was that if five hundred were wired immediately, I would fly back. The money being wired, I returned and was met by Mr. Fejos, who escorted me into the presence of

Mr. Laemmle, Jr., who cannot possibly have forgotten. If he has, Mr. Fejos is easily available by cable. Possibly you will apologize but I doubt it. What is needed is an apology from life itself for the existence of your type.

Now as to your libel that though I have prospered, I have neglected an indigent brother. Although this has nothing to do with my charge against Universal, I will trouble to dispose of it and I will do it in this way. If you can induce my friend, Roy Howard of the New-York-World-Telegram or the Editor of the Los Angeles Times, whom I do not know, or O. O. McIntyre,[3] to receive and privately verify proof from me as to the falsity of the rumor you circulate, and you will agree to publicly apologize, I will satisfy any and all of these, and quickly.

As for your charges—to wit—that my letter was prompted by shallow and bitter envy of Miss Hurst, who, as you say is a great and original and honorable authoress, whereas I am a clown and mentally unbalanced—supposing I grant you both. How can that affect my direct charge that either Mr. Laemmle or Universal, or both—(if you were Vice President at the time, as I see you are now, I suppose I should have included you)—stole the essence of my novel, Jennie Gerhardt, and in making a moving picture entitled Back Street by Fannie Hurst, made it the essence of her alleged moving picture and exhibited it as such. Here is a non-sequitur I do not grasp unless you are just saying anything to distract attention from a fact.

And in passing let me correct the impression you seek to convey, that I wrote Miss Hurst. At the time that Messrs. Walsh, Baird, Hume and Cameron considered the case, they, themselves, addressed letters to Universal and Miss Hurst, and were answered by lawyers. My reference to Miss Hurst's reply is either from a letter from her lawyer, a Mr. Stern, to Arthur Carter Hume, of Walsh, Baird, Hume and Cameron, or a conversation had by Arthur Carter Hume with Mr. Stern. Only once did Miss Hurst write me, and that was some years ago. She wrote a personal letter praising a short story of mine called Married, and with the exception of thanking her for her letter to me, I have never written her.

In regard to your threat to give your letter to the public—this is, as above stated, granted, but on the condition that it be joined in such publicity with my letter to Mr. Laemmle, and this, my reply to your letter to me. Otherwise, I shall be compelled to publicize all three myself.

P. S. For the life of me I cannot fathom your psychopathic delight in addressing me as Teddy. Does it really thrill you so much?

P. P. S. As to your knightly threat to in the future defend all authors from whom I may possibly take things—how about beginning at home? I am an author and Universal or Mr. Laemmle, Jr., or both, have stolen the essence of a book from me. How about making me author no. 1, and apologizing to me for taking my work from me?

1. Cochrane's letter to Dreiser, which Dreiser is here replying to, has not been found. There is no indication that either Dreiser or Universal made their exchange of letters public aside from Dreiser sending some copies of his side of the correspondence to friends.

2. The Hungarian born Fejos (1897–1963) immigrated to America in 1923 and began directing for Universal in 1928; the three films named by Dreiser appeared in 1928 and 1929.

3. Howard (see Dreiser to Roy W. Howard, 29 October 1931) was publisher of the *New York World-Telegram* and part owner of the Scripps-Howard newspaper chain; McIntyre (1884–1938) was a popular syndicated newspaper columnist. For Dreiser's support of his brother Rome, see Dreiser to Arthur Pell, 5 November 1926.

To Arnold Gingrich [TC-DPUP]

Gingrich (1903–1976) founded the Chicago-based magazine Esquire *in 1933. The stage version of* Tobacco Road *(1932), based on the novel by Erskine Caldwell (1903–1987), opened in New York in December 1933 and was hugely successful, running for more than seven years. Both the New York production and its touring companies encountered attempts to censor the play's frank sexual scenes and language.*

Mt. Kisco, N. Y.
October 31, 1935.

Dear Gingrich:

I was not in New York when your wire asking me to protest against the suppression of Tobacco Road by Mayor Kelly of your city, came.[1] Now that it is before me, I am, of course, moved to protest as I am moved and do protest as many of these mental outrages as I hear of.

Only recently I read that Pearl Buck's Good Earth had been barred by the City School Superintendent of Kansas City from the schools of that center,[2] while in Massachusetts I am legally charged with having, through an American Tragedy, brought about the murder of the latest Massachusetts Tragedy victim.[3]

Here in New York when Tobacco Road was about to fail I did my best to arouse public interest in it and certainly partially succeeded in so doing. To me it is a great play and a great piece of American dramatic realism. To bar it from the American stage is to throw open the door to ignorant attacks on mental achievements of all kinds. What I suspect is that it is the Catholic Church, which, endangered by any show of real intelligence anywhere, is determined to fight all mental progress here and throughout the world.

If it is not too late you can use as much or as little of this as you choose.

1. Gingrich had wired Dreiser on 23 October c/o Simon & Schuster. Edward Kelly (1876–1950), the longtime (1933–47) mayor of Chicago, saw a touring company performance of the play in Chicago in late October and had it closed. A legal challenge to his action was successful and it soon continued its run.

2. The *New York Times* of 19 October 1935 reported that the much-applauded novel *The Good Earth* (1931) by Buck (1892–1973) had been banned in a Kansas City high school.

3. Unidentified.

To Donald P. McCord   [TS-DPUP]

For McCord, see Dreiser to Donald P. McCord, 12 June 1920. Dreiser, George Douglas, and McCord (who had a home in Pasadena) frequently discussed philosophical ideas during the half-year Dreiser had recently spent in Los Angeles.

THEODORE DREISER

Mt. Kisco, New York
November 26, 1935

Dear McCord,

This is certainly a belated acknowledgement of your invitation to breakfast back in October; but you know that not answering simply meant that it was impossible, with the packing and the trip ahead of us, to get around to it.[1] When we started out, as we were packing the two cars in the morning, we decided that we would call you up. Once we were actually started we arranged to stop by, but as usual in such cases we did not get started until noon. We were delayed so much that we did not get any further than Salton Sink in Southern California that day and only took breakfast in Yuma the following morning, so you can judge for yourself. But I missed seeing you and have thought of you often. Now I wish that you could come to this neighborhood so that we could continue our ironic discussions. I have had several letters from George and in one he mentioned quite enthusiastically that he had been over there to dinner. I wonder how you like my friend Calvin Bridges?[2] I admire him enormously and it is not admiration alone that I feel but something deeper. If you see him repeat this to him, and if you see George remember me to him.

It is sharp and brisk here, with nothing but leafless trees in sight and snow on the ground, but now that I am back here I am again intrigued by it just as I was when I first came here. It is a beautiful section of Westchester and I wish you might come here. That does not mean that I have changed my view about Los Angeles. It is just as charming as ever and I am planning either to sell or lease this place and move out there because we have a place in Montrose that is charming and we might as well occupy it when conditions permit.[3] Curiously, when I was talking to Millikan[4] at Cal-Tech he suggested that I move out there. The argument was that apart from the climate, the intellectual life was broadening out and offered ample mental and social possibilities and I think he is right.

We had an interesting and in many ways an exciting trip. When we got half way through Arkansas an unbelievable flood rain set in and fairly drenched the car from the middle of Arkansas to Knoxville, Tennessee. In Memphis the down pour was so immense that it flooded the streets and wherever there was a depression which could be flooded there were two or three feet of water. However, on reaching Knoxville the sun came out and it was as warm as June. I put the top of my roadster down and enjoyed the weather until we reached Chambersburg, Pennsylvania, where we parked for the night. But the next morning cold, gray November weather was upon us and has remained more or less in force ever since.

How are the stars and how do you and George get along? I know very well that you do not condone his editorial service, but what else do you find in him? To me he is an enigma. He has a searching mind stocked with an enormous amount of information, and can recall at a word apparently, thousands of paragraphs from the distinguished literature of the world. He writes doggerel when he chooses and in the same day or hour exquisite poetry. One which he penned to me on leaving was really beautiful.

Do write me. Forgive us for not making breakfast and if you do come East, promise to come and see me.

Affectionately,
Dreiser

Excuse this typing. I am breaking in a new secretary.[5]

1. Dreiser and Helen drove from Los Angeles to New York.
2. For Bridges, see Dreiser to George Douglas, 15 February 1935, n. 5.
3. During their first stay in Los Angeles, in 1919–22, Helen had acquired several lots in Montrose, a small town in the foothills of the San Gabriel Mountains, about ten miles north of Los Angeles.
4. For Millikan, see Dreiser to George Douglas, 15 February 1935, n. 5.
5. Dreiser has entered the postscript by hand.

To Henry Von Sabern [TC-DPUP]

Von Sabern, a sculptor, was a member of the San Francisco bohemian group which included the poet George Sterling and the journalist George Douglas. Dreiser first met him in San Francisco in the fall of 1920.

Mount Kisco, New York
December 23, 1935

Dear Von Sabern:

You often promised to write me during the past fifteen years but this is the first and probably the last communication which I will have from you. I really might as well look on it as your last will and testament. Just the same, merely to look at it is a happy reminder of the times we have met in San Francisco. The last time, we all climbed up to your lookout over San Francisco Bay. I felt as much at home as though I had worked in it for years. For me, it carried fully the feeling of harmony which exists between you and myself. As a matter of fact, it seemed to contain most of the charm that existed in the San Francisco of the 20's, when Sterling and yourself, and George were such busy [word missing].

Later we went through the house with your wife and I was so soothed and really comforted by the aesthetic peace which radiates from everything she touches. It was beautiful.

Helen and I crossed from Los Angeles to New York in about eleven days.[1] We used both cars and made sort of a caravan of it. I found the southern route wonderful—through Yuma, El Paso, Texarkana, and so on. The only break in the charm of the journey was when we arrived in middle Pennsylvania, and it was suddenly cold. All the delightfulness of the southland gone.

My stay in Los Angeles from May to October was crowded with entertainment and profit. By degrees George and I gathered around us a few intellectuals and rehashed the world together. It was really very comforting, and from being truly sick in May, I became well and strong, and accomplished a very great deal of what I was seeking to accomplish. As you know from George, we talked about you a great deal before we arrived in San Francisco and afterward. Here in Mount Kisco I am keeping as much as possible to myself, although working in the same field but I hope to have done with it once and for all, and then I shall return to my novels. I understand how you feel about George and it is quite accurate, but for all the Brahman in him he creates an atmosphere where intellectuals like ourselves can live.

Regards,

1. See Dreiser to Donald P. McCord, 26 November 1935.

1936

To Jerome S. Blum   [H-AAA]

Blum, an artist whom Dreiser had met in Chicago in 1913 (see Dreiser to Arthur Davison Ficke, 21 September 1916, n. 2), was a patient in the Bloomingdale Mental Hospital, White Plains, N.Y. Dreiser wrote an appreciative essay on Blum's work for the April 1929 issue of Vanity Fair.

THEODORE DREISER

Mt. Kisco

Feb 24—1936

Jerry Dear:

I read your letter carefully and weighed all of your comments and your needs.[1] But Jerry, the one man in all the world who can get you out of Bloomingdale—and most quickly is *Jerry Blum*—in *person*. And he is thoroughly capable of doing it. Don't forget who you are—your real mentality, genius, force, and that your attitude toward *yourself* and all others is what will clear your path for you. No one is plotting against you Jerry—*no one*. And you know that. It is a mood you have given way to. *Don't accept it.* Don't accept any thought that suggests to you that you are being plotted or conspired against. And don't listen to anyone in that place who suggests that. Or to yourself if such a thought slips in. Be yourself. Be *Jerry Blum* the artist and thinker. Take yourself in hand. Realize your own genius and force & and that no one is plotting or would want to plot against you. You came to me once before and I told you this *same thing*. I am retelling it to you *now*. You have pictures to paint. Ideas to break out. Think constructively for yourself, forget persecution, concentrate on your work, and you will convince anyone that you belong *outside*—not in. Shut out—*slam the door* on every *idea* of persecution. I respect you. I care for you & I am coming to see you.

Dreiser

1. Blum had written Dreiser on 10 February 1936 asking for aid in gaining his release from Bloomingdale Hospital.

To Claude Bowers [TS-LLIU]

For Dreiser and Bowers, see Dreiser to Claude Bowers, 22 May 1924. Bowers, who was American ambassador to Spain, had written a lengthy letter to Dreiser on 10 January 1936 describing the Spanish political situation.

THEODORE DREISER

Mt. Kisco, New York
February 26, 1936

Dear Bowers:

A letter from you is like a half-dozen of the best pages of Tacitus. You tell all and how! Following your letter and its presentation of conditions, the Spanish elections, fully set forth in the TIMES, authenticate all of your political geography and your predictions.[1] No wonder you write fascinating histories. The only advantage I see in your being ambassador to Spain is that it may result in a modern picture of Spain that will be honest, glittering, and full of real information for foreigners. How you do get around! All of your letters, as you know, are strictly confidential, as far as I am concerned; but if only you would allow me to peddle occasionally the information you provide without indicating the source! It would do so much good in certain radical quarters. But I don't suppose you would trust anybody to do that. If you ever do, trust me.

Why don't you write and tell me how the American scene looks to you, and what is likely to happen to Roosevelt? For the life of me, I cannot see how you can stay out of it. It's a wonder you don't resign, or get Roosevelt to let you resign, and come over here and help stir up the animals. He is a dunce if he doesn't make you do it. And that might lead to that walk up to the White House door.[2]

The best book I ever read on Spain was George Borrow's THE BIBLE IN SPAIN. What a wonderful thing! He was paid by the English Bible Society to do it.[3]

Well, this is enough, except to say thanks and I miss you on the old home ground. Don't get lost, and, whatever you do, don't become either a Spanish grandee or a bull-fighter.

Give my regards to Mrs. Bowers and to Pallas Athena II.

As ever,
Dreiser

To Don Claudio Boweroso:

1. The formation of the Spanish republic in 1931 was followed by a series of unstable governments. The elections of early 1936, to which Dreiser refers, had provided the Popular Front, consisting largely of Communists and other leftist parties, a controlling majority. Still to come in July 1936, however, was a right-wing rebellion against this government, led by Francisco Franco and thus the beginning of the Spanish Civil War. Bowers remained a strong supporter of the Loyalist cause throughout the war.

2. Dreiser appears to be implying that if Bowers entered national politics in support of Roosevelt's impending drive for a second term, it might lead to later consideration as a presidential candidate.

3. *The Bible in Spain* (1843), a colorful account of Borrow's adventures in Spain during the late 1830s while an agent of the English Bible Society.

To Otto Kyllmann [TS-TU]

THEODORE DREISER

Mount Kisco, New York
April 15, 1936

Dear Kyllmann,

Thanks for your note in regard to *Sister Carrie*. I understand now that both Paramount and Metro-Goldwyn-Mayer would do it, but there is still an objection on the part of Will Hays to its morality,[1] and that has to be overcome in some way. My personal feeling is that it isn't a case of its morality as much as it is of its economic implications which disturbs the Hays office. It is an actual fact that ever since 1914 when the movies began to get under way in this country, this book has been dickered for by one of the movie companies on the average of twice a year, and yet it has never been filmed.

By the way, do you have any dealings with CIN of Prague? They published six books of mine beginning with the *American Tragedy* I think, back in 1926 or 1927. They admit owing me $4000 in schillings, but they have never communicated with me, or sent me any statements, or even a letter. It just occurs to me that you or your firm might know some reliable Englishman in Prague who would take this matter in hand, and compel these people to straighten this thing out in some way. If you do know of someone, let me know; but if you don't, don't bother to answer.

Incidentally, thanks very much for the books.

Regards,
Dreiser

I will pay the person who straightens it out a commission of 10%.

1. For Hays and *Sister Carrie*, see Dreiser to Otto Kyllmann, 9 September 1935.

To Mrs. Jerome S. Blum [H-AAA]

Jerome Blum was still in a mental hospital; Francis Blum, his wife, was nick-named Frank. For Dreiser and the Blums, see Dreiser to Jerome S. Blum, 24 February 1936.

Thursday
[Oct. 22, 1936][1]

Dear Frank:

It's fine of you to write me so affectionately and to offer me one of Jerry's paintings. Of course I'd like to have it and yet I feel not at all entitled to it. Jerry gave Helen once a beautiful South Sea thing that I love to look at as I do all of his things. Poor Jerry! When I think of his vigorous, searching, flashing mind it makes me angry as well as sad to think how life can do. I would go to see him as you know but when I do—and come away I am shaken deeply by the contrast—and more by the dread, fierce processes of life. If only they would discover some chemical that would rearrange things, for it can only be a chemical derangement brought about by emotional pressures. For our emotions are chemical in their origin and it is they that break us.

We had a good time, didn't we. I think your place is so inviting and re-freshing. And your friends. How gay they were. Mrs. Lucius (?) or Luscious (?). Which?

Sure I'll write people in S.F. & tell them about the exhibit. As a matter of fact I have already written one man and today or tomorrow I'll write three more. His things are so beautiful, they should sell easily.

Listen: when you're up at White Plains on Friday—or the next one—why not call up (Mt. Kisco 5413) and if were going to be in come up. And when I'm in New York—now that I have your telephone number I ring & maybe we can go to dinner or just *blather*. I'm glad you like your new job & that you have it. I see by the papers that owing to some phase of parsimony a number of people died. But since I never trust the papers it means almost nothing.

Affectionately

T.D.

I must say you look O.K. It must be due to your almost militant virtue.

1. Dated on the holograph in a hand other than Dreiser's.

1937

To Paul E. Lacosky [TC-DPUP]

Dreiser corresponded with Lacosky, a Catholic priest, sporadically between 1919 and 1937 on a variety of philosophical ideas.

June 24, 1937.

My dear Father Lacosky:

The book came, was autographed and sent back before your letter arrived so I had no chance to comment on my 1925 letter to you.[1] As to that I am inclined to feel that you may have misinterpreted it—the last sentence or two, anyhow, or rather that I misinterpreted myself to you. I have a bad habit of occasionally setting down any passing romantic thought of mine and passing it off as a real one—the picture in that letter of myself as an aged and wandering penitent is of that sort—blague. Alas I was born and remain a questioning realist, rarely if ever satisfied with appearances. Philosophically a mechanist, I grant to the great process or machine whatever values it appears to establish in me or others. Nor do I venture to charge it with any basic deficiencies, since, as I well know, all this may be a seeming—wholly unreal as I sense reality. And I love its beauty and am grateful.

In the main life has been good to me and this despite the fact that as one of its products I seem to myself to be poorly fabricated. But I do not blame it on anyone. The process is too intricate for me to judge. Just the same I take no great meaning from it unless eating, laboring and playing about as men and animals do has meaning.

What you say about psychiatry interests me much.[2] I have myself felt for a long time that psychiatric treatment is so much a problem of understanding, of instinctively knowing or intuiting the proper course. Even though on occasion "knowing" may lead to surgery and the sugar explosion.[3] I have an enormous reverence for both Freud and Adler[4]—refusing as I do to charge every frustration to sex, although I see where sex is the cause of many. And I am willing to and do believe that a person of good personality rather than one of uninspired learning should prove more successful trying to help people. But chemistry and surgery appear to be helping also.

I wonder what your book will be like. If you are ever in New York, perhaps you will drop me a note—better before hand than on arrival—and share a dinner with me. Table philosophy at times is very comforting, as you know.

My very best wishes,

1. On 23 April 1937, Lacosky sent Dreiser a copy of *An American Tragedy*, in which he had pasted a 1925 Dreiser letter to him for Dreiser to autograph. Then, in a letter of 13 June 1937, Lacosky also asked Dreiser to comment, when he inscribed *An American Tragedy*, on the 1925 letter.

2. Lacosky, who was serving as chaplain in a Hammond, Indiana, mental institution, had commented in his 13 June letter that psychiatrists seemed to perform a function that any person of intelligence and insight might duplicate.

3. It is not clear what Dreiser means by "sugar explosion."

4. In addition to Sigmund Freud (1856–1939), the founder of psychoanalysis, Dreiser refers to Alfred Adler (1870–1937), an early disciple of Freud who later argued with him over the issue of the overriding importance of sexual repression in neuroses.

To Joseph Fischler [H-LLIU]

A rare comment by Dreiser on African Americans. For Fischler, see Dreiser to Joseph Fischler, 30 May 1935.

THEODORE DREISER

July 12—'37

Dear Fischler:

Thanks for the Paul Williams article.[1] It is honest, moving and informing. It ought to be reprinted and distributed. I not only *like* but *respect* the Negros. They are kind, durable, never deeply resentful philosophic and willing to work. The "lazy, trifling Negro" tradition does not go down with me. I have seen too much of how willingly and faithfully they fulfill their obligations.

Thanks.

And my regard

Dreiser

And they have a racial genius for making life more pleasing and bearable.
50 W. 77th N.Y.C

1. Paul R. Williams's "I Am a Negro" in the July 1937 issue of the *American Mercury*.

To Joseph Freeman [H-CU]

Freeman (1897–1965), one of the founders of New Masses *in 1926, was a Communist Party literary spokesman during much of the 1920s and 1930s.*

THEODORE DREISER

Aug 25—'37

Dear Freeman:

I have been meaning to answer your request for an article,[1] but a lot of things have interfered, travel here and there and a big job of my own. Intellectually nor propagandistically have I ever been able to understand the indifference of the Communists to my book *Tragic America*.[2] While it was still in manuscript I showed it to Browder[3] and an associate and friend of his. But while both regretted deeply that it had not been written by a comrade (and this because as it stood with but few changes it would have proved so useful to the party!)—neither suggested its use—nor was one word said in its defense after it appeared. And it was deliberately suppressed—as was *The Case of Clyde Griffiths*—(a Communist interpretation of An American Tragedy) two years ago.[4] Yet both are now constantly referred to [word missing] ideal implements of the cause in this country—should they be seized upon as such. Naturally after two such efforts both still available I am not much moved to work out material of the same character. It would be simpler to do something about what is.

I hear that you and Charmion Habicht are married.[5] I offer my congratulations and sincere good wishes.

Theodore Dreiser

I am here at the Long Island Biological Laboratory[6] but mail should be addressed to 50 W. 77th St. where it is picked up for me.

Regards

1. Freeman had written on 2 August 1937 asking for an article and suggesting as a topic recent changes in the American novel.
2. An attack on the inequities of the American capitalistic system, published in 1931.
3. Earl Browder (1891–1973), head of the Communist Party in America.
4. A translation from the German of the 1930 Lina Goldschmidt–Erwin Piscador heavily communistic dramatic version of *An American Tragedy*; its Broadway production, sponsored by the Group Theatre, opened in March 1936 and closed after three weeks.
5. Freeman had married the American artist Charmion von Wiegand Habicht (1899–1993) in 1934.

6. Dreiser was spending a month at the Carnegie Biological Laboratory at Cold Spring Harbor (on Long Island) as a guest of Calvin Bridges (see Dreiser to George Douglas, 15 February 1935, n. 5).

To William C. Lengel [TS-WCLUP]

THEODORE DREISER

November 17, '37

Dear Lengel,

I find that I haven't a copy of the criticism by Joe Breen of the filming of Sister Carrie.[1] Will you be good enough to let me have one. In connection with this I have been thinking of pictures or plays that have been acceptable in the play and picture field. Consider Boy Meets Girl where the seduced girl with child is the chief character, also Sailor Beware with prostitutes and their money labors as the source of all the humor.[2] Also, how about Tobacco Road in its fourth year?[3] Also Madame X with murder to prevent a man talking as its theme and the murderess dying on the stage,[4] or Mae West in Come Up Some Time[5] or Jennie Gerhardt or An American Tragedy both filmed by the movies.[6] Murder, sudden or delayed death, unsanctioned sexual relations are certainly the most common of all movie material. There was one movie, fairly good, I can't recall the name, in which a man and a woman, both wanted by the police, meet on ship, indulge in an unsanctioned sex affair and subsequently go to their respective deaths in San Francisco. Their spirits even clink glasses at a smart saloon after their death.[7] The picture was very popular. Under the circumstances, I am not in the mood to take the Hay's decision lieing down.

Regards,

T.D

1. Jack Warner, of the Warner Brothers film studio, had asked Joseph Breen of the Hays Office (see Dreiser to Theodore Kiendl, 18 August 1930, n. 7) for an opinion on whether *Sister Carrie* could be filmed under current Hays Office restrictions. Warner sent Breen's largely negative reply to Lengel, and on 30 October 1937 Lengel had sent it on to Dreiser.

2. *Boy Meets Girl*, a 1937 film involving gang warfare in New York; *Sailor, Beware!* a successful 1933 play noted for its bawdiness.

3. For *Tobacco Road*, see Dreiser to Arnold Gingrich, 31 October 1935.

4. Initially a 1910 play by Alexandre Bisson, it was revived in 1927 and then produced as a movie in 1937; Dreiser appears to be referring to the 1927 theatrical revival.

5. Not a film or play, as Dreiser suggests, but rather a version of the suggestive tag line associated with West and first used by her in the movie *She Done Him Wrong* (1933); for West, see Dreiser to Otto Kyllmann, 9 September 1935, n. 2.

6. Both were filmed by Paramount, *An American Tragedy* in 1931 and *Jennie Gerhardt* in 1933.

7. *One Way Passage*, a 1932 movie starring William Powell and Kay Francis for which Robert Lord won the Oscar for best screenplay.

To Robert H. Elias [TS-Cor]

Dreiser and Elias (1914–), who had written a Columbia M.A. thesis on Dreiser, met in October 1937. Elias would also complete in 1948 a University of Pennsylvania doctoral dissertation on Dreiser, which was published in 1949 as Theodore Dreiser: Apostle of Nature. *On 15 November 1937, Elias wrote Dreiser that he was writing an article on Dreiser for the magazine* Avocations *and requested information on the translation of his works.*

THEODORE DREISER

116 West 11 Street
November 17, '37

Dear Mr. Elias,

All of my books with the exception of the short stories Rub-A-Dub,[1] Tragic America, A Traveler at Forty and Moods have been published in Sweden, Denmark, Germany and Austria, and Russia. Rub-A-Dub, Tragic America, A Traveler at Forty and Moods have been published in England. Sister Carrie and Jennie Gerhardt have been published in Japan without my consent. The Financier has been published in Spain. This same book and An American Tragedy have been published in Italy and I understand a number of the others but without my consent. All of the novels have been published in Czecho-Slovakia. An American Tragedy, Jennie Gerhardt have been published in Hungary. I have no authorized publishers in South America but I hear that Sister Carrie and Jennie Gerhardt are on sale there. An American Tragedy, Sister Carrie, Jennie Gerhardt, The Financier and Twelve Men are published in France. This is the best information I can give you.

The name Cowperwood is pronounced Cooperwood.

My agent, Mr. Lengel whose address is 1560 Broadway, Room 511 A, has not been able as yet to place your thesis. But he likes it very much and thinks that someone will take it. I will call him up and ask him to write you.

I enjoyed the evening very much and would be glad to see you again. One of these evenings when I am having a group here, I will telephone or wire you and perhaps you can come down.

Cordially,

Theodore Dreiser
Gramercy 7–3768

1. Dreiser means his collection of philosophical essays *Hey Rub-a-Dub-Dub* (1920).

1938

To Richard L. Simon   [TC-DPUP]

Simon had asked Dreiser to comment on the advance sheets of Daughter, *a novel by Bessie Breuer (1893–1975) which Simon & Schuster was to publish later in 1938. Breuer had a varied literary career, including periods as an expatriate in France and as a Hollywood scriptwriter.*

116 W. 11th St.,
New York City
March 28, 1938

Dear Mr. Simon,

I have looked over Bessie Breuer's book, and I don't want to say anything about it if you are going to use it for publicity. The following is a purely personal and private opinion and not for anyone but you.

I realize very well that the problems and people which are presented in this book do exist and that there is a real theme in the miserable confusion which results from conditions which are truly modern—I might say that this baffled, frustrating search for emotional satisfaction and secure human relationships has the cruelest results for weak, tender temperaments which constantly reach out for love and companionship which will strengthen and harden them. However, I do feel that the reflection of this situation and of the life in general involving it in this book is so partial, so one-sided that it is scarcely justifiable. Specifically, the mother seems to me an extremely false drawing and the same of the daughter and the father—the ingrown, neurotic and negative side of human psychology. It seems scarcely possible that a person should grow into an artistic sensitivity which the daughter displays, a consciousness of the facts of existence without finding more to ease and justify her life, and especially without being able to display more positive emotional force.

I mean to say usually in life when one encounters such people who have so little to offer in the way of attractive and humane force, who lead narrow, ingrown lives, without justification to themselves or anyone else, their reflections on the state of nature, their reactions to art, their taste in music and books and natural beauty are equally heartless. Their lack of positive ability to reach out and try to make something of themselves, admire something enough to ape it, at least, would, it seems to me, be like an armor plate which would keep them from appreciating or being hurt in the same degree on the negative side. People who are so dead to the world are usually equally dead to themselves, and can scarcely generalize about themselves.

And as for any justification to such life as this picture gives, I cannot see it at all. There is no beauty where there is no warmth or strength or living force, or active desire.

A small point which I cannot get is this—why would a woman whose whole life was sex, like the mother, be so blind, and how could her husband be so blind, as to wreck their marriage in this conscious, even self-conscious and almost righteous way. Such things don't happen, without passion, with just brittle sexual gestures. If she was sentimental enough to idealize her home, child, husband and social scheme, she wouldn't go after this false and curiously ambitious sexual release or suffer so acutely—at any rate not for long. And even an immature person like the daughter, if she had any taste for romance, taste for nature, admiration for lusty healthy life which she displays but is not able to encompass for herself, could not so acutely display such a complete lack of feeling for other people, and such an unproductive waste. Tragedy is always two-sided. It has a true side, a sort of Achilles' heel in the person to whom it happens—like a desire, or ambition, or security or position. A person wildly caught up in the convulsive insanities of nature and life enough so as to act consciously or unconsciously will not be surprised at the lack of success and satisfaction if they have so eloquent an imagination as to see this all taking place outside them to other things and people. Tragedy happens to the blind spot, the unguarded, the ignorant. A person who can sympathize with art and nature does not do so without a positive seeking force which has warmth and fire and fuel to burn in life. Shallow temperaments suffer in a shallow way, with shallow words and gestures. Cold people, like these, suffer coldly. They are hot enough as far as sex is concerned. But that is not necessarily emotion. The real development or net in which it seems to me such people as Miss Breuer find themselves is scarcely mentioned. Even the life of the senses, of the sensations over any period, has as much variety as what is actually reflected, and as much life. Here, it is like the curves of a snail-shell, riding frantically around into nothing, whereas the details of suffering and the intensity of feeling would indicate a trip in the opposite direction. This daughter, yearning so for warmth and love and returned emotions, sees the difference between her life and what she wants. And as much as she desires to that degree will she desert her old life for a new one, but she does not. In the same way, emotional wounds are healed, and without effort, in their own time.

Sincerely,

To Edward M. Dreiser   [TC-DPUP]

Dreiser's sister Mame had asked Dreiser for more financial aid for her care of their brother Rome, who had been living with her in New York since 1930. Ed, Dreiser's youngest brother, had been an actor early in his career, but after an accident in 1912 became a textile appraiser. For Ed, see also Dreiser to Edward M. Dreiser, 11 February 1924.

Mount Kisco
April 16, 1938

Dear Ed,

This enclosed letter from Mame about Rome has just reached me. Why can't you do something to help in this situation? Beginning as far back as 1915 I helped Mame and Brennan and Emma when they were in difficulties over and over again.[1] Beginning with 1927 when Rome was down and out in Chicago I began to take care of him[2] and continued to take care of him until just about a year ago when my affairs got so bad that I could not do all the things I have been called upon to do. And since then I have sent them small sums when I could afford it. My original proposition to Mame was, back in 1930, that I agreed with her that if she would take care of Rome personally I would give her $10 a week, and I so did until my finances got so bad that I could not go on with it to the same extent.

I cannot possibly see now, in the face of all this, and whatever personal charges you have to make against Rome, that in this situation you could not help Mame a little. He can't last much longer and I certainly will do what I can. But for once in your life what's the matter with you coming to the front? I wouldn't say this except that I am almost completely broke and worried with endless financial troubles and responsibilities of my own. Whether you refuse or don't refuse please be good enough to let me know what your answer is.[3]

Best regards,

1. Emma was the model for Carrie in *Sister Carrie* and Mame and Brennan the models for Jennie and Lester Kane in *Jennie Gerhardt*; Dreiser had in particular helped Mame for many years.
2. For the onset of this support, see Dreiser to Arthur Pell, 5 November 1926.
3. Ed replied on 20 April 1938 that he was hard up and could not help more than he had in the past.

To Edgar Lee Masters [H-HRHUT]

Dreiser and Masters (1869–1950), the author of Spoon River Anthology (1915), had met in Chicago in 1912 (see Dreiser to William C. Lengel, after 31 March 1913, n. 4); they remained in touch over the years but did not become close until they met again in New York in December 1937. Dreiser was attracted by Masters's independent spirit and dour temperament, and the two men maintained strong ties until Dreiser's death.

THEODORE DREISER

April 26—'38

To Edgar, the Poet:

I have read and reread the five sonnets.[1] They are clear to me—not obscure. And they voice in lovely ways a stern, feverish and consuming reality. You can be proud of them. Furthermore your reactions these days are vivid and moving. This cycle should condense into a valuable volume. And probably be issued at a time when it will be properly appreciated—after all the minor flies have spun to their meaningless end.

Edgar Lee Masters, Dreiser, and His Secretary Harriet Bissell, Iroki, Summer 1938.

Your care for my personal welfare touches me. But as yet I am managing fairly well. It is this long depression. Actually one year ago, due to the rise in stock values I was well out of the red. Everything could have been worked out perfectly—the carrying of this place[2] and all. As it is the drop has reversed the situation. But I hope to pull through—sell this place & live peacefully ever after. But thanks to you just the same.

Affectionately
Dreiser

Should the sheriff suddenly appear I'll wire you.

1. In a letter of 23 April 1938, Masters had enclosed five sonnets on love. Masters often enclosed manuscript poems in his letters to Dreiser.
2. Iroki, Dreiser's home in Mount Kisco, New York.

To A. Heller [TC-DPUP]

A. Heller, who is probably Abraham M. Heller (1896–1975), a rabbi and a writer and lecturer on Jewish subjects, had reported to Dreiser in a letter of 16 May 1938 that after one of his lectures a member of the audience had stated that "'the greatest men of America are antisemites; look at Th. Dreiser. . . .' I replied that the aesthetical personality as well as the social & political philosophy of a great artist is to be found in his works, and I challenged the gentleman to show me one deliberately antisemitic passage in any of your works. —I wonder whether I was right."

THEODORE DREISER

Mt. Kisco
N. Y.
May 25—1938

Dr. A. Heller:

Dear Sir: There are no anti-semitic passages in my works. And if anyone thinks that basically I am anti-semitic he or she should read *The Hand of Potter*. Played successfully in Germany during 1929–30–31 it brought about the banning of my books on the ground, I hear, that I am a Jew, which does not happen to be the case.[1] However I did say that as Jews settle different lands they should blend as do most other races with the people of their chosen country. I have often argued for a Jewish father land—to be established in international agreement—where their common language, religion and traditions—assuming they prefer these—could be maintained—a source from which their race culture could flow out to others. For this I have been freely denounced although I still see nothing wrong with it.[2]

Very truly

Theodore Dreiser

1. Dreiser made this claim about the cause of the banning of his works in Germany on several occasions during the 1930s; see Dreiser to George Douglas, 14 January 1935, in Elias, *Letters*, II, 714–15.

2. For a similar comment by Dreiser on Zionism, see Dreiser to Ludwig Lewisohn, 5 July 1933.

To William C. Lengel [H-DPUP]

Dreiser sailed for France on 13 July 1938 and spent almost a month in Europe, speaking at the Paris conference of the International Association of Writers for the Defense of Culture, visiting Barcelona and seeing firsthand the effects of the Spanish Civil War, and spending some time with John Cowper Powys in Wales.

French Line

S.S. NORMANDIE

July 16—'38

Dear Will:

Thanks for the last phone call & the previous efforts. It all came up so sudden and the pressure was so great that I finally decided to go, though whether I can do any good remains to be seen. It's the League of American Writers and the American League Against War and Fascism Plus the French Comitte for Coordination and Information that is back of it all—thats in back of an International Peace Conference that assembles in Paris and holds meetings July 23–24.[1] The two American groups, plus the International Association of Writers, whose office is in Paris (29 Rue d'Anjou), plus one Paul Aragon, editor of Ce Soir, a Paris afternoon paper are collectively the people who have engineered my going.[2] Aragon is coming to Havre to meet me. They say his paper has a very large circulation and he may have some information for me that will be interesting. I'll see. On board I've been conversing with Herman F. Reissig, (Rev.) Dr. Jesse [illegible] & Langston Hughes who are members of the two American groups.[3] Nothing new in them—yet. I understand that Aragon is the one who wants me to go to Spain—probably to be blown up for the sake of the news—and that René Blech—Secy of the International Writers is willing to pay the freight. So—any day now.

To my astonishment I have met nine people I know on this boat—Jack Cosgrave, Marian Powys and her son Peter, Margaret Canty, a woman I

Dreiser in Paris,
July 1938.

knew in London, Madam Clayburgh, Reginald Wright Kauffman and his wife. (Do you remember him—author of The House of Bondage!) and Sam Groskopf—a German-Jewish—now French Jewish trader whom I first met in Los Angeles.[4] And there are celebrities galore—Joe Schenck, Charlie Chaplin, Paul Goncourt and others.[5]

By the way—as to my mail hold all personal letters for me until I return or give other directions. (I may cable before you get this.) Anything that looks pure business let Harriet[6] open & then forward to me. Unless I cable another address—mail can go to *18 Place* Vendome, c/o Llewellyn.

Regards to the family and you of course

Dreiser

1. These sponsoring organizations of the peace conference were either communist or on the extreme left, as were most of its participants. Encouraged by the Soviet Union, left-wing groups throughout the world had formed a popular front to fight what was believed to be a conspiracy by the Western capitalist powers and fascist countries to isolate and destroy the Soviet Union in a new world war.

2. Dreiser means Louis (not Paul) Aragon (1897–1982), one of the founders of literary surrealism, a communist, and the editor of *Ce Soir*.

3. Herman F. Reissig (1899?–1985), clergyman and author, and Langston Hughes (1902–1967), African American poet.

4. John O'Hara Cosgrave (1864–1947) edited *Everybody's*, a Butterick magazine, during the period Dreiser edited Butterick's *Delineator;* Marian Powys, a sister of Dreiser's friends John Cowper and Llewelyn Powys; Margaret Canty—unidentified; Alma Clayburgh (1882?–1958), a wealthy New Yorker who had in 1929 contributed to Dreiser's scheme to bring the Russian ballet to America; Reginald Wright Kauffman (1877–1959), a popular novelist whom Dreiser had known when both wrote for *Ainslee's* in the late 1890s (his *The House of Bondage* appeared in 1921); Samuel Groskopf, a German-born businessman, then resident in Paris.

5. Joseph M. Schenck (1876–1961), Hollywood executive and founder of Twentieth Century–Fox studios; Chaplin (1889–1977), the famous actor; Paul Goncourt—probably Joseph Paul-Boncour (not Goncourt) (1873–1972), French minister of foreign affairs during the early 1930s.

6. Harriet Bissell (1914–), Dreiser's secretary from November 1935 until his departure for California in late 1938.

To Edgar Lee Masters [H-HRHUT]

French Line
S.S. NORMANDIE
July 16th '38

Dear Doctor Masters:

They descended on me last Sunday with telegrams and cablegrams and in Fords and trucks and by Wednesday noon last they had me piled on this boat, bags and all, bound for Paris and worse Spain and maybe London. Dear Doctor, you never [word missing] such goings on! It may not even be legal! But here I am, entirely surrounded by salt water and steadily nearing France. Any cries I may utter don't carry no distance at all. It's these here [illegible]. There I was peaceful as you saw, doing nothing to nobody and now look at me! I haven't even got the right clothing. No cuff-buttons for my shirts. Not even the right socks or ties. All I got is instructions. I'm to say I represent the American Writers League and the American League For War and Fascism—no—wait a minute—I see now it's the American League *Against* War and Fascism and everywhere I go I'm to say that I'm for *Peace*. That's it—*Peace*. And I'm to say it hard-like. If anybody hits me I'm to repeat it—hard—and then cable them what happens. That's all I got to do. And for that I get my room and meals over and back. And I'm to keep my ears open and hear what I see. And if it's anything terrible I'm to cable that. But otherwise I ain't got nothin' else at all to do—just to keep my ears open and say Peace—particularly if they hit me.

Well, Doctor Masters, I've been feelin so troubled about this—so kinda sick in my insides, that I thought I better write you right away and ask you about it. In the first place, Doc, I don't really belong to either of these companies—in fact I ain't ever joined nothin yet. But the truth is Doc, they talked so loud and fast and all at once, like—they even hollered—that I got sorta confused,—hipponosed maybe an' the next thing I knew I was in the truck an' they were telling me that I had promised an' not only that but that I had signed something and that if I tried to get out they'd have me arrested. So here I am—locked in this here room with salt water all around. I can hear it & smell it. They say I can write all the letters I want, Doc—but that they wont do me no good. That I've signed and they've got me in their legal possession and that when I get over in France they're goin to take me somewhere and stand me up and when they say "*say Peace*" I gotta say it. Now Doc, you know ordinarily I'm for Peace—plenty of it—but this here way of makin me say it don't seem quite natural. So, Doc, I thought I'd try to write you anyhow and ask you what you'd prescribe.

You might wire if you can only find out where I am.

Your old patient
D

To Caroline McCormick Slade [TC-DPUP]

On his return from Europe, Dreiser saw President Franklin D. Roosevelt on 7 September to solicit his support in a plan for humanitarian aid proposed by the Loyalist government. Roosevelt recommended that such an effort be conducted by a committee of prominent citizens, and it was on this basis that Dreiser asked Rufus M. Jones (1863–1948), a Quaker leader, for suggestions. Mrs. Slade (1874?–1952) had been active in both suffragette reform and Republican politics. Dreiser had difficulty persuading several of those whom he asked to accept (Mrs. Slade herself declined) and the plan foundered. In December 1939, however, Roosevelt himself requested that the International Red Cross supervise a Spanish humanitarian relief program similar to the one Dreiser had transmitted to him.

George Washington Hotel,
Lexington Ave., & 23rd St.,
New York City
[28 September 1938][1]

Dear Mrs. Slade:

Rufus Jones of Haverford College suggested that I get in touch with you with regard to the matter which I am about to outline.

This summer I spent a few days in Barcelona, and while I was there I talked with Negrin and Del Vayo, the chief ministers of Loyalist Spain.[2] They outlined a plan to me which would effectually relieve the miserable conditions of the great mass of the Spanish people *on both sides* of the war.

This country and the American countries as a group have access to a great quantity of surplus supplies of all kinds—wheat, coffee, cotton and sugar and so on. This material is not being used over here, and Negrin and Del Vayo suggested that it might be possible for this material to be shipped to Spain and distributed to the civilian population, especially the women and children, in both Rebel and Loyalist territory and without regard to political or religious affiliations.

Conditions, as you no doubt are aware, are very bad; there is intense suffering now, and the certainty of famine and starvation this winter for at least five million people, if something is not done to alter the situation. In Loyalist Spain alone there is a population of twelve million, of whom three and one half million are refugees without any means whatever, and of these a half million are young children. Private efforts to help these people made by those sympathetic to the Loyalists are really insignificant compared to the actual need. They have no soap and as a result of this lack an epidemic of skin infections is wide-spread. There is no meat, no milk or other dairy products, and really nothing to eat except vegetables, and these are scarce and insufficient. There is no cotton for clothes, sheets, and other needs.

The same situation is approximated on the Rebel side, for, as is generally known, the aid given to Franco[3] by Italy and Germany has been mostly military and there has been little if no provision for the civilian population. And, of course, as a result of the war, all the normal procedures have been interrupted and it is impossible for the population on either side to sustain itself through its own efforts.

Negrin and Del Vayo suggested that I see President Roosevelt with a view to getting some method of shipping and distributing surplus supplies. I talked with the President about this two weeks ago, and he gave his hearty approval to the idea and offered his cooperation. The first step in putting the plan into effect, he said, would be to get a committee of not more than three or four people. The committee would present the plan to him and he would meet with them and place at the committee's disposal the aid of various government offices, and also, he would aid the committee personally. In getting the committee together, I have approached the Right Reverend John Ryan of the Catholic University in Washington,[4] and Rufus Jones of Haverford, and both have accepted. Mr. Jones has been in Washington and has talked further with the President about the enterprise, and it is now suggested that Norman Davis, of the Red Cross,[5] be a member of the Committee. Mr. Jones and Mr. Davis suggested that I get in touch with you, as he thought you would make a very valuable member of the committee. And that is what I am asking—will you be a member of this committee?

Mr. Jones, as you know, is a member of the Friends' Service Committee, and they are already equipped, in both Rebel and Loyalist Spain, to handle the distribution of these supplies when they are obtained. The President suggested that the shipping could be conducted through France on account of some agreement which this country has with the French government. I do not propose to be a member of the committee because I feel that I am too well identified with the Loyalist side of the war to help. And as soon as the committee is formed I propose to drop out of the picture.

If you care to be a member of the committee, I am not in a position to say exactly what you would have to do. That will be up to the committee and Mr. Roosevelt. But I am certain that being on the committee will not involve any great expense. I suppose you would have to make a trip to Washington for the preliminary meeting at least.

Since I first discussed this plan with the President the situation has altered considerably. If a general European war ensues, I very much fear for the result of the plan. But in any event, if anything is to be done, it must be done at once, not only because of the fear of a general war but because winter and the resulting famine are getting closer every day to the Spaniards. And, as I pointed out before, aid on a large scale, such as only a nation and not any private organization could give, would be of any value in this situation.

I understand that you plan to return to New York at the end of the week. Could you give me your answer before then if possible, so that I may tell Mr. Jones and the Right Reverend Ryan? I would be very glad to discuss this with you further, when you get back to town.

Very truly yours,

1. Although the letter is undated, Dreiser's secretary noted in a letter to Mrs. Slade on 10 October 1938 that Dreiser's initial letter about the Spanish humanitarian relief plan had been sent to her on 28 September 1938.

2. Juan Negrin (1891–1956), the premier, and Julio Alvarez del Vayo (1891–1974), the foreign minister, of Loyalist Spain.

3. General Francisco Franco (1892–1975), leader of the rebel forces and later Spanish head of state.

4. Ryan (1869–1945), a Catholic educator, was also an expert on labor law and a New Deal supporter.

5. Davis (1878–1944), an American diplomat, had been appointed head of the American Red Cross by Roosevelt earlier in the year.

To Edgar Lee Masters [H-HRHUT]

Dreiser and Helen had arrived in the Los Angeles area in early December 1938 and settled in Glendale, northeast of the city. They had also lived in Glendale in 1921 during their first extended stay in California.

253a Lorraine St,[1]
Glendale, Calif
Dec 7—'38

Fairest Edgar:

To Portland first & then to here. This is the extreme west end of Glendale where the mountains begin. I have a bungalow through which the sun shines. Monday when I arrived here it was 89. Today—noon—it is 84—but dry heat. This region is strangely beautiful. The people in Hollywood almost entirely loose straw. Here in Glendale all seems solid bourgeois—and farmerish and with means to live. For myself I am seeking quiet and—here at least—finding it. But I miss you and Alice.[2] That constant palaver over the old engaging problem! I laugh and laugh. But as against the ordinary run of things how wonderful to be able to laugh ironically and yet kindly. Here—as in N.Y. is a constant palaver about this & that. But there are some people to know. My friend McCord[3] just left here—after bringing mail. And Calvin Bridges is destined to show up.[4] If only you were here—you and the hen—and we would argue out under the trees.

See Harriet if you can.[5] A note addressed to her care of the Geo. Washington Hotel will reach her. Don't say I asked you to. I feel as though she were a child of mine and I am in nowise deserting her or leaving her in any difficult situation & have no intention of so doing.

Love to both of you.

T.D

1. Dreiser misspelled this street name until early 1939, when he began to spell it correctly as "Loraine" (see Dreiser to William Watters, 22 March 1939).
2. Alice Davis, with whom Masters lived from 1936 to 1943. Her nickname (see below) was Hen.
3. See Dreiser to Donald P. McCord, 26 November 1935.
4. See Dreiser to George Douglas, 15 February 1935, n. 5.
5. See Dreiser to William C. Lengel, 16 July 1938, n. 6.

To Edgar Lee Masters [H-HRHUT]

Since Masters was often in financial difficulties, Dreiser sought to aid him in finding profitable outlets for his work.

253 W. Lorraine
Glendale
Dec 30—'38

Dear Von Masters:

Thanks for the Puckett arias.[1] They thrill me and still me, as 'twere. And sorry I am that you cant move out here for I truly believe it would have the usual value of an extreme change—bubbles the blood and so the imagination. All things are charged against this area but I avoid all save the simpler—really the simp-lest social phases. Glendale—while an important part of Los Angeles—is a sober sturdy realm. On its extreme northern edge under the mountains am I—as many as eight miles from Hollywood—nine from the business heart of L A. A charming furnished bungalow as full of sunlight as a beach is mine for $40.00 a month. Heat, light, telephone, distilled water bring it probably to $50.00.

Of course a car of some kind is indispensible. I have a Ford. No charge for garage. Gas 16 cts a gallon. Food is much cheaper than in N.Y. I should say at least 30%. Entertainment for me is the sunshine and the sub-tropic vegetation & the real beauty of the same. Such skies! Such a climate! Perhaps 65 to 70 by day, 40 at night. Blankets. A small fire in the evening. And you no me. I avoid all but selected friends. And I love to walk—as much time as I can spare. No parties. No gossip. I lived just so 3 years here once, in this same Glendale, & worked out two books. Yet if one takes a car & rides, the scene is amazingly varied. There is no such city anywhere that I have ever seen. Not anywhere.

Speaking of *The Spoon River Anthology* and Rupert Hughes I sincerely doubt if he can do anything for you.[2] He was a factor but I hear no more. A new crowd is in. The New York banks—Chase, National City Central-Hanover, Morgan own the movies—all of them. They called 5% or change the management. I know Walter Wanger, Joseph Cohen, Jesse Lasky, Joseph Schenck and some others personally.[3] One of the livest today—and young-est—is Wanger. I thought, with your consent, I'd speak to him about Spoon River. If he is not interested, there is an under surface advisor in M.G-M by the name of Philbrick, who is English and literary.[4] I will talk to him. Of course if you wish I'll speak to Hughes and he may do something. But I hear that he is not much listened to.

My darling Calvin Bridges died here in Holy Angels Hospital last week.[5] He was so wonderful. Such a truly great spirit. I arrived just in time to talk with him for the last time. He was never rational again after I left him that time though I saw him every other day. I had the gratification of telling him again how deeply and truly I cared for him—how wholly beautiful his great mind was to me. Now he is gone.

I have tacked the hen coop with its poetic gourd on the wall beside me.[6] Fail not! Keep watch and ward! And thou spiest a cock in the offing—*Fire!*

Love & best wishes always

Dreiser

1. Masters enclosed in his letter to Dreiser on 26 December 1938 a series of rhymed couplets by "Lute Puckett," a figure he had created for the expression of irreverent and lewd themes.

2. Masters, who had for some years sought to interest producers in a dramatic or film adaptation of his still popular *Spoon River Anthology* (1915), had mentioned in a letter of 27 December that he was thinking of writing Rupert Hughes about the idea. Hughes (1872–1956) had a multifaceted career as a historian, musicologist, playwright, and—since the early 1920s—scriptwriter.

3. Wanger (1894–1968) was production chief at Paramount and later a major independent producer; for Lasky, see Dreiser to Jesse L. Lasky, 14 March 1926; Schenck (1876–1961) had helped found both United Artists in 1924 and Twentieth Century–Fox in 1935. For Joseph Cohen, Dreiser probably meant Harry Cohn (1891–1958), founder and head of Columbia Pictures.

4. Unidentified.

5. For Bridges, see Dreiser to George Douglas, 15 February 1935, n. 5.

6. Unclear, but perhaps the comment contains an allusion to Masters's companion Alice Davis; see Dreiser to Edgar Lee Masters, 7 December 1938, n. 2.

1939

To Edgar Lee Masters   [H-HRHUT]

THEODORE DREISER

253 W. Lorraine
Glendale
Jan 3—'39

Edgar Dear:

I am so sorry to read of your state and mood.[1] It is outrageous that all your great gifts you should be brought to such a pass. I spoke to you of my troubles once—how much of all that I had was so swiftly swept away between '29 and '31. Since then I have been trying to readjust things so as to be able to live simply while I attempt to recover a portion of my economic safety. It is not easy. This last year, and the loss of that since and the negligence & I think hostile, attitude of my publishers, has done much to frustrate me. How glad I will be, if I succeed in selling something of mine here, to discharge my tenants from the Mt Kisco house and reopen it as a haven for a few of those whom I so much admire—just a place to come and stay indefinitely and work in peace. I used to aid Calvin Bridges and my friend Davis (Hubert) the painter.[2] The big studio in West 57th was a refuge in many ways for so many—and I enjoyed and profited by it, as who wouldn't? In your case though I feel that some practical thing can be turned forthwith. I just wrote an introduction to the philosophy of Thoreau—(a 30 thousand word group of selections illustrating his philosophy which I made)—and for the which,—the combination of the two,—I was paid $500.[3] It was not hard—very agreeable—Longmans, Green are putting out a series. They want some one to do Emerson and who else but you should do it. I am writing Harriet to go and see them and urge them to come to you.[4] Incidentally, if you will send me a brief outline of a possible script of Spoon River I will certainly go to Wanger & some others and see what I can do.[5]

Here is something else. You say you cannot afford to come to L.A. I have a friend—Maj. D. P. McCord—the brother of my *Peter* (in 12 Men). He is a retired army Doctor.[6] He is all alone in a charming house in Pasadena—has a telescope. Books, food etc and loves company but has scarcely anybody. I am positive that he would share that house which has two or three large bedrooms, two baths, a living room, dining room, kitchen, lawn garage for almost nothing—say $20 or $25 a month. Besides he has a car and loves literature. He would be honored to have you, I know, and with you there, I would have you, too. We could proceed to make a small circle. I don't know whether you know Upton Sinclair personally or his wife.[7] But they are decent people, and never take the floor and keep it. They are available. So are a number of the scientists at Caltech—the good ones—Borsook, Sturtevant, Painter.[8] And at Mt. Wilson are Hubbell[9] and large group of stationary and visiting astronomers all of whom are available. If you know & like Rupert Hughes[10] he is here & will introduce a world of movieites of all degrees and descriptions. And from here you will do as well as from New York. I'll be delighted to stir things up for you & when I get a slightly larger place here to share my bed & board. Anyhow and at once—I'll work on this Emerson thing and you write & tell me how you react to the McCord idea.[11]

Whatever you do—*don't* die. Your the most fascinating figure & temperament in all living American letters and I'll miss you past all explaining.

Affectionately

Dreiser

1. Masters had complained about his financial problems in several of his letters to Dreiser of the previous month.

2. For Bridges, see Dreiser to George Douglas, 15 February 1935, n. 5; Dreiser admired the work of the painter Hubert Davis (1902–77), who in 1930 published *The Symbolic Drawings of Hubert Davis for An American Tragedy*, with a preface by Dreiser.

3. *The Living Thoughts of Thoreau Presented by Theodore Dreiser* was published by Longmans, Green & Co. in late March 1939.

4. Harriet Bissell, Dreiser's secretary. Masters did prepare the Emerson volume in the Living Thoughts Library; it appeared in March 1940.

5. See Dreiser to Edgar Lee Masters, 30 December 1938.

6. For McCord, see Dreiser to Donald P. McCord, 12 June 1920.

7. For Sinclair, see Dreiser to Upton Sinclair, 8 October 1914; Mary Sinclair (1882–1961).

8. Henry Borsook (1897–1984), a biochemist; Alfred H. Sturtevant (1891–1970), a geneticist; probably T. S. Painter (1889–1969), who though a distinguished geneticist at the University of Texas, visited Cal Tech on occasion.

9. Dreiser means Edwin P. Hubble (1889–1953), an astronomer at the Mt. Wilson Observatory in Pasadena and one of the leading figures in the field during this period.

10. See Dreiser to Edgar Lee Masters, 30 December 1938, n. 2.

11. Masters, replying on 9 January 1938, thanked Dreiser for the suggestion but declined on the grounds that he did not believe himself sufficiently "pliable" to move.

To Rufus M. Jones [TS-Hav]¹

Jones, whom Dreiser had corresponded with during the fall of 1938 about aid to Spain (see Dreiser to Caroline McCormick Slade, 28 September 1938), was a distinguished Quaker author and scholar, with special interest in the mystical side of Quakerism. Dreiser had written him on 1 December 1938 seeking advice about the Quaker background of The Bulwark. *When Dreiser revised and completed* The Bulwark *in 1945, he drew on Jones's work. It is not known what two letters Dreiser refers to in his first paragraph.*

THEODORE DREISER

253A, West Loraine,
Glendale, Calif.
Jan. 27, 1939.

Dear Dr. Jones:

I am sending two letters to you which I would like to have you look over.

I can't tell you how much this interests, and I may say thrills me, because I feel that the Quaker Faith is the only true exposition, and, in so far as it is carried out, realization of Christianity in the modern world. However, when I say Christianity, I mean social ethics and equity introduced into life according to scientific principles as I now, at last, understand those to be. Of all things your books in their entirety should be used, as you know.

Don't bother to answer this letter. I merely wanted to urge you to move in the matter in so far as your much over-burdened life will permit. The world needs a revival of this kind and there is nothing else that it needs so much.

Affectionately and with admiration.
Theodore Dreiser

1. Published in Gerhard Friedrich, "The Dreiser-Jones Correspondence," *Bulletin of Friends Historical Association* 5 (Spring 1957): 23–34.

To William Watters [TS-UV]

Dreiser attempted for several years during the late 1930s and early 1940s to interest a film company in My Gal Sal, *a movie version of Paul Dresser's life based on his portrayal of Paul in "My Brother Paul" (in* Twelve Men *[1919]) and containing a number of Paul's songs. Twentieth Century–Fox bought the rights in 1941 and the film appeared in 1942. Watters, a New York–based agent, had apparently inquired about the state of the project.*

THEODORE DREISER

253 West Loraine,
Glendale, Calif.
March 22, 1939.

Dear Mr. Watters:

I want to explain to you the present situation in regard to the story of Paul Dresser's life. A story has been worked out from my My Brother Paul, plus all the available material about him existing in family files, plus any and all of his songs. These have been rolled into one and a story has been constructed, which is the authentic story of Paul's life. There can be only one.

As it stands, I, while I am the executor of Paul Dresser's estate, which includes all royalties from his songs (most of which go to Paul's family) do not have the exclusive rights on this complete story, nor will I realize as much on it as I would on any other of my stories. There are existing contracts between myself and my sister and a third party[1] which cover the whole thing. There are also contracts between these three interested parties and the music publishers who control Paul's songs. The songs are all tied up with the picture and the whole thing is quite complicated. This naturally makes the profits limited for any and all interested parties, and that is the reason that this particular story has to be handled in a different manner than any other of my stories.

At the present time Mr. A. Dorian Otvos has the exclusive on this idea and is working on it from all angles here in Los Angeles.[2] During the time of his contract it has been agreed that no agent will handle it unless that agent be employed by Mr. Otvos.

I want to give you this information so that complications will not arise during present negotiations.

Very truly yours,
Theodore Dreiser
A. Dorian Otvos,
1345 N. Hayworth Ave.,
Hollywood, Calif.

By the way Otvos is not interested in Radio or anything that I might do for that—and I have radio talks—short on literature in San Francisco, Portland and Salt Lake City.[3]

1. The sister Dreiser refers to is Mame; the "third party" was probably Helen.

2. Otvos (1890–1945) wrote popular music in his native Hungary as well as for Broadway shows before he became a Hollywood agent; it was in fact Donald Friede (see Dreiser to Donald Friede, 22 March 1934), who formerly had worked for the Liveright publishing firm and was now a Hollywood agent, who negotiated the sale to Twentieth Century–Fox.

3. The postscript is in Dreiser's hand.

To Edgar Lee Masters   [H-HRHUT]

THEODORE DREISER

April 12,'39

Dear Edgar:

This graveyard business has had an occasional thought from me. Having officiated on various occasions my conclusion was that the best way to arrange things was to ascend to heaven in a chariot of fire. Failing that cremation seemed next best. I once inquired as whether I might dig a family vault at Mt. Kisco. Answer: No. You must deal with a licensed undertaker and an incorporated graveyard company—otherwise you would injure their business.

Incidentally, speaking of living with me—I think I told you I once thought of turning the place (Mt. Kisco) into a kind of art roost; but the more I thought it, the more I was sure it would turn *me* into a hotel manager with a group of dissatisfied tenants, certain in the end to sue and denounce me. My last plan was to work and earn a large sum of money and then invite those that I admired most to live there, *free,* while I hid in the bushes—or joined some war somewhere. Object? Peace.

This town grows apace. 20,000,000 will live here, sure. But *lethargy* will be its full name. All who come here come to lie down & take the count—die & go to heaven (this being heaven). They come with enough to conclude their days in peace. I marvel at the L.A. papers. They reflect this mood exactly. Personally my work room is my complete world. I hear of all sorts of people being here, but avoid contacts. Letters keep me in touch with real people.

As ever

Dreiser

Your Easter hymn should have been entitled *The Hen is Risen.*[1]

1. The "Easter Hymn" is apparently Masters's "Why We Know Not," a poem on the meaning of death which he sent Dreiser on 30 March 1939. "Hen" was the nickname of Masters's companion Alice Davis; see Dreiser to Edgar Lee Masters, 7 December 1938, n. 2.

To Gabriel Lapicque [TC-DPUP]

Lapicque was an undergraduate at Colby College, Waterville, Maine.

253 West Loraine,
Glendale, Calif.
April 13, 1939.

Dear Mr. Lapicque:

For some reason or other your letter has been mislaid. I am sorry and hope that this will still be of use to you.

I was never directly influenced by Zola. When I first went into the newspaper business in Chicago and St. Louis there was considerable talk of his books and his method but I did not read anything of his until after I had written Sister Carrie. But even when I did read him I found absent from his work the artistic and emotional responses which make for contrast and were outstanding in Balzac, Hugo, de Maupassant, Dostoievski and others.

As for Nietzsche, I was entirely unaware of his philosophy until I had written The Financier and The Titan and several other of my works.[1] Even when I did read him I did not accept his suggestion of a mass production of super-men. It seemed to me that they would cancel out and advantage society very little if any.

In the main I think that my reaction to life was direct and both realistic and naturalistic, in that it included not only the surface actions of people but their emotions which are the basis of their actions.

From the point of view of construction—the physical structure of the novel—I think that Balzac, more than Thackeray or Dickens or Hugo or Tolstoy—all of whom I had encountered—was of more help. I liked his method of illustrating as he went with philosophy, poetry, criticism. While the form and technique of the novel came from abroad, America was the life canvas which fascinated me and still does.

I trust this will be of some help. As you see I am here in Glendale, on the west coast, so, seeing me in New York is out. But any questions (within reason) that you may care to forward will get my attention.

Very truly,

1. This claim is not entirely accurate, since Dreiser appears to have read at least the introduction to H. L. Mencken's study of Nietzsche, *The Philosophy of Friedrich Nietzsche* (1908), in late 1909, some years before he began work on the Cowperwood Trilogy. See Dreiser to Mencken, 6 December 1909, in Riggio, *Dreiser-Mencken Letters*, I, 41.

To William C. Lengel [TS-WCLUP][1]

1426 North Hayworth Ave.,
Hollywood, Calif.[2]
May 6, 1939.

Dear Lengel:

For some time I have been wanting to write you about my present un-happy relationship with Simon and Schuster.

As you know, their present attitude toward me, and their attitude, re-ally, ever since I went in there, has been amazingly antagonistic. It may be nothing more than a suspicion but I have had the feeling all along that the dreadful deal I got on my left over Liveright books, which they were supposed to stock and sell for me on a 15% royalty, was arranged between Pell and themselves through Mr. Shimkin, and that all along he has been a cause as well as a party to their attitude toward me.[3] Having signed the contract, however, and gotten in there, I had no immediate way of getting out. Now, because of other developments, one or two of which you have pointed out to me, I may be in a position to pay them either in cash or publication securities, the sum they have asked and agreed to take, which is $10,000.

One thing that may make it possible for me to do this is the very likely sale of Sister Carrie here.[4] Another thing is the rise of the cheap paper book publication companies to which you called my attention several years ago. I am satisfied that the best move that I could possibly make now would be to get one of these 25 cent book houses to take over all of my books and issue them either serially or as a set at 25 cents a volume, because on the strength of that they should be able to get a wide pre-publication subscrip-tion either for the sets or parts of it.[5]

If a worth while advertising campaign by one of these houses were launched it should bring in money enough to repay me what I will have to pay Simon and Schuster to bring my books back to life, as well as make a lot of money for the publishing house, because, of course, I would accept a very low royalty which should run for the life of the books. In connection with that, of course, I would insist on reserving the right to issue, after a period of time, an expensive set of my books—and since you were the one who first pointed out to me that a cheap issue of a number of my books would be of value, I feel that you are the one who could take charge of this and put it over for me.

As I can show you, if I come to New York in connection with it, I have literally an enormous collection of letters, and a great quantity of them within the last three or four months—and all wildly enthusiastic about one or another of the books from the first to the last and coming from all parts of the world. Many of the writers are highly incensed because in each case they have discovered that the books are not only not to be found in the libraries or the book stores but that they are not even to be had on order from Simon and Schuster. They literally will not supply them.

That, in connection with this constant under-cover talk about my anti-Judaism which consisted of the mild correspondence I once had with Hutchins Hapgood,[6] has caused all sorts of people who are inimical to me—writers and what not—to not only play this up but exaggerate it in every quarter, so that I feel that Simon and Schuster may themselves be joined with this issue to the end of taking me off the market entirely. It may be that they identify me with Germany and have decided to include me in their campaign against Teutonic Culture. However, that really leaves me no door except the one I am proposing to you because at the present time no high cost book house is going to take over all of my books and issue them, and so place me before the public again. Besides, I am much more sympathetic with the cheap book idea since it brings within easy reach of the masses the total worth while literature of the world which should be theirs. I think it is the next obvious progressive step in connection with literature in general, and I would like to have my works shared.

Now in connection with this, what I would like you to do would be to consult with one and another of these low priced book companies, the best one first, of course, and see how it would respond to this idea. Since each volume would sell at 25 cents I would want to know what they would look upon as a fair percentage to pay me and whether or not they would really indulge in a preliminary publicity campaign, perhaps in connection not only with me but some others whose works they would like to issue cheaply in this way.

In order to impress the public as to the value of this idea, a really worth while campaign would be the most important phase of it, as this would be the thing that would sell complete sets in quantity as opposed to a lesser sale for single volumes. It is on the cheap sets, I am sure, that they would make really more.

Now as to this, there is another matter which has something to do with it. Since there is a likelihood of Sister Carrie being released through the movies, a special edition of the book should come out simultaneously with the release of the picture. At 25 cents a copy it should prove of great value and would help to sell not only the other volumes but the sets as a whole. I have no idea when this release will be, but if it goes through, action in connection with this phase of it should be immediate.

I feel that nothing should be said to Simon and Schuster in any way, at this time. Negotiations with them should wait until you have an offer that is worth while. Also it would be better, I think, if word as to these negotiations could be kept from them in every way until we are ready to act.

As to your commission, I don't know whether or not you would think 10% of whatever I get worth while or not. But I must re-emphasize the fact that in connection with all this a real publicity campaign would have to be undertaken. If that cannot be absolutely guaranteed I would not feel this move worth much of anything.

Regards.

Dreiser

Enclosed is the most recent letter concerning *Moods* and some of my other books.[7]

1. Published in Louis Oldani, "Dreiser and Paperbacks: An Unpublished Letter," *Dreiser Newsletter* 6 (Fall 1975): 1–9.
2. Dreiser and Helen had moved in early May to an apartment in Hollywood.
3. Dreiser's arbitration settlement with Horace Liveright in 1934 gave him ownership of his books in their possession, and his contract with Simon & Schuster, signed not long after, provided that they market these books. Arthur Pell (see Dreiser to Arthur Pell, 25 May 1931) was president of Liveright at that time; Leon Shimkin (see Dreiser to M. Lincoln Schuster, 27 August 1935, n. 3) was a partner in Simon & Schuster.
4. Although Dreiser at this time was negotiating with several studios, the issue of the film rights to *Sister Carrie* was not settled until the fall of 1940 when RKO, which had acquired an option on them in February 1940, completed the deal.
5. Nothing came of this idea; the first paperback of a Dreiser novel did not appear until the Pocket Books edition of *Sister Carrie* in 1949.
6. Hapgood's "Is Dreiser Anti-Semitic?" *Nation* 140 (April 1935): 436–38, which contains letters exchanged between Hapgood and Dreiser in 1933 on Dreiser's purported anti-Semitism, received much attention on its appearance.
7. The postscript is in Dreiser's hand.

To Dayton Stoddart [TS-DPUP]

Stoddart, a writer on New York show business, published a book on the entertainment magazine Variety *in 1941 and a novel in 1945.*

THEODORE DREISER

1426 North Hayworth,
Hollywood, Calif.
May 10, 1939.

Dear Stoddart:

Thanks for your letter and I'll write you about that later. Also I will let you know what I can find out about the movie situation in so far as you are concerned, but will you do this for me, if it is not too much trouble?

Get me the names of a number of fairly recently organized non-Jewish publishers. I am thinking of changing from Simon and Schuster to another concern but there is no use of my going to Scribners or Harpers or MacMillan's. They are too conservative.

What I want is a young house with some money and a willingness to undertake a new kind of proposition which I have ready to present to them.

Incidentally, can you tell me whether W. W. Norton or anyone connected with his organization in a financial control sense is Jewish? All this is strictly private. Don't mention it to anybody because I will have trouble enough without that arranging my [word missing?] changes.

Regards,
Dreiser

You don't *casually* observe *Parades*—you televise as well as psychologize those mechanical social organs.[1] Or, perhaps I had better say, organisms. Once your arrive as a novelist you will simultaneously arrive as a critic—an ironic howitzer.

Don't drink any more than will further your career as a writer.[2]

I had to move over here, because my studio calls are a little too numerous & the driving distance too great.[3]

1. In an undated letter to Dreiser, Stoddart had noted observing a recent New York political parade.
2. The postscript is in Dreiser's hand.
3. Dreiser also added this sentence in the margin.

To Dayton Stoddart [H-DPUP]

1426 N. Hayworth
June 22nd 39

Dear Stoddart:

Didn't I write you about your Broun article.[1] I'm sorry, for I enjoyed it much & sent it on to a number of others—among them Annie Riley Hale—Broun's ex-mother-in-law. It please her enormously. I feel if you had given the Broun paper a somewhat more serious and substantial ending it might have been published. What mince-meat you make of him.

—I would write oftener but the truth is that I'm harried by endless duties—and work. Believe it or not I'm up at 7.30 as a rule & at my desk at nine. What between writers—callers from the East—movie consultations, my meals, my own particular job I work until evening. Publicly it looks as though I had nothing to show for it but I have—as time will prove—unless I die suddenly.

Wish you were living out here. But that's selfish in one sense, for you'd find it awfully thin picking mentally. Painfully so.

This is a selfish, self-concentrated, mean, loafing town. The business & political world is hard boiled & cruel. The movies are solidly Jewish. They've dug in, employ only Jews with American names and buy only what they cannot abstract & disguise. And the dollar sign is the guide—mentally & physically. That America should be led—the mass—by this direction is beyond all believing. In addition they are arrogant, insolent, and contemptuous. But I'm not telling you anything. This I judge will be their future land.

Don't think I don't miss your dynamic presence. I do. I may be back next fall.

Regards
T.D.

Do you ever see Duffy.[2] He's a nice guy.

1. Heywood Broun (1888–1939), the well-known columnist for the *New York World-Telegram* and other newspapers. Stoddart had sent Dreiser a copy of an article dealing principally with Broun's recent conversion to Catholicism. Dreiser had known Broun, also a staunch socialist, since the early 1920s.
2. Dreiser had renewed his association with Richard Duffy, his old friend from the turn of the century, when both were living at New York's George Washington Hotel during the early fall of 1938.

To Richard Duffy [TS-CU]

For Dreiser's renewal of his friendship with Duffy, see Dreiser to Dayton Stoddart, 22 June 1939, n. 2. During the late 1920s, Dreiser, following the great success of An American Tragedy and the increased popularity of his work abroad, was often mentioned as the author who might be the first American to receive the Nobel Prize in Literature. However, in 1930, the prize was awarded to Sinclair Lewis, largely, it appears, because his blatant satire of American middle-class life appealed to the anti-American sentiments of the prize committee.[1]

THEODORE DREISER

1426 North Hayworth,
Hollywood, Calif.
August 1, 1939.

Dear Duffy:

Thanks for your gracious letter.

The situation in regard to the Nobel prize is as follows. In 1928—two months before the prize was awarded, the New York papers—all of them—announced (as seemingly, a tip from Sweden) that the prize was coming to me. Two months later it was awarded to Sinclair Lewis. Then next (in so far as America was concerned) it was awarded to Eugene O'Neill who not only wrote me but said in the Press that he thought it was going to me—not him. Next—several years later it was awarded to Pearl Buck who also announced, as you know, that it should have gone to me. Lastly there was Somerset Maugham, whom you mention.[2]

Just what the Swedish point of view in regard to me is, I don't know. Perhaps the Nobel Committee has been informed that I am wild Red—regardless of how little I personally qualify for the job. I do not know what your plans are but if you feel like challenging the committee I would be interested to learn what the particular mental angle is that prompts this. There must be one. But I do not expect that I will be awarded the prize.

The humorous story pays its way out here with laughter.

I recall, always, our evening conferences in the bar and my room. You are as delightful a conversationalist and story teller as any I have ever known,—I think the best. Briggs is not man-of-the-world enough to appreciate your charm.[3] But there must be a bureau manager who is. I'll inquire.

As always,
Dreiser

P. S. Tell Roberts that I have run into Angna Enters and it looks as though she might make an impression in the moving picture business. If she should get the part of Carrie, I think there will be a new star made.[4]

P. P. S. You will be interested in the enclosed particularly since it comes from Indianapolis via New York. Young Chaliapin is a remarkable portrait painter and has achieved an arresting and striking likeness.[5] It is going to be photographed for the Press here. I have been sitting two hours a day for a week, and like it and him very much.

1. See Rolf Lundén, "Dreiser and the Nobel Prize," *American Literature* 50 (May 1978): 216–29.
2. Lewis won the Nobel Prize in 1930, O'Neill in 1936, and Buck in 1938; Maugham (an Englishman) did not receive a Nobel Prize.
3. Dreiser had attempted to interest Ernest Briggs (1900–1971), who ran the lecture bureau managing Dreiser's lecture tours, to arrange some lectures for Duffy.
4. Roberts has not been identified. Enters (1907–89), a dancer, writer, and painter; Dreiser came to admire her work during the 1930s when she often gave dance recitals in New York.
5. Boris Chaliapin (1907–79), a Russian-born portrait painter.

To George T. Bye [H-DPUP]

Bye (1887–1957), a New York agent, placed much of Dreiser's magazine writing during the 1920s and 1930s. Encouraged by Bye, Dreiser had prepared an outline for a sketch entitled "Orville Signs the Checks" for the Reader's Digest's *"Unforgettable Character" series. On 24 October 1939, Bye reported that the* Digest *had declined the project but went on to note that he and William C. Lengel, who often acted as Dreiser's agent, had "agreed to pool our forces to make some deals for you." He went on to present Lengel's idea that Dreiser write a sketch of his brother Paul for the* Digest *series.*

THEODORE DREISER

Oct. 29—'39

Dear Bye:

It's fine of you and Lengel to get together in this way and, of course, it's ok with me. There are many angles—articles, radio, movies assignments, lectures—whatever you choose to undertake. As for this Readers Digest article, I had no idea until I read the editors statement in your letter that the *uplift* was involved. (Public virtue). I thought Orville would be acceptable as a contrast.

However, heres the trouble with *My Brother Paul*. It's 11000 words long. How is that to be condensed into 3,000? Also, would the editor want a condensation of what is really a well known character sketch. I could, of course, condense it some and have another person suggest more & better ways, but I have a really virtuous character who appeals to me & might appeal to the editor *if it could* be a woman.

When I was a kid—and very poor (age 15) an old maid school-teacher at Warsaw Ind, Agnes Fielding,[1] took a quite loving—really motherly interest in me. She braced me up and when I had to leave school in my 1st year high, came to me and explained the things she thought I could do for myself to insure my going up not down. There were a lot of small town depreciations due to family poverty & ignorance which she brushed away as worthless & nothing to bother about—told me the story of her own life & and two years later followed me to Chicago & finding me working for 5.00 a week in a wholesale hardware house made me quit and go to the University of Indiana, at her expense. She knew David Starr Jordan & wrote him about me and gave me a letter to present to him.[2] (I had contracted consumption.) After that one year at college I did well enough,—saw her once and later (1897) started saving money to pay her back. However, by the time I was ready to do anything, she had married and—of all things—at her age died of childbirth. Before that she had become Supt. of a Chicago High School.

I never forgot her—how could I. A beautiful temperament—a sort of fairy god mother in this naughty world. Perhaps the editor of the Digest might not object to a study of her.

Regards—to you and Will.

Let me know

Dreiser

1. Dreiser means Mildred (not Agnes) Fielding, his teacher during his freshman year (1885–86) at Warsaw's Central High School. Dreiser also recalls her in *Dawn* (1930), 274–77.

2. Dreiser was a student at Indiana University during the 1889–90 academic year; Jordan (1851–1931), who was later to achieve national prominence as the first president of Stanford University and as a peace advocate, was then president of Indiana.

To Patrick Coakley [H-Hun]

Patrick was the young son of Elizabeth Coakley (1903–1985), who herself was the sister of Patrick Kearney, the actor/playwright who adapted An American Tragedy *for the stage in 1926. Dreiser met Elizabeth Coakley in Los Angeles during the summer of 1939; they remained close until his death.*

THEODORE DREISER

Hollywood, Calif
Nov. 27—39

Dear Mr. Coakley:

As per your request I am enclosing a bow tie which I trust will meet your needs.[1] For one so young as yourself it seems a little mature (to me) but as you age, assuming that you keep it, it may not prove unsuitable. However, if you insist on wearing it now, I can only wish you luck. Avoid gangs. And if taken unaware defend it stoutly. You will need to. And remember courage is the better part of valor.[2] But rocks and clubs also help.

With both awe and admiration I remain,

Very Truly
Theodore Dreiser

1. Dreiser had become partial to bow ties during the early 1930s.
2. A variation on Falstaff's "The better part of valor is discretion" (*Henry IV,* Part One, Act 5, Scene 1).

1940

To Joseph Fischler [H-LLIU]

For Fischler, see Dreiser to Joseph Fischler, 30 May 1935.

THEODORE DREISER

1426 N. Hayworth
Hollywood
Jan 12—1940

Dear Fischler:

Did I write you about your *Brazil* how much I thought of it.[1] It is so—not only informative, but interpretive. I feel as though it had passed from being a name to an attractive and worthwhile reality. And now I wish I might see it. I also feel that you should submit it to some magazine like the *North American Review* or *Current History* and see if one will not publish it.[2] It is too good to rest in any drawer. Furthermore your style—and it is a style—is lucid, smooth, pleasing, like a good drink. I should like to see it published—*much*.

Meanwhile all I can say is that I am here. I have gathered fascinating material for a, to me, important book and am now condensing it into chapters.[3] Otherwise there exists for me a constant byline of dickering. At least 5 scripts of books or original stories are always on tables here—office or editorial. There are conferences, excitement, objections, Mr. Hays,[4] the Catholic Church, the interests and then quiet. There is never an hour when forty or fifty thousand ($) are not right around the corner. But there they stay.

Then there are requests—for opinions, criticisms, reviews, autographs—to meet people, to dine. But I duck as much as possible. I am enclosing samples.[5] The S&S thing you might return.[6] Sometimes I wish I could get you to represent me in my publishing relations in NY. I am far away & the average agent is—well—he is—thats about all.

Regards
Dreiser

1. Fischler had sent Dreiser the manuscript of his essay "Brazil" on 20 December 1939.
2. The essay does not appear to have been published.
3. Dreiser's philosophical study, *The Formula Called Man*.

4. For Hays, see Dreiser to Theodore Kiendl, 18 August 1930, n. 7.

5. Dreiser enclosed in this letter a copy of a letter sent to Ed Smith, dated 9 January 1940, in response to Smith's request for a contribution to the Finnish Relief Fund. This letter also appeared in the San Francisco *People's World*, 12 January 1940, and in Elias, *Letters*, III, 864–65.

6. Dreiser's publisher, Simon & Schuster; the "thing" Dreiser refers to has not been identified.

To Bernard G. Ulizio [H-KSU]

Ulizio (1889–1969), who made and lost several fortunes, was a well-known collector of Victorian and modern authors. For Dreiser's earlier efforts to sell his manuscripts, see Dreiser to Walter W. Lange, 20 October 1922.

THEODORE DREISER

24 January 1940

Dear Mr. Ulizio:

Thank you for your very kind letter.[1] Unfortunately, quite all of my original Mss are in storage in New York City and to get one out I shall personally have to return there. However, should you choose one of the major Ms, which is what, I fancy, interests you, I would make the trip without extra charge. The principal Mss that still belong to me are:

1. An American Tragedy	5,000
2. The "Genius"	4,500
3. The Titan	3,000
4. Dawn. Being Vol 1 of my autobiography	2,500
5. Newspaper Days (Originally published as *A Book About Myself*.)	2,000
6. A Hoosier Holiday	1,800

There is, however, the 1st typed copy of *Sister Carrie*, the original of which now belongs to the N. Y. Public Library and is no longer for sale, which I will sell for $1,800. This is of especial interest because it is the text from which the 1st American Edition was set. It bears a large number of corrections and cuts in my own hand writing. Also a number more made with my consent by the late Arthur Henry, my friend, and at that time, literary advisor.[2] Collectors place a high value on it.

Apart from these I have only a number of the shorter of my mss included in such books as Free and Other Stories; *Chains*—(a book of short stories) Twelve Men, A Gallery of Women, Plays of the Natural and the *Supernatural*

268 • *Theodore Dreiser*

and The Color of a Great City. These, with some exceptions, I will sell for 500.00 each.

Whether any of these fall within your price range or not[3] it pleases me to know that both you and Vice Chancellor Berry think so well of some of my work, and I will be glad to accommodate you.[4]

Cordially
Theodore Dreiser

Jennie Gerhardt was sold years ago.

1. In a letter of 18 January 1940 Ulizio explained that he chaired a committee responsible for purchasing a gift for Maja Leon Berry, a prominent judge (a vice chancellor), and that since Berry was himself a collector, Ulizio had suggested the acquisition of a Dreiser manuscript.

2. Henry (see Dreiser to Richard Watson Gilder, 12 December 1899, n. 1) encouraged Dreiser to write *Sister Carrie* and aided him its revision; Dreiser dedicated the novel to him.

3. Ulizio replied on 9 February 1940 that the committee had decided that Dreiser's prices were indeed beyond their budget.

4. Dreiser wrote in the margin next to this sentence: "Several Mss were burned."

To Karl W. Fischer [TCopy-DPUP]

Dreiser was increasingly sensitive about the belief that he was the sole author of "On the Banks of the Wabash." He apparently had a number of copies made of his letter to Fischer, a reporter for the Indianapolis News, *to distribute to various figures who might have an interest in the matter.*

COPY

1426 North Hayworth,
Hollywood, Calif.
March 7, 1940.

Dear Mr. Fischer:

It troubles me no little that William E. Wilson, in his book "The Wabash", should have credited me with the authorship of On The Banks Of The Wabash.[1] No rhymed verses on any topic ever made a song. The song is the singer—his music—not the words alone, ever. If so, Swanee River would be famous today *without the music*. So would *Annie Laurie*. So would *On The Sidewalks of New York*.[2]

Try and believe that or even think it. I contributed roughly—not exactly—the first verse and chorus. My brother, Paul, provided *the music*, the second verse and the title. His reputation as a writer of popular and widely distributed songs—My Gal Sal, Just Tell Them That You Saw Me, The Letter That Never Came, The Blue and The Gray, The Pardon Came Too Late, The Convict and The Bird, etc. etc., aided as much as anything else to carry On The Banks Of The Wabash to a swift and deserved popularity. And I was conscious of that when I penned—roughly—the verse and the chorus that I did.

So why say of me that I wrote the song? He wrote it. His loving and poetic temperament is in the words of the whole song, the title, and, above all, the music. In this connection it strikes me that only a reputation influenced commentator could think or feel otherwise.

The cause, however, of this controversy springs from the time factor involved in this story. The fact is that, when I wrote TWELVE MEN, which included the portrait of My Brother Paul, I was relatively little known in this country, and, when I described in that portrait how I had contributed some of the words as brothers do sometimes during the course of their companionship, I had no least idea that it would ever mean anything to anyone. My brother, Paul, was famous and I was his struggling younger brother. I am sure it pleased him very much that I had anything to do with it at all. Anyway, that is what he conveyed to me. If, on the other hand, I had written My Brother Paul after I had achieved an international literary reputation I certainly would never have as much as mentioned the fact that I had contributed one word,—for, knowing the weight of influence that goes with a wide reputation, as I came to know it later, I would then have understood how a part of the public, at least, might have swung to the belief that I not only claimed the song, but that I had written it, of course. There was no lie told, but, had I realized for an instant that with some my statement might have taken a little of the glitter from my brother, I certainly would not have written what I did.

Lastly I wish to emphasize how truly sorry I am that I ever mentioned it. My very good and loving brother did more for me in every way than ever I was privileged to do for him and I wish that the fact might be strongly emphasized. He is a living and precious force to me. His songs still thrill hundreds of thousands as they do me. And if you will be good enough to publicize this in Indiana and elsewhere I will be deeply grateful.

Theodore Dreiser

1. William E. Wilson (1906–?), *The Wabash* (New York: Farrar & Rinehart, 1940), 314.
2. Dreiser refers to "Way Down Upon the Sewanee River" (1851), by Stephen Foster; "Annie Laurie" (late eighteenth century), attributed to William Douglas; and "On the Sidewalks of New York" (ca. 1890s), by James W. Blake and Charles E. Lawler.

To William C. Lengel [H-WCLUP]

1426 N. Hayworth
Mch 9—1940

Dear Will

How are you? Regardless of business (although I wish you were making a million a year) I think of you constantly. You in and out like the family cat or dog but whatever happens around and at home here. I didn't write you but I've been sick for 6 weeks—flat on my back for about four and since then up and around a few hours each day, slowly but steadily improving. Fluritis is how I describe—sunshine & flowers notwithstanding. I notice people die of pneumonia out here as easily and gracefully as they do anywhere—from the north pole to the equater.

How are you? How are all the ulcers—big and little? I remember among other things that you used to suffer from migraine—that dreadful head-ill. And then only the other day my local doctor told me that oxygen—the good old oxygen tank variety—if used for as much as three to five minutes would abolish any case of migraine anywhere. And you had to suffer terribly even though tank oxygen has been around all the time—since as long ago as 1900—if not before! He says it is the complete answer. That's one "case" where ignorance isn't bliss.

But how is Nelle.[1] And William L. Junior? I think of them too. And the business. Anything doing in that line?

I assume you read that I "sold" Sister Carrie. The exact fact is that R.K.O took a 90 day option on it—handing over $3000—a total loss if they don't buy.[2] Meantime they've publicized it—engaged the Spivaks (whose work I admire very much) to do the script and a well thought of director by the name of *Sisk* to direct it.[3] And they have slated *Ginger Rogers* for Carrie. Who is to play Hurstwood and who Drouet is now being debated. Once they spoke of Barrymore—but he is out. Edwin Arnold is also being discussed as Hurstwood.[4] Can you think of anyone for Drouet or Hurtswood?[5] I so rarely see a movie I cant even guess.

As I say I'm still a little down under but feeling much better. A few more weeks & I think I'll be going strong.

As you know—or ought to—I'm a red hot red and may spend my last days in jail. If so I'll feel privileged and honored. If you want to read a revealing and convincing book get Hewlett Johnson's—"*The Socialist Sixth of the World.*" He is the Dean of Canterbury Cathedral, England and the book (English Edition) is labeled—"*Not for sale in England.*"[6] And the contents show why. That set of imperialistic swine in the South of England are presented as is—snout, tail and paunch. Also what Russia presents in the way of contrast.[7]

Love & best wishes. I wish I might see you.

D—

Coincidence? I had no sooner signed the R.K.O. option than Columbia which a year ago last January agreed to buy it—(Cohan talking to me personally),[8] & later let it slide, phoned to say that if it was still for sale they wished to buy—at once. Would bring contract & check to the house at once. Same price—if necessary 5000 more. But it was gone. Now they are discussing my short story called *The Hand!*[9]

1. Lengel's wife.

2. RKO did purchase *Sister Carrie* (for $40,000) in the fall of 1940, but the film was not made until 1952.

3. Samuel (1899–1971) and Bella (1899–1990) Spewack (not Spivak) had collaborated in writing many successful Broadway plays and Hollywood scripts. (When Paramount finally made the film in 1952, as *Carrie*, the screenplay was by Ruth and Augustus Goetz.) Dreiser probably means Douglas Sirk (1900–87), who had directed films in Germany and had immigrated to the United States in 1937.

4. Three successful films actors of the day: Rogers (1911–95) had made her reputation in musical comedy but had recently taken on more dramatic roles (see also Dreiser to Ginger Rogers, 15 May 1943); John Barrymore (1882–1942) was one of the major Shakespearean actors of his generation; and Edward (not Edwin) Arnold (1890–1956) was a character actor of note.

5. Lengel, in a letter of 19 April 1940, suggested Irene Dunne for Carrie, Charles Laughton for Hurstwood, and George Raft for Drouet.

6. Johnson (1874–1966), known as the "Red Dean," had achieved notoriety for his unqualified endorsement of communism in his *The Socialist Sixth of the World* (1939).

7. Dreiser added in the left-hand margin next to this paragraph: "Idea for book— America! Keep Out!!"

8. Dreiser means Harry Cohn (1891–1958), the head of Columbia Pictures.

9. An uncharacteristic story by Dreiser because of its Poe-like Gothicism, "The Hand" was published initially in 1919 and collected in *Chains* (1927).

To Stanley M. Moffat [TC-DPUP]

Still seeking release from his contract with Simon & Schuster, Dreiser had turned to the New York law firm of Moffat and Sanford for advice.

1426 North Hayworth,
Hollywood, Calif.
March 21, 1940.

Dear Mr. Moffat:

My quarrel with Simon and Schuster began immediately after the signing of the contract, Sept. 28, 1934. Previous to that—sometime in August, 1934 at their complimentary dinner, Simon and Schuster (M. Lincoln Schuster, Richard L. Simon, Leon Shimkin, their business manager, and all present)[1] pictured verbally all they intended to do. Later, on Sept. 5, 1934, my lawyer, Arthur Carter Hume of Yonkers, working with their lawyer, drew up the "Tentative and Provisional Memorandum of Proposal" from Simon and Schuster, Inc., which you will find in this file. It preceded the signing of the contract, and furnishes the ground of my complaint, which you will find fully outlined in the enclosed correspondence which begins with a letter from Mr. Leon Shimkin and is followed by an answer from me. Having read that you will see of what I complain.

The remainder of the correspondence fairly clearly demonstrates that apart from selling off (remaindering) all of the Horace Liveright stock and taking over an arrangement previously made with Doubleday-Doran by Horace Liveright, Inc., they did nothing. But as you will see from some correspondence with Doubleday-Doran dated February, 1939, they, Simon and Schuster, after collecting $4,000 in royalties from Doubleday-Doran and with $361.20 still due them from the same source, wish to charge me $10,114.39 for my books and plates in order to let me clear out. And this in the face of the fact that illegally they failed to live up to the Provisional Agreement of Sept. 5, 1934. Also, illegally, sold to old book sellers all the old Liveright stock on which I was entitled to a royalty of 15%—and, in the face of the fact that Doubleday-Doran—without a dollar's worth of advertising—they have succeeded in selling 47,424 copies of four of my novels, they have insisted that not one other of all my other books could be made to sell and that it was for this reason they allowed them to go out of print.

Yet I notice that Random House, which prints a Dollar Edition of Sister Carrie sells 700 a year and that without any advertising. Also that all of the old book stores in the United States do a lively business in second hand copies of my books—good copies of any of them bringing the original new book store or publishing price and often more. In fact in many old book stores here in Los Angeles there are Dreiser Shelves (I can furnish photographs of the same) and charge as high as $5.00 for an ordinary Liveright copy of most of my books.

What I really want is to frighten these people into letting me go for a thousand or two dollars at the most. If I can get a low release price I can, with a new book now almost ready,[2] get an American publisher who will push my books. All the more can I do this because this next Fall or winter the film version of Sister Carrie will be released—possibly that of The "Genius" and these should bring my works into the lime-light again.[3]

Thanks for your interest in regard to the house and thanks thanks for your interest in this matter also. Before you do anything about it, please let me know what you feel about it and what you think the prospects are for a successful closing of the entire relationship between myself and Simon and Schuster.

I want to caution you about the shrewdness of these people. For instance, this is what I have found to be uniformly true: If an author is to be sought or cajoled into turning over a book, Mr. Schuster invariably writes the letter: If it is a problem of sales and possible profit to be worked out Mr. Simon does it: If an author is to be refused or rejected or dealt with in any clear practical way, Mr. Shimkin does it, but no letter is ever signed collectively. These are always individual letters without any suggestion of firm authority.

As you will notice, if you examine their Spring list, they have drifted a long way from any worth while literary standards.

There is one other thing: For a long time, on my demand, they agreed to insure my plates separately for me. Since then, as these letters show, they have put in some cheaper method and I wish you would find out what that is—how my plates are insured and whether in my name or theirs and what it is costing me.

1. See Dreiser to M. Lincoln Schuster, 7 August 1935.
2. Dreiser's philosophy book, *The Formula Called Man*.
3. Although RKO had taken an option on *Sister Carrie* (see Dreiser to William C. Lengel, 9 March 1940, n. 2), the film was not to be made until 1952. *The "Genius"* was never filmed.

To Edgar Lee Masters   [H-HRHUT]

Masters wrote Dreiser on 30 April 1940 that he had just finished reading Forgotten Frontiers: Dreiser and the Land of the Free *(1932), by Dorothy Dudley (1894–1962), and had liked it. The book combines an often inaccurate biographi-*

cal account of Dreiser with a vigorous defense of his work and a celebration of his importance.

May—13—40

Dear Edgar:

Your letter about *Forgotten Frontiers* is naturally pleasing to me as it will be to Dorothy Dudley. She worked so hard on it and recieved nothing for her pains—exactly nothing. From the first there was trouble—as there usually is with anything connected with me. I couldn't find certain letters she wanted. The publishers objected to various paragraphs. Ernest Boyd,[1] whom she persuaded to read it gave an unsatisfactory verdict. The publishers that did bring it out split up; Harrison Smith disliked her & the book (I think):[2] I tried to get Pell (the successor of Liveright to issue it.[3] No go. Simon & Schuster the same. Finally I bought for Dorothy—some 700 or 800 sheets of the work & now I don't know where they are. Burton Rascoe once said that if she had put my name on it and carried Forgotten Frontiers as a second line it would have sold (?)[4] I like the book but—it seems to be thoroughly dead. So there. . . . But now that you praise it maybe someday, some publisher will pick it up and reissue it.[5] As for me, accept for Dorothy I don't really care. Its a good book. But if there is no public interest why bother. Just the same I'm grateful to you for writing about it, as you have, to me.

And now the war! Maybe when it's all over this mush of books and publicity (inane publicity) will end? How about a 1000 years of lazy indifference to things mental—or a degraded mass suppressed and ill used by a few dogmatic tyrants and their comfortable favorites. It may be. Only what difference will it make to us. We will not be here. Maybe no trace of anything we said or did. I ponder each day about it all. I see such interesting people go and new, interesting people come. And unless there is some intelligence—or semi-intelligence that gets some pleasure out of staging all this, I can not think why anyone of us are here. Nothing is really accomplished—unless the pleasure of walking in the sun is cosmically important.

But———But———But

But me no buts.

And thanks just the same.

Love—from

T.D
Hollywood

1. For Boyd, see Dreiser to Ernest Boyd, 1 May 1931.

2. Smith (1888–1971), later the longtime editor of the *Saturday Review of Literature*, founded the publishing firm of Harrison Smith in 1931 with Robert Haas as co-owner.

3. For Arthur Pell, see Dreiser to Arthur Pell, 25 May 1931.
4. For Burton Rascoe, see Dreiser to Burton Rascoe, 13 April 1931.
5. Dudley did reprint her study in 1946 under the title *Dreiser and the Land of the Free*.

To Joseph Fischler [H-LLIU]

After a period of little military activity during the winter of 1939–40, the Germans invaded Norway and Denmark in April 1940 and shortly afterward outflanked the French Maginot Line defenses and commenced a full onslaught on Belgium and northern France. The British forces in France were evacuated at Dunkirk during 24 May–4 June.

1426 N. Hayworth
Hollywood
June 8—1940

Dear Fischler:

It's nice to have news of you. The whirling lunacies of these days make realistic words such as yours welcome. Out here, except in exceptionally private circles it is impossible to express yourself comfortably. Rows spring up on every hand—bad feeling is created. Out here the KKK parades openly in sheets & pillow cases with eye holes cut in them. They are looking for undesirable aliens. At the same time the legionaires evesdrop at every point hoping to contact the 5th column.[1] The press outdoes itself in the matter of originating misleading headlines. Every front page must indicate an allied success in the top line no matter what the second or others reveal. And strikers, however American, and however just their cause, are "sabotaging democracy." Meantime the movie magnates seize the occasion to rush out all shelved anti-Nazi and spy pictures the while they fire actors & patriotically cut salaries. Civilization is on the brink. The naked Senegambians[2] on the French front line—with knives two feet long—are finding that out. They have experienced French civilization in Africa.

However, the stores keep open and their is a campaign on here to persuade American housewives to buy and eat more of the surplus food and other products produced during the past ten years in order to prevent them falling into the hands of the jobless who cannot buy—or being thrown into the sea. The brains of the 60 families are beginning to function at last.[3] Saluting the flag is compulsory and the American flag trust is seeking to make a home flag display compulsory. So you see how a few sane words now & then help. What will happen when Hitler takes France and that noblest hand-out man of all, Mussolini, enters the war, I cant think.[4] For he intends that his share shall be safe and easy. It looks as though some

sane and economic thinking & producing will have to be brought about by
someone if another panic isn't suddenly and painfully evoked. Roosevelt
reminds me of a Rah-Rah cheer leader but nothing more. One thing that
interests me is this. If Hitler takes France what becomes of the enormous
Catholic properties & investments there? Will Mussolini want a share? I
would like to make an intelligent comment on all this but I can think of
no intelligent thing to say.

Thanks for your letters.

And my best wishes, of course

Dreiser

1. A Fifth Column consists of residents of a country at war who are disloyal to
their own government. The term originated during the Spanish Civil War, when
the fascist leader General Franco claimed that on his attack of Madrid with four
columns of troops, a fifth column would arise within the city.

2. Gambian natives of the French West Africa colony of Senegal serving with
the French army and noted for their ferocity in combat.

3. Ferdinand E. Lundberg (1905–95) had argued in his book *America's 60 Families*
(1937) that the country was controlled economically and politically by an elite
group of wealthy families.

4. Indeed, Mussolini brought Italy into the war as an ally of Germany on 10 June
1940, two days after Dreiser wrote this letter.

To Dayton Stoddart [H-DPUP]

1426 N. Hayworth
Hollywood
June 8—'40

Dear Stoddart:

I'd have written before but I've been and still am pressed on all sides for
a large variety of things, which keeps a secretary going & myself dictating
& scribbling. I wont discuss the insane show now on, but enjoyed your
comment on Roosevelt.[1] The local lunacies are too numerous, too cruel &
too fantastic to enumerate. . . . As for your book, if you care to send it on, or
parts of it, I'll do my best. I was very sorry about the first failure in connection with it, but I feel better now and working better. It sounds interesting
and with your gift for irony and blague it should be.[2]

I'm sorry to hear your so hard pressed. That phase of really good writing
has always depressed me. So many really able men have had to put up such
rugged fights. When I was editing I did my very best for those whose work
I truly admired. After I got out I could do nothing, of course. And I had
several bad periods—amazingly so. But, some how I pulled through. Since

coming out here, I have managed, (because of the sale of Sister Carrie)[3] to clear up several bad property tangles, pay up some back alimony and lay aside enough (or nearly) to buy my way out of S & S. If some form of panic doesn't ensue during the coming year—and it well may, I'll be able to finish the work I undertook about six years ago without fretting.[4] But if one comes all bets are off. I'll be in my old Sullivan Street quarters.[5]

Do you ever see Duffy?[6] I always liked him but I never hear. Or Harriet Bissell?[7] She is a lively, fighting cockerell if ever there was one. In case your book is not easy to ship I'm enclosing something to help defray the charges. And I'm wishing you the best of luck always.—

Dreiser

1. In an undated letter, Stoddart had written Dreiser that a "major reason for switching from Roosevelt [was] the admission of many ordinary people that though they were on WPA, etc., he had done no good."

2. Stoddart was working on a book about Broadway entitled *Broadway War to War* and had asked Dreiser to read a portion of it. Dreiser had neglected to do so but now accepts the task.

3. Dreiser had sold an option on the movie of *Sister Carrie* to RKO in February 1940 and was in the process of finalizing the sale.

4. Dreiser's book of philosophy, *The Formula Called Man.*

5. At the turn of the century, Sullivan Street was in a run-down area of Greenwich Village; Dreiser apparently lived there briefly during the spring and summer of 1895, after he had left his job on the *New York World* and before he began editing *Ev'ry Month.*

6. For Dreiser's renewed friendship with Richard Duffy, see Dreiser to Dayton Stoddart, 22 June 1939, n. 2.

7. For Bissell, see Dreiser to William C. Lengel, 16 July 1938, n. 6.

To William C. Lengel [H-WLCUP]

Lengel, acting as Dreiser's agent, had received a commission from Oskar Piest (1898–1987), proprietor of the small Veritas Press, for Dreiser to write a book opposing America's entrance into the European war. The work, America Is Worth Saving, *which Dreiser then prepared with the aid of several helpers, evolved into a pro-Communist, anti-British diatribe. During 1935–39, the Soviet Union strongly endorsed the Popular Front, a policy which encouraged Communist Party organizations around the world to cooperate with democratic governments for the defeat of fascism. The Soviet-Nazi pact of August 1939, however, both alienated Western democracies from the Soviet Union and changed the Communist Party line to that of the threat which imperialistic Western powers, and especially Great Britain, posed to the Soviet Union. This change in policy no doubt intensified Dreiser's already strong Anglophobia and encouraged him to undertake the project.*

THEODORE DREISER

1426 N. Hayworth Ave
Hollywood, Calif
July 10—1940

Dear Will:

Your notes and the offer from the Veritas Press for a book by me to be entitled *Keep Out* or better yet *"America! Keep Out,"* dated July 6 recieved yesterday.[1] I have studied it carefully and *Can Do* (Deliver) but not earlier that Sept. 1st next. Research is required and not a little assembling of data. If the Sept. 1st date is satisfactory I will proceed and deliver.

However, to make sure that we understand each other, I am enclosing a list of chapter topics, which shows quite accurately how the subject matter will run. Also that it will take about 60,000 words to cover it. I don't know whether the volume will have permanent value or not, but it may have. At least a few center shots will be recorded. Please ok chapter list & return with contract.

As for the terms, they are satisfactory and for the record I will repeat them here:—

$1,000 on my acceptance of the commission—which I hereby accept.

$2,000.00 on delivery of the completed manuscript.

$2,000 on publication or six weeks after delivery of the manuscript; whichever date may be earlier.

You are to forward contract and check for $1000.00 payable to me on reciept of this letter or wire which precedes it.

Fortunately I like the idea and have considerable data of my own. Also two capable newspaper researchers who I will employ on receipt of check.[2]

I am happy that you are my agent in this transaction, that you are doing so well & and I will try not to disappoint you.

Regards and Luck to you
Theodore Dreiser

1. The title of the book on publication in January 1941 was *America Is Worth Saving*.

2. Dreiser appears to be referring to Esther McCoy (1904–89) and Lorna Smith (1897–1981), both of whom had newspaper experience. Also aiding him in research and composition was Cedric Belfrage (1904–90), an English writer then living in Hollywood. All three were on the left, though only McCoy was a communist.

To William C. Lengel [H-WCLUP]

THEODORE DREISER

Aug 5—'40

Dear Will:

I have just signed all three copies of the contract & sent one to Mr. Piest along with an answer to his very nice letter to me. Six chapters are done— except for revision—and re-revision and 6 or 7 more will be done by Aug 16 or 17. The remaining 7, 8, 9, or 10 will be done & in your hands by Sept 15th I am sure. As you know I have two researchers, and incidentally editors & writers—digging out & arranging data under various heads or chapters. My job is to co-ordinate and resay the facts as I wish to co-ordinate & say them. No easy job. About 9 hours a day.

Saturday I recieved the idea for a movie which I read with care, but, it is not anything I could do.[1] That would require a trained script writer of who there are at least a score out here. Their prices range from 2 to 40 thousand dollars per script. Ben Hecht is one. McArthur is another. Kaufmann another.[2]

To me it sounds like another "Doctor Ehrlich"[3] but I am not the man. It does not, as I see it, contain the so necessary drama or tragedy of the *individual*. I may be wrong.

Speaking of *America! Keep Out* or *America! Awake & Live*, if the book is as forceful & definite as I expect to make it, it may cost me my honest English Publishers—Constable & Co. I have just recieved an editorial by Kyllman[4]—so savagely destructive of Hitler & all he stands for (Death to all Germans) that when he reads some of my Anti-English comments I am through—I think. However, as you know, my convictions are not for sale. Yet, I never had a better publisher than Constable—and never will have one, I know.

Regards & best wishes
Dreiser

1. Lengel had written Dreiser on 2 August 1940 asking if he might be interested in writing a story synopsis for a movie being planned by the Hungarian producer Theodore A. Benedek. The movie was to seek to demonstrate the falsity of the belief that there were superior and inferior blood types and was to have as its climax a blood transfusion.

2. Ben Hecht (see Dreiser to Ben Hecht, 28 November 1915) and his frequent collaborator Charles McArthur (1895–1956) were successful Broadway and Hollywood writers during the 1920s and 1930s. By "Kaufmann," Dreiser may mean

either George S. Kaufman (1889–1961), best known as a Broadway playwright and director but also a screenwriter, or Reginald Wright Kauffman (1877–1959), a prolific popular novelist and writer of screenplays.

3. *Dr. Ehrlich's Magic Bullet*, a popular film of 1940 based on the life of Paul Ehrlich, the German bacteriologist who had discovered a cure for venereal disease.

4. For Otto Kyllmann (not Kyllman), see Dreiser to Otto Kyllmann, 23 February 1927.

To William C. Lengel [H-WCLUP]

THEODORE DREISER

Aug 10–1940

Dear Will:

I think you will see where Mr. Piest ideas come in when you read chapters 4, 5, 7, 15, 17 and 19.[1] They are indicated at various points—in various chapters of the book. For Mr. Piest's & your illumination I have revised (re-arranged) the list of chapters with explanatory notes. This coming week (latter part) I will send you duplicates of chapters 1 to 8 inclusive. The others a little later. Do not forget that I personally am not *sure* that the dream of Jefferson, Washington, Paine, Franklin and others will ever come to pass but—if our capitalists & financiers will do as much—(even 2/3rd as much)—for the American worker as Russia does for her workers it may. Certainly tying up with England & Mr. Morgan[2] won't do it.

However, no fear. This will be an interesting book. If Mr. Piest doesn't want it he can tell me after reading the first eight chapters & *studying this outline*.[3] I have no thought of changing this. If he does not see what he wants here—now is the time to speak. If we cannot agree on what the book should contain—ditto. As I told you I will not write in anything that goes against my personal convictions. At the present time it looks to me as though we were being tricked into a dictatorship—which should bring revolution—or, the end. Personally I feel that Roosevelt should be defeated. He has a pro-England complex which is the same as a pro-corporation or dictator complex—Dr. Hitler.

Regards,

Dreiser

1. Piest believed that portions of *America Is Worth Saving* which he had seen were not only too pro-communist but also possibly libelous. He was additionally troubled that the work's radicalism might endanger his position as an alien seeking citizenship.

2. John Pierpont Morgan (1867–1943), head of the House of Morgan banking empire, which was widely believed to have had a role in America's entrance into World War I in order to ensure the safety of its British loans.

3. Dreiser enclosed in this letter a list of the book's chapter titles and a brief summary of each chapter. Although the nineteen chapters of the published version of *America Is Worth Saving* maintain this outline of their contents, the chapter titles themselves differ to a considerable degree.

To William C. Lengel [TC-WCLUP]

After receiving the full manuscript of America Is Worth Saving *in late September, Piest backed away from proceeding. As he explained to Dreiser in a letter of 24 October 1940, because it was rumored that Veritas was a Nazi propaganda organization, he thought it best that Dreiser publish his book with "an established American publishing house" and was therefore seeking, with the aid of Frederick V. Field (see Dreiser to Frederick V. Field, 6 November 1940), to arrange for its transfer to a firm of this kind.*

THEODORE DREISER

1426 North Hayworth,
Hollywood, Calif.
Sept. 7, 1940.

Dear Lengel:

Well this is Saturday, Sept. 7, and here are 7 more chapters and the balance—the remaining two will go to you (Airmail) Tuesday evening of the 10th or Wednesday A. M., the 11th. And that fulfills my end of the bargain so far as the Nov.[1] 15th date goes. You will never know the stress and strain that has gone with this—the people employed—the data collected—the typing and retyping and cost of it all. But I feel that you should know because it has been a staggering job—one of the most strenuous I ever undertook. Thank god it is over—or practically over. Tuesday will be the end.

Interestingly enough after editing and retyping I haven't found much to change and hope there will be nothing—once it gets in type. The two chapters still coming to you are (15) What Should Be The Social and Economic Objectives of the American People and (19) Are The Masses Worth Saving? They will be all right. As for any additional work—editing and revising proofs, I doubt if there will be much unless you people go in for changes which I hope you wont. The stuff is all too true and sound. However, before calling on me for very much, you had better read the balance of this letter which concerns time, price, distribution, etc. and strikes me as very important.

To begin with there are four things that occur to me: (1) The title should be: *Is Democracy Worth Saving?*[2] I think that fits the book best. Next (2) the question of publication date is of extreme importance—not only because of the speed with which America is moving toward war—and likewise toward Fascism at home which will make such books unpublishable—but also because of the elections in November. Obviously the book can do its greatest amount of good during the month preceding the elections, to make readers realize what sort of platforms their candidates must have to be worthy of support. And since it appears that both Roosevelt and Wilkie are determined to put us in the war—if they can—immediately after election, the book would at that point lose its main significance even if it could be published.[3]

(2) Bound up with this is the question of price. I notice that the publication of Allsop and Kintner's American White Paper in the form of a paper-bound "document"—at, I believe, 75¢—has been very successful.[4] Whatever be the objections to a paper bound book, is it not something which under the present very abnormal conditions should be given careful thought? Because the whole message of this book is directed at the ordinary American masses—and they cannot afford more than, at most $1—and the message is useless unless given *now*, without the smallest unnecessary delay. For this reason it seems to me unwise to publish the book at a high price, cloth-bound, with the idea of a paper cheap edition later. There may be no *later*. And the vital thing is to get the book in as many hands as possible as long as possible before the elections. Therefore I cannot but feel that if there are to be two editions, the cheap one *must* be brought out at the same time as the expensive one.[5]

(3) It has been pointed out by a not unobservant friend that there is every chance of the British Embassy, through its consulates all over the country, trying to buy up every copy of the book to prevent its immediate distribution to the people. If the first edition were one of 10,000, say at $1, it would certainly be worth $10,000 to the British in the present crisis to keep it off the market until another edition could be printed—which might just give them enough delay to render the message less harmful. Therefore—and this again is tied up with price—it might be worth considering to print a very large first edition, and have plenty of copies in reserve for immediate sending out. Such an edition could be sold without any difficulty at all *provided it was cheap enough in price.*

A friend of the man who advised me concerning what the British Embassy might do wrote him several days ago as follows:

"I have talked with several leaders of the peace movement, who are now in Chicago, and all are wildly enthusiastic about the possibilities of a book of this kind by a man of Dreiser's standing. All say that if it were priced low enough—*anything up to $1*—they could sell it like hot cakes by the tens of thousands. These peace organizations have been set up now in almost every community in America and could be cooperated with to the limit with tremendous results. The Los Angeles peace group says that through its various affiliates it is confident that it could sell 15,000 copies at $1. If one city could do that—think of the national possibilities! None of this would be true with a book at a higher price than $1."

So you see how others see it. Read these, think it over and let me know.

Dreiser

P.S. Enclosed is another letter about my book Forgotten Frontiers which I hope you haven't forgotten. I'd like to see it published.[6] Next, Simon and Schuster have an offer for 10,000 moving picture edition of SISTER CARRIE—the money earned to apply on my debt to them—5% royalty on a cheap edition. Should I take it?[7]

1. Lengel has written "Sept ?" in the margin; 1 September was the date agreed upon for delivery of the manuscript and Dreiser had in fact almost met this deadline.

2. Modern Age, which replaced Veritas as the publisher of *America Is Worth Saving*, found this title too negative and asked that it be changed.

3. Both Franklin D. Roosevelt and Wendell L. Willkie (1892–1944), the Democratic and Republican candidates in the 1940 presidential election, argued for American support of the British war effort. In fact, the change in publishers resulted in the book not appearing until after the election, on 20 January 1942.

4. Joseph Alsop (1910–1989) and Robert Kintner (1909–1980), *American White Paper: The Story of American Diplomacy and the Second World War* (New York: Simon & Schuster, 1940).

5. Despite this plea, Modern Age brought out *America Is Worth Saving* only in hardback and priced it at $2.50.

6. For *Forgotten Frontiers*, see Dreiser to Edgar Lee Masters, 13 May 1940.

7. Of course, since the film of *Sister Carrie* was not made until 1952, this edition did not appear.

To Frederick V. Field [TC-DPUP]

American Peace Mobilization, an organization consisting of leftists and isolationists united in this instance by their opposition to America's entrance into the war, was founded in Chicago in late September 1940, with Field (1905–2000), a member of the Vanderbilt family, as executive secretary. Dreiser, though not present at this meeting, accepted one of its vice presidencies.

1426 North Hayworth,
Hollywood, Calif.
Nov. 6, 1940.

Dear Mr. Field:

I haven't willingly neglected your very complimentary letter of November 1—last. It is pressure of work and engagements here that has made it, so far, impossible. I'm so glad you like the book so much and that you feel it may be of use in your great campaign to keep us out of war and more particularly out of England's purely selfish entanglements.[1] It was, as you may or may not know, a rush order or job with a time limit of six weeks placed upon it. The only reason I undertook it at all was because, for so long, I have resented the conniving and traitorous interference of England in our American affairs, as much as I have resented our American lick-spittle attitude toward all that the English titled class chooses to assume in regard to itself. As a nation we appear to know nothing of its history, its imperialistic and what is worse its tyrannical attitude toward labor, democracy and social equity in general and its unaltered and unaltering determination to abolish democracy not only in Europe but throughout the entire world. So I took time off to do what I could.

As for Mr. Piest, his intentions were excellent I think, but his political security was much too slight for the job in hand.[2] What was worse, I was not the one—only he appears not to have known this—to whittle, let alone hew, the book to make it conform to his political necessities. That he did not know this was none of my doings—I thought he did and that that was why he selected me.

However, no great harm has been done him, I think, and I, thanks to him and to you, have at last been permitted to say what I know and think of England.

Just now, by the way, I have your telegram concerning change of radio time and will be at the radio studio at 1.45 P. M. on Saturday.[3] It will be a pleasure to meet you and I hope, of course, to say something that will advantage this Peace Movement of yours.

Sincerely and cordially,

1. Field, who had aided in the transition of publishers from Veritas to Modern Age, was reading a manuscript copy of *America Is Worth Saving* for possibly libelous statements.

2. See Dreiser to William C. Lengel, 10 August 1940, n. 1.

3. Dreiser flew to Washington and on 9 November spoke at an American Peace Mobilization mass meeting and also gave a radio address.

To Heath Bowman [TC-DPUP]

The Indiana-born Bowman (1910–?) had included a chapter titled "The Wrong Side of the Tracks" dealing with Dreiser's Warsaw, Indiana, boyhood in his Hoosier (Indianapolis: Bobbs-Merrill, 1941), 202–15. Almost all of Bowman's account was drawn from Dreiser's autobiography Dawn (1931).

1426 North Hayworth
Hollywood, California
November 19, 1940

Dear Heath Bowman:

This chapter of yours concerning me is very sensitive, understanding, and generous,—rich in feeling, and naturally I am grateful to you for your very great care in the matter.[1] As you know though, a summary of special data excerpted from as large a volume as DAWN can easily effect a harsher impression than would a reading of the entire volume. Thus a very few lines in this chapter—the last five lines on page 231; lines 15–20 on page 232 and lines 22–24 on the same page seem to me to overemphasize *some* of the then current conduct of the older girls—none of whom were there for more than brief visits. Perhaps I am still over sensitive in regard to that period but it seems to me the fault may lay in the brevity as well as the force of your characterization—no space for any exculpatory comment. For instance, the girls were unquestionably not any bolder or freer than some other girls of their age in the town, but, in the first place, they were comparative strangers, no worth while social connections; in the next their parents were not as well to do or locally as well placed financially, and this made the criticism of the stranger easier. Curiously, the one who brought the illegitimate child into the world married soon after and at 37 had turned to Christian Science and at 45 had been a Christian Science Healer of repute in the church.[2] The other three married not so long after, and as conventionally and happily as any.

Several other things, the way you report the nude bathing of young men and girls in the Tippecanoe one might conclude that the local newspaper attack was a direct consequence of one or more of the sisters in those pleasurable outings. My personal conviction is that their presence and the reported bathing were in no way related. To make this clearer might help. Possibly the bathing incident might be omitted.

Somewhere in this chapter it seems to me should come a presentation of the binding affection of my mother over her children and their response. This in one sense was the reason for all the comings and goings and hence the cause of a lot of the trouble for her and themselves.

As far as unpleasant feeling toward Indiana is concerned, I have never entertained any, although the attitude of the State has been somewhat unfriendly toward me. Therefore the note of bitterness that I detect in your chapter seems out of place. Have you by any chance read A HOOSIER HOLIDAY?[3]

Please be sure that with these exceptions I find no fault with your summary. Your approach, as I have said, is at once sensitive, understanding and richly sensitive—beautiful, I feel in its all embracing humanity. I am fortunate in finding so informed and considerate an interpreter.[4]

Truly,

1. On 12 November 1940 Bowman had sent Dreiser for his approval the chapter from *Hoosier* on Dreiser's Warsaw boyhood.
2. Dreiser's sister Sylvia (1866–1945).
3. Dreiser's often genial account, published in 1916, of an automobile trip from New York to various Indiana towns during the summer of 1915.
4. Bowman replied on 26 November 1940 that he was revising the chapter in response to Dreiser's comments.

To Frederick V. Field [TC-DPUP]

Field was preparing a lecture campaign by various speakers on behalf of the aims of American Peace Mobilization.

1426 North Hayworth,
Hollywood, Calif.
Nov. 25, 1940.

Dear Mr. Field:

I feel that we are not fighting the battle to keep America out of the war in the right way. For the arch enemy of Democracy—here as anywhere, but particularly here in America—is England. And by England I do not mean the deceived and all but obliterated mass of English people—but the oligarchy snob-ocracy that is in armed and financed control of the English people and that never intends that they shall be anything other than servants and slaves of the same. I have pointed this out in my book—*Is America Worth Saving.*[1] I have pointed it out in my speeches and radio addresses and will continue to do so. But I am but one man. You—and by you I mean the American Peace Mobilization—have scores or hundreds of speakers, or can have. But unless they are seriously instructed as to the points they have to make,—the *facts* they have to emphasize,—they will make no headway against British propaganda in this country which has finally caused ten thousand out of every ten thousand and one of our Americans to believe in the top mental grasp, by Britain, of everything that concerns man and his destiny here on earth. In spite of all the lousy plots indulged in by England against America—the Tories of this country—our American money gang has always wished we had a court, like England, so that it could gather round and be permitted to bask in the radiance of the Emperor or Empress of India—the while the noble British Navy helped the American Army to put aspiring American labor in its place as the slave (nothing more) of American and British wealth—joined as these now are, in one royal tyranny over the aspirations of all but their parading 5%.

The condition of the masses in England is terrible and has ever been since the industrial age set in and English finance and manufacture was joined up with English royalty to put the common man in a corner—as a servant and nothing more. And that fact should be emphasized because it can be proved.

Furthermore, as you know, from my book, the 500,000,000 Imperial British subjects outside of the British Isles have no representation in the British Parliament. They are really the unrepresented subjects of the British Foreign Office, directed as that is by the British Cabinet which is directed by British Big Business which enforces its will on British Royalty. They are suffering, as our 13 colonies suffered before our American Revolution, from taxation without representation. And the more backward colonials—those of India, Burmah, Egypt and the British African colonies, are deliberately kept backward by His Majesty's Imperial Government, and are uniformly the victim of overwork, starvation wages and so starvation.

As I pointed out in my Washington radio address,[2] England hates Democracies. It has betrayed all those of Europe just as it has betrayed Canada, Australia, New Zealand and South Africa. It pillaged and destroyed the Orange Free State of South Africa in order to steal its diamond mines. And all of its smaller colonies like the working districts of Northern England are veritable shambles of poverty and degradation—overlorded by British gun boats, British marines, a sycophantic and toady British Governor and his little court of loafing British visitors and pleasure seekers.

And that, in sum, is the British Democracy and Civilization that we are being called upon to break our peace for—to spend our money on, at the same time that we are called upon to adequately defend ourselves.

Under the circumstances I think your speakers everywhere should be called upon to hammer home these facts to our deluded and really half hypnotized—certainly propaganda doped Americans—in the hope that they can be awakened to the immense economic and social disaster that threatens them. They will be bled white—and if England wins—turned over to our money and power crazed 60 families[3] who will gladly join up with a triumphant British Royalty in order to put over us a dictatorship of the money lords of both lands—in other words to abolish democracy as we know it and replace it with the wage slavery and enforced ignorance which England knows and loves and now fights to maintain.

If your speakers can be persuaded to set forth these truths, America may yet be awakened to what awaits her in case she fails to grasp these same, and better, aid in her own defense.

Sincerely,

1. The title of *America Is Worth Saving* before its final change into the published title.

2. For Dreiser's Washington radio address, see Dreiser to Frederick V. Field, 6 November 1940, n. 3.

3. For the "60 families," see Dreiser to Joseph Fischler, 8 June 1940, n. 3.

1941

To Stanley M. Moffat [TC-DPUP]

Although Dreiser was increasingly eager to end his relationship with Simon &
Schuster, he was thwarted by his financial obligations to the firm. It was not until
the fall of 1941 that he finally reached a settlement with Simon & Schuster and
was thus able to move to Putnam's. See also Dreiser's earlier letter to Stanley M.
Moffat, 21 March 1940.

1015 N. King's Rd.,
Hollywood, Calif.[1]
Jan. 27, 1941.

Dear Mr. Moffat:

I have your letters of Jan. 22.[2]

In regard to a final settlement between myself and Simon & Schuster, I feel that a hard and fast contract with them at this time would be a rather difficult thing for me to take on. In the first place I have no assurance that I will make money on my new book.[3] I hope I will. But one never knows about these matters, especially about a book of that character, and with feeling running as high as it is now. Still, if I did make money on the book, I would be only too glad to liquidate my indebtedness to them as quickly as ever I could.

I think it would be o. k. to make some new agreement with them, setting aside formally the old contract, but I would like to get the best possible terms I can, just in case things did not go swimmingly for me. I mean the lowest rate of interest (if indeed interest is demanded) and the lowest payments to be met, etc. etc.

In this connection I would like to warn you against the lawyer, Rein- heimer.[4] He was the lawyer whom I engaged to represent me in a disagree- ment I had with Piscator, the playwright who dramatized a version of An American Tragedy. (It was called The Case of Clyde Griffiths).[5] Later I found out that he was at the very same time representing Milton Schubert, the producer,[6] who was doing his best to drive a hard bargain with me and collecting from both of us. So I have no faith whatsoever in the man. This is for your information.

If you can work out something tentative with Simon and Schuster await- ing a conference between you and me, before any definite action were taken, I will be in New York for a few days around March 6th or 7th—if that is not too late—and we can go over the whole matter.[7]

The third and fourth clauses of your letter seem to be fair enough. In connection with the third, I am sure they could sell all the old copies if they tried in any way.

I certainly am not willing to do anything about Clause 5. It is unreasonable.[8]

There is another matter about which I would like to consult you. There is a picture called *Back Street* taken from a book by the same name written by Fannie Hurst. It is soon to have a grand opening in Florida (Second production).[9] This book, and the picture taken from it, are a direct steal from my story *Jennie Gerhardt*. In the past I had some correspondence with Fannie Hurst regarding it, and also wrote Carl Laemmle, once President of Universal Pictures. I wish you would read these two books and give me your legal as well as literary opinion as whether my opinion is correct. If you think I have a clear case of plagiarism I would like to do something about it. Regardless of how close the books are, the pictures are *very* close. The first steal of Back Street was movied here in 1931. I did not hear of it—or "get it" until 1933 or 4. The first and second moving pictures of Back Street should be run and compared the same afternoon with the movie of Jennie Gerhardt. Fannie Hurst claimed through her lawyer, a Mr. Stern, that she had nothing to do with the picturization which is very like Jennie Gerhardt. All she did was to take the money. What she really did in Back Street was to take the German-American family pictured in Jennie Gerhardt and transpose or transubstantiate it into Jews. The underlying idea is the same throughout.

I will send on the books, trusting you will be able to read them.

Will be glad to see you—and regards.

1. Bolstered financially by the sale of *Sister Carrie* to RKO, Dreiser and Helen purchased a house on Kings Road in Hollywood. This was to be Dreiser's home address until his death in December 1945.

2. Moffat wrote two letters to Dreiser on 22 January—one about a Grosset & Dunlap reprint of *Sister Carrie* and another about the Simon & Schuster settlement.

3. *America Is Worth Saving*, which, in fact, had a small sale.

4. Howard E. Reinheimer (1899–1970), a prominent New York lawyer specializing in theater and film copyright law.

5. Erwin Piscator and Lina Goldschmidt (see Dreiser to Joseph Freeman, 25 August 1937, n. 4) had collaborated in preparing the 1936 Broadway adaptation of *An American Tragedy*. Piscator, however, later claimed that since he had written the final script, he should receive all its author royalties, and he threatened to sue Dreiser over the issue.

6. Schubert, a member of the powerful Schubert theatrical family, had produced *The Case of Clyde Griffiths* in collaboration with the Group Theatre.

7. Dreiser was making the trip to New York to address the American Council on Soviet Relations on 28 February 1941.

8. Simon & Schuster's settlement plan, as outlined by Moffat in his letter of 22 January, had five clauses: clause three allotted Dreiser's future royalties from books already published by Simon & Schuster to payment of Dreiser's indebtedness to the firm; clause four provided for the liquidation of Dreiser's debt at the time he moved to another firm; and five requested that any royalties paid to Dreiser for new books published by a new firm be dedicated to the reduction of the debt.

9. See Dreiser to Carl Laemmle, Jr., 23 August 1935. Both productions of *Back Street* were by Universal, the first in 1932 starring Irene Dunne, the second in 1941 with Margaret Sullavan.

To Mary Francis, Sylvia, and Edward M. Dreiser [TS-EU]

Dreiser's agent Donald Friede sold My Gal Sal, *a film biography of Paul Dresser, to Twentieth Century–Fox in early March 1941. Believing that the film would increase the popularity of Paul's songs, Dreiser sought a new agreement with the surviving Dreiser siblings concerning the administration of Paul's estate.*

THEODORE DREISER

1015 N. King's Rd.,
Hollywood, Calif.
March 22, 1941.

Dear Mame, Syl and Ed:

It is necessary, on account of the expiration of my administration letters, to appoint someone else in this immediate situation to administer un-administered properties, such as future royalties, etc. on the songs of Paul. I cannot be reappointed without considerable delay, whereas a new person can be appointed immediately. It would help me greatly at this point if you would appoint Helen. She is here on the ground and can attend to everything, under my supervision. Naturally, I will dictate the policy right along, through her. It is quite a job and requires time and a certain business sense, and I think she is the right party at this time. She will naturally have to go under bond and everything must be accounted for anyway to the Government and to everyone else. She will not charge anything for her services in this matter. She says she is willing to do it if it is perfectly satisfactory to all concerned. Not otherwise.

If this is agreeable to you, Ed, Mame and Syl, it is to me. If so, please convey the acceptance by telephone immediately to Mr. Stanley Moffat of Moffat & Sanford, 342 Madison Avenue, New York City. He will then send you a form to sign. There should be no delay of any kind, for the whole matter should go forward at once out here. If she is not agreeable to you, then appoint someone else immediately. I cannot do it at this time. But if you appoint someone back there, it will make for delays, confusion, explanations, this and that, which will be very bad. Helen is here and she is taking care of many matters already in connection with this picture.

I will appreciate a quick decision on this matter.

Sincerely,
T. D. (Theodore Dreiser)

(Copy to Mame, Syl.)

P.S. For this appointment it is not necessary to secure the signatures of anyone other than Mame, Syl, Ed and myself.

To William C. Lengel [TS-WLCUP]

While Dreiser's negotiations with Simon & Schuster continued, he was also seeking to finalize an agreement with Putnam's for the American rights to his works and to complete both The Formula Called Man *and* The Bulwark. *Lengel was acting as Dreiser's agent in the effort to arrange a contract with Putnam's.*

THEODORE DREISER

1015 N. King's Rd.,
Hollywood, Calif.
July 5, 1941.

Dear Lengel:

In regard to the Simon and Schuster contract, I haven't a copy here. Stanley Moffat of Moffat and Sanford, 342 Madison Avenue, has it. Borrow it and make two copies and send me the typing bill. Simon and Schuster are trying to pile on interest at 5% and their lawyer's bill, but Moffat is fighting them, and so holding up the Putnam deal.

As to *The Mechanism Called Man*,[1] yes, I can send on a half dozen chapters and will. You read *Good and Evil*. You sold it to the North American Review. All of the others have been published—one in The American Mercury. The other four in Esquire.[2] What I will do now is to stop and assemble all of the chapters since all of the material for each is typed. It is—for me—a question of the most effective arrangement of the points made under each chapter head. There are all of 40 chapters. However, each has a separate and highly individual interest at the same time that all, collectively, not singly, establish,—that man, as well as the material universe of which he is a part, are both organisms or mechanisms put together by an immaterial and creative power which works through matter and energy as man works in and through clay or wood and stone.

As for the next work, I am strongly urged to finish The Bulwark and feel now that I had better do so. I would like to see Putnam take over such bound works as Simon and Schuster have on hand and advertise them along with the philosophy book. Why not talk over the situation with him. I want only a fair contract as I wrote you. The right to publish eventually a complete set of my books should be worth something to Putnam. One thing I do wish to do is to discard Hey-Rub-a-Dub-Dub as a book, and put the one-act plays that are in that in the book called *Plays of the Natural and Supernatural*.[3] I may use one essay that is now in *Hey! Rub-a-Dub-Dub* in *The Mechanism Called Man*. By the way, Simon and Schuster liked that title very much. I once thought of using *The Myth of Reality*. Also *You, the Phantom*. I can't feel that any of your titles have any particular kick. *The Myth Called Man* or *Man, the Myth*—one or the other—would be better. I'll see if I can think of anything else.

Regards,

Dreiser

P. S. I am enclosing a letter from Jacques Chambrun, Inc. 745 Fifth Ave. NYC., I think it refers to the thing started in *The Readers Digest*. (They rejected my idea) If it is not that, see what it is. Perhaps you can split the commission.[4]

T.D.

1. One of the working titles of *The Formula Called Man*. The book was not published in Dreiser's lifetime; when his draft of its various sections was published in 1974, edited by Marguerite Tjader Harris and John McAleer, the work was titled *Notes on Life*.

2. The essays are: "Good and Evil," *North American Review* 246 (Autumn 1938); "The Myth of Individuality," *American Mercury* 31 (March 1934); and (in *Esquire*) "An Address to Caliban," 2 (September 1934), "You, the Phantom," 2 (September 1934), and "Kismet," 3 (January 1935). Only three essays of this kind in *Esquire* have been identified.

3. *Hey Rub-a-Dub-Dub* (1920) contains three one-act plays: "The Dream," "Phantasmagoria," and "The Court of Progress."

4. Jacques Chambrun, an agent, was attempting to interest Dreiser in preparing an article for the "My Most Unforgettable Character" series in *Reader's Digest*. For Dreiser's earlier relationship to this series, see Dreiser to George Bye, 29 October 1939.

To Charles E. Yost [TC-DPUP]

Dreiser had met Yost in 1919 in Fayette, Ohio, where Yost edited a weekly news-
paper; Yost was a great admirer of Dreiser's work, and the two men corresponded
frequently over the years.

1015 N. King's Rd.,
Hollywood, Calif.
July 17, 1941.

Dear Yost:

Its gratifying to hear from you again. And the fact that your wife died
and that you are so unsettled saddens me.[1] Yet, personally the approach of
death doesn't trouble me as it once did. Life tapers off rather decently for
most of us, and when I consider the arrogance, the follies and the cruelties
that go with so many temperaments, I'm damned glad that all have to die.
Consider 150 or 200 years of Louis XIV or Captain Mussolini or Ivan the
Terrible or Dr. Hitler or our own select band of corporation bandits. Plainly
the creative force is exercising not only great wisdom and true justice in
limiting the duration of everything. For, by so doing, it is limiting mischief
and that is putting it mildly. Its too bad death can't catch more undertakers
before they rob so many of our heirs and assigns.

Well, anyhow—as to the book—I would have written you about it but I
had so much trouble getting it published at all and was so sure beforehand
that it was to be ignored or slammed by the press, that I decided not to
bother anyone much. I have so few friends in the corporation press today
that only word-of-mouth will do any of my books any good, and so—the
silence. *Time*, the weekly, called it a *tract*. I got about eight lines.[2]

But I'm glad you like it. I had to have a very great deal of research done
before I could move at all. Curiously, although it has been published 9
months now,[3] it is only recently that I have begun to get complimentary
letters—although one pro-Britisher wrote to say that plainly I am a para-
noiac. So you see the lean goes with the fat. As for courage—if you call
being provoked and enraged until you begin to squawk,—courage,—well,
yes, I have that kind,—if that's what it is.[4]

Anyhow, thanks. And my love and best wishes. I often wish you were
around where I could talk to you.

1. Yost reported in his letter to Dreiser of 12 July 1941 that his wife had died
the previous November and that he had just finished reading *America Is Worth
Saving*.

2. "Counsel from Hollywood," *Time* 37 (3 February 1941): 74–76.

3. Since *America Is Worth Saving* was published on 20 January 1941, six months would be more correct.

4. It appears strange that Dreiser does not mention in connection with *America Is Worth Saving* that Nazi Germany had invaded the Soviet Union on 22 June 1941, an event that transformed Great Britain and the Soviet Union into allies and thereby weakened Dreiser's argument in his book that Britain was the enemy of the Soviet Union.

1942

To Edgar Lee Masters [H-HRHUT]

The attack on Pearl Harbor on 7 December 1941 and the war with Japan that followed occasioned some panic in California because of a fear that the Japanese might invade the West Coast.

[13 March 1942][1]

Dear Edgar:

Irony, sardonic laughter and flaming rage are truly outstanding gifts of yours, and I most sincerely hope that a collection of your letters, apocryphal poems, published and unpublished documents of various kinds are collected by some lover [word missing] letters & life and stored in some library or university for future readers to look at. They are interesting, amusing illuminative and almost quite always thrilling. Certainly my files—when they go to some university as they presently will—will contain—with your permissions—your communications to me. If your answer is *no* I'll try & dig them out & burn or return them. But, like Dean Swift & Voltaire you should let them ride.[2] What harm! They will help & entertain many. As for the rest what harm.

Well, how art thou Edgar? Hale and incorrigible? I hope and also I know so. You will never change, glory be, and I only wish I could see more of you. Out here all is rather dead at the moment since there is serious evidence to the effect that a Japanese onslaught—Pearl Harbor style—is in the immediate offing—about the middle of April. At the moment the state is planning to move all children to government camps in the Sierras East of here until the fate of the coast is settled. All school children at this hour are being supplied with metal identification tags to be worn about the neck. Citizens are being advised to apply for instruction in self-defense, the art of smothering fire bombs etc. Trains appear to be pouring in soldiers but as for aeroplanes, submarines, battleships etc the general feeling is that the supply is insufficient—in other words we are to get the worst of it! As for myself I am stocking up with a repeating rifle, one repeating revolver and a fair supply of ammunition with which to welcome the visitors as they invade this street if they do. If only I could bag two or three before I am bagged I wont feel so bad. One can only die once.

Curiously I hear that Washington knows. Also General Motors, the Duponts, the Metropolitan Life Insurance Co, the Railways etc. 19 Pullman car trains leave daily for the East—or Middle West. Real estate sales

& rentals are already down to nothing. Many small stores have shut up. And all I can see is that the general population lacks the fighting spirit to make such an invasion immensely costly. They either do not believe it will come—or if they do they talk as though we cannot hope to win!—must lose heavily, which is certainly the tragic mood. So we sit & wait. If I am cleaned out you can remember that I tried to do something to the enemy first. But our Navy! And our Army! My God!

How is the Hen? Regards to her. And Harriet.[3] Once in a blue moon I have a short word from her. Is she ok? Working? Cheerful? I hope so. She is a brave, aggressive kid & I will always like her. Let me have a word at your convenience. And always

Love—
from
T.D
1015 N. Kings Rd. Hollywood.
Friday March 13th (Everybodys lucky day.)

1. The date on the first page of this letter is in Masters's hand, but Dreiser himself has also dated it at its close.

2. Dreiser appears to be referring to the realization by Swift and Voltaire that their letters to others would play important roles in their posthumous fame.

3. Alice Davis, Masters's companion (see Dreiser to Edgar Lee Masters, 7 December 1938, n. 1), and Harriet Bissell, Dreiser's former secretary (see Dreiser to William C. Lengel, 16 July 1938, n. 6).

To William C. Lengel   [H-DPUP]

Dreiser had signed a contract with Putnam's in November 1941 for delivery of The Bulwark *on 1 June 1942. He made little progress on the novel, however, until Marguerite Tjader Harris arrived in Los Angeles in August 1944 to aid him in its preparation.*

THEODORE DREISER

July 1—'42

Dear Lengel:

The book is not ready yet and will not be for some time.[1] Not that I am not working on it or getting along with it but it is a very intimate and touchy problem in connection with religious family life—and, like the American Tragedy I find it difficult. I think I wrote Balch[2] that for a while I was down with intestinal flu and could do nothing. However that was some time ago & since I have been working—but slowly since it is slow—this close psychologic interpretation. If it will ease Balch's mind or yours I am willing, to return the $1000 advance providing when the Ms is handed over the advance money is returned to me. That will leave the contract intact and I will do my best to get along.

I hope you are not still sick or—if you are, that you are improving. Let me know. And my best to Nelle[3] and your son Bill.

Dreiser
1015 N. King's Rd
Hollywood

1. On 29 June 1942, Lengel's assistant had written Dreiser reminding him of the contract deadline for the submission of *The Bulwark*.
2. Earle H. Balch (1893?–1977), vice president of Putnam's.
3. Lengel's wife.

To William C. Lengel [TS-WCLUP]

THEODORE DREISER

1015 N. King's Rd.,
Hollywood, Calif.,
July 18, 1942.

Dear Will:

I am shocked and very sorry to hear of the long operation you had to undergo and that it will be some time, as naturally it would be, before you are up and around.[1]

I marvel at your physical strength. I have never had but two operations—one lasting 30 minutes and one an hour. And because of the latter I was kept in bed a little over a week (appendicitis). Naturally you will be some time down but I certainly do hope this winds up operations for you. You have had so much trouble in one way and another.

As for myself, just now I am feeling fairly well,—The amount of desk work I have to do dragging me down a little. But I'm getting along with the novel and am told that it reads very well. Of course its all interesting to me or I wouldn't be writing it. I hope when you get on your feet you will be interested to take a look at My Gal Sal which is still running here and throughout the rest of the country.[2] I was surprised and pleased at the skilful way the Fox company developed Paul's life story as well as the gay nineties, and particularly his Gal Sal. It's truly charming and gay.

Anyhow—and regardless of that—I hope you are up and around soon and that your operation troubles are over for good.

Affectionately,
Dreiser

1. Lengel's assistant wrote Dreiser on 6 July 1942 that Lengel had undergone a six-hour operation.
2. The film was released in May 1942.

To Charles W. David [TS-DPUP]

Robert H. Elias, who had been working on Dreiser's biography for some time, was also completing his Ph.D. at the University of Pennsylvania while teaching there. Elias, his dissertation director Professor Sculley Bradley (1897–?), and David (1885–1984), a professor of history at the University of Pennsylvania as well as the university's director of libraries from 1940 to 1955, had encouraged Dreiser to deposit his literary estate in the university library, and Dreiser had begun shipping material to it in April 1942.

1015 N. King's Rd.,
Hollywood, Calif.,
July 30, 1942.

Dear Mr. David:

I am sorry I did not answer your letter before.[1]

As to the Mencken letters I am perfectly willing to have Mr. Mencken supplied with photostats of my letters from him in exchange for my letters to him, which he is sending you.[2]

In connection with paragraph 3 of your July 7th letter, there will be additional shipments to you from time to time. However, I do not have a full set of American first editions of my books, particularly Sister Carrie. The firsts that I sent you were all that I had.[3] Also there are some foreign editions, which were published without my consent, as for instance, Spanish, Italian, Chinese, Russian, etc. etc., which I have never had.

In connection with DAWN (MS) which I listed in my letter-agreement, I have been holding it back owing to the fact that I have had an offer for it which I am considering. Should it be sold, however, a photostat can be made of it before delivery.[4]

In checking the contents of the trunks in my possession I did not come across my file of EVERY MONTH. I think it is there somewhere, however, and as soon as I can find the time for a thorough search I will write you about it.[5]

Is the Literary Department of your university interested in Charles Fort,—his life and works?[6] I have some material that relates to him, and Tiffany Thayer, the author of *Thirteen Women* and the alleged head of the Fortean Society, has more.[7] As a matter of fact, against the wishes and the Will of Mrs. Charles Fort, he is said to have taken 10,000 notes which Fort had made on scientific and historic data, which he evidently intended to incorporate in future volumes. Thayer was asked by the lawyer of Mrs. Fort to return this data to me but he refused to do so. Perhaps he would be willing to turn it over to the University of Pennsylvania. If so, I would gladly add my collection to his, for, to me, it is highly important that it should be examined and a study of it made for publication.

Yours very sincerely,

Theodore Dreiser

1. David had written on 7 July 1942 raising several questions about the material which the library had been receiving from Dreiser.

2. Dreiser had accepted Mencken's idea that each of them should have copies made of the letters to them by the other and that they should then exchange the copied letters (see also Riggio, *Dreiser-Mencken Letters*, II, 673–78).

3. In his 7 July letter to Dreiser, David had asked when the library could expect to receive additional material, especially more first editions of Dreiser's works.

4. In a letter to Dreiser on 4 August 1942, David vigorously protested this arrangement. Dreiser in his reply of 11 August relented and indicated that he would indeed send the manuscript to Pennsylvania. In the end, however, the sale to another party went through, and at present the *Dawn* manuscript is in the Lilly Library of Indiana University and a photographic copy is in the University of Pennsylvania Library.

5. David had also asked, in his letter of 7 July, about Dreiser's file of *Ev'ry Month* for the years he edited it (1895–97). Dreiser apparently failed to find this material, since the copies of the journal in DPUP were laboriously gathered over many years after his death.

6. For Dreiser and Fort, see Dreiser to John Cowper Powys, 12 December 1930.

7. Dreiser engaged in an extended feud with Thayer (1902–1959), a writer of often salacious novels who had helped found the Fortean Society in 1931, over control of Fort's papers. Thayer's novel *Thirteen Women* appeared in 1932.

To Charles Laughton [TS-UCLA]

The British-born Laughton (1899–1962) had been a major Hollywood star since the early 1930s. Elizabeth Coakley (see Dreiser to Patrick Coakley, 27 November 1939) had been aiding Dreiser in adapting a number of his short stories into screenplays.

THEODORE DREISER

1015 N. King's Rd.,
Hollywood, Calif.,
Nov. 13, 1942.

Dear Mr. Laughton:

I am taking the liberty of sending you a synopsis, or perhaps I had better say a rough moving picture script, of a short story of mine—THE HAND— which now leads the current BOOK-OF-THE-MONTH Club selection of the best American short stories (168 all told) which has been combined in one volume and of which 400,000 copies have been issued. The book is entitled THIS IS MY BEST—edited by Whit Burnett.[1]

This story needs an exceptionably able actor to play it, and it occurred to me that you might possibly be interested in a part of this kind. Therefore, I am sending it to you with the request that you read it.

I remember your very excellent work in PAYMENT DEFERRED, as well as many other fine performances you have given—HENRY THE EIGHTH being one of my favorites—but I have never forgotten your work in PAYMENT DEFERRED.[2] This story of mine has much of the same fateful theme as that, and, in my opinion, would make a great picture for you, if it were handled by an able director.

Will you be so kind as to read it? And if you are not interested, will you please return it to me?

Yours very sincerely,
Theodore Dreiser

1. *This Is My Best* (1942), edited by Whit Burnett (1899–1973). Dreiser is not quite accurate in describing Burnett's collection, since its stories were the "best" only in the sense that each author selected for inclusion the story he considered "closest to his heart." For an earlier possible film version of "The Hand," see Dreiser to William C. Lengel, 9 March 1940.

2. *Payment Deferred*, originally a 1931 Broadway production and then a Hollywood film of 1932; *The Private Life of Henry VIII*, a British film of 1933. "The Hand" resembles *Payment Deferred* in that both stories involve protagonists who murder for money.

1943

To Rufus M. Jones [TS-Hav]¹

Dreiser turned to Jones, with whom he had worked in 1938 on a plan for Spanish Civil War relief (see Dreiser to Caroline McCormick Slade, 28 September 1938), for information on specific aspects of Quaker belief and practice as he wrote The Bulwark. *Jones replied on 30 April, describing the various Quaker schools and colleges in the Philadelphia area and referring Dreiser to the chapter on education in his* Later Periods of Quakerism *(1921).*

THEODORE DREISER

1015 N. King's Rd.,
Hollywood, Calif.,
April 23, 1943.

My dear Jones:

It is a long time since we undertook to impress the Rockefellers and the Catholic Church,² but I not only have thought of you often but do think frequently of your temperament and your social import.

I happen to be writing a novel that involves Friends or Quakers, and I want to ask you this question: What educational institutions in the Philadelphia, New Jersey & Eastern Pennsylvania area were either influenced or controlled by Friends between the years 1885 and 1900? The reason for the question is that I want to establish in my own mind, and possibly in the book, how liberal or illiberal (from the Sectarian point of view) were these schools, if any. I am concerned only with Friends' schools or schools that were influenced by them in one way or another, which were in existence in that period within one hundred miles of Philadelphia. Friends' schools or colleges farther away do not interest me so much, although, if you will, you might name a few.

How are you? I hope strong and active.

When I think of you and contrast you with the average so called Christian, I am inclined to use language that your temperament would not countenance. But I still and always will hold you in my very highest esteem. Regards.

And all my best wishes—
Theodore Dreiser

1. Published in Gerhard Friedrich, "The Dreiser-Jones Correspondence," *Bulletin of Friends Historical Association* 5 (Spring 1957): 23–34.

2. Dreiser refers to his effort to enlist Monsignor John Ryan, a Catholic priest, and Nelson Rockefeller in a committee to aid Spanish Civil War civilians; see Dreiser to Caroline McCormick Slade, 28 September 1938.

To Ginger Rogers [TCopy-Hun]

Rogers (1911–95), who had become a star during the 1930s as Fred Astaire's dancing partner, had recently undertaken more dramatic roles. No reply by Miss Rogers has been found.

COPY

THEODORE DREISER

1015 North King's Rd.,
Hollywood, California
May 15, 1943.

Dear Ginger Rogers:

I thought it very gracious on your part to allow me to explain CINDER-ELLA THE SECOND to you personally—even though five eighths of the explaining was done by Elizabeth Coakley.[1] It is pleasant at times to be a mere bystander. It certainly was on that occasion.

The reason for this letter is that, in the time that has elapsed since talking to you, I have had time to think over the story as a whole, and it has occurred to me that the love contacts are not sufficiently numerous to make it as effective as it might be. In my desire to remedy that I have worked out several strong situations which bring the lovers together in the middle of the story.

So . . . before making up your mind finally, I would like the privilege of submitting to you a revised script, with these scenes in their proper place. After that, an early decision would be very appreciated by

Yours very truly,
Theodore Dreiser

P.S. Needless to say, I found your home delightfully arresting, and the hour that Mrs. Coakley and I spent there will be aesthetically remembered.

Cordially,
Th.D.

1. Among the screenplays at DPUP is *"Cinderella the Second* / An Original Story for the Screen / by / Theodore Dreiser / Script / by / Elizabeth Coakley." The story is a lightweight romantic comedy involving a young actress. For Elizabeth Coakley, see Dreiser to Patrick Coakley, 27 November 1939. Also see letters to Elizabeth Coakley in *New Letters*, Vol. II.

To Emerson S. Van Cleave [TC-DPUP]

Van Cleave, a teacher at Southern Illinois Normal University (in Carbondale, Illinois) and like Dreiser a native of Terre Haute, wrote Dreiser a long undated letter in which he discussed Dreiser's depiction in Dawn *(1931) of his boyhood there in the 1870s.*

1015 N. King's Rd.,
Hollywood, Calif.,
Sept. 28, 1943.

Dear Mr. Van Cleave:

Your letter is very interesting and I am glad you wrote me.

As to Merom Bluffs, I think I wont move them again. I think I'll just leave them where they are.[1]

About Eugene Debs, I only knew him after he became famous and came east to speak in New York City and some surrounding places.[2] Personally I found him not only an extremely sympathetic and informed man but a magnetic temperament which, if it had not been for his interest in working humanity, which you seem to think should be discarded, he might have attained to some important political position in this country. In my estimation, he should have. My father knew him and his family and several of my friends seem to have been actually and admiringly in touch with him. I only wish that life had treated him better than it did.

As for my visiting Terre Haute, for some reason or other, my birth place has never taken to me. This opposition seems to have sprung from my desire to see Paul's birthplace purchased as a memorial since a considerable sum of money was raised for some purpose in connection with him. Also, perhaps, because I suggested and re-suggested the affectional and historical value of removing his remains from Chicago and placing him in the small plot of ground that surrounds that house. However, the authorities there do not seem to think that this was where he was born, and since I did not know that, I probably spoke out of turn.[3] These are the only reasons why I have not visited there. There are no others. And sometime I may find it convenient to go back and look the place over.

Thank you very much for your interesting information and your invitation.

Yours very truly,

1. In *Dawn*, Dreiser had placed Merom Bluffs near Vincennes, Indiana; Van Cleave had pointed out that they are actually near Sullivan, Indiana.

2. Van Cleave had asked if Dreiser had known Eugene Debs, the famous labor leader, who was born and raised in Terre Haute (for Dreiser and Debs, see Dreiser to Eugene Debs, 17 October 1922). Dreiser's account of his impression of Debs is based on the Debs of the late 1890s and the turn of the century, after he gained national prominence as the head of the American Railway Union and especially after he ran for president in 1900 on the ticket of the Social Democratic Party, a precursor of the Socialist Party.

3. For Dreiser's efforts on behalf of a Paul Dresser memorial, see Dreiser to Edward M. Dreiser, 11 February 1924.

1944

To Claude Bowers [TS-LLIU]

Bowers's failure to reply to Dreiser's July 1938 request for aid in entering war-torn Spain had angered Dreiser. (Bowers at the time was American ambassador to the Loyalist government of Spain.) Bowers, learning of Dreiser's feelings some years later, sought, in a letter of 27 March 1944, to discover their source. For Dreiser's earlier relationship to Bowers, see Dreiser to Claude Bowers, 22 May 1924.

THEODORE DREISER

1015 N. King's Rd.,
Hollywood, 46, Calif.,
April 14, 1944.

Dear Bowers:

Through your friend, Mr. Kuper,[1] I have your letter of March 27. My resentment or grievance (non existing at this date) relates to the fact that when I was in Paris in 1938 representing the League of American Writers at the International Peace Conference, being held there at that time,[2] I was asked by that organization to, if possible, visit Loyalist Spain, and, after seeing what I could of conditions there, report later to it in New York, if I would. Knowing no one of any import in France at the time other than Madam Clayburgh,[3] who had crossed with me on the Normandie, I consulted with her and was advised by her that you were in the south of France, either on the French or the Spanish side of the Franco-Spanish boundary line and that you would be the one to obtain for me a passport if anyone could. Accordingly I wrote—I forget now whether it was one or two letters but I think two—the first one telling you of my presence and work there in Paris—the second (a little later) explaining that I had been asked to visit Loyalist Spain and inquiring whether you could be of any service to me in that direction. Though I heard from you in regard to the first letter, I heard nothing in regard to the second, which same puzzled me not a little.

Later, however, in Paris I was introduced to a secret Loyalist group there who saw to it at once that I was provided with the necessary credentials, and, better still, guides and well wishers inside the Loyalist field. Later I returned to Paris and via England to the United States. Naturally I was a little irritated since Madam Clayburgh had emphasized to me your cordiality and hospitality to her on some visit she appeared to have paid you some time before on one of her previous visits to Paris.

However, let that be as it will. You may have written me and I never received it. Or you may not have received my letter. If I spoke to anyone it probably was to Bob Heinl[4] whom I afterwards met somewhere. Certainly I do not recall speaking of it to any other. Anyhow, it is of no consequence now and I am not harboring any ill will. In fact I was glad to learn that after the Loyalist collapse you had been favored by our government with another international mission[5]—a tribute which must have sprung from services worthy of it.

But let us forget this. It is not and has not been of sufficient import to warrant any enduring feeling on my part. Rather I prefer to think of your silence as due to some miscarriage on the part of the French mail service.

Sincerely and cordially,
Theodore Dreiser

1. Theodore F. Kuper (1886–1981), a Thomas Jefferson scholar and a friend of Bowers since the 1920s.
2. See Dreiser to William C. Lengel, 16 July 1938.
3. For Alma Clayburgh, see Dreiser to William C. Lengel, 16 July 1938, n. 4.
4. For Heinl, see Dreiser to Robert D. Heinl, 30 September 1924. Heinl, like Bowers and Dreiser, was an Indiana native.
5. Bowers served as ambassador to Chile from 1939 to 1953.

To Alfred A. Knopf [TS-HRHUT]

Elias did not win the Knopf Fellowship, but his biography, Theodore Dreiser: Apostle of Nature, *was nevertheless published by Alfred A. Knopf in 1949.*

Hotel Commodore
New York, N. Y.
May 28, 1944

Dear Knopf:

Robert H. Elias, of the University of Pennsylvania, tells me that he is applying for an Alfred A. Knopf Fellowship in Biography for a work tentatively titled "Theodore Dreiser: Critic of Society," and he wants me to write you what I think of his literary ability and scholarship.

I think he ought to be awarded a fellowship, because, on the basis of what I have seen him do, I think he will write a good book. I have known him since 1937, when he sent me the thesis he had written about me for a Master's degree at Columbia.[1] Frankly, I was astonished and not a little impressed by his estimate of me and my work. I told him at that time that his study of me was the most careful examination of the material and the best weighing of it that had been done. All the ideas were carefully evaluated, yet so readably presented—and quite correct, I felt. I said his book ought to be published. He insisted, however, that there was more to do, and continued digging into my past and assembling various data from interviews with me and from scattered articles, addresses, and letters. In 1941 I opened all my files to him, and he spent the summer at my place in Hollywood putting everything in order—filing, indexing, and taking notes. All this material, consisting of some manuscripts, first editions, and my entire correspondence, I have since given to the University of Pennsylvania, where Elias is teaching and is in charge of the cataloguing of my collection. He is proceeding with his biographical researches there and has my permission to make use of any material he wants, subject, of course, to my final approval for its reproduction.

If it is ever right for an author to encourage any one of his critics or any interpretation of his own work, I would say that Elias's work ought to be encouraged. He is, temperamentally, fitted to complete this book. He has imagination and an intelligent, philosophical turn of mind. His research is honest and thorough; his judgments are fair—I may say he understands my work and what I am trying to do. And his writing is vivid and colorful. I think that's what you want.

Sincerely yours,
Theodore Dreiser

1. See Dreiser to Robert H. Elias, 17 November 1937.

1945

To Malcolm Elwin [TS-HRHUT]

Elwin (1902–73), a British biographer and critic, was preparing a biography of Llewelyn Powys, who had died in 1939. It appeared in 1946 as The Life of Llewelyn Powys.

THEODORE DREISER

1015 N. King's Rd.,
Hollywood, 46, Calif.,
Jan. 27, 1945.

Dear Mr. Elwin:

Thank you very much for your letter and your appreciation of my work.

As to Llewelyn, yes, I first met him in San Francisco through his brother, John Cowper Powys. He came to the St. Francis Hotel where Helen and I were stopping. Helen was ill in bed at the time, and the two boys called on us.[1]

When they both walked into the room, it was as though, between the two of them, all that was beautiful, intelligent and worth while contemplating in the way of thought and spirit suddenly swept into the room. Jack with his profound knowledge of philosophy, poetry, literature, along with the magic common touch which he has never lost,—Llewelyn with his great child-like beauty—physical as well as spiritual—his massive head of golden curls, his beauty loving eye lit up by a smile that contained all the sunshine in the world. I thought, as I looked at them in their interesting loose fitting hand woven English tweeds, and observed the rhythm and freedom of their movements, that they were about as complete a pair as I have ever seen. Once seen together, one can hardly separate one from the other, although each is the opposite pole of the other in philosophy and thought, but not in spirit.

I wrote an introduction to Llewelyn's first book—EBONY AND IVORY— at that time because I liked the book so much.[2] And I still like it, as well as all of his other books. His last book—LOVE AND DEATH—I think is one of the most beautifully tragic books I have ever read, and one in which the true spirit of Llewelyn comes through with great clarity and force.[3]

I wish you success with your book about Llewelyn.

Sincerely,
Theodore Dreiser

1. Dreiser met John Cowper Powys in 1913 in Chicago (see Dreiser to John Cowper Powys, 12 December 1930); the San Francisco meeting with Llewelyn occurred in October 1920.

2. Dreiser is referring to the American edition of *Ebony and Ivory*, which was published in early 1923 with an introduction by him.

3. *Love and Death: An Imaginary Autobiography* (1939).

To Robert H. Elias [TS-Cor]

Dreiser is replying to a series of questions by Elias, who was preparing his biography.

1015 N. King's Rd.,
Hollywood, 46, Calif.,
Jan. 28, 1945.

Dear Elias:

I did write the title SISTER CARRIE on a piece of paper as Rascoe says, but it was in New York, not in Cleveland.[1] It was at the time I lived up on 102nd St. facing Central Park, West. It was not entitled "The Flesh & The Spirit". Where did you get that?[2]

I met Loeb around 1912 or 13, maybe a little before. He wrote me a letter, which should be in the files somewhere, after he had seen some article of mine somewhere.[3] We started a correspondence which led to a friendship which lasted over quite a period.

I did not drive a street car in Brooklyn. That is from SISTER CARRIE. I rode on a car in Toledo during a strike. (As Reporter).[4]

As to a set of my books, well that is something on which I will have to cash in. It is my one good shot at this time and I have an exclusive arrangement with an agent just now who is determined and confident that he can sell a large number (number guaranteed) to either Marshall Field or another firm which really has the quantity of paper necessary.[5] It seems to come down to that one point. Who has the paper? However, I would like to let these people try in this regard before I do anything on my own. In the meantime I am not obligated to Putnam's any more as I have repaid them their advances made on The Bulwark and the General Contract for all of my books. (They have done nothing for me financially or otherwise). It is now possible for me to get a real deal on my set, which will be my next move. (Confidential, of course.) However, I appreciate your interest.

And I am glad that you are doing so well with your project. With kindest regards.

Sincerely,
Theodore Dreiser

1. In his *Theodore Dreiser* (1925), Burton Rascoe (see Dreiser to Burton Rascoe, 13 April 1931) had claimed (p. 37) that Dreiser began *Sister Carrie* in Cleveland.

2. As Elias explained in his letter to Dreiser on 4 February 1945, "The Flesh and the Spirit" appears as the novel's title on the contract which Doubleday, Page prepared for Dreiser's signature. Dreiser crossed this title out and substituted his original title, *Sister Carrie*. Doubleday, Page probably derived its title from a motif in the novel's chapter titles.

3. Dreiser is probably in error, since the two men corresponded initially in 1919 and met briefly in 1923.

4. See Dreiser's article "The Strike To-Day," *Toledo Blade*, 24 March 1894; republished in T. D. Nostwich, ed., *Theodore Dreiser: Journalism, Vol. One: Newspaper Writings, 1892–1895* (Philadelphia: University of Pennsylvania Press, 1988).

5. A wartime shortage of paper had led to restrictions in publishing; Marshall Field, the Chicago department store, at this time included book publishing among its ancillary enterprises.

To Edgar Lee Masters   [H-HRHUT]

[30 January 1945][1]

Dear Edgar:

Merry Xmas and a happy 1945! Also down with the Germans and the Japs! Incidentally I now retail that since last I wrote I've had not only a continuous and unbroken chest cold but tooth trouble to the extent of having four of my good solid teeth extracted—each extraction three weeks later than the last one. Diagnosis—as usual—a poisening cyst at the root of each tooth. Hence neuralgic pains, colds, general lassitude. Well, the cysts are out but the neuralgic pains are not wholly gone by any means and my cold is right here as I write. [Cough! Cough! Cough!] However I feel that I'll be coming round for the weather here is perfect—like the best days in June & July in New York. Incidentally Edgar I'd like to know how you are. The last word I had was that you were not particularly better yet not so worse either. Personally I'm loaded down with all sorts of letters and requests which require time to read and result in nothing. The only letters I open with happy interest are those from you and Jack over in Wales. He's still translating Rabelais into the Welsh which would make even Rabelais laugh.[2] But that's Jack—the wilder the idea the better. As far as yours truly & you—well I'll be here until May when I may have to go to N.Y. (My books.[3] And if so I'll be breezing in on you and hope to find you as ironic and as cynically amusing as you have been ever since the first hour I laid eyes on you. And something tells me you will be. So, darling, pending my survival of various ills I'll be seeing you. And here's life, lust & length of days.

ThD.

1. Dated in brackets on the holograph in a hand other than Dreiser's; the date is roughly in accord with Dreiser's greeting in his initial sentence.

2. John Cowper Powys (see Dreiser to John Cowper Powys, 12 December 1930) did not publish a Welsh translation of Rabelais, though in 1948 his *Rabelais, His Life: The Story Told by Him . . .* did appear.

3. Dreiser appears to be referring to the possible publication of an edition of his complete works (see Dreiser to William C. Lengel, 17 November 1945); the trip did not materialize.

To Robert H. Elias [TS-Cor]

Continuing his querying of Dreiser, Elias wrote him on 4 February 1945 asking a number of questions about his life and work and appending to his letter an additional thirty-one numbered questions. Helen replied on 15 February and appended to her letter Dreiser's dictated responses to Elias's questions. It has been thought best to present this material in the following manner: Helen's letter appears initially; Elias's questions and Dreiser's replies follow in the document which Helen entitled "Robert H. Elias Questionnaire." Within this document, however, Elias's questions are in brackets, since the questions are not by Dreiser. Dreiser's responses to Elias's questions, however, since they are similar to other correspondence by him over the years which took the form of a dictated letter to a secretary who then typed the final version, constitute a letter by Dreiser and are presented as such.

THEODORE DREISER

1015 N. King's Rd.,
Hollywood, 46, Calif.,
Feb. 15, 1945.

Dear Mr. Elias:

I am enclosing answers to some of the questions which you have asked Mr. Dreiser. It is the best I can do about getting answers from him.

He is so completely absorbed in his book[1] and the many pressing social problems that he feels compelled to do something about, that it is almost impossible for him to go back and go over specific detailed matter in connection with events which happened so long ago. For instance, he says that he cannot possibly go over the photostats which you sent. However, he does identify the "As If In Old Toledo" article and the strike article and the mind reading hypnotism one.[2] In fact I have heard him tell about that one many times.

I wish I could be of more help to you but it is almost impossible to pin him down to questions. The only time for it is in the evening and he is utterly tired at that time. My job, too, is terrific.

However, if there is anything urgent, just write about it and I will try to get the information for you, sooner or later.

With kindest personal regards.

Sincerely,
Helen Dreiser

Robert H. Elias Questionnaire.

[1. John W. Grant in a letter to you harks back to childhood days and asks whether you recall the following rhymes. Do you recall them, and to what do they relate?

> "The festive Dudelet
> With his poodlet
> Took a walklet down the streetlet
> Dude got so rudelet
> Cop nabbed the Dudelet:
> And stuck him in the cooler with his poodlet."]

1. I do not recall them and do not know to what they relate.

[2. When did you first meet Maud Powell, and where? To what extent did she encourage you in your career? Is it true that she was one of the first to perceive your artistic bent?]

2. She came into Ev'ry Month to see me. She knew Arthur Henry, and he had told her he was a friend of mine. She was interested in the character of the magazine, etc. etc. I encouraged myself in my career. Henry was one of the first interested in my career and he told Maud Powell about me.[3]

[3. You wrote under the pseudonyms of Edward Al and Stanley Wils at one time. Edward Al is signed to book reviews in *Ev'ry Month*. Stanley Wils supposedly was signed to dramatic criticism? In what publication?]

3. Don't remember using name of Stanley Wils. Used Edward Al because one was my brother's name and Al was the name of another brother.

[4. Concerning Toledo days: (a) How did you happen to know Frank Cook, of the *Commercial*, who gave you a letter of introduction to the railroad to get you to Buffalo?

(b) Who was J. T. Hutchison?

(c) Was the Wood County Herald an actual paper, and did you actually do work for it during the street-car strike?]

4. Don't recall how I happened to know Frank Cook.

(b) Hutchinson came from a little town about 25 miles from Toledo. He came to Chicago and did a few days work on the Globe. Left and wanted me to come up to this small town and edit paper up there. I went up there and thought the town was too small,—so I did not stay.[4] Went on to Toledo and got a job on Blade.

(c) Wood County Herald might have been the name of the small town paper. I was not interested at all.[5]

[5. Concerning *Sister Carrie:* (a) Did the original character or characters upon the facts of whose life or lives you drew for Hurstwood ever commit suicide? (I ask this, because in "A Touch of Human Brotherhood," *Success* for March 1902, you report a talk with the Captain of the "Curious Shifts of the Poor" chapter, and he says men don't give up their lives, no matter how bad.)]

5. I took Hurstwood from a bowery type. Manager of Hannah and Hogg's.[6] Suicide fictional, although lots of people commit suicide.

[6. Am I right in believing that in November, 1902, you lived at 210 Sumac Street in Philadelphia and at that time became acquainted with Coates? (I have a letter to one "Coates" with the address 210 Sumac St., "City," and wonder whether that means Philadelphia.)]

6. Address on Sumac likely. City Philadelphia where I became acquainted with Coates.[7]

[7. If you were working in Philadelphia then, I assume it was for the *North American*. I have been through the files for around then and can find no signed article. But in December of 1902 there is an article on "Tupenny Tube War" in London (Morgan vs. Yerkes). Do you recall whether you wrote that? Or what you did write?]

7. I wrote four or five philosophic speculations on life for North American.[8] 20 dollars each was paid for them. Don't remember "Tupenny Tube War".

[8. After this did you get your job on the New York Central?]
8. Yes.

[9. Does The "*Genius*" contain a fairly accurate account of your own difficulties in this period? For example:

(a) Didn't you, like Eugene Witla, wander south into Tennessee, Kentucky, and Mississippi? (Stopping in Phila. en route back). *Genius*, p. 288–91.

(b) Did Eugene's state of mind and health represent yours? (p. 301) That is, upon your return to NY.

(c) Had you, too, once consulted an astrologer and, in Chicago, a palmist who foretold certain troubles and distress when you would reach a certain age?

(d) Did you, too, have a plan like Eugene's Sea Island Development Co? Was that why you were interested in the Henry Bros.' Yakima Orchards?

(e) Who was the original of Hudson Dula? He seems to have been a close friend of yours, who, I judge, got you a job after your work on the NY Central.]

9. No.

(a) Didn't go into those states at all.

(b) Entirely possible but I don't recall that I was painting myself exactly. Was simply painting an artist.

(c) Don't recall.

(d) Was never interested in it. Henry told me about it.[9]

(e) Don't recall Hudson Dula. Got my own job.[10]

[10. For what paper did you do Page Specials after the Railroad? In May, 1904, you contributed "Sailors' Snug Harbor" to a Sunday *New York Tribune*. Was that the paper?]

10. Don't recall doing that article for Tribune.[11]

[11. Who got you that job?]

11. Got it myself tracking around from one door to another.

[12. To what editor or publication did you send your poem (or "Mood") "They Have Nourished As an Abundant Rain"? I haven't yet located it.)]

12. Can't possibly recall.[12]

[13. Who got you your job at Smith's: was it yourself or a friend?]

13. Richard Duffy, running Ainslee's told me that Street and Smith needed a man and it might be to my advantage to go down and see them, which I did. They wrote me a letter and Mr. McLean put me on.

[14. I've been looking through the files of *Smith's Magazine*. I notice that when changes in management were made, there was adopted the policy of having an introductory editorial in each issue, an editorial which would discuss the stories within. Was that innovation your idea? And were the editorials yours or Ormond Smith's?]

14. Don't recall.[13]

[15. I notice a similar policy pursued on *The Broadway Magazine*. Some of the editorials stressed the fact that this was a magazine for and of New York, portraying the city in all its variety. Sounds like you. Was it you? Did you, too, adopt the policy of getting readers to send in their ideas and criticisms?]

15. Ben Hampton advertised the magazine in some of the papers and he may have suggested to people to bring in ideas, but most people brought in ideas anyway.[14]

[16. *Delineator:* Was the idea for the Child Rescue Campaign yours? Who else was especially active in promoting it?]

16. Yes. Myself and advertising department.[15]

[17. Was *The Rake* (a book you destroyed) about any subject you later dealt with in another novel?]

17. No. Never dealt with subject later.[16]

[18. You were, in 1908, working on something called *A Solution in Exile*. What became of that? Was it an early title for *Jennie*?]

18. Don't remember. No, it was not Jennie.[17]

[19. What became of the story of a Puritan you were doing around 1916–23?]

19. May have torn it up. Don't remember.[18]

[20. The *"Genius"* seems to have been completed between *Jennie* and *The Financier*. Did the original MS bear the present ending, with Eugene staring out into "the sparkling deeps of space"? In fact, were any revisions made at the time or year of publication?]

20. Started Jennie. Went to Dodge and got my books back. Had a little money from Butterick and was free to do something. Got stuck at one point on Jennie. Started The "Genius". Finished "Genius". Started Jennie again and finished it.[19]

[21. You once planned a volume entitled *The King Is Naked*. Did that become *Hey Rub-a-Dub-Dub*? If not, what was it?]

21. Yes.

[22. In it there was, I think, an essay entitled "To Be or Not To Be." Was this, then written, eventually published in *Esquire* as "Kismet"?]

22. No. Kismet was written and published shortly afterward.[20]

[23. I believe you completed both *Dawn* and *Newspaper Days* around 1920. To what extent was *Dawn* later revised for publication? I am thinking especially of remarks on Russia (p. 22—chapter 4, paragraph 3) and the last three chapters, containing remarks on individualism (p. 578) and the meaning of life (p. 588). They seem more characteristic of 1931.]

23. Dawn was not finished in 1920. Dawn was written and finished before publication.[21]

[24. In the early 1920s you were working on a play with Dietrichstein. Was it a dramatization of *The "Genius"*? If not, what was it?]

24. Yes, it was a dramatization of The "Genius".[22]

[25. You were then also working on something called *Her Boy?* What was this? And do you have the MS?]

25. Don't recall it.[23]

[26. What is the movie script *Tobacco*, or *Revolt*, about? Duke? And do you have that MS?]

26. Tobacco was about the war between the growers and the owners. Yes.[24]

[27. (a) In the magazine *Your Life* for January 1938 you published an article entitled "Lessons I Learned from an Old Man." It told how you had been sent by the editor of a Western daily to ask a retired manufacturer his opinion concerning a proposed terminal. Although you were impressed by his age, his wealth, his home, his personality, etc., you were not allowed to write of them, but had to confine yourself to his replies regarding the terminal. The man is called Mr. Y—. Since the story sounds as though it happened in St. Louis, I doubt it is Yerkes. Who was that great personage?

(b) And is this article something originally part of *Newspaper Days* or something written much later for magazine publication?]

27. He was the head of a large wooden ware company. Cannot remember his name. Not connected with Newspaper Days. It was an interview.

[28. When did the idea of *An American Tragedy* occur to you as a subject for a novel? I believe you had cut out clippings of case at time of Gillette's trial. But what brought it to mind, if anything did?]

28. The idea of a novel called An American Tragedy did not occur to me until four or five years after the Grace Brown Gillette case, although I read about the case at the time it happened (around 1905) and was greatly interested in it.

[29. What was Author's Holding Co. and your part in it?]

29. Liveright thought Author's Holding Company a good way to protect my property if anything happened to the Liveright Corporation. I was all there was to it.

[30. Do you have in your possession the MSS of *The "Genius"* and *An American Tragedy*? If not, who does? And are they, if in the East, consultable?]

30. Yes.

[31. Is Eleanora R. O'Neill McQuaid living? If so, I think she'd be worth talking with. Where could I reach her?

And is Arthur Henry's wife or daughter accessible, and how?]

31. Do not know.[25]

1. With the aid of Marguerite Tjader Harris, Dreiser was attempting to complete *The Bulwark*.

2. "As If in Old Toledo," *Toledo Blade*, 28 March 1894; and "Jules Wallace, Faker, Fraud, Medium, Healer," *St. Louis Republic*, 9 September 1893. The first article is republished in T. D. Nostwich, ed., *Theodore Dreiser: Journalism, Vol. One: Newspaper Writings, 1892–1895* (Philadelphia: University of Pennsylvania Press, 1988).

3. For Arthur Henry, see Dreiser to Richard Watson Gilder, 12 December 1899, n. 1. Maude Powell (1867–1920) was a well-known violinist. Dreiser included sections about her work in two articles of the time: "Our Women Violinists," *Puritan* 2 (November 1897); 34–35; and "American Women Violinists," *Success* 2 (30 September 1899): 731–32. Both articles are republished in Yoshinobu Hakutani, ed., *Art, Music, and Literature, 1897–1902: Theodore Dreiser* (Urbana: University of Illinois Press, 2001.)

4. Dreiser is referring to an incident in St. Louis (not Chicago), when he journeyed with Hutchinson (not Hutchison) to Grand Rapids, Ohio, to examine the possibility of taking over the newspaper there.

5. From Grand Rapids, Dreiser and Hutchinson traveled to Weston, Ohio, where the *Wood County Herald* was for sale.

6. The Chicago saloon managed by L. A. Hopkins, the prototype of Hurstwood.

7. For Coates, see Dreiser to Joseph H. Coates, 19 September 1903.

8. No articles by Dreiser in the *North American*, a Philadelphia newspaper, have been identified.

9. Henry had moved to Yakima, Washington, in 1905 where he went into the real estate business with his brother; Dreiser had later invested in one of the firm's properties.

10. Dula may be roughly based on Richard Duffy (see Dreiser to Richard Duffy, 25 May 1898), who was one of Dreiser's closest friends during this period and who did help him get a job at Street & Smith's publishing firm when he left the New York Central. See also Dreiser's response to question 13.

11. Dreiser's "When the Sails Are Furled: Sailor's Snug Harbor" appeared initially in *Ainslee's* 2 (January 1899); it was reprinted in the *New York Tribune* Magazine Section on 22 May 1904.

12. The first publication of this poem appears to be in the 1926 edition of *Moods*.

13. The *Smith's* column "What the Editor Has to Say" is by Dreiser during the period he was responsible for the contents of the magazine, from June 1905 to June 1906. Ormond G. Smith (1860–1933) was one of the proprietors of Street & Smith, the publisher of *Smith's Magazine*.

14. Benjamin B. Hampton (1875–1932) owned the *Broadway*; the introductory editorial comments to each issue of the magazine during the period of Dreiser's editorship, from April 1906 to June 1907, are by Dreiser.

15. For the Child Rescue Campaign, see Dreiser to Dear Sir, 15 November 1907.

16. Elias appears to be asking about an early autobiographical novel which Dreiser later destroyed, but both he and Dreiser may also be referring to another work titled *The Rake*, based on the famous Molineux murder case of 1899, which he worked on in 1915 and which is extant in DPUP in fragmentary form.

17. No work by Dreiser titled "A Solution in Exile" had been identified.

18. Solon Barnes, the Quaker protagonist of *The Bulwark*, a novel Dreiser began in 1916 and worked on sporadically until he completed it in late 1945, is a puritan in the sense that he holds strict views on proper belief and behavior.

19. The accepted scenario for the composition of these works is that Dreiser completed *Jennie Gerhardt* in December 1910 and then immediately began writing *The "Genius,"* finishing it in late spring 1911. After writing both *The Financier* and *The Titan*, he revised the conclusion of *The "Genius"* in early 1914.

20. *Hey Rub-a-Dub-Dub* was published in 1920; "Kismet," which was to be a chapter in Dreiser's philosophical work *The Formula Called Man*, appeared in *Esquire* in January 1935.

21. Dreiser appears to have completed a full draft of *Dawn* by 1920, but he revised and cut this version extensively before it was published in 1931.

22. Leo Ditrichstein (as he was more commonly known)(1865–1928) was a successful Broadway actor and playwright during the 1910s and 1920s.

23. Dreiser wrote a draft of the unpublished story "Her Boy," which deals with the origins of criminal behavior, during 1919–20; the draft is in DPUP.

24. For Dreiser's involvement in *Tobacco*, see Dreiser to S. Anargyros, 30 December 1932.

25. Eleanora O'Neill was a longtime friend, especially during Dreiser's Greenwich Village years of 1914–19. Maude Wood Henry (1873–1957) was Arthur Henry's first wife; Elias did interview her.

To Rufus M. Jones [TS-Hav]¹

Dreiser had reached the final stages in the writing of The Bulwark. *Although Jones replied on 13 April 1945 that Dreiser's distinction between Quakers and Protestants was correct, the passages that Dreiser includes in his letter do not appear in the published novel.*

1015 N. King's Rd.,
Hollywood, 46, Calif.,
April 10, 1945.

Dear Mr. Jones:

I would like to ask you a question in connection with the text of the book I am now writing.

I am writing about a mill-town section of the village of Segookit, Maine, and where I speak of "Christian *and* Quaker Americans," is this correct? In other words, are Quakers considered Christian or are they considered Deists? I know there has been much controversy on this subject in the past, but I would like to know if the following statements are correct.

"However the standards of these (mill-town) people, come by as they might have been, were looked upon as lower and socially more negligible than those of the Christian (Protestant) and Quaker Americans of Segookit, who in turn were considered as always beyond the reach of the minds and temperaments of these particular Canadians (mill-town people).

And later, in my script:

"And this, in the eyes of the remainder of the community was truly a great ill which was to be fought by Friends *and* Christians (Protestants) alike."

(Of course the words in parentheses are not in the script.)

And, are these two statements contradictory? "Friends and all Christians alike" and "Christian *and* Quaker Americans"?

I will appreciate very much an answer from you on this point. And with kindest personal regards.

Sincerely,
Theodore Dreiser²

1. Published in Gerhard Friedrich, "The Dreiser-Jones Correspondence," *Bulletin of Friends Historical Association* 5 (Spring 1957): 23–34.
2. Dreiser also wrote by hand in the left-hand margin: "*I hope that all is well with you.*"

To Otto Kyllmann   [TS-TU]

Kyllmann's bitterness in early 1941 *over Dreiser's anti-British position in* America
Is Worth Saving *had not prevented the two men from reassuming their former
business and (to some extent) personal relationship.*

THEODORE DREISER

1015 N. King's Rd.,
Hollywood, 46, Calif.,
June 11, 1945.

Dear Kyllmann:

First let me say Congratulations and Good Cheer to you, now that the
terrible war in Europe is over.[1] I am so happy to realize that the actual firing
on London has ceased. God grant that it will never happen again.

Next, I want to let you know that I am publishing THE BULWARK
this Fall,[2] my novel about the Quakers—three generations in the United
States. I started this book years ago but have just now finished it. I feel that
it is a book that the English people might easily take to.

If you are interested I can send you a script to read.

Then in the Spring 1946 I will put out A TRILOGY OF DESIRE,
of which I have just finished the third volume—THE STOIC.[3] THE FI-
NANCIER was the first volume—THE TITAN, the second, and now THE
STOIC, the third. I wrote you once about it back in 1932 and sent on a few
chapters for you to read. Someone there wrote a criticism of it.[4] However,
I finished the book just now and will put it out with the other two volumes
in a special edition. Three volumes about Frank Algernon Cowperwood.
Do you think you would be interested in looking over the manuscript? If so
I can send it on a little later, as soon as I finish the last three chapters.

I think the small objections made by your critic in 1932 have been
outlived now that so much has happened in the past 13 years. Anyway, I
will be glad to hear about this from you, after you have read the script.

Another matter that I am interested in is the publication of all of my
books in a uniform set. I have had several propositions made to me in
this regard in the United States, but, as you know, there has been a paper
shortage over here, which has prohibited the publication of this set as yet.
However, I think this difficulty will soon be overcome, especially if the
books can be issued a few each year, but in a uniform edition.

Do you think you would be interested in this project? Or, what are the
chances for it at this time in England?[5]

It seems to me that I should have a larger English reading audience. And it may be that a set of my complete works at this time would create it. However, there is The Bulwark, and the TRILOGY OF DESIRE in the Spring of 1946.

What do you think about them?

I hope this letter finds you well and in good spirits, now that V E DAY actually arrived.

With kindest regards and love to you. Helen joins me in this.

Sincerely,
Dreiser

P. S. I get statements from Curtis Brown,[6] but, I must say, the sales are very small. Why is this? And don't you think they can be improved?

1. The European phase of World War II ended on 7 May 1945; the Pacific phase continued to 14 August 1945.

2. *The Bulwark* did not in fact appear until March 1946; Constable published the English edition in 1947.

3. Because Dreiser decided in December 1945 to revise the conclusion of *The Stoic*, this portion of the novel was incomplete at his death on 28 December. The American edition of *The Stoic* was published in November 1947; Constable declined to issue an English edition.

4. See Dreiser to Otto Kyllmann, 15 June 1932.

5. Constable did not act on this suggestion.

6. Dreiser's British agent.

To Robert H. Elias [TS-Cor]

THEODORE DREISER

1015 N. King's Rd.,
Hollywood, 46, Calif.,
July 7, 1945.

Dear Elias:

Thanks for your letter with enclosures and for your congratulations, etc.

Yes, I finished THE BULWARK, and it has been placed for publication with Doubleday Doran.[1] The amazing part of it is that they have guaranteed 150,000 copies the first year, should the sale warrant that many. I don't think there's another publisher who could make such a guarantee. They seem to be the only publishing house with enough paper.

I am now working on THE STOIC and I expect to finish in two months.

It *is* a little astounding that I can do all of this work, but I am doing it, and it seems to be going very well. Doubleday Doran has the first refusal on my next book (which will be THE STOIC,—that is after THE BULWARK). THE BULWARK will most likely come out in the fall, possibly November. Then it may be followed by THE STOIC in the spring, 1946.[2] Judging from the letters I have received in the past years, THE STOIC has a waiting public too. I think it will be good to bring both of these books out soon.

Doubleday Doran and Company are also interested in a full set of my works, and while I appreciate very much your suggestions about the University Press, I still do not think they would be able to handle the distribution these books, in my opinion, should have. As you know, I suffered long and bitterly by being shelved so many years, and I am hardly in the mood for no promotion and slow distribution. I need a progressive publisher at this time,—someone who will really do a job. This I feel Doubleday Doran might do if they do well with the two novels. And I am inclined to give them a trial.

Anyway, I would not want to do anything in connection with this matter now. I want to see what happens with the two books first. Then I will be in a better position to judge what to do.

I appreciate your letter very much, and the news therein. Glad you saw Mencken. And Heilbrunn.[3] And here's my very best wishes to you and them.

Sincerely,
Theodore Dreiser

1. By the time *The Bulwark* was published in March 1946, Doubleday, Doran & Co. was reorganized as Doubleday & Co.

2. For this timetable, see also Dreiser to Otto Kyllmann, 11 June 1945, n. 2–3.

3. Dr. L. V. Heilbrunn (1892–1959), a biologist whom Dreiser had met in 1928 at Woods Hole Marine Biology Laboratory; Heilbrunn was living in Philadelphia.

To William Z. Foster [TC-DPUP][1]

Although Dreiser actively supported many communist causes and served on many communist-controlled organizations during the 1930s, he did not formally join the party. (He had approached Earl Browder [1891–1973], then head of the party, in early 1932 about joining, but Browder, doubting Dreiser's ability to toe the party line, dissuaded him from applying.) In April 1945, however, Dreiser wrote to the Los Angeles office of the party indicating a desire to become a member. With the aid of the Hollywood scriptwriter and communist John Howard Lawson, whom he had known for many years (see Dreiser to Lawson, 10 August 1928), as well as other local communists, a letter of application was prepared by early July and signed by Dreiser. By this time, Browder was in the process of being removed as head of the American communist movement, to be replaced by William Z. Foster (1881–1961). Although Dreiser's letter to Foster more closely resembles conventional party phraseology than Dreiser's usual prose, it nevertheless constitutes one of the most important political statements of his later career.[2]

THEODORE DREISER

Hollywood, California
July 20, 1945

Dear Mr. Foster:

I am writing this letter to tell you of my desire to become a member of the Communist Political Association.

This request is rooted in convictions that I have long held and that have been strengthened and deepened by the years. I have believed intensely that the common people, and first of all the workers,—of the United States and of the world—are the guardians of their own destiny and the creators of their own future. I have endeavored to live by this faith, to clothe it in words and symbols, to explore its full meaning in the lives of men and women.

It seems to me that faith in the people is the simple and profound reality that has been tested and proved in the present world crisis. Fascism derided that faith, proclaiming the end of human rights and human dignity, seeking to rob the people of faith in themselves, so that they could be used for their own enslavement and degradation.

But the democratic peoples of the world demonstrated the power that lay in their unity, and a tremendous role was played in this victory by the country that through its attainment of socialism has given the greatest example in history of the heights of achievement that can be reached by a free people with faith in itself and in all the progressive forces of humanity—the Soviet Union. The unity of our country with the great Soviet Union is one of the most valuable fruits of our united struggle, and dare not be weakened without grave danger to America itself.

Communists all over the world have played a vital part in welding the unity of the peoples that insures the defeat of Fascism. Theirs were the first and clearest voices raised against the march of aggression in China, Ethiopia and Spain.

Dr. Norman Bethune, the great pioneer in saving war wounded through the use of the blood bank, died in China helping the free peoples of that country withstand the Japanese hordes years before the democratic countries came to their aid. His dying request was that it be made known that since many years he had been a Communist.[3]

Out of the underground movements of tortured Europe, Communists have risen to give leadership in the face of terror and all-pervading military suppression. Tito of Yugoslavia won the admiration of the world for his leadership of his people to victory. The name of Stalin is one beloved by the free peoples of the earth. Mao-Tse-tung and Chou-En-lai have kept the spirit of democracy and unity alive in China throughout the years that divisive forces have split that country asunder.[4]

In the United States, I feel that the Communists have helped to deepen our understanding of the heritage of American freedom as a guide to action in the present. During the years when Fascism was preparing for its projected conquest of the world, American Communists fought to rally the American people against Fascism. They saw the danger and proposed the remedy. Marxist theory enabled them to cast a steady light on the true economic and social origins of Fascism; Marxism gave them also a scientific understanding of the power of the working people as a force in history which could mobilize the necessary intelligence, strength and heroism to destroy Fascism, save humanity, and carry on the fight for further progress.

More than 11,000 Communists are taking part in that struggle as members of the armed forces of our country. That they have served with honor and patriotism is attested to even by the highest authorities of the Army itself.

More and more it is becoming recognized in our country that the Communists are a vital and constructive part of our nation, and that a nation's unity and a nation's democracy is dangerously weakened if it excludes the Communists. Symbolic of this recognition was the action of the War Department in renouncing discrimination against Communists in granting commissions. A statement signed by a number of distinguished Americans points out that "the Army has apparently taken its position as a result of the excellent record of Communists and so-called Communists, including a number who have been cited for gallantry and a number who have died in action."

It seems to me that this ought to discredit completely one of the ideological weapons from the arsenal of fascism that disorients the country's political life and disgraces its intellectual life—red-baiting. Irrational prejudice against anything that is truly or falsely labeled "Communism" is absurd and dangerous in politics. Concessions to red-baiting are even more demoralizing in the field of science, art and culture. If our thinkers and creators are to fulfill their responsibilities to a democratic culture, they must free themselves from the petty fears and illusions that prevent the open discussion of ideas on the adult level. The necessities of our time demand that we explore and use the whole realm of human knowledge.

I therefore greet with particular satisfaction the information that such leading scientists as the French physicist, Joliot-Curie, and the French mathematician, Langevin, have found in the Communist movement, as did the British scientist Haldane, some years ago, not only the unselfishness and devotion characteristic of the pursuit of science, but also the integration of the scientific approach to their own field of work with the scientific approach to the problems of society.[5]

I am also deeply stirred to hear that such artists and writers, devoted to the cause of the people, as Pablo Picasso of Spain and Louis Aragon of France, have joined the Communist movement, which also counts among its leading cultural figures the great Danish novelist, Martin Anderson Nexo, and the Irish playwright, Sean O'Casey.[6]

These historic years have deepened my conviction that widespread membership in the Communist Political Association will greatly strengthen the American people, together with the anti-fascist forces throughout the world, in completely stamping out fascism and achieving new heights of world democracy, economic progress and free culture. Belief in the greatness and dignity of Man has been the guiding principle of my life and work. The logic of my life and work leads me therefore to apply for membership in the Communist Political Association.

Sincerely,

1. Published in the *Daily Worker* (New York), 30 July 1945, 5, and in Donald Pizer, ed., *Theodore Dreiser: A Selection of Uncollected Prose* (Detroit, Mich.: Wayne State University Press, 1977), 330–33. The *Daily Worker* publication differs from Dreiser's TC letter in that all references to Dreiser's wishing to become a member of the Communist Political Association have been revised to Communist movement, organization, or party to reflect recent changes in the party's leadership and official title.

2. See also Donald Pizer, "'The Logic of My Life and Work': Another Look at Dreiser's July 20, 1945, Letter to William Z. Foster," *Dreiser Studies* 30 (Fall 1999): 24–34. Dreiser's letter is published here as well.

3. A Canadian-born physician who was a pioneer in the development of the blood bank, Bethune (1890–1939) died while serving with the Chinese communist army.

4. Josip Broz (1892–1980), the communist dictator of Yugoslavia from 1945 until his death, adopted the name "Tito" during the war when fighting the Germans; Mao Tse-tung (1893–1976), leader of the Chinese Communist Party during the 1930s and then head of the People's Republic of China until his death; Chou En-lai (1898–1976), premier and foreign minister of the People's Republic of China from 1949 until his death.

5. Frédéric Joliot-Curie (1900–1968), the son-in-law of Marie Curie and himself a 1935 Nobel Prize–winning physicist; Paul Langevin (1872–1946), a French physicist; and John Burdon Sanderson Haldane (1892–1964), a British geneticist.

6. The world-famous painter Picasso (1881–1973), who joined the party shortly after the end of the war; Aragon (see Dreiser to William C. Lengel, 16 July 1938, n. 2), a party activist for several decades; Nexo (1869–1954), Danish novelist; and O'Casey (1884–1964), Irish playwright.

To William Z. Foster [TC-DPUP]

Foster replied to Dreiser's letter of 20 July 1945 on 7 August, welcoming him as a party member and outlining both the recent accomplishments and future efforts of the party.

> 1015 N. King's Rd.,
> Hollywood, 46, Calif.,
> August 16, 1945.

Dear Foster:

I was very much interested in your very broad and socially human comment on the proper force of the Communist Party in this country and elsewhere. I read it with very great interest and profit, and I wish, if you write anything more in connection with movements for the party in this country, that you would have a copy sent to me. As a member I would like to know the party direction and its achievements.

I am so glad that you are at last head of it, which is where you belonged long ago. And I was very much interested in your analysis and demolition of Browder's compromises.[1]

Please make a note of my address, and if anything of interest comes up, have someone let me know.

Thank you very much for your letter to me.

> Sincerely,

1. Following a reversal in the Soviet Union's strategy of an international Popular Front (see Dreiser to William C. Lengel, 10 July 1940), Earl Browder, who had earlier vigorously supported this policy, was, on 26–28 July, formally dismissed as head of the American communist movement and replaced by Foster. Dreiser not only supported this change in policy but also found Foster far more personally congenial than Browder.

To William C. Lengel [TC-DPUP]1

Lengel, who had helped negotiate Dreiser's relationship with Putnam's, was trou-
bled by his switch to Doubleday, Doran for the publication of The Bulwark *and*
The Stoic *and expressed his concern to Dreiser in a letter of 15 November.*

1015 N. King's Rd.,
Hollywood, 46, Calif.,
Nov. 17, 1945.

Dear Lengel:

I have just received your letter dated November 15th in regard to THE
BULWARK and THE STOIC. Yes, I am very glad to say they are both
finished, although I do find myself rather tired from the strain.

About my leaving Putnam's, I am sorry that this has affected you in the
way it has. But I had to find a more enterprising publisher. Putnam's did
nothing, whatsoever, for my books, the ones they had on hand, and the
ones they could have done something about. I had letters from them asking
over and over for THE BULWARK. In fact, at the time that I got stuck on
the book and could not finish it, I was worried quite a lot by the fact that I
had not fulfilled my contract with them by delivering the book at a certain
time. (There was even danger of legal action). I offered to pay back their
advance to me. They accepted it without a word of regret. In fact, they
seemed rather glad to get it back. I found relief in this act, and it was not
long before I was able to progress with the writing of the book.

But before this, I asked them over and over to do something about the
circulation of my books, the reprinting of some of them so they would not go
out of print altogether. Nothing was done. Nothing of any kind. I received
letters from all over the country from students (an entire new reading public)
asking where my books could be purchased. They were out of print, most of
them, and the only place they could get a book was in a second hand store.
This was during the finest book selling period in history. And it did me much
more harm than the receipts of THE BULWARK can make up for.

When there was any discussion of a reprint of any story they were always
willing to accept the very minimum charge—a policy I have never followed.
And in this last instance of a check to me for $25 from the American Mer-
cury for my story "Convention", I exchanged telegrams and letters with the
American Mercury myself and the price of $100 was agreed on over a year
ago for the story. Over a year later I receive a check for 1/3 of the amount
paid for it.2 This is simply negligent business methods. Someone somewhere
in the firm does something, and no one knows why.

I need a much more enterprising firm. I need someone who will really promote my works, and I intend to have someone like that. If it is not Doubleday-Doran, then I will find someone else. But, so far, it does look like Doubleday, Doran & Co. were alive. They are doing a lot for their books, it seems to me. I do not have all the time in the world to wait for someone to realize what there is in a set of books of mine. And as far as Putnam's is concerned, if they discussed a set of my works with you, it is the first I have heard of it. They outlined no such extensive plan to me. And, even now, in the face of THE BULWARK coming out, there is an opportunity for someone to get out reprints of my books to be sold along with it. But I have not heard of anyone in Putnam's suggesting any such thing. They do not seem to realize that there is an existing market for my books. I know it because of the many letters I receive from all parts of the country, as well as from abroad.

And I do not feel that I can work with a firm which does not have any vision of its own. I feel that I am justified, from the lack of interest in my books in the past, to change publishers. Anyway, it is what I have done. I can only say that I am sorry it affected you as it did.

Hoping this finds you well. And with my warmest regards always.

Sincerely,

1. This letter is in DPUP as an enclosure in Dreiser's letter to his lawyer, Stanley M. Moffat, on 17 November 1945, in which he explained that he was sending Moffat a copy of the letter because Earle Balch, of Putnam's, "wrote lately saying that he had had luncheon with you and that you expressed amazement at my changing publishers. And so I thought you might like to see what I consider my reasons for changing."

2. Dreiser's "Convention" appeared initially in the *American Mercury* in December 1925 and was republished in his story collection *Chains* (1927). Dreiser is referring to its further republication in *The American Mercury Reader*, ed. Lawrence E. Spivak and Charles Angoff (Philadelphia: Blakeston, 1944). Dreiser's position is that Putnam's should have acted as his agent in negotiating a price for the story that he and the magazine would then share.

To James T. Farrell [TS-JTFUP]

Dreiser had met the Chicago novelist Farrell (1904–79), a warm admirer of his work, in 1936. In June 1945, Farrell, at Dreiser's request, had advised him about possible revisions of The Bulwark *manuscript and was now performing a similar role with* The Stoic. *On 19 December 1945 Farrell wrote Dreiser a long critique of the novel, in which he especially recommended revising its conclusion, and it was while Dreiser was engaged in this task that he died on 28 December.*

THEODORE DREISER

1015 N. King's Rd.,
Hollywood, 46, Calif.,
Dec. 14, 1945.

Dear Farrell:

I hope you received the telegram I sent you about the Broadcast. It was very good, especially your part in it, as I wrote you.[1]

About the Danish Publisher, you do not mention his name. He may be the one I have, or had there. Gyldendalske-Boghandl. My Danish agent is David Grunbaum and he is located in Copenhagen. However, if your new Publisher would like to write me I will be glad to hear from him and learn what he has to suggest.[2]

You may certainly keep THE STOIC until the end of the year, as you wish. At that time I would like you to please give it personally to Mr. Donald Elder of Doubleday Doran,[3] instead of sending it back here to me.

And here's wishing you many happy Holiday Greetings, and a good year—all year—in 1946.

Sincerely,
Dreiser

1. On 9 December 1945 Farrell had spoken at length about Dreiser's work on the popular radio program "Invitation to Learning."

2. Farrell had written Dreiser on 8 December 1945 that he had recently met a Danish publisher in New York who was interested in publishing *The Bulwark* in Denmark.

3. Elder (1913–65) was Dreiser's editor at Doubleday, Doran for both *The Bulwark* and *The Stoic*.

To Otto Kyllmann   [TS-TU]

THEODORE DREISER

1015 N. King's Rd.,
Hollywood, 46, Calif.,
Dec. 22, 1945.

Dear Kyllmann:

As far as I can see, the contract for THE BULWARK seems all right. I am therefore signing the enclosed copy and returning it to you. Also, under separate cover, I am mailing to you the final galleys of the book which will come out over here March 21. They are o. k. but should be scanned carefully, naturally, for any slight printer's mistake, before being set up.

When do you think you will get to the publication of the book? It seems to me that it would be better to get it out as soon as you can.

How are you personally? I hope this note finds you really well, and very happy, in spite of all the difficulties England has to face, through and after such a war. A war of any kind is a terrible thing, but one of that magnitude is not easy to recover from, in all the countries which participated. It has left its scar on every soul in America, I am sure. What a dreadful thing! I hope that peoples everywhere will begin to realize what a devastating thing it all is, and at least begin to learn that peoples on this small planet of ours should live together, work together, and cooperate. Heavens!—why not?

Do write me as soon as you receive this and send me the signed contract, and also give me some word of yourself.

With the kindest of regards and personal good wishes, I remain.

Sincerely,
Dreiser

P. S. I have always wanted a pleasing presentation of my book MOODS which would include all of the poems, a number of which were added to the Simon and Schuster edition, but which resulted in an ungainly, heavy volume hard to hold by anyone. Couldn't you get me up a volume on thin but durable paper and with an attractive light weight cover, and by that I do not mean a paper cover but some flexible material that would be agreeable to the reader, and something that would be sufficiently light weight to avoid tiring the reader?[1]

1. Dreiser's book of poetry, Moods, was published in 1926 by Boni and Liveright; new, enlarged editions appeared in 1928 (also by Boni and Liveright) and 1935 (by Simon & Schuster). Constable had in 1929 published an English edition of the 1928 Boni and Liveright edition, but it did not act on Dreiser's suggestion for a new version of the 1935 edition.

INDEX

DONALD PIZER, Pierce Butler Professor of English
emeritus at Tulane University, has published widely on
late nineteenth- and early twentieth-century American
literature. Among his books are *The Novels of Theodore Dreiser:
A Critical Study* (1976); *Theodore Dreiser: A Selection of
Uncollected Prose* (1977); *Theodore Dreiser: A Primary
Bibliography and Reference Guide*, with Richard Dowell and
Frederic E. Rusch (1991); and—also with Frederic E. Rusch—
Theodore Dreiser: Interviews (2004). He is a Guggenheim
Fellow and has also received senior research fellowships
from the National Endowment for the
Humanities and the American Council
of Learned Societies.

The University of Illinois Press
is a founding member of the
Association of American University Presses.

Composed in 10.5/13 Goudy Old Style
by Jim Proefrock
at the University of Illinois Press
Manufactured by Thomson-Shore, Inc.

University of Illinois Press
1325 South Oak Street
Champaign, IL 61820-6903
www.press.uillinois.edu